NEGOTIATION

SECOND EDITION

by

ALAN SCOTT RAU
Robert F. Windfohr & Anne Burnett Windfohr Professor of Law
The University of Texas at Austin School of Law

EDWARD F. SHERMAN
Professor of Law
Tulane University School of Law

SCOTT R. PEPPET
Associate Professor of Law
University of Colorado School of Law

This edition is the successor to John S. Murray, Alan Scott Rau, & Edward F. Sherman, Processes of Dispute Resolution: The Role of Lawyers, first published in 1989 (2nd Edition 1996)

NEW YORK, NEW YORK
FOUNDATION PRESS

2002

Reprinted in part from Rau, Sherman & Peppet, Processes of Dispute Resolution, Third Edition © 2002
By Foundation Press

Foundation Press, a division of West Group, has created this publication to provide you with accurate
and authoritative information concerning the subject matter covered. However, this publication was not
necessarily prepared by persons licensed to practice law in a particular jurisdiction. Foundation Press
is not engaged in rendering legal or other professional advice, and this publication is not a substitute
for the advice of an attorney. If you require legal or other expert advice, you should seek the services of
a competent attorney or other professional.

                        395 Hudson Street
                        New York, NY 10014
                        Phone Toll Free 1–877–888–1330
                        Fax (212) 367–6799
                        fdpress.com

ISBN 1–58778–093–3

 TEXT IS PRINTED ON 10% POST
CONSUMER RECYCLED PAPER

PREFACE

This paperback dealing with negotiation was originally written as a chapter of our coursebook, *Processes of Dispute Resolution: The Role of Lawyers* (Third edition), which is designed for a course on the full range of alternative dispute resolution procedures. With a growing number of law school courses and seminars focusing specifically on the negotiation process, we thought it might be useful to reprint it separately, for use by instructors who wish to focus only on negotiation.

The teaching of negotiation must, of course, reflect at several points an awareness of the issues raised by the use of "alternative" processes generally. Alternative methods of dispute resolution have become part of the processing of a wide range of disputes in our society. Hundreds of thousands of disputes are voluntarily submitted to mediation each year through community dispute resolution centers, other non-profit institutions, and a growing host of entrepreneurial providers. In a sizable number of state and federal courts, dispute resolution procedures are invoked as part of the litigation process. Private companies and governmental agencies have adopted "system designs" incorporating ADR procedures to prevent, or to resolve, the inevitable disputes that arise in their operations. Arbitration has expanded from such traditional fields as labor and construction to a wide range of contractual services such as investments, banking, health care, and employment. It is obvious that lawyers today must have a grounding in ADR in order to provide adequate advice and representation in many areas of the law.

Lawyers must also understand the negotiation process and the opportunities and risks inherent in bargaining. Too often attorneys—even attorneys who have negotiated throughout their professional careers—have little understanding of what they're doing as they bargain. This book aims to provide an analytic structure to help make sense of negotiation, as well as various readings to provoke thinking and discussion about bargaining in legal disputes. In addition, we have included more than the usual dose of material on the legal and ethical aspects of bargaining so that students can see how negotiations are regulated within the profession and how other areas of law, such as torts, contracts or civil procedure, impact legal bargaining.

A note on form: We have substantially edited most cases and selections to delete unnecessary material. Deletions of text due to our editing are indicated by spaced asterisks. Citations in the text, and footnotes from the text, have usually been omitted without indication. Where footnotes to selections do appear, however, we have retained the number they have in the original material. A reader desiring to use the opinion as a research tool can, of course, go to the official case reporters.

We have benefited from the helpful comments and critiques of many colleagues and students who have used the prior editions of this book. We are also extremely grateful to those whose conscientious and able research and administrative assistance made completion of this book possible—in particular Christina Garcia, Chris Piazzola, Sandy Schmeider, Shawn Stigler, Mary Pace, Jonae Harrison, Janice Sayas, Pat Smith and Pat Floyd.

A.S.R.

E.F.S.

S.R.P.

January, 2002

ACKNOWLEDGMENTS

The following authors and publishers gave us permission to reprint excerpts from copyrighted material; we gratefully acknowledge their assistance.

CHAPTER I

PEANUTS cartoon reprinted by permission of United Features Syndicate, Inc.

Llewellyn, The Bramble Bush: On Our Law and Its Study 12 (1960). Reprinted by permission of Oceana Publications, Inc.

Miller & Sarat, Grievances, Claims, and Disputes: Assessing the Adversary Culture, 15 Law & Soc'y Rev. 525, 526-27, 531-33, 536-46, 561-64 (1980-81). Reprinted by permission of the Law and Society Association.

Galanter, Reading the Landscape of Disputes: What We Know and Don't Know (And Think We Know) About Our Allegedly contentious and Litigious Society, 31 UCLA L. Rev. 4, 13-14 (1983). Originally published in 31 UCLA L. Rev. 4, copyright © 1983, The Regents of the University of California. All rights reserved.

Auerbach, Justice Without Law? 10, 12-13, 78 (1983). From Justice Without Law? by Jerold S. Auerbach. Copyright © 1983 by Oxford University Press, Inc. Reprinted by permission.

Trubek, Sarat, Felstiner, Kritzer & Grossman, The Costs of Ordinary Litigation, 31 UCLA L. Rev. 72, 84, 89, 122 (1983). Originally published in 31 UCLA L. Rev. 4. copyright © 1983, The Regents of the University of California. All rights reserved.

Newman, Rethinking Fairness: Perspectives on the Litigation Process, 94 Yale L.J. 1643, 1644-45 (1985). Reprinted by permission of The Yale Law Journal Company and William S. Hein Company from The Yale Law Journal, Vol. 94, pages 1643-1659.

Gulliver, Disputes and Negotiations: A Cross-Cultural Perspective 13 (1979).

Brazil, The Attorney as Victim: Towards More Candor About the Psychological Price Tag of Litigation Practice, 3 J. Legal Prof. 107, 109-10, 114-117 (1978-79).

Fuller, The Forms and Limits of Adjudication, 92 Harv. L. Rev.. 353, 364-71, 382-85, 393-400, 403 (1978). Copyright © 1978 by the Harvard Law Review Association. Reprinted with permission.

The Role of Courts in American Society: Final Report of Council on the Role of Courts, 102-114, 120-21 (Jethro K. Lieberman ed. 1984).

Fuller, Collective Bargaining and the Arbitrator, Proceedings of the 15th Annual Meeting, National Academy of Arbitrators 8, 39-41 (1962). Reprinted with permission. Chapter 2, pages 8, 29-33, and 37-48 and 34-41 from Collective Bargaining and the Arbitrator's Role (Proceedings of the 15th Annual Meeting National Academy of Arbitrators), by Lon L. Fuller. Copyright © 1962, by The Bureau of National Affairs, Inc. Washington, D.C. 20037.

Chayes, The Role of the Judge in Public Law Litigation, 89 Harv. L. Rev. 1281, 1298-99 (1976). Copyright © 1976 by the Harvard Law Review Association.

Fiss, Against Settlement, 93 Yale L.J. 1073, 1075-78, 1082-90 (1984). Reprinted by permission of The Yale Law Journal Company and William S. Hein Company from The Yale Law Journal, Vol. 93, pages 1073-1090.

Edwards, Alternate Dispute Resolution: Panacea or Anathema , 99 Harv. L. Rev.. 668, 678-79 (1986). Copyright © 1986 by the Harvard Law Review Association.

Galanter, The Day After the Litigation Explosion, 46 Maryland L. Rev. 3, 32-37 (1986).

Burger, Isn't There a Better Way?, March 1982, ABA Journal, The Lawyers Magazine, 274-75 (1982).

Friendly, Some Kind of Hearing, 123 U. Pa. L. Rev. 1267, 1287-90 (1975).

Terry Leap, Tenure, Discrimination, and the Courts 16-17 (1993).

CHAPTER II

Cartoon, used by permission of United Media.

Lax & Sebenius, The Manager as Negotiator 90-102 (1986). From The Manager as Negotiator by David Lax and James Sebenius. Used by permission of Simon and Schuster.

Bazerman & Gillespie, Betting on the Future: The Virtues of Contingent Contracts, Harvard Business Review 155, 156-160 (Sept.-Oct. 1999). Copyright © 1999 by the Harvard Business Review.

Falk, The Art of Contract Negotiation, 3 Marquette Sports L.J. 1, 12-14 (1992). Copyright © 1992 by the Marquette Sports Law Journal. Reprinted by permission of the Marquette Sports Law Journal.

Wetlaufer, The Limits of Integrative Bargaining, 85 Georgetown L.J. 369, 374-375 (1996).

Menkel-Meadow, The Transformation of Disputes by Lawyers: What the Dispute Paradigm Does and Does Not Tell Us, J. of Disp. Res. 25, 31-33 (1985). Copyright © 1985 by the Journal of Dispute Resolution. Reprinted by permission of the Journal of Dispute Resolution.

Lax & Sebenius, The Power of Alternatives or the Limits of Negotiation, 1 Neg. J. 163, 169-170 (1985). Reprinted by permission of Plenum Publishing Corp.

Fisher, Ury & Patton, Getting to Yes 3-4 (2d ed. 1991). Excerpts from GETTING TO YES 2/e by Roger Fisher, William Ury and Bruce Patton. Copyright © 1981, 1991 by Roger Fisher and William Ury. Reprinted by permission of Houghton Mifflin Company. All rights reserved.

Gifford, A Context-Based Theory of Strategy Selection in Legal Negotiation, originally published in 46 Ohio St. L.J. 41, 48-52 (1985). Used by permission of the Ohio State Law Journal.

Goodpaster, A Primer on Competitive Bargaining, J. Disp. Res. 325, 346-348 (1996). Reprinted by permission of the Journal of Dispute Resolution.

Schelling, The Strategy of Conflict 22-28 (1960). Reprinted by permission of the publisher from "An Essay on Bargaining" in THE STRATEGY OF CONFLICT by Thomas C. Schelling, pp. 22-28, Cambridge, Mass.: Harvard University Press, Copyright © 1960, 1980 by the President and Fellows of Harvard College, Copyright © renewed 1988 by Thomas C. Schelling.

Fisher, Ury & Patton, Getting to Yes 7-9 (2d ed. 1991). Excerpts from GETTING TO YES 2/e by Roger Fisher, William Ury and Bruce Patton. Copyright © 1981, 1991 by Roger Fisher and William Ury. Reprinted by permission of Houghton Mifflin Company. All rights reserved.

Edwards & White, The Lawyer as Negotiator 115-116 (1977). Reprinted from The Lawyer as Negotiator, Edwards & White, Copyright © 1977, with permission of the West Group.

Lax & Sebenius, The Manager as Negotiator 132-134 (1986). From The Manager as Negotiator by David Lax and James Sebenius. Used by permission of Simon and Schuster.

Fisher, Beyond Yes, 1 Neg. J. 67, 67 (1985). Reprinted by permission of Plenum Publishing Corp.

Fisher, Ury & Patton, Getting to Yes 40-50 (2d ed. 1991). Excerpts from GETTING TO YES 2/e by Roger Fisher, William Ury and Bruce Patton. Copyright © 1981, 1991 by Roger Fisher and William Ury. Reprinted by permission of Houghton Mifflin Company. All rights reserved.

Menkel-Meadow, When Winning Isn't Everything: The Lawyer as Problem-Solver, 28 Hofstra L. Rev. 905, 915-918 (2000). Used by permission of the Hofstra Law Review Association.

Raiffa, Post-Settlement Settlements, 1 Neg. J. 9-12 (1985). Reprinted by permission of Plenum Publishing Corp.

Fisher, Comment, 34 J. of Legal Educ. 120, 121 (1984). Reprinted by permission of the Journal of Legal Education.

Bazerman, Gibbons, Thompson & Valley, Can Negotiators Outperform Game Theory?, in Halpern & Stern (eds.), Debating Rationality: Nonrational Aspects of Organizational Decision Making 78 (1998). Reprinted by permission of the ILR Press.

Korobkin, A Positive Theory of Legal Negotiation, 88 Georgetown L.J. 1789, 1821-1829 (2000).

Thompson & Nadler, Judgmental Biases in Conflict Resolution and How to Overcome Them, in Deutsch & Coleman (eds.), The Handbook of Conflict Resolution: Theory and Practice 213, 224-225 (2000).

Mnookin & Ross, Barriers to Conflict Resolution: Introduction, in Arrow et al. (eds), Barriers to Conflict Resolution 7-8 (1995).

Luce & Raiffa, Games and Decisions 95 (1957).

Lax & Sebenius, The Manager as Negotiator 157-160 (1986). From The Manager as Negotiator by David Lax and James Sebenius. Used by permission of Simon and Schuster.

Pruitt, Strategic Choice in Negotiation, 27 Am. Behavioral Sci. 167-194 (1983).

Shell, Bargaining for Advantage: Negotiation Strategies for Reasonable People 12-14 (1999). Used by permission of Penguin Putnam Inc.

Morris, Sim & Girotto, Time of Decision, Ethical Obligation, and Causal Illusion: Temporal Cues and Social Heuristics in the Prisoner's Dilemma, in Kramer & Messick (eds.), Negotiation as a Social Process 210-213 (1995).

Heumann & Hyman, Negotiation Methods and Litigation Settlement Methods in New Jersey: "You Can't Always Get What You Want," 12 Ohio St. J. Disp. Resol. 253, 262-265 (1997). Reprinted by permission of the Ohio State Journal of Dispute Resolution.

Mnookin, Peppet & Tulumello, Beyond Winning: Negotiating to Create Value in Deals and Disputes 321-322 (2000). Reprinted by permission of the publishers from BEYOND WINNING: NEGOTIATING TO CREATE VALUE IN DEALS AND DISPUTES, by Robert H. Mnookin, Scott R. Peppet, and Andrew S. Tulumello, Cambridge, Mass.: Harvard University Press, Copyright © 2000 by Robert Mnookin, Scott R. Peppet and Andrew S. Tulumello.

Condlin, Bargaining in the Dark: The Normative Incoherence of Lawyer Dispute Bargaining Role, 51 Md. L. Rev. 1, 71-72 (1992).

Birke & Fox, Psychological Principles in Negotiating Civil Settlements, 4 Harv. Neg. L. Rev. 1, 7-12, 14-20, 42-47, 48-51 (1999).

Thompson & Nadler, Judgmental Biases in Conflict Resolution and How to Overcome Them, in Deutsch & Coleman (eds.), The Handbook of Conflict Resolution: Theory and Practice 213, 214-219 (2000).

Kahneman & Tversky, Conflict Resolution: A Cognitive Perspective, in Arrow et al. (eds), Barriers to Conflict Resolution 47 (1995).

Ross, Reactive Devaluation in Negotiation and Conflict Resolution, in Arrow et al. (eds), Barriers to Conflict Resolution 34-40 (1995).

Allred, Anger and Retaliation in Conflict: The Role of Attribution, in Deutsch & Coleman (eds.), The Handbook of Conflict Resolution: Theory and Practice 236, 243-244 (2000).

Adler, Rosen & Silverstein, Emotions in Negotiation: How to Manage Fear and Anger, 14 Neg. J. 161, 167-177 (1998). Reprinted by permission of Plenum Publishing Corp.

Tjosvold & Huston, Social Face and Resistance to Compromise in Bargaining, 104 J. of Soc. Psychol. 57, 59 (1978). Reprinted by permission of Heldref Publications and the Journal of Social Psychology.

Heumann & Hyman, Negotiation Methods and Litigation Settlement Methods in New Jersey: "You Can't Always Get What You Want," 12 Ohio St. J. Disp. Resol. 253, 262-265 (1997). Reprinted by permission of the Ohio State Journal of Dispute Resolution.

Gifford, Legal Negotiation: Theory and Applications 21 (1989). Reprinted from Legal Negotiation: Theory and Applications, Gifford, 1989 with permission of the West Group.

Mnookin, Peppet & Tulumello, The Tension Between Empathy and Assertiveness, 12 Neg. J. 217, 218-226 (1996). Reprinted by permission of Plenum Publishing Corp.

Allred, Distinguishing Best and Strategic Practices: A Framework for Managing the Dilemma Between Creating and Claiming Value, Neg. J. 387, 388-390 (2000). Reprinted by permission of Plenum Publishing Corp.

Stone, Patton & Heen, Difficult Conversations 37-40, 167-168 (1999). Copyright © 1999 by Douglas Stone, Bruce Patton and Sheila Heen. Used by permission of Penguin Putnam Inc.

Nyerges, Ten Commandments for a Negotiator, 3 Neg. J. 21 (1987). Reprinted by permission of Plenum Publishing Corp.

Menkel-Meadow, Teaching about Gender and Negotiation: Sex, Truths, and Videotape, Neg. J. 357, 358-359, 364 (2000). Reprinted by permission of Plenum Publishing Corp.

Rhode, Gender and Professional Roles, 63 Fordham L. Rev. 39, 42-43 (1994).

Rack, Negotiated Justice: Gender and Ethnic Minority Bargaining Patterns in the Metro Court Study, 20 Hamline J. Pub. L. & Pol. 211, 222-236 (1999).

Watson, Gender Versus Power as a Predictor of Negotiation Behavior and Outcomes, 10 Neg. J. 117, 119 (1994). Reprinted by permission of Plenum Publishing Corp.

Rubin & Sander, Culture, Negotiation, and The Eye of the Beholder, 7 Neg. J. 249 (1991). Reprinted by permission of Plenum Publishing Corp.

Lewicki & Litterer, Negotiation 166-169 (1985).

Ayres, Further Evidence of Discrimination in New Car Negotiations and Estimates of Its Cause, 94 Mich. L. Rev. 109, 120 (1995).

Adler & Silverstein, When David Meets Goliath: Dealing With Power Differentials in Negotiations, 5 Harv. Neg. L. Rev. 1, 29-48 (2000).

Farnsworth, Precontractual Liability and Preliminary Agreements: Fair Dealing and Failed Negotiations, 87 Colum. L. Rev. 217, 239-242 (1987). This article originally appeared at Colum. L. Rev. 217 (1987). Reprinted by permission.

Longan, Ethics in Settlement Negotiations: Forward, 52 Mercer L. Rev. 807, 810-829 (2001).

Crystal, The Lawyer's Duty to Disclose Material Facts in Contract or Settlement Negotiations, 87 Kentucky L.J. 1055, 1059-1074 (1998-99).

Rosenberger, Laissez-"Fair": An Argument for the Status Quo Ethical Constraints on Lawyers as Negotiators, 13 Ohio St. J. on Dis. Resol. 611, 638 (1998).

White, Machiavelli and the Bar: Ethical Limitations on Lying in Negotiation, Am. B. Found. Research J. 921, 927-938 (1980).

Applbaum, Ethics for Adversaries: The Morality of Roles in Public and Professional Life 5-6 (1990).

Raiffa, The Art and Science of Negotiation 142-144 (1982). Reprinted by permission of the publisher from THE ART AND SCIENCE OF NEGOTIATION: HOW TO RESOLVE CONFLICTS AND GET THE BEST OUT OF BARGAINING by Howard Raiffa, pp. 142-144, Cambridge Mass.: The Belknap Press of Harvard University Press, Copyright © 1982 by the President and Fellows of Harvard College.

Gordon, Private Settlement as Alternative Adjudication: A Rationale for Negotiation Ethics, 18 U. Mich. J. L. Ref. 503, 530 (1985).

Steele, Deceptive Negotiating and High-Toned Morality, 39 Vand. L. Rev. 1387, 1402 (1986).

Alfini, Settlement Ethics and Lawyering in ADR Proceedings: A Proposal to Revise Rule 4.1, 19 N. Ill. U. L. Rev. 255, 270-271 (1999).

Perschbacher, Regulating Lawyers' Negotiations, 27 Ariz. L. Rev. 75, 133-136 (1985).

Rubin, A Causerie on Lawyers' Ethics in Negotiation, 35 La.L.Rev. 577, 591-592 (1975).

Mnookin, Peppet & Tulumello, Beyond Winning: Negotiating to Create Value in Deals and Disputes 286-293 (2000). Reprinted by permission of the publishers from BEYOND WINNING: NEGOTIATING TO CREATE VALUE IN DEALS AND DISPUTES, by Robert H. Mnookin, Scott R. Peppet, and Andrew S. Tulumello, Cambridge, Mass.: Harvard University Press, Copyright © 2000 by Robert Mnookin, Scott R. Peppet and Andrew S. Tulumello.

Fisher, A Code of Negotiation Practices for Lawyers, 1 Neg. J. 105-110 (1995). Reprinted by permission of Plenum Publishing Corp.

Epstein, Post-Settlement Malpractice: Undoing the Done Deal, 46 Cath. U. L. Rev. 453, 453-460, 463-464, 472-474 (1997).

Kramer, Consent Decrees and the Rights of Third Parties, 87 Mich. L. Rev. 321, 324-331 (1988).

Kull, Restitution as a Remedy for Breach of Contract, 67 S. Cal. L. Rev. 1465, 1512-1514 (1994).

Sherman, From Loser Pays to Modified Offer-of-Judgment Rules: Reconciling Incentives to Settle with Access to Justice, 76 Tex. L. Rev. 1863, 1863-1877 (1998). Copyright © 1998 by the Texas Law Review Association. Used by permission.

Michaels, Rule 408: A Litigation Mine Field, 19 Litig. 34, 34-38, 71 (Fall 1992).

Brazil, Settling Civil Disputes 44-46 (1985). Published by the American Bar Association.

Panel Discussion, Comments by Judge Hubert L. Will, The Role of the Judge in the Settlement Process (Federal Judicial Center 1983).

Panel Discussion, Comments by Judge Alvin B. Rubin, The Role of the Judge in the Settlement Process (Federal Judicial Center 1983).

Schuck, The Role of Judges in Settling Complex Cases: The Agent Orange Example, 53 U. Chi. L. Rev. 337, 344-348 (1986). Reprinted by permission of the University of Chicago Law Review.

Sherman, Court-Mandated Alternative Dispute Resolution: What Form of Participation Should be Required?, 46 SMU L. Rev. 2079, 2094-2096, 2103-2108 (1993).

*

SUMMARY OF CONTENTS

*

TABLE OF CONTENTS

*

TABLE OF CASES

Principal cases are in bold type. Non-principal cases are in roman type. References are to Pages.

*

NEGOTIATION

*

CHAPTER I

LAWYERS, LITIGATION AND PROCESS

A. INTRODUCTION

"What, then, is this law business about? It is about the fact that our society is honeycombed with disputes. Disputes actual and potential; disputes to be settled and disputes to be prevented; both appealing to law, both making up the business of the law. But obviously those which most violently call for attention are the actual disputes, and to these our first attention must be directed. Actual disputes call for somebody to do something about them. First, so that there may be peace, for the disputants; for other persons whose ears and toes disputants are disturbing. And secondly, so that the dispute may really be put at rest, which means, so that a solution may be achieved which, at least in the main, is bearable to the parties and not disgusting to the lookers-on. This doing of something about disputes, this doing of it reasonably, is the business of law. And the people who have the doing in charge, whether they be judges or sheriffs or clerks or jailers or lawyers, are officials of the law. *What these officials do about disputes is, to my mind, the law itself.*"[1]

This book is about the ways in which those "in charge" of "doing something about disputes" help to resolve those disputes. In particular, it is about the choices that lawyers make in helping to "put at rest" the disputes in which their clients have become involved.

Lawyers make choices about the appropriate process for resolving disputes even as they handle the most routine cases—in writing a letter suggesting possible settlement options for a divorce case, filing a lawsuit for a personal injury claimant, requesting arbitration under the provisions of a supply contract, filing a request for a waiver of a local zoning restriction, or asking a former school board member to mediate a dispute between a parent group and the elementary school principal. Often, however, such

---

1. Karl Llewellyn, The Bramble Bush:
On Our Law and Its Study 12 (1960).

"choices" are made instinctively and without a great deal of reflection. Legal education—beginning with the traditional first-year curriculum and continuing through many advanced courses and extracurricular programs— may well have socialized the attorney into accepting litigation as the default process, that is, the normal, routine way in which client problems are to be resolved. The dominance of the "case book" and the hallowed "case method," while reflecting the importance of court decisions within the common law system, conveys the impression that a court is the inevitable forum for resolving disputes between individuals. Legal training may well focus intensively on the intricacies of the litigation process—but it will rarely address the strengths and weaknesses of litigation as only one among many processes available to resolve disputes.

During the last few decades, however, increased concern has been expressed by both the professionals who are engaged in litigation and the public at large about our judicial system. Litigation has been criticized as being too slow and costly and as failing ultimately to provide a resolution of disputes that is fair and that the parties will respect—as being, in short, "formal, tricky, divisive, time-consuming, and distorting."[2] Clients have begun to demand attention to process issues, and many now expect their lawyers to be familiar with the full range of alternative processes available for dispute resolution. And lawyers, trying to respond to this challenge, have begun to treat process as an important variable in the dispute resolution equation. This book seeks to give lawyers greater awareness of the process choices they make, and to expand their understanding of, and ability to use, a wide range of available dispute resolution processes.

We will be looking more closely at the litigation process in the next section. Our first step, however, is to develop some background understanding of conflict and the lawyer's role in its resolution. The typical lawyer probably gives very little thought to the nature of conflict—for example, how a dispute arises, or how and why a person decides to come to an attorney for help with a particular dispute. The lawyer is likely to take the dispute as a "given," turning immediately to the processing of the dispute in order to arrive at a satisfactory resolution. Yet any human problem will have traversed a long route and gone through a complex transformation before arriving at the lawyer's office. Understanding the social context out of which a dispute has arisen may help us in choosing and applying the appropriate process.

Richard E. Miller and Austin Sarat, Grievances, Claims, and Disputes: Assessing the Adversary Culture

15 Law & Soc'y Rev. 525, 526–27, 531–33, 536–46, 561–64 (1980–81).

One of the most important characteristics of dispute processing is the degree to which it emphasizes or requires adversariness. The comparison of

---

2. Lieberman & Henry, Lessons from the Alternative Dispute Resolution Movement, 53 U.Chi.L.Rev. 424, 427 (1986).

mediation and other techniques is frequently structured as a comparison between conciliation and contention. Criticism is often directed against legal professionals and legal processes for unnecessarily intensifying hostility between disputants. * * * [T]his intensification occurs because lawyers treat disputes through the adversarial forms prescribed by the legal order and thus remove them from their natural context.

Many theoretical statements about dispute processing reflect this concern for its adversarial elements. Theories of dispute transformation examine techniques for "heating up" or "cooling down" disputes. Dispute processing researchers typically favor methods of resolution which minimize adversarial elements; informality and reconciliation are preferred over formality and coercion. Dispute processing research has thus acquired its own ideology, which, apart from its intrinsic merits, further obscures the social context of disputing. It denies, implicitly, that disputes and disputing are normal components of human association.

Disputes begin as *grievances*. A grievance is an individual's belief that he or she (or a group or organization) is entitled to a resource which someone else may grant or deny. People respond to such beliefs in various ways. They may, for example, choose to "lump it" so as to avoid potential conflict. They may redefine the problem and redirect blame elsewhere. They may register a *claim* to communicate their sense of entitlement to the most proximate source of redress, the party perceived to be responsible. As Nader and Todd suggest,

> The grievance or preconflict stage refers to a circumstance or condition which one person ... perceives to be unjust, and the grounds for resentment or complaint.... The grievance situation ... may erupt into conflict, or it may wane. The path it will take is usually up to the offended party. His grievance may be escalated by confrontation; or escalation may be avoided by curtailing further social interaction....

Consumers, for example, make claims when they ask retailers to repair or replace defective goods. Claims can be rejected, accepted, or they can result in a compromise offer.

If the other party accepts the claim in full and actually delivers the resource in question in a routine manner ("Yes, we'll repair your new car; just bring it in"), there is no dispute. Outright rejection of a claim ("The car was not defective; it broke down because of your misuse") establishes an unambiguous dispute; there are now two (or more) parties with conflicting claims to the same resource. A compromise offer ("We'll supply the parts if you will pay for the labor") is a partial rejection of the claim, which initiates negotiation, however brief, and thus constitutes a dispute. * * * *A dispute exists when a claim based on a grievance is rejected either in whole or in part.* It becomes a civil legal dispute when it involves rights or resources which could be granted or denied by a court.

* * *

The manner and rate at which disputes are generated is sometimes taken as an indicator of societal "health." This view is most characteristic of the work of historians writing about World War II. They presented a picture of American society as a stable balance between conflict and calm, a society in which all disputes were resolved within a framework of consensus. Some may question the validity of that picture as a description of *any* period in American life, but the experience of the last two decades has certainly undermined both the social basis upon which the balance of conflict and calm may have existed and its viability as an ideology or a system of legitimizing beliefs. We increasingly hear the voices of those who perceive and fear the growth of an "adversary society", a society of assertive, aggressive, rights-conscious, litigious people ready and eager to challenge each other and those in authority. Images of our allegedly unprecedented assertiveness, or the ingenious ways which we have found to fight each other, flow through the popular culture, from *New Yorker* cartoons about children threatening to sue their parents for forcing them to drink their milk to palimony suits against celebrities.

There is, of course, another view of contemporary American society, a view which suggests that we are in fact, relatively uncontentious and even passive. Americans are said to be reluctant to admit that their lives are troubled and conditioned to accept circumstances and treatment which are far from ideal. Since our institutions respond slowly, inefficiently, and reluctantly, we learn not to complain, not to pursue our grievances or claim our rights. Even when we do, we find that appropriate institutions do not exist. As our society becomes ever more complex and expansive, it becomes easier to avoid conflict or to ignore it merely by moving on. People unable or unwilling to assert their rights or defend their interests may be easily victimized by self-interested organizations seeking to perpetuate a social and economic status quo. Proponents of this view typically question the adequacy of existing political, social, and economic arrangements to achieve justice.

It is ultimately both an empirical question and a matter of definition as to whether ours is a society of rights consciousness and conflict, or one of acquiescence and equilibrium.

* * *

DESCRIBING THE STRUCTURE OF CONFLICT: GRIEVING, CLAIMING, AND DISPUTING

Grieving

Disputes emerge out of grievances. Consequently we look first to the incidence of grievances to establish the baseline potential for disputes. There is, however, a conceptual problem. Grievances are composed of concrete events or circumstances which are relatively objective, but they are also composed of subjective perceptions, definitions, and beliefs that an event or circumstance is unwarranted or inappropriate. Individuals may react differently to the same experience. One buyer of a defective good may find it unacceptable and remediable; another may regard the bad purchase as "inevitable" and "lump it" or write it off to experience. According to our definition the first individual has a grievance; the second does not. Grievance rates reflect both the occurrence of certain events and a willingness by the participants to label those events in a particular way. * * *

Claiming

Given the perception that some event or circumstance is unacceptable and remediable, we can ask how assertive those who experience grievances are in seeking a remedy. Possible responses, as previously mentioned, range from avoidance, through repair without direct confrontation, registering a claim, to a demand for monetary compensation. Unless a claim is made, a dispute cannot occur. Other responses, such as avoidance, may be accompanied by feelings of bitterness or resentment which could lead to later conflict.

* * *

The Role of Lawyers and Courts

The language of rights and remedies is preeminently the language of law. One might logically ask where, in all of this, the law and legal institutions play a role. There is relatively little empirical work on the role of lawyers and courts in disputing. An assessment of the role of law, legal institutions, and legal services in the development of, or response to, conflict requires us to confront the problem of baselines.

[The authors then analyze the results of a telephone survey of approximately 1000 randomly-selected households in each of five federal judicial districts. In this survey grievances involving less than $1000 were screened out.]

Examining [Figures 1A and 1B], we find that relatively few disputants use a lawyer's services at all. Lawyers were used by less than one-fourth of those engaged in the disputes we studied. There are, however, two significant exceptions to the pattern. The role of lawyers is much more pronounced in post-divorce and tort problems. In the former, the involvement of lawyers is a function of the fact that many of these problems, e.g., adjustment in visitation arrangements or in alimony, *require* court action. In the latter, the contingent fee system facilitates and encourages lawyer use.

Few disputants (11.2 percent) report taking their dispute to court. Excluding post-divorce disputes, where court action is often required, that number is approximately 9 percent. These findings do not mean that courts or lawyers play a trivial role in middle-range disputes. Claims are made, avoided, or processed at least in part according to each party's understanding of its own legal position and that of its opponent; that understanding reflects both the advice that lawyers provide and the rights and remedies which courts have in the past recognized or imposed.

Figure 1A. A Dispute Pyramid: The General Pattern
No. per 1000 Grievances

Court Filings	50
Lawyers	103
Disputes	449
Claims	718
Grievances	1000

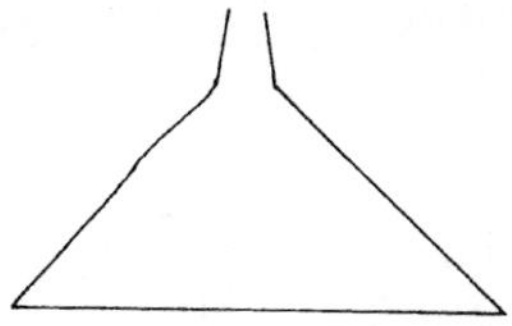

Figure 1B. Dispute Pyramids: Three Deviant Patterns
No. per 1000 Grievances

	Tort	Discrimination	Post-Divorce
Court Filings	38	8	451
Lawyers	116	29	588
Disputes	201	216	765
Claims	857	294	879
Grievances	1000	1000	1000

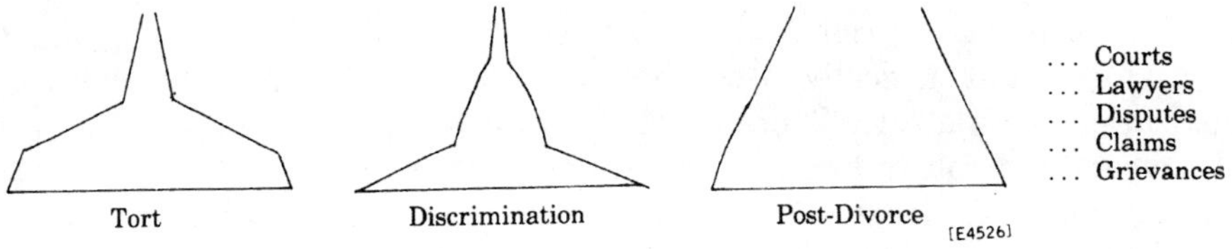

Tort   Discrimination   Post-Divorce   [E4526]

... Courts
... Lawyers
... Disputes
... Claims
... Grievances

Summary

We can visualize the process of dispute generation through the metaphor of a pyramid (see Figure 1A). At the base are grievances, and the width of the pyramid shows the proportions that make the successive transitions to claims, disputes, lawyer use, and litigation. Figure 1B presents three contrasting patterns—the disputing pyramids for torts, post-divorce, and discrimination grievances.

Torts show a clear pattern. Most of those with grievances make claims (85.7 percent), and most claims are not formally resisted (76.5 percent result in immediate agreement). As a result, disputes are relatively rare (23.5 percent of claims). Where they occur, however, lawyers are available, accessible, and are, in fact, often employed (57.9 percent). Moreover, the same can be said for the employment of courts (at least in comparison with other problems). The overall picture is of a remedy system that minimizes formal conflict but uses the courts when necessary in those relatively rare cases in which conflict is unavoidable.

The pattern for discrimination grievances is quite different. Seven of ten grievants make no claim for redress. Those who do are very likely to have their claim resisted, and most claimants receive nothing. Only a little more than one in ten disputants is aided by a lawyer, and only four in a hundred disputes lead to litigation. The impression is one of perceived rights which are rarely fully asserted. When they are, they are strongly resisted and pursued without much assistance from lawyers or courts. Of course, we do not know how many of these or any other grievances would be found meritorious in a court of law. Nonetheless, as perceived griev-ances, they are a source of underlying tension and potential social conflict.

Post-divorce problems engender high rates of grievances, claims, and disputes, and are characterized by frequent use of lawyers and courts. As a result, almost half of all grievances lead to court involvement. While the court's activity in many, possibly most, of these cases is more administra-tive than adjudicative, this is, at least formally, the most disputatious and litigious grievance type we have measured.

Dispute pyramids could be drawn for the other types of problems, but they would all be quite similar: high rates of claims (80 to 95 percent of grievances), high rates of disputes (75 to 85 percent of claims), fairly low proportions using a lawyer (10 to 20 percent of disputants), and low litigation rates (3 to 5 percent of disputants). Indeed, the most striking finding in these descriptive data is again the general uniformity of rates at each stage of the disputing process across very different types of middle-range grievances.

* * *

We have found that, when measured against a baseline of perceived injustices or grievances, disputing is fairly common. But we are in no position, absent historical or comparative data, to determine just how substantial or significant it is. Our own belief is that where there are grievances there ought to be claims and that where there are claims, conflict is not necessarily an undesirable or unhealthy result. Those who fear conflict or who advocate acquiescence in the face of grievances fear threats to the social status quo. They bear a substantial burden in showing how people benefit from lumping or enduring injurious experiences or the denial of rights or how the status quo is served in the longer run as frustrations increase and legitimacy decreases. Indeed, it may be that the most significant aspect of our data, at least to those interested in argu-ments about the adversary culture, is the relatively low grievance rate for most of the transactions or relationships which we studied. Either those transactions are routinely efficient and satisfactory or people are reluctant to perceive or acknowledge trouble as it occurs. The incidence of social conflict ultimately hinges both on the rates at which injurious experiences are inflicted upon people and on what people define as acceptable perfor-mance of obligations or tolerate as acceptable conditions of life. The fact that almost 60 percent of our respondents report no recent middle-range grievance indicates a relatively low level of "injury" and/or a relatively high level of satisfaction or acquiescence.

Levels of "real" and perceived injuries, and the way people respond to them, are not self-generating. Economic, social, and political forces shape the context in which problems are perceived and conflicts generated, just as they affect the kind and amount of problems which occur. Thus we found, for example, that grievance rates were affected not only by the risk factors of particular transactions, statuses, and relationships, but also by edu-cational levels and legal contacts. Particular concerns and not others come to be seen as worthwhile; particular responses and not others are legitimated; and those who declare trouble or who participate in conflict are differentially rewarded or stigmatized.

We wonder whether a survey of discrimination problems conducted twenty or thirty years ago would have found, as we did, that female-headed households reported a higher incidence of such problems or that blacks with such grievances were more likely to make a claim for redress. Not only have social and economic changes increased the number of women at risk of discrimination in employment or housing, but concomitant political and cultural changes have brought both increased sensitivity to and legislative condemnation of such discrimination. We have no basis on which to speculate about changes, if any, in blacks' "sensitivity" to racial discrimination, but social and political developments clearly have both reflected and enhanced the willingness and ability of blacks to resist such behavior.

Sex discrimination is a classic example of a movement from unperceived injurious experiences (unPIES) to perceived injurious experiences (PIES), which Felstiner *et al.* argue lies at the heart of the process through which new grievances emerge and new types of disputes arise. With each newly recognized injurious experience comes a strengthened or reinforced sense of harm and entitlement, both of which prepare the way for higher rates of grievances and conflict. Such cultural labeling is often matched by the use of official declarations, particularly the declaration of legal rights, as a device to regulate grievance perception and the response to grievances. The political forces that lead to declaration of legal rights may also result in the establishment of specialized remedy systems. Such systems may arise from other sources as well, such as an economic incentive to share risks. In any case, it is possible that the balance of rights declared and remedies provided is important in cueing responses to middle-range problems.

Problems differ in terms of the availability and kind of *institutionalization of remedy systems*. By institutionalization of remedy systems we mean the extent to which there are well-known, regularized, readily available mechanisms, techniques, or procedures for dealing with a problem. Take, for example, automobile accident and discrimination problems. The remedy system for auto accidents is highly institutionalized. There are routinized, well-known, and widely available procedures for dealing with such problems. The problem itself is one which has been recognized and acknowledged in the society for a long time and the principles—at least, the legal principles—involved are relatively settled. The result is a high claim rate, a low dispute rate, and considerable success for claimants.

The same cannot be said for discrimination problems. Neither a clear and widely accepted definition of discriminatory behavior which creates an entitlement to redress nor notions about appropriate kinds of redress have yet evolved. Existing legislated definitions are not well understood by the public, and those definitions are themselves in flux. Furthermore, remedy systems are less well developed and certainly less accessible. One simply doesn't pick up the phone and call one's insurance agent about a discrimination problem, and the principles governing redress are both rather unsettled and highly controversial. Under these circumstances, it is not surprising that, while quite a few households report some discrimination grievance, only three in ten of these asked for any redress of their grievance.

[The authors had earlier suggested other possible explanations for the low level of "claiming" for discrimination grievances:

Perhaps a lack of assertiveness has more to do with the substance of the problem itself. In discrimination situations it seems easier for those who believe that they have been unfairly denied a job or home just to keep on looking. Securing a job or home is likely to be much more pressing and important than filing a claim for something which is made undesirable by the very act that generates the grievance. "I need a job, and who would want to work there anyway" would not be an inexplicable response. * * *

Furthermore, there may be some stigma attached to the grievance itself or to the act of assertion. Victims, for example, may blame themselves for the unfair treatment. In discrimination grievances, especially, victory may turn into defeat. Those who are assertive, even if vindicated, are branded as troublemakers. Furthermore, grievants may be uncertain about the fit between their own perceptions and definitions of grievances and those embodied in statutes or otherwise recognized in their community. Indeed, both the law and popular expectations in this area of relatively new rights appear unsettled. Many who experience discrimination problems are, as a result, uncertain whether their grievance constitutes a sustainable claim.]

The institutionalization of remedies affects grievance perception, claiming, and disputing in two ways: first, by legitimizing action, and second, by shaping the objective probabilities of success should action be taken. The institutionalization of remedies alone suggests that the frequency and importance of a problem, as well as the appropriateness of action taken in response to it, is recognized. Where remedies are institutionalized, the probability of successful action can be more accurately assessed and prospective action thereby more clearly shaped and considered. Higher levels of institutionalization, everything else being equal, would be associated with higher rates of grievance perception and claiming, lower rates of disputes, and higher rates of success in recovery for meritorious claims.

Disputing is minimized where remedies are most and least institutionalized. Conflict can be avoided where automatic remedies are provided for felt grievances or where the demand for redress is discouraged by making it uncertain and hard to obtain. It is easier, on the whole, for societies to declare rights than to provide remedies; indeed, the development of remedies almost inevitably lags substantially behind the recognition of rights. The inability to vindicate rights discourages their expression and thus helps avoid a precondition for overtly adversarial relations. At the same time, of course, the gap between rights and remedies contributes to feelings of frustration and alienation which breed adversity between individuals and institutions. It is this tension which drives the development of remedy systems. Where rights are not realized or realizable over a long period of time and among a substantial portion of the population, where raised expectations are disappointed, interpersonal conflict is discouraged at the price of social and political strain. The balance of rights recognized and remedies provided is, in our view, important to an understanding of the generation of disputes and adversarial behavior.

NOTES AND QUESTIONS

1. Whether an individual even perceives that he has been "injured" may depend on his background and circumstances. A cancer victim previously exposed to asbestos may fail to perceive that he is ill; a consumer may fail to appreciate that a product is dangerous or not working as it is intended to. And among those experiences which *are* perceived as "injurious" "some may be seen as deserved punishment, some as the result of assumed risk or fickle fate"; only a limited number will be seen as a violation of some right or entitlement for which another person is responsible (that is, the subject of a "grievance"):

> [C]haracterization of an event as a grievance will depend on the cognitive repertoire with which society supplies the injured person and his idiosyncratic adaptation of it. He may, for example, be liberally supplied with ideological lenses to focus blame or to diffuse it. * * *
>
> The perception of grievances requires cognitive resources. Thus Best and Andreasen found that both higher income and white households perceive more problems with the goods they buy and complain more both to sellers and to third parties than do poor or black households. It seems unlikely that this reflects differences in the quality of goods purchased. Similarly, Curran reports that better educated respondents experience more problems of infringement of their constitutional rights.

Galanter, Reading the Landscape of Disputes: What We Know and Don't Know (And Think We Know) About Our Allegedly Contentious and Litigious Society, 31 U.C.L.A.L.Rev. 4, 13–14 (1983). See also Best & Andreasen, Consumer Response to Unsatisfactory Purchases: A Survey of Perceiving Defects, Voicing Complaints, and Obtaining Redress, 11 Law & Soc'y Rev. 701 (1977); Felstiner, Abel, & Sarat, The Emergence and Transformation of Disputes: Naming, Blaming, Claiming . . . , 15 Law & Soc'y Rev. 631 (1980–81).

Finally, even perceived grievances may not become the subject of complaints or claims. Despite much talk about our "litigious" society, many Americans seem reluctant to voice grievances. To do so, after all, may require them to acknowledge—both to themselves and to others—that they have been bettered by others or that they have allowed themselves to be victimized. See, e.g., Kristin Bumiller, The Civil Rights Society: The Social Construction of Victims 109 (1988) ("people who have experienced discriminatory treatment" feel that asserting their legal rights "would force them to justify their worthiness against a more powerful opponent"; they "reluctantly employ the label of discrimination because they shun the role of the victim"); Abel, The Real Tort Crisis—Too Few Claims, 48 Ohio St.L.J. 443 (1987).

Should the legal profession play any role in this process by which grievances and claims are generated? How does the relationship between "sensitivity" to grievances and disputes affect a lawyer's practice? His relationship with the client?

2.   The Miller and Sarat data suggest that lawyers may play a less significant role in processing disputes than is commonly thought. Even where a grievance has crystallized into a "dispute," it may be brought to a lawyer's office less than a quarter of the time. Even in tort cases or in post-divorce conflicts, a sizable minority of disputants may choose not to seek legal help. What might account for this choice? Do disputants have an effective alternative?

3.   Miller and Sarat state: "Claims are made, avoided, or processed at least in part according to each party's understanding of its own legal position and that of its opponent; that understanding reflects both the advice that lawyers provide and the rights and remedies which courts have in the past recognized or imposed." The notion that dispute resolution may take place "in the shadow of the law" is central to the lawyer's role in negotiation as well as in the other dispute resolution processes that we will be considering here. The authors imply, however, that the advice of lawyers may in some way be different from the rights and remedies expressed by courts. Why might this be true? It has been suggested that lawyers in consumer disputes often see their major role to be that of "gatekeepers" to the legal system: The individual client may be "cooled out"—discouraged from pressing claims that the lawyer feels may not be in the client's best interests to pursue, or that the lawyer *himself* for one reason or another would rather not pursue. See Macaulay, Lawyers and Consumer Protection Laws, 14 Law & Soc'y Rev. 115 (1979).

B.   Courts and Litigation

1.   The Dimensions of Litigation

Jerold S. Auerbach, Justice Without Law?

10, 12–13 (1983).

Americans prefer to stand apart, separated from their ancestors, contemporaries, and descendents. Individualism means freedom—above all, the freedom to compete, acquire, possess, and bequeath. It is precisely this freedom that our legal system so carefully cultivates and protects. In a society where the dominant ethic is competitive individualism, regulated by the loose ground rules of the Darwinian struggle (with special protection reserved for crippled corporate giants), social cohesion is an enduring problem. Even as litigiousness expresses, and accentuates, the pursuit of individual advantage, the rule of law helps to hold such a fractured society together. At the least (usually it is also the most), people can agree upon how they will disagree. In a restless, mobile society of strangers, the staple scene of Western movies is perpetually reenacted: an American, at the first sign of danger, reaches for his (hired) gun and files a lawsuit. Yet contradictions abound. Our individualistic society encourages the assertion of legal rights as an entitlement of citizenship, but distributes them according to the ability to pay. Conflict is channeled into adversary proceedings with two combatants in every legal ring; but beyond the implicit assumption that every fight and any winner is good for society, the social good is ignored. Litigation is the all-purpose remedy that American society provides to its aggrieved members. But as rights are asserted, combat is encouraged; as the rule of law binds society, legal contentiousness increases social fragmentation.

* * *

The consuming American reverence for legal symbols and institutions slights the manifold ways in which law not only reinforces, but imposes, an atomistic, combative vision of reality. "Sue Thy Neighbor" is the appropriate modern American inversion of the Biblical admonition. So a newspaper photograph shows an angry woman, her face contorted with rage, who points menacingly at a cowering man, whose hands are raised in retreat and surrender. A judge looks on impassively, an American flag at his side. "If thy neighbor offend thee," the caption reads, "don't turn the other cheek. Slap him with a summons. And take him to Small Claims Court." It is only a blurb for a television special report, but the line between soap opera and reality is hopelessly blurred. Viewers are promised "a free course in self-defense," evidently a requirement for life among neighbors. (With neighbors like these, of course, enemies are superfluous.) Armed with the sword of litigation, Americans can wage ceaseless warfare against each other—and themselves.

NOTES AND QUESTIONS

1. Auerbach's image of a rights-obsessed, combative, litigious American society is certainly a familiar one in popular culture. After having spent some time in law school, does this ring true to you? Or does it strike you as something of a caricature? Does the picture he draws seem consistent with the data collected by Miller and Sarat on disputing patterns in America?

2. The rhetoric of the preceding excerpt may obscure one crucial fact: Even where disputants do have recourse to the courts, "full-blown" adjudication remains extremely rare. In the early 1980s the Civil Litigation Research Project (CLRP), sponsored jointly by the U.S. Department of Justice and the University of Wisconsin, compiled data about civil litigation in state and federal courts in five federal judicial districts. The following excerpt is based on data published in the Project's Final Report.

David M. Trubek, Austin Sarat, William L.F. Felstiner, Herbert M. Kritzer & Joel B. Grossman, The Costs of Ordinary Litigation

31 U.C.L.A. L.Rev. 72, 89, 122 (1983).

What happens in ordinary litigation? There is a popular image that litigation involves extensive pretrial activity and protracted trials. Our data suggest the contrary. Trials are rare, pretrial activity modest, and most cases terminate through settlement negotiations.

Less than 8% of the cases in our sample went to trial. In another 22.5%, the judge dismissed the complaint or rendered judgment on the merits without a trial. The most frequent mode of termination is voluntary agreement between the parties, which occurred in over 50% of the cases. Our data suggest civil judges and juries provide final, authoritative third party dispute processing in less than a third of the cases. More often, the courts serve as the background for bargaining between the parties. Bargaining occurs "in the shadow of the law," but is conducted primarily, if not exclusively, by the parties and their lawyers.

* * *

One of the most striking aspects of our study of litigation was that bargaining and settlement are the prevalent and, for plaintiffs, perhaps the most cost-effective activity that occurs when cases are filed. This will come as no surprise to litigators, but it is remarkable how seldom this fact is taken into account in discussions of the litigation crisis, costs of litigation, and the need for "alternatives to litigation."

Much of the literature advocating alternatives to litigation naively assumes that what occurs in courts is adjudication, in the classical sense. Since "adjudication" by definition uses judicial time heavily, the literature deduces that increased litigation will increase court budgets dramatically. Since adjudication presents an imposed, rather than a bargained or mediated solution, many observers believe it to be ineffective for the resolution of certain kinds of disputes. Finally, if adjudication is expensive and intrusive, then what is needed, so it is argued, are cheaper, more flexible "alternatives." But if in the world of ordinary litigation judges rarely reach formal decisions on the merits, the parties negotiate, albeit "in the shadow of the law," judges actively intervene to encourage settlement, and settlement is the rule, not the exception, then perhaps the whole reform debate falls wide of the mark. Perhaps the right approach is not to reach for wholly new institutional alternatives to a hypothetical process of adjudication, but to understand the non-adjudicative dimensions of litigation, to see how and why they work, and to seek to make this dimension of the litigation process even more central and effective.

NOTES AND QUESTIONS

1. A similar picture appears in a more recent study drawn from business litigation in the state courts of Rhode Island. In civil cases "in which there was at least one business entity on each side," less than 3% of the cases even reached the opening of trial—suggesting strongly that "business litigation in state court is overwhelmingly resolved in the shadow of the law, rather than through the formal legal process." The authors of the study also argue that economic trends may help to explain litigation rates— and in particular that

> less litigation will be observed in expanding industries than in stagnant or contracting ones. As firms fight over a shrinking economic pie, short-term gains and the bottom line will be emphasized sometimes at the cost of healthy long-term relationships. * * * Expanding conditions mean that the short-term value of winning a case in court will likely be less than either the potential profits from a future relationship with the party or simply the return on resources invested elsewhere. Our data provide modest support for the hypothesis.

Ross E. Cheit & Jacob E. Gersen, When Businesses Sue Each Other: An Empirical Study of State Court Litigation, 25 Law & Social Inquiry 789, 797, 807 (2000).

2. Would you expect that we would see different rates of settlement in cases involving different areas of law? The CLRP data indicate that while the "trial rate" for torts cases was 10%, by contrast 25% of domestic relations cases, and 15% of civil rights and discrimination cases, were "tried." Of course, "the higher 'trial rate' in domestic relations reflects the requirement of a formal resolution in divorce cases; while the court record may show an event that is labeled as a trial, it is typically nothing more than the ratification of a settlement agreed upon by the parties." Kritzer, Adjudication to Settlement: Shading in the Grey, 70 Judicature 161, 164 (1986).

3. The CLRP data also suggest that even where a lawsuit has been filed, the lawyers involved are likely to devote as much or more time to settlement than to actually "trying" the case in the traditional sense. When asked how they allocated their time in the cases being studied, lawyers reported spending 15% of their time on "settlement discussions." In addition, we can assume that a substantial proportion of their time nominally devoted to other activities, such as conferring with the client (16%), investigating the facts (12.8%), and engaging in legal research (10.1%), must have been directly aimed at reaching a settlement.

These results underscore even further the complementary relationship between litigation and negotiation: The CLRP study suggests that just as negotiation is an integral part of the dynamic of the litigation process, conversely, litigation may be just one stage—one strategic move—in the ongoing process of negotiation. Professor Marc Galanter has coined the term "litigotiation" to refer to this "single process of disputing in the vicinity of official tribunals"—"the strategic pursuit of a settlement through mobilizing the court process." Galanter, Worlds of Deals: Using Negotiation to Teach about Legal Process, 34 J.Legal Educ. 168 (1984). As a practical matter, then, in our system a lawsuit may be little more than a rather pointed way of opening negotiations—one way of bringing the other party to the bargaining table, where the real work of dispute resolution takes place.

4.   A careful study of the much-publicized "litigation explosion" acknowledges that there has been an increase over the last century in the per capita filings of civil cases in both state and federal courts. However, "there is no evidence to suggest an increase in the portion of cases that runs the whole course. * * * [T]he percentage of cases reaching trial has diminished." On the other hand, for the small minority of cases that *do* run the full course, adjudication is likely to be "more protracted, more elaborate, more exhaustive, and more expensive." Galanter, Reading the Landscape of Disputes: What We Know and Don't Know (And Think We Know) About Our Allegedly Contentious and Litigious Society, 31 U.C.L.A. L.Rev. 4, 43–44 (1983). Perhaps of even greater interest is a comparison of American litigation rates with rates in other countries. The evidence suggests that the rate at which Americans use the civil courts "is in the same range as England, Ontario, Australia, Denmark, [and] New Zealand," although far higher than in Japan, Spain, and Italy. Id. at 55. The inclusion of Spain and Italy—societies that are not usually considered models of harmony and lack of contentiousness—may suggest the danger of facile "cultural" generalizations about litigation patterns.

5.   The words "adjudication" and "litigation" are often casually used as if they were interchangeable, and you may see examples of this confusion in material quoted throughout this book. "Adjudication" refers to the process by which final, authoritative decisions are rendered by a neutral third party who enters the controversy without previous knowledge of the dispute. The third party's solution may, if necessary, be enforced by recourse to governmental sanctions; he may (but need not) have the authority to resolve the dispute according to a set of objective norms and following an elaborate procedure for the presentation of arguments and proof. In this sense, private arbitration shares with the official court system some of the characteristics of dispute settlement through "adjudication." In "litigation," by contrast, the parties invoke the official court mechanism; as we have already seen, however, "litigation" need not lead to any final third-party decision. The dominance of negotiation and settlement has focused attention on what Trubek calls the "non-adjudicative dimensions of litigation." In addition, a number of mechanisms which aim at resolving disputes short of trial—such as the mini-trial, court-administered arbitration, or the summary jury trial—are closely connected to and may be considered part of the litigation process.

2.   The Limits of the Judicial Process

The high prestige and symbolic importance that Americans attach to the formal court system have never been incompatible with an intense awareness of the limitations and inadequacies of the litigation process. In 1850 Abraham Lincoln wrote in notes for a law lecture, "Discourage litigation. Persuade your neighbors to compromise whenever you can. Point out to them how the nominal winner is often a real loser—in fees, expenses, in waste of time."

Recent attention to the shortcomings of litigation also begins with complaints about the frequent delay and expense of legal proceedings, as does this excerpt from a speech by Judge Jon Newman of the Second Circuit:

> Whether we have too many cases or too few, or even, miraculously, precisely the right number, there can be little doubt that the system is not working very well. Too many cases take too much time to be resolved and impose too much cost upon litigants and taxpayers alike. No one should have to wait five years for a case to come to trial, but many litigants in this country face this reality. Legal expenses should not exceed damage awards, yet in the asbestos litigation morass, for example, those expenses total $1.56 for every $1 provided to a victim. If long delays and high litigation costs were aberrational, systemic change could safely be avoided. But we know the problem is more serious. Even if the modern defenders of our current litigation level are right, systemwide averages should not obscure the long delays and high costs imposed upon hundreds or thousands who use or participate in the litigation process and the losses endured by those who are deterred from seeking redress in court.[3]

Moreover, the impact of delay and expense in litigation is not equally allocated. In a personal injury case, delay before trial will affect a plaintiff with mounting medical bills and without substantial resources far more than it will affect the defendant. And particularly where legal services are not available on a contingent fee basis, the costs of litigation may have made the courts inaccessible to large sections of the poor and middle class. As former President Derek Bok of Harvard has commented, "There is far too much law for those who can afford it and far too little for those who cannot."[4]

NOTES AND QUESTIONS

1. The portion of suits that are "pursued through the full possibilities of contest" has indeed continued to decline—but Professor Galanter has suggested that there may be other explanations for this besides a decrease in the "appetite for litigious combat": "[I]t may be that more contest can be packed into earlier stages; or that increased transaction costs mean that parties can afford less contest than they would prefer." Galanter, The Life and Times of the Big Six: Or, The Federal Courts Since the Good Old Days, 1988 Wisc. L. Rev. 921, 951. Might this indicate that settlement is not always an unmitigated virtue—and that it might often be instead mere acquiescence in a lesser evil?

3. Newman, Rethinking Fairness: Perspectives on the Litigation Process, 94 Yale L.J. 1643, 1644–45 (1985).

4. Bok, Law and its Discontents: A Critical Look At Our Legal System, 38 Record of the Ass'n of the Bar of the City of New York 12, 13 (1983).

2. The New York City Health Code requires window guards for apartments with children under the age of ten. The board of a co-operative apartment building in New York voted to charge the cost of installation to the individual residents who needed such guards, rather than having the cost shared by everyone in the building; however the owner of a ninth-floor loft apartment, whose child was a month old, refused to pay. The co-op's law firm devoted a number of hours to settlement attempts and when this failed, the co-op brought a lawsuit against the owner. The New York Civil Court ruled in favor of the co-op; this was reversed, but on further appeal to the Appellate Division, the original ruling was reinstated. The contract by which the owner had acquired the apartment provided that the losing party in any litigation was to be responsible for the winner's attorneys' fees, and so further litigation then ensued concerning responsibility for the co-op's legal fees. Throughout all the stages of this suit the board paid its attorneys a total of $73,547, but it was ultimately held that it could recover only $30,000 of this from the owner of the apartment. In addition, the owner had paid around $30,000 to *his own* attorneys. It had originally cost $909 to purchase and install child-proof window guards across the 32 windows of the apartment in question. A full account appears in Lambert, "Ever Hear the One About the Lawyers and Window Bars?," Wall St. J., March 23, 1994, p. A1; see also Owners Corp. v. Diacou, N.Y.L.J., Feb. 23, 1994, p. 21.

What could possibly account for this behavior?

3. The CLRP study suggests that by contrast to such aberrant cases, the typical lawsuit is in fact

> a "paying" proposition for the parties. The average plaintiff will recover some portion of the amount claimed, and the amount recovered will significantly exceed the money and the value of time spent on the case. Even the defendants can be said to have "gained" from the litigation, at least in the sense that their litigation expenditures are less than the amount by which plaintiff's claim was reduced during litigation.

However, while it may be true that litigation typically "pays" in the sense of yielding net monetary benefits, the study left open the question whether "these gains are wiped out by negative non-monetary features of the litigation experience." Trubek et al., 31 U.C.L.A.L.Rev. at 84.

4. One study has estimated that the total expenditure nationwide for tort litigation in state and federal courts in 1985 was between $29 billion and $36 billion. Of this amount, plaintiffs received "about $14 to $16 billion in net compensation, after deducting all their litigation costs." James S. Kakalik & Nicholas M. Pace, Costs and Compensation Paid in Tort Litigation vi–ix (Rand 1986).

5. The more burdensome the prospect of litigation, of course, the more likely it becomes that the judicial process will be invoked strategically— that is, for purposes that have little or nothing to do with obtaining a favorable judgment.

In 1983 Seward Johnson, an heir to the Johnson & Johnson fortune, died and left virtually all his $400 million estate to his third wife, who had once worked in the Johnson household as a maid. His children hired Alexander Forger, of the New York firm of Milbank, Tweed, Hadley & McCloy, to challenge the will, and the ensuing will contest became "the largest, costliest, ugliest, [and] most spectacular" in American history:

> [I]t was dubious that Milbank could knock out one will, let alone the long line of them Seward had signed over the years. Forger must have known from the outset that the children could never actually win their case; the object had to be settlement. But for that to work, Milbank needed a scorched-earth brand of litigator, someone who could make life so miserable for [the widow and the executor of the estate] that they would eventually have to surrender. The more wretched they could be made to be, the higher the price they'd pay.

David Margolick, Undue Influence: The Epic Battle for the Johnson & Johnson Fortune 12, 198 (1993).

6. A recent survey of business attorneys and nonlawyer executives indicated that virtually all the executives (96%) and inside counsel (91%) thought that less than half of suits involving a business are "resolved at an appropriate cost"; 86% and 79% respectively thought that less than of half of suits involving a business are "resolved within an appropriate amount of time." In addition, only 28% of executives and 38% of inside counsel believed that the legal system correctly determines the truth more than half the time (the comparable figure for outside counsel was only 40%). "Indeed many respondents laughed cynically when the proposition was posed to them." John Lande, Failing Faith in Litigation? A Survey of Business Lawyers' and Executives' Opinions, 3 Harv. Neg. L. Rev. 1, 29, 35–36 (1998).

The delay and expense associated with litigation are largely a function of the limited resources that we are willing to allocate to the judiciary, and of our highly stylized and structured trial procedure. There are other shortcomings of the judicial process, however, which may be less contingent and more fundamental.

In resolving a dispute a court is likely to rely on the use of objective, abstract "rules." Not even the most conscientious fact-finder can come away from a trial with more than the most limited, partial view of any given situation; out of the complexity and messiness of a dispute, out of an infinite variety of elements, the court will select just what seems relevant to enable it to place the dispute into one of several pre-existing "categories" (for example, "this is an action based on anticipatory repudiation of an executory contract"). The appropriate rule to govern the category is then neatly applied. Courts will only rarely be willing to use more person-oriented norms of conduct. Only exceptionally, for example, will a court feel able to consider (at least openly) the personal characteristics of the disputants, the human texture of their relationship, what may be in their long-term interest, or what they themselves may perceive as critical to their own dispute. In this process, the disputants themselves participate only secondarily. The lawyers and judge are the principal actors; the parties themselves speak and act only within court-imposed restrictions.

One consequence is that the court's solution may not be particularly well-adapted to the parties' needs. It is certainly not likely to be as appropriate or efficient as something that the parties familiar with the situation might have worked out for themselves. A related point is that the range of remedies available to a court is traditionally limited. A court will reduce most claims to the payment of money or the transfer of goods; it necessarily avoids person-or relationship-oriented relief. It may not, for example, call for an apology, expression of regret, or acknowledgment of fault, although this might be the relief that would most satisfy a hurt or angry plaintiff. "Claims for personal injury are treated as if the issue is how to put a dollar price on pain and suffering, while claims essentially based on insult and psychic hurt are not dealt with well, if they are recognized at all."[5] Nor, in a commercial dispute, is a court in any position to try to "salvage" the deal by calling for the restructuring or renegotiation of the transaction for the future.

In addition, a court's decision is "binary" in character:

[T]he "verdict of the court has an either/or character; the decision is based upon a single, definite conception of what has actually taken place and upon a single interpretation of the legal norms." This implies that adjudication operates largely in terms of black and white: This is the rule, that is not; this rule is superior to or more compelling than that one and therefore the latter is overridden; these facts are more probably correct, those are less probably, and therefore the latter are rejected; this disputant is in the right, the other is in the wrong.[6]

Even in jury trials "in the great majority of the cases, perhaps 80% to 85%, the verdict is a clear victory for one side and a clear loss for the other."[7]

The result is not only to limit the court's creativity in the matter of remedies. Often, the "either/or" nature of adjudication may also polarize the parties and drive them still further apart. The dynamic of litigation brings with it a need for self-justification and for the strategic escalation of struggle; being caught up in the process is likely to be an intense, emotionally charged experience which can generate considerable antagonism. The

---

5. Wagatsuma & Rosett, The Implications of Apology: Law and Culture in Japan and the United States, 20 Law & Soc'y Rev. 461, 494 (1986); see also Note, Healing Angry Wounds: The Role of Apology and Mediation in Disputes Between Physicians and Patients, 1987 J. of Dispute Res. 111.

6. P.H. Gulliver, Disputes and Negotiations: A Cross–Cultural Perspective 13 (1979).

7. Samuel Gross & Kent Syverud, Don't Try: Civil Jury Verdicts in a System Geared to Settlement, 44 U.C.L.A. L. Rev. 1, 46–47 (1996). The authors term a "loser" a litigant "who does less well than she could have by accepting an available settlement offer from the opposing side (and a 'winner' is someone who does better by that standard) considering both the judgment and the cost of obtaining it."

parties may finally lose sight altogether of the problem that gave rise to the dispute in the first place. Nor is it only the behavior and attitude of the disputants that may be affected; as the following excerpt suggests, the process may affect their representatives as well.

Wayne D. Brazil, The Attorney as Victim: Towards More Candor About the Psychological Price Tag of Litigation Practice

3 J. of the Legal Profession 107, 109–10, 114–117 (1978–79).

Some form of manipulation is a very real component of the professional lives of most litigators every day. The targets of the litigator's manipulatory efforts include people, data, documents, precedents, institutions—virtually everything that can be moved to serve some purpose. The potential human subjects of the litigator's manipulations are almost countless: clients, witnesses, opposing counsel, judges, clerks, jurors, expert consultants, court reporters, even colleagues.

* * *

It is commonly believed by many litigators that to simply turn over all the relevant data to a consultant expert is to flirt with disaster: namely, the possibility that your expert will reach a negative conclusion about the role of your client. To reduce the chances of such an eventuality, many litigators carefully control the flow of information to their consultants. They first forward the data that would support a positive conclusion. Their hope is that the expert will form a positive opinion, will identify with the attorney's client, and will develop an ego investment in the positive conclusion that the attorney wants reached. Thereafter, the attorney may feed the expert some negative data about the client's conduct in order to prepare the expert to withstand cross-examination. By the time the expert receives the bulk of the negative information (at least so goes the litigator's theory of manipulation), he has so heavily identified with the client's position and has invested so much of his own professional ego in his positive opinion that all his impulses are in the direction of defending rather than reevaluating that opinion. Thus the lawyer hopes to capitalize on the expert's relatively predictable reactions to cognitive dissonance.

* * *

I believe that "money" and "winning" are the primary motivations of a high percentage of the litigators who are most comfortable with their work and the current system of dispute resolution. The people who seem least disturbed by litigation and best adapted to its pressures are not people to whom justice and esthetics are the paramount values, but are people who thrive on competition and doing battle, who are thoroughly engaged by gamesmanship, who love the taste of victory, and to whom the power and status that accompany wealth in our culture are very important. * * *

I find some support for these generalizations in the ways many litigators measure their professional success. For too many attorneys, success is not primarily seen as a function of how close to a just result was achieved for their clients. Indeed, some attorneys have retreated so far back into mystical (and self-serving) veneration for the adversary process that they insist that justice is whatever result the system produces and that they would violate their role if they even tried to determine what a "fair" result would be. Instead of measuring success by fairness of result, the adversary system encourages its participants to estimate their achievements by determining how much more they got for their client than his just deserts, by how much better they did for their client than other attorneys might have done and than opposing counsel did for her client, and by how much money they made. The system, in short, is seen as rewarding competitors and winners, not humanists, esthetes or moralists. And the pressures the system imposes track the reward it offers. Since rewards go to the competitors and the winners, the pressures are to compete and to win. Woe to the peaceful. Woe to those to whom constant competition is not comfortable and to whom victory is less important than justice. They are the ones who will be most distorted and strained by a litigation practice.

Most of my suggestions about the psychic implications of the manipulative and exploitative behavior of litigators originate in my own experiences. * * * Every time I manipulated a person or a precedent, tried to exploit an opponent's weakness, or failed to disclose some clearly important information (case, argument, or evidence), I felt not only dishonest, but also in some measure distorted, alienated from the kind of human being our culture has taught me to respect and to strive to be. When I wanted to be open, candid, and cooperative I felt pressure to be closed, self-conscious, and contrived. I emerged from encounters with other lawyers where I had hidden some weakness in my own case or postured for some tactical advantage feeling lessened, cheapened, degraded, and shaken. Even when my tactics were completely "successful," I felt discomfort, dissatisfaction, and unhappiness. I did not like myself in this role and did not respect the product of my professional endeavors. * * *

My manipulations and concealments not only eroded my self-respect, but also subtly discolored my feelings about others. The human subjects of my manipulatory tactics were converted in my eyes, by the process of manipulation itself, into something different from me, something less complex and sacred, something more like the inanimate objects in my environment that I move around more or less at will to satisfy myself. Manipulation, in short, bred objectification. If the people I manipulated were not fully reduced to inanimacy, they at least tended to become children in my clouded psychological vision—children in the old pejorative sense of only partial people, people not to be related to as equals. This kind of objectification of others probably leads to objectification of self and, thus, to the final closing of the circle of alienation. It must be very difficult to regularly view others as incomplete and manipulable without gradually coming to view oneself that way.

* * *

What assurance can an attorney who lives in a manipulation-oriented world for eight to ten hours a day have that she will be able to shift to another interpersonal gear in the evenings and on weekends? My experiences and my observations of other attorneys suggest that there is a very real danger that the modes of behavior that begin as adaptations to a special professional setting will gradually expand to fill virtually all of the lawyer's interpersonal space. Subtly, we may come to view all people as proper subjects for manipulation and become suspicious that all people will manipulate us if the opportunity and need arises. If manipulation and suspicion extend into our personal lives, they inevitably will bring with them their psychological baggage: a tendency to objectify and devalue others which invites a general cynicism and sense of alienation from the entire social fabric. The product of all this is hardly attractive: a person distorted and alone, unhappy with himself, suspicious of and separated from others.

Recent discussions of adjudication frequently sound other themes as well. One such theme suggests that there may be "functional" limits on the types of disputes that courts can appropriately handle—that is, that there are types of disputes that are inherently unsuited to resolution through the judicial process. What are these limits, and what effect might they have on a lawyer's choice of process for resolving a client's dispute? These questions are explored in the following excerpts.

Lon Fuller, The Forms and Limits of Adjudication
92 Harv. L. Rev. 353, 364–71, 393–400, 403 (1978).

* * * This whole analysis will derive from one simple proposition, namely, that the distinguishing characteristic of adjudication lies in the fact that it confers on the affected party a peculiar form of participation in the decision, that of presenting proofs and reasoned arguments for a decision in his favor. Whatever heightens the significance of this participation lifts adjudication toward its optimum expression. Whatever destroys the meaning of that participation destroys the integrity of adjudication itself.

* * *

When I am entering into a contract with another person I may present proofs and arguments to him, but there is generally no formal assurance that I will be given this opportunity or that he will listen to my arguments if I make them. (Perhaps the only exception to this generalization lies in the somewhat anomalous legal obligation to "bargain in good faith" in labor relations.) During an election I may actively campaign for one side and may present what I consider to be "reasoned arguments" to the electorate. If I am an effective campaigner this participation in the decision ultimately reached may greatly outweigh in importance the casting of my single vote. At the same time, it is only the latter form of participation that is the subject of an affirmative institutional guarantee. The protection accorded my right to present arguments to the electorate is almost entirely indirect and negative. The way will be clear for me, but I shall have to pave it myself. * * * The voter who goes to sleep before his television set is surely not subject to the same condemnation as the judge who sleeps through the arguments of counsel.

Adjudication is, then, a device which gives formal and institutional expression to the influence of reasoned argument in human affairs. As such it assumes a burden of rationality not borne by any other form of social ordering. A decision which is the product of reasoned argument must be prepared itself to meet the test of reason. We demand of an adjudicative decision a kind of rationality we do not expect of the results of contract or of voting. This higher responsibility toward rationality is at once the strength *and the weakness* of adjudication as a form of social ordering.

* * *

Now if we ask ourselves what kinds of questions are commonly decided by judges and arbitrators, the answer may well be, "Claims of right." Indeed, in the older literature * * * courts were often distinguished from administrative or executive agencies on the ground that it is the function of courts to "declare rights." If, then, we seek to define "the limits of adjudication," a tempting answer would be that the proper province of courts is limited to cases where rights are asserted. * * *

Is this a significant way of describing "the limits of adjudication"? I do not think so. In fact, what purports here to be a distinct assertion is merely an implication of the fact that adjudication is a form of decision that defines the affected party's participation as that of offering proofs and reasoned arguments. It is not so much that adjudicators decide only issues presented by claims of right or accusations. The point is rather that *whatever* is submitted to them for decision, tends to be converted into a claim of right or an accusation of fault or guilt. This conversion is effected by the institutional framework within which both the litigant and the adjudicator function.

* * *

I have suggested that it is not a significant description of the limits of adjudication to say that its proper province lies where rights are asserted or accusations of fault are made, for such a statement involves a circle of reasoning. If, however, we regard a formal definition of rights and wrongs as a nearly inevitable product of the adjudicative process, we can arrive at what is perhaps the most significant of all limitations on the proper province of adjudication. Adjudication is not a proper form of social ordering in those areas where the effectiveness of human association would be destroyed if it were organized about formally defined "rights" and "wrongs." Courts have, for example, rather regularly refused to enforce agreements between husband and wife affecting the internal organization of family life. There are other and wider areas where the intrusion of "the machinery of the law" is equally inappropriate. An adjudicative board might well undertake to allocate one thousand tons of coal among three claimants; it could hardly conduct even the simplest coal-mining enterprise by the forms of adjudication. Wherever successful human association depends upon spontaneous and informal collaboration, shifting its forms with the task at hand, there adjudication is out of place except as it may declare certain ground rules applicable to a wide variety of activities.

* * * [T]he point I should like to stress is that the incapacity of a given area of human activity to endure a pervasive delimitation of rights and wrongs is also a measure of its incapacity to respond to a too exigent rationality, a rationality that demands an immediate and explicit reason for every step taken. Back of both of these incapacities lies the fundamental truth that certain kinds of human relations are not appropriate raw material for a process of decision that is institutionally committed to acting on the basis of reasoned argument.

THE LIMITS OF ADJUDICATION

Attention is now directed to the question, what kinds of tasks are inherently unsuited to adjudication? The test here will be that used throughout. If a given task is assigned to adjudicative treatment, will it be possible to preserve the meaning of the affected party's participation through proofs and arguments?

* * *

Some months ago a wealthy lady by the name of Timken died in New York leaving a valuable, but somewhat miscellaneous, collection of paintings to the Metropolitan Museum and the National Gallery "in equal shares," her will indicating no particular apportionment. When the will was probated the judge remarked something to the effect that the parties seemed to be confronted with a real problem. The attorney for one of the museums spoke up and said, "We are good friends. We will work it out somehow or other." What makes this problem of effecting an equal division of the paintings a polycentric task? It lies in the fact that the disposition of any single painting has implications for the proper disposition of every other painting. If it gets the Renoir, the Gallery may be less eager for the Cezanne but all the more eager for the Bellows, etc. If the proper apportionment were set for argument, there would be no clear issue to which either side could direct its proofs and contentions. Any judge assigned to hear such an argument would be tempted to assume the role of mediator or to adopt the classical solution: Let the older brother (here the Metropolitan) divide the estate into what he regards as equal shares, let the younger brother (the National Gallery) take his pick.

As a second illustration suppose in a socialist regime it were decided to have all wages and prices set by courts which would proceed after the usual forms of adjudication. It is, I assume, obvious that here is a task that could not successfully be undertaken by the adjudicative method. The point that comes first to mind is that courts move too slowly to keep up with a rapidly changing economic scene. The more fundamental point is that the forms of adjudication cannot encompass and take into account the complex repercussions that may result from any change in prices or wages. A rise in the price of aluminum may affect in varying degrees the demand for, and therefore the proper price of, thirty kinds of steel, twenty kinds of plastics, an infinitude of woods, other metals, etc. Each of these separate effects may have its own complex repercussions in the economy. In such a case it is simply impossible to afford each affected party a meaningful participation through proofs and arguments. * * *

We may visualize this kind of situation by thinking of a spider web. A pull on one strand will distribute tensions after a complicated pattern throughout the web as a whole. Doubling the original pull will, in all likelihood, not simply double each of the resulting tensions but will rather create a different complicated pattern of tensions. This would certainly occur, for example, if the doubled pull caused one or more of the weaker strands to snap. This is a "polycentric" situation because it is "many centered"—each crossing of strands is a distinct center for distributing tensions.

Suppose again, it were decided to assign players on a football team to their positions by a process of adjudication. I assume that we would agree that this is also an unwise application of adjudication. It is not merely a matter of eleven different men being possibly affected; each shift of any one player might have a different set of repercussions on the remaining players: putting Jones in as quarterback would have one set of carryover effects, putting him in as left end, another. Here, again, we are dealing with a situation of interacting points of influence and therefore with a polycentric problem beyond the proper limits of adjudication.

* * *

It should be carefully noted that multiplicity of affected persons is not an invariable characteristic of polycentric problems. This is sufficiently illustrated in the case of Mrs. Timken's will. * * * This insistence on a clear conception of polycentricity may seem to be laboring a point, but clarity of analysis is essential if confusion is to be avoided. For example, if a reward of $1000 is offered for the capture of a criminal and six claimants assert a right to the award, hearing the six-sided controversy may be an awkward affair. The problem does not, however, present any significant polycentric element as that term is here used.

Now, if it is important to see clearly what a polycentric problem is, it is equally important to realize that the distinction involved is often a matter of degree. There are polycentric elements in almost all problems submitted to adjudication. * * * It is not, then, a question of distinguishing black from white. It is a question of knowing when the polycentric elements have become so significant and predominant that the proper limits of adjudication have been reached.

The Role of Courts in American Society: Final Report of Council on the Role of Courts

102–114, 120–21 (Jethro K. Lieberman ed. 1984).

Which types of cases are and which are not fit for courts? We note at the outset that we can give no definitive answer to the question. Indeed, we believe that there is no single answer; rather, a number of criteria dictate various axes of inclusion and exclusion. What follows are meant as suggestions, not prescriptions. At best we can offer a series of observations that should help organize the inquiry.

* * *

These criteria can be grouped loosely in two categories; functional criteria and prudential criteria. Because no mathematical exactitude is possible, we state these criteria in the form of questions whose answers can be given only as a matter of degree.

FUNCTIONAL CRITERIA

By functional criteria we mean those factors that make a court peculiarly suited (or unsuited) to hear the matter in controversy. Here we are asking whether the court, as a particular type of governmental institution, is competent to hear and determine the dispute.

1. Objectivity

Does the dispute demand detached objectivity, in both reality and appearance? As we have seen, independence and impartiality are hallmarks of courts, and party participation in giving proof and making arguments are basic attributes of the judicial process that courts employ. In combination, the politics, psychology, and process are calculated to assure close, balanced, and open-minded scrutiny to contested claims. These in turn give integrity and respect to judicial decisions. When it is important for a decision to have the kind of integrity that the nature of the court and its process impart, the court is the proper forum. This criterion of objectivity surely applies in life-and-death cases, in constitutional claims, and in cases where liberty is at stake. It may or may not apply in cases turning on a dispute over a sum of money.

2. Necessity for Authoritative Standards

Can authoritative and ascertainable standards be applied to the facts of the dispute to produce a principled resolution? Courts are not as well suited as other institutions to adjudicate disputes in the absence of an ascertainable and authoritative standard. This inability is evident in disputes that present issues involving multiple criteria that cannot be weighed and ranked on an objective scale (e.g., selecting the position of players on a football team, picking the winner of a beauty contest).

To speak of authoritative and ascertainable standards is to speak in terms of degree, not mathematical precision. An authoritative standard can but need not be "black letter law." It may be a legal standard, as in a statute, or a private standard, as in a contract. It may be written, as in the commands of a constitution, or it may be found in the logic of common law decision or in the culture or traditions of a people. Likewise, to be ascertainable means to be capable of being discerned, possibly after some struggle. Of course an ascertainable standard may be one that is precisely spelled out, as in a statute of limitations that tells exactly after which date an action may no longer be pursued. But vague constitutional language like "due process of law" is, for all its frequent opaqueness, no less a standard that a court can apply. If some authoritative and ascertainable standard can be applied to a dispute to produce a principled resolution, the dispute likely belongs in court.

Nevertheless, not every "standard" capable of being applied by some person is proper for application in court. Thus courts are reluctant to intervene in questions of academic scholarship, not because professors do not use standards to evaluate student performance, but because the standards are not capable of easy or formulistic expression for application by an outsider. Compare, for example, a mathematics examination with an examination testing the student's knowledge of French literature. The math exam may call for answers that are ascertainable according to an authoritative standard; i.e., only one correct answer is possible for each question and any person knowledgeable in mathematics could state beforehand a precise formula for uncovering it. If a professor were to give a student a bad grade in the face of correct answers, a court could arguably intervene. But the French examination would pose an intractable difficulty: assuming that it did not call for such exact answers as a poet's birthdate, a court would have no standard to apply.

* * *

PRUDENTIAL CRITERIA

By prudential criteria, we mean those factors that make a court more or less suited than other institutions to hearing and resolving a dispute, given that on any view the court is competent to adjudicate the issue in controversy.

1.   Costs

In a dispute over a monetary claim, is the cost of judicial resolution disproportionately large in relation to the amount at stake? When the dispute involves only money and the cost of determining the controversy is out of proportion to the amount at stake, some process of deciding that is less expensive and less time-consuming than adjudication should be sought * * *.

2. Particularized Consideration

Does the type of case typically present only repetitive kinds of factual or administrative questions not calling for particularized consideration of legal issues in each case? The deliberateness and individuated assessment associated with the judicial process may be of little use and may even be extraneous when courts are called upon to process en mass types of cases that pose only routine and repetitive issues. * * * In short, cases that do not require particularized consideration do not routinely call for courts. Examples are found in the administration of estates, in the determination and payment of various forms of public benefits, and in the routine disposition of traffic cases in lower courts.

3. Preference of the Parties

Would a sounder resolution of the controversy likely be achieved through a process giving effect to the parties' preferences rather than through the imposition of a third-party judgment? When the best solution is closely tied to giving effect to the parties' own preferences and utilities, bargaining rather than adjudication is desirable. A clear example is the case Fuller posed of the apportionment of paintings by a will * * *.

* * *

4. Vitality of Another Institution

Would judicial resolution of the matter at hand likely impair the vitality of an existing institution with means of dealing with the matter? When a decision would closely affect the continued vitality of another valued institution—a family, a school, a private political party—a court should supplant the traditional decision maker only in compelling cases. As one court put it in hearing a dispute over academic standards: "(I)n matters of scholarship, the school authorities are uniquely qualified by training and experience to judge the qualifications of a student, and efficiency of instruction depends in no small degree upon the school faculty's freedom from interference from other noneducational tribunals."

* * *

This rule can be illuminated further by considering a few cases in which courts have been invited to intrude on that great bastion of private autonomy, the family. Traditionally, courts have refused to adjudicate disputes and grant legal relief between members of an intact family. Thus, in McGuire v. McGuire [157 Neb. 226, 59 N.W.2d 336 (1953)] the court refused to order a husband, financially able to do so, to provide more adequately for his elderly wife, who was compelled to live in meager circumstances in a rundown house without indoor plumbing. The court based its refusal to intervene on the observation that the couple were still living together as husband and wife. Although the wife's claim would have been cognizable had she been separated from her husband, her demand for support here was not properly resolvable in a judicial forum because it was "a matter of concern to the household." * * *

A few years ago, Justice Rehnquist issued a broad warning against adjudication of claims that "can only disrupt ongoing relations" because "the very crystallization of the parties' differences in the adversary process may threaten the future of the institutional relationship." Others, while acknowledging the importance of preserving the family, have advocated a more particularized analysis in each case. They would balance the likely harm that judicial intrusion into family matters would cause against the damage resulting from refusal to redress an individual family member's claim.

* * *

5.   Immediate Resolution of a Specialized Problem

Is the controversy one that arises in a specialized area when an immediate, on-the-spot decision that must be final is necessary? Even though a dispute is justiciable and serious, courts are not the best forum when the decision calls for an expert, on-the-scene determination and when delaying matters to get a more careful and accurate judgment from the courts will destroy the values that immediate finality would assure. A clear example of this type of case is the athletic contest during which it is claimed that an official made an erroneous call.

* * *

CASES IN WHICH COURTS SHOULD PLAY A BACKUP ROLE

1.   Child Custody Cases

Courts now determine custody disputes. Does an analysis of the factors favoring and disfavoring judicial handling of the disputes support the conclusion that courts are the right place for these disputes to be resolved?

a.   Factors Favoring Court Determination

(i) When parents disagree about the custody of a minor child, an institution enjoying high public confidence must resolve the disagreement.

(ii) Society has a deep interest in protecting children; it is essential to assure that injury to them is kept to a minimum. Courts can insist that the proceedings protect the child.

(iii) Some believe that the judicial process, with its emphasis on decency and dignity, may impart these qualities to the outcome.

b.   Factors Opposing Court Determination

(i) In child custody disputes, "the actual determination of what is in fact in the child's best interest is ordinarily quite indeterminate." Because the standard of decision is so amorphous, courts are not able to apply it in a judicious way.

(ii) Determining the best interest of the child in part requires predicting future behavior patterns and interpersonal relationships, work in which courts do not excel.

(iii) Because the parties' own preferences and utilities are so crucial to the best possible outcome, the court's process is not especially useful. In these cases, consensual agreements may yield greater permanency than imposed arrangements.

(iv) Adversary adjudication intensifies frictions and exposes private affairs to no useful end in reaching the decision.

c.   How the Courts May Be of Use

The foregoing list of pros and cons suggests that the court is not the proper institution to *make* the decision but is the proper forum to help *guide* the parties to reach their own decision. Obviously if the parents have reached no agreement, a dispute remains that urgently requires settlement. It seems far better to enlist the court than an administrative agency in the search for private agreement: The court process will ensure a modicum of decorum and decency along the way, and the court's imprimatur will be more convincing than a bureaucrat's. Courts thus have an important backup role to play in related-party cases, not "because judges can deftly resolve domestic controversies, but [because] . . . the very threat of their being called upon to do so can expedite negotiated settlement."

* * *

CASES NOT SUITABLE FOR COURTS

An ingenious enough lawyer can fashion any quarrel into the form of a legal dispute—or so it might seem. But few would argue that the courts should be open to hear any matter; problems that have not been shaped into disputes resting on a claim of legal entitlement ought not be aired in court. A matter may be of pressing moral concern, and proponents may make moral claims to remedial action by other institutions. Unless the moral claim is rooted in a legal entitlement, however, it is unsuited to judicial resolution. * * *

A second type of case that might be deemed unsuitable for the courts, no matter which view of courts' role is adopted, is that which raises issues that policy-makers would prefer to leave to the unfettered discretion of the individual. In fact, this category of cases—simple examples of which are claims based on breach of promise to marry or alienation of affection—is more properly seen as embracing matters that legislators on policy grounds would prefer not to see raised legally at all than as cases that jurispruden-tially courts are unequipped to handle. Another example is the difference between fault and no-fault regimes in divorce law. If fault is an issue, then the question must be adjudicated—was the defendant guilty of adultery or abusive behavior or some other conduct that the law lays down as grounds for divorce? But cause is not a universal necessity: the legislature may decide, as many legislatures have decided, that a couple may divorce without assigning causes, leaving only disputes over the estate and custody of the children to be resolved in court. Diverting factual issues to other forums or denying the issues justiciability is one way of avoiding the difficulties that especially arise when adjudication must touch ongoing relations.

NOTES AND QUESTIONS

1. Exactly what does Brazil appear to mean by "manipulation"? And just what is wrong with it?

2. Just how may "problems" be "shaped into disputes resting on a claim of legal entitlement"? How would Professor Fuller have responded to such a question?

3. The problem of Mrs. Timken's will and its unsuitability for adjudication were explored further in another article by Professor Fuller, Collective Bargaining and the Arbitrator, Proceedings, 15th Annual Meeting, Nat. Academy of Arbitrators 8 (1962). Professor Fuller suggested that the typical cases falling neatly within the competence of the adjudicative process tend to be cases that call for a decision of "yes or no," or "more or less." By contrast, the available solutions in the Timken case "are scattered in an irregular pattern across a checkerboard of possibilities." To try to effect an "equal division" of the paintings within the framework of the adjudicative process would run into the difficulty that "meaningful partic- ipation by the litigants through proofs and arguments would become virtually impossible. There is no single solution, or simple set of solutions, towards which the parties meeting in open court could address themselves. If an optimum solution had to be reached through adjudicative procedures, the court would have had to set forth an almost endless series of possible divisions and direct the parties to deal with each in turn."

Professor Fuller also cautioned that he was not asserting

that an agency called a "court" should never under any circumstances undertake to solve a "polycentric" problem. Confronted by a dire emergency, or by a clear constitutional direction, a court may feel itself compelled to do the best it can with this sort of problem. All I am urging is that this sort of problem cannot be solved within the procedural restraints normally surrounding judicial office. Courts do in fact discharge functions that are not adjudicative in the usual sense of the word, as in supervising equity receiverships or in setting up procedures for admission to the bar. What I ask is clear thinking about the limits of the adjudicative process and about the value of those limits in the perspective of government as a whole. Thus, what I have said is relevant to the question whether courts should undertake to rewrite the boundaries of election districts to make them more repre- sentative of the distribution of population. It does not, however, pre- emptively decide that question.

Id. at 39–41.

4. Do you agree that courts assume "a burden of rationality not borne by any other form of social ordering"? What appears to be meant here by "rationality"? As we proceed through these materials, you might consider in what sense "rationality" plays a more limited role in other dispute-resolution processes such as negotiation, mediation, and arbitration.

5. Does Professor Fuller's exclusive focus on "polycentricity" lessen the usefulness of his analysis in evaluating the appropriateness of adjudication? In what ways might the functional and prudential criteria suggested by the Report of the Council on the Role of Courts be more helpful? Does the choice of the members of a college golf team involve "polycentricity"? Is this choice any more suitable for adjudication than is the choice of the members of the football or baseball team? See Eisenberg, Participation, Responsiveness, and the Consultative Process: An Essay for Lon Fuller, 92 Harv.L.Rev. 410 (1978).

6. One way that a court may handle polycentric problems is to encourage parties to negotiate a resolution acceptable to them. The degree of judicial involvement in negotiation will vary from judge to judge, as well as across different subject areas. To a large extent, however, the litigation system relies on the negotiating ability and judgment of lawyers to provide fair, efficient, and durable solutions to disputes.

Consider, for example, the case of Mrs. Timken: The substantive law of wills, and the threat that a court may step in and itself resolve the dispute between the two museums, is likely to assure that negotiation and a satisfactory settlement take place. Compare also the discussion of the "backup" role of courts in child custody cases in the Report of the Council on the Role of Courts. This also seems to be the prevailing way in which ongoing remedies are worked out in the "public law" or "institutional reform" litigation that places so much strain on the Fuller model of adjudication. In these complex cases, which typically challenge the operation and organization of public schools, mental hospitals, or prisons, the litigation system provides a framework within which the parties can bargain:

> The court will ask the parties to agree on an order or it will ask one party to prepare a draft. * * * The draftsman understands that his proposed decree will be subject to comment and objection by the other side and that it must be approved by the court. He is therefore likely to submit it to his opponents in advance to see whether differences cannot be resolved. Even if the court itself should prepare the initial draft of the order, some form of negotiation will almost inevitably ensue upon submission of the draft to the parties for comment.

> The negotiating process ought to minimize the need for judicial resolution of remedial issues. Each party recognizes that it must make some response to the demands of the other party, for issues left unresolved will be submitted to the court, a recourse that is always chancy and may result in a solution less acceptable than might be reached by horse-trading. * * * Indeed, relief by way of order after a determination on the merits tends to converge with relief through a consent decree or voluntary settlement. And this in turn mitigates a major theoretical objection to affirmative relief—the danger of intruding on an elaborate and organic network of interparty relationships.

Chayes, The Role of the Judge in Public Law Litigation, 89 Harv.L.Rev. 1281, 1298–99 (1976).

3.   THE CASE FOR THE JUDICIAL PROCESS

Owen M. Fiss, Against Settlement

93 Yale L.J. 1073, 1075–78, 1082–90 (1984).

In a recent report to the Harvard Overseers, Derek Bok called for a new direction in legal education.[1] He decried "the familiar tilt in the law curriculum toward preparing students for legal combat," and asked instead that law schools train their students "for the gentler arts of reconciliation and accommodation." He sought to turn our attention from the courts to "new voluntary mechanisms" for resolving disputes. In doing so, Bok echoed themes that have long been associated with the Chief Justice,[4] and that have become a rallying point for the organized bar and the source of a new movement in the law. This movement is the subject of a new professional journal, a newly formed section of the American Association of Law Schools, and several well-funded institutes. It has even-received its own acronym—ADR (Alternative Dispute Resolution).

The movement promises to reduce the amount of litigation initiated, and accordingly the bulk of its proposals are devoted to negotiation and mediation prior to suit. But the interest in the so-called "gentler arts" has not been so confined. It extends to ongoing litigation as well, and the advocates of ADR have sought new ways to facilitate and perhaps even pressure parties into settling pending cases.

[Professor Fiss discusses amendments to Rule 16 and Rule 68 of the Federal Rules of Civil Procedure intended to "sharpen the incentives for settlement." See Appendix A, infra.]

The advocates of ADR are led to support such measures and to exalt the idea of settlement more generally because they view adjudication as a process to resolve disputes. They act as though courts arose to resolve quarrels between neighbors who had reached an impasse and turned to a stranger for help. Courts are seen as an institutionalization of the stranger and adjudication is viewed as the process by which the stranger exercises power. The very fact that the neighbors have turned to someone else to resolve their dispute signifies a breakdown in their social relations; the advocates of ADR acknowledge this, but nonetheless hope that the neighbors will be able to reach agreement before the stranger renders judgment. Settlement is that agreement. It is a truce more than a true reconciliation,

1. Bok, A Flawed System, Harv. Mag., May–June 1983, *reprinted in* N.Y.St.B.J., Oct. 1983, at 8, N.Y.St.B.J., Nov. 1983, at 31, *excerpted in* 33 J.Legal Educ. 570 (1983).

4. See, e.g., Burger, Isn't There a Better Way?, 68 A.B.A.J. 274 (1982); Burger, Agenda for 2000 A.D.—A Need for Systematic Anticipation, 70 F.R.D. 83, 93–96 (1976).

but it seems preferable to judgment because it rests on the consent of both parties and avoids the cost of a lengthy trial.

* * *

In my view, however, this account of adjudication and the case for settlement rest on questionable premises. I do not believe that settlement as a generic practice is preferable to judgment or should be institutionalized on a wholesale and indiscriminate basis. It should be treated instead as a highly problematic technique for streamlining dockets. Settlement is for me the civil analogue of plea bargaining: Consent is often coerced; the bargain may be struck by someone without authority; the absence of a trial and judgment renders subsequent judicial involvement troublesome; and although dockets are trimmed, justice may not be done. Like plea bargaining, settlement is a capitulation to the conditions of mass society and should be neither encouraged nor praised.

By viewing the lawsuit as a quarrel between two neighbors, the dispute-resolution story that underlies ADR implicitly asks us to assume a rough equality between the contending parties. It treats settlement as the anticipation of the outcome of trial and assumes that the terms of settlement are simply a product of the parties' predictions of that outcome. In truth, however, settlement is also a function of the resources available to each party to finance the litigation, and those resources are frequently distributed unequally. Many lawsuits do not involve a property dispute between two neighbors, or between AT & T and the government (to update the story), but rather concern a struggle between a member of a racial minority and a municipal police department over alleged brutality, or a claim by a worker against a large corporation over work-related injuries. In these cases, the distribution of financial resources, or the ability of one party to pass along its costs, will invariably infect the bargaining process, and the settlement will be at odds with a conception of justice that seeks to make the wealth of the parties irrelevant.

The disparities in resources between the parties can influence the settlement in three ways. First, the poorer party may be less able to amass and analyze the information needed to predict the outcome of the litigation, and thus be disadvantaged in the bargaining process. Second, he may need the damages he seeks immediately and thus be induced to settle as a way of accelerating payment, even though he realizes he would get less now than he might if he awaited judgment. All plaintiffs want their damages immediately, but an indigent plaintiff may be exploited by a rich defendant because his need is so great that the defendant can force him to accept a sum that is less than the ordinary present value of the judgment. Third, the poorer party might be forced to settle because he does not have the resources to finance the litigation, to cover either his own projected expenses, such as his lawyer's time, or the expenses his opponent can impose through the manipulation of procedural mechanisms such as discovery. It might seem that settlement benefits the plaintiff by allowing him to avoid the costs of litigation, but this is not so. The defendant can anticipate the plaintiff's costs if the case were to be tried fully and decrease his offer by that amount. The indigent plaintiff is a victim of the costs of litigation even if he settles.

* * *

Of course, imbalances of power can distort judgment as well: Resources influence the quality of presentation, which in turn has an important bearing on who wins the terms of victory. We count, however, on the guiding presence of the judge, who can employ a number of measures to lessen the impact of distributional inequalities. He can, for example, supplement the parties' presentations by asking questions, calling his own witnesses, and inviting other persons and institutions to participate as amici. These measures are likely to make only a small contribution toward moderating the influence of distributional inequalities, but should not be ignored for that reason. Not even these small steps are possible with settlement. There is, moreover, a critical difference between a process like settlement, which is based on bargaining and accepts inequalities of wealth as an integral and legitimate component of the process, and a process like judgment, which knowingly struggles against those inequalities. Judgment aspires to an autonomy from distributional inequalities, and it gathers much of its appeal from this aspiration.

* * *

THE LACK OF A FOUNDATION FOR CONTINUING JUDICIAL INVOLVEMENT

The dispute-resolution story trivializes the remedial dimensions of lawsuits and mistakenly assumes judgment to be the end of the process. It supposes that the judge's duty is to declare which neighbor is right and which wrong, and that this declaration will end the judge's involvement (save in that most exceptional situation where it is also necessary for him to issue a writ directing the sheriff to execute the declaration). Under these assumptions, settlement appears as an almost perfect substitute for judgment, for it too can declare the parties' rights. Often, however, judgment is not the end of a lawsuit but only the beginning. The involvement of the court may continue almost indefinitely. In these cases, settlement cannot provide an adequate basis for that necessary continuing involvement, and thus is no substitute for judgment.

The parties may sometimes be locked in combat with one another and view the lawsuit as only one phase in a long continuing struggle. The entry of judgment will then not end the struggle, but rather change its terms and the balance of power. One of the parties will invariably return to the court and again ask for its assistance, not so much because conditions have changed, but because the conditions that preceded the lawsuit have unfortunately not changed. This often occurs in domestic-relations cases, where the divorce decree represents only the opening salvo in an endless series of skirmishes over custody and support.

The structural reform cases that play such a prominent role on the federal docket provide another occasion for continuing judicial involvement.

In these cases, courts seek to safeguard public values by restructuring large-scale bureaucratic organizations. The task is enormous, and our knowledge of how to restructure on-going bureaucratic organizations is limited. As a consequence, courts must oversee and manage the remedial process for a long time—maybe forever. This, I fear, is true of most school desegregation cases, some of which have been pending for twenty or thirty years. It is also true of antitrust cases that seek divestiture or reorganization of an industry.

The drive for settlement knows no bounds and can result in a consent decree even in the kinds of cases I have just mentioned, that is, even when a court finds itself embroiled in a continuing struggle between the parties or must reform a bureaucratic organization. The parties may be ignorant of the difficulties ahead or optimistic about the future, or they may simply believe that they can get more favorable terms through a bargained-for agreement. Soon, however, the inevitable happens: One party returns to court and asks the judge to modify the decree, either to make it more effective or less stringent. But the judge is at a loss: He has no basis for assessing the request. He cannot, to use Cardozo's somewhat melodramatic formula, easily decide whether the "dangers, once substantial, have become attenuated to a shadow," because, by definition he never knew the dangers.

* * *

Settlement also impedes vigorous enforcement, which sometimes requires use of the contempt power. As a formal matter, contempt is available to punish violations of a consent decree. But courts hesitate to use that power to enforce decrees that rest solely on consent, especially when enforcement is aimed at high public officials, as became evident in the Willowbrook deinstitutionalization case[33] and the recent Chicago desegregation case. Courts do not see a mere bargain between the parties as a sufficient foundation for the exercise of their coercive powers.

* * * Of course, a plaintiff is free to drop a lawsuit altogether (provided that the interests of certain other persons are not compromised), and a defendant can offer something in return, but that bargained-for arrangement more closely resembles a contract than an injunction. It raises a question which has already been answered whenever an injunction is issued, namely, whether the judicial power should be used to enforce it. Even assuming that the consent is freely given and authoritative, the bargain is at best contractual and does not contain the kind of enforcement commitment already embodied in a decree that is the product of a trial and the judgment of a court.

---

33. New York State Ass'n for Retarded Children, Inc. v. Carey, 631 F.2d 162, 163–64 (2d Cir.1980) (court unwilling to hold governor in contempt of consent decree when legislature refused to provide funding for committee established by court to oversee implementation of decree). The First Circuit explicitly acknowledged limitations on the power of courts to enforce consent decrees in Brewster v. Dukakis, 687 F.2d 495, 501 (1st Cir.1982), and Massachusetts Ass'n for Retarded Citizens, Inc. v. King, 668 F.2d 602, 610 (1st Cir.1981).

JUSTICE RATHER THAN PEACE

The dispute-resolution story makes settlement appear as a perfect substitute for judgment, as we just saw, by trivializing the remedial dimensions of a lawsuit, and also by reducing the social function of the lawsuit to one of resolving private disputes: In that story, settlement appears to achieve exactly the same purpose as judgment—peace between the parties—but at considerably less expense to society. The two quarreling neighbors turn to a court in order to resolve their dispute, and society makes courts available because it wants to aid in the achievement of their private ends or to secure the peace.

In my view, however, the purpose of adjudication should be understood in broader terms. Adjudication uses public resources, and employs not strangers chosen by the parties but public officials chosen by a process in which the public participates. These officials, like members of the legislative and executive branches, possess a power that has been defined and conferred by public law, not by private agreement. Their job is not to maximize the ends of private parties, nor simply to secure the peace, but to explicate and give force to the values embodied in authoritative texts such as the Constitution and statutes: to interpret those values and to bring reality into accord with them. This duty is not discharged when the parties settle.

* * * To be against settlement is not to urge that parties be "forced" to litigate, since that would interfere with their autonomy and distort the adjudicative process; the parties will be inclined to make the court believe that their bargain is justice. To be against settlement is only to suggest that when the parties settle, society gets less than what appears, and for a price it does not know it is paying. Parties might settle while leaving justice undone. The settlement of a school suit might secure the peace, but not racial equality. Although the parties are prepared to live under the terms they bargained for, and although such peaceful coexistence may be a necessary precondition of justice,[35] and itself a state of affairs to be valued, it is not justice itself. To settle for something means to accept less than some ideal.

* * *

THE REAL DIVIDE

To all this, one can readily imagine a simple response by way of confession and avoidance: We are not talking about those lawsuits. Advocates of ADR might insist that my account of adjudication, in contrast to the one implied by the dispute-resolution story, focuses on a rather narrow

---

35. Some observers have argued that compliance is more likely to result from a consent decree than from an adjudicated decree. See O. Fiss & D. Rendleman, Injunctions 1004 (2d ed. 1984). But increased compliance may well be due to the fact that a consent decree asks less of the defendant, rather than from its creating a more amicable relationship between the parties. See McEwen & Maiman, Mediation in Small Claims Court: Achieving Compliance Through Consent, 18 Law & Soc'y Rev. 11 (1984).

category of lawsuits. They could argue that while settlement may have only the most limited appeal with respect to those cases, I have not spoken to the "typical" case. My response is twofold.

First, even as a purely quantitative matter, I doubt that the number of cases I am referring to is trivial. My universe includes those cases in which there are significant distributional inequalities; those in which it is difficult to generate authoritative consent because organizations or social groups are parties or because the power to settle is vested in autonomous agents; those in which the court must continue to supervise the parties after judgment; and those in which justice needs to be done, or to put it more modestly, where there is a genuine social need for an authoritative interpretation of law. I imagine that the number of cases that satisfy one of these four criteria is considerable; in contrast to the kind of case portrayed in the dispute-resolution story, they probably dominate the docket of a modern court system.

Second, it demands a certain kind of myopia to be concerned only with the number of cases, as though all cases are equal simply because the clerk of the court assigns each a single docket number. All cases are not equal. The Los Angeles desegregation case, to take one example, is not equal to the allegedly more typical suit involving a property dispute or an automobile accident. The desegregation suit consumes more resources, affects more people, and provokes far greater challenges to the judicial power. The settlement movement must introduce a qualitative perspective; it must speak to these more "significant" cases, and demonstrate the propriety of settling them. Otherwise it will soon be seen as an irrelevance, dealing with trivia rather than responding to the very conditions that give the movement its greatest sway and saliency.

* * *

In fact, most ADR advocates make no effort to distinguish between different types of cases or to suggest that "the gentler arts of reconciliation and accommodation" might be particularly appropriate for one type of case but not for another. They lump all cases together. This suggests that what divides me from the partisans of ADR is not that we are concerned with different universes of cases, that Derek Bok, for example, focuses on boundary quarrels while I see only desegregation suits. I suspect instead that what divides us is much deeper and stems from our understanding of the purpose of the civil law suit and its place in society. It is a difference in outlook.

Someone like Bok sees adjudication in essentially private terms. The purpose of lawsuits and the civil courts is to resolve disputes, and the amount of litigation we encounter is evidence of the needlessly combative and quarrelsome character of Americans. Or as Bok put it, using a more diplomatic idiom: "At bottom, ours is a society built on individualism, competition, and success." I, on the other hand, see adjudication in more public terms: Civil litigation is an institutional arrangement for using state power to bring a recalcitrant reality closer to our chosen ideals. We turn to the courts because we need to, not because of some quirk in our personalities. We train our students in the tougher arts so that they may help secure all that the law promises, not because we want them to become gladiators or because we take a special pleasure in combat.

To conceive of the civil lawsuit in public terms as America does might be unique. I am willing to assume that no other country—including Japan, Bok's new paragon[43]—has a case like *Brown v. Board of Education* in which the judicial power is used to eradicate the caste structure. I am willing to assume that no other country conceives of law and uses law in quite the way we do. But this should be a source of pride rather than shame. What is unique is not the problem, that we live short of our ideals, but that we alone among the nations of the world seem willing to do something about it. Adjudication American-style is not a reflection of our combativeness but rather a tribute to our inventiveness and perhaps even more to our commitment.

NOTES AND QUESTIONS

1. When, if at all, is it appropriate to rely on "private," non-official processes to resolve disputes in which "public" values are implicated? When should the diversion of such disputes from the court system be discouraged? Despite Professor Fiss's suggestion to the contrary, it would be highly unlikely that anyone interested in dispute resolution today would "lump all" such cases together. Can we find techniques or approaches that might moderate any tension between the need to articulate and uphold societal values and the potential advantages of alternative processes? These are all questions that will recur constantly throughout these materials: You should not lose sight of them as you proceed to consider the variety of the available means of dispute resolution.

2. Judge Harry Edwards tells the story of a seminar conducted by the Carter Center at Emory University, which brought together people on both sides of the tobacco controversy. As described by former First Lady Rosalynn Carter, "when those people got together, I won't say they hated each other, but they were enemies. But in the end, they were bringing up ideas about how they could work together." Judge Edwards comments:

> This result is praiseworthy—mutual understanding and good feeling among disputants obviously facilitates intelligent dispute resolution—but there are some disputes that cannot be resolved simply by mutual agreement and good faith. It is a fact of political life that many

43. As to the validity of the comparisons and a more subtle explanation of the determinants of litigiousness, see Haley, The Myth of the Reluctant Litigant, 4 J. Japanese Stud. 359, 389 (1978) ("Few misconceptions about Japan have been more widespread or as pernicious as the myth of the special reluctance of the Japanese to litigate."); see also Galanter, Reading the Landscape of Disputes: What We Know and Don't Know (And Think We Know) About Our Allegedly Contentious and Litigious Society, 31 U.C.L.A.L.Rev. 4, 57–79 (1983) (paucity of lawyers in Japan due to restrictions on number of attorneys admitted to practice rather than to non-litigiousness).

disputes reflect sharply contrasting views about fundamental public values that can never be eliminated by techniques that encourage disputants to "understand" each other. Indeed, many disputants understand their opponents all too well. Those who view tobacco as an unacceptable health risk, for example, can never fully reconcile their differences with the tobacco industry, and we should not assume otherwise. One essential function of law is to reflect the public resolution of such irreconcilable differences; lawmakers are forced to choose among these differing visions of the public good. A potential danger of ADR is that disputants who seek only understanding and reconciliation may treat as irrelevant the choices made by our lawmakers and may, as a result, ignore public values reflected in rules of law.

Edwards, Alternative Dispute Resolution: Panacea or Anathema, 99 Harv. L.Rev. 668, 678–79 (1986).

3. Does it follow from the views expressed by Professor Fiss that all cases of "imbalances of power" (such as consumer claims) and all cases implicating public values (such as racial discrimination) must reach court judgment? For example, does the critical importance of *Brown v. Board of Education* mandate that all discrimination disputes need judicial attention? Once a body of law has become well-developed and the applicable principles clearly defined, might not other processes be as good or better in resolving specific recurring problems?

4. Is it likely that a settlement arrived at through the participation and with the consent of the parties may often appear more satisfying to them than the result of adjudication? In what ways—other than in the sense that (in Fiss's grudging terms) it helps them to "secure the peace" at an acceptable cost? These too are questions that you should return to continually as we proceed through the following chapters.

5. More generally, where does the average plaintiff or defendant fit into a view of dispute resolution (such as that advanced by Professor Fiss) that rests so completely on the public interest? Surely the community's need for the open development and enforcement of public values should not "trump" in all cases the individual's choice of process? Cf. Carrie Menkel–Meadow, Whose Dispute Is It Anyway?: A Philosophical and Democratic Defense of Settlement (In Some Cases), 83 Georgetown L.J. 2663, 2669 (1995): "I fear, but am not sure, that this debate can be reduced to those who care more about the people actually engaged in disputes versus those who care more about institutional and structural arrangements."

6. The influence of the judicial process radiates far beyond the impact of litigation—actual or threatened—on the parties immediately involved. Beyond the effect on the individual disputants, one must consider what has been called the "general effects" of public adjudication that result from the communication to *others* of information about litigation. These effects are the subject of the following excerpt.

Marc Galanter, The Day After the Litigation Explosion

46 Maryland L.Rev. 3, 32–37 (1986).

Special effects [arising from litigation] are changes in the behavior of the specific actors involved in a particular lawsuit—like the Princeton club [an all-male college eating club votes to admit women in response to the filing of a sex discrimination suit against the college] or the University of Georgia [dismissed English professor who refused to pass failing athletes receives $2.75 million verdict] or the plaintiffs who sued them. We can, in theory at least, isolate various kinds of effects on the subsequent activity of such actors. An actor may be deprived of resources for future violations. This is *incapacitation*. Or the result of litigation may be increased *surveillance* which renders future offending behavior less likely. The Georgia case dramatically illustrates this surveillance effect. Or the offending actor may be deterred by fear of being caught again. This is *special deterrence*. Or, the experience of being exposed to the law may change the actor's view that it is right to exclude women or pass failing athletes or whatever. This is *reformation*.

In addition to these special effects on the parties before the court, there may be effects on wider audiences that we may call general effects. Litigation against one actor may lead others to reassess the risks and advantages of similar activity. We see this displayed in our Cape Cod [bar owner, fearing law suits, teaches employees how to recognize intoxicated customers] and Madison Parks [city removes asphalt from children's play areas in parks because liability insurance settlements are high] examples. This is *general deterrence*. It neither presumes nor requires any change in the moral evaluation of the acts in question, nor does it involve any change in opportunities to commit them. It stipulates that behavior will be affected by acquisition of more information about the costs and benefits that are likely to attach to the act—information about the certainty, celerity, and severity of "punishment," for example. Thus the actor can hold to what Hart called the "external point of view," treating law as a fact to be taken into account rather than a normative framework that he is committed to uphold or be guided by. The information that induces the changed estimate of costs and benefits need not be accurate. What a court has done may be inaccurately perceived; indeed, the court may have inaccurately depicted what it has done.

On the other hand, communication of the existence of a law or its application by a court may change the moral evaluation by others of a specific item of conduct. To the extent that this involves not the calculation or the probability of being visited by certain costs and benefits, but a change in moral estimation, we may call this general effect *enculturation*. There is suggestive evidence to indicate that at least some segments of the population are subject to such effects. Less dramatically, perceiving the application of law may maintain or intensify existing evaluations of conduct, an effect that Gibbs calls *normative validation*.

In addition to these effects on the underlying behavior, litigation may produce effects on the level of disputing behavior. It may encourage or discourage the parties to a case from making (or resisting) other claims. And generally it may encourage claimants and lawyers to pursue claims of a given type. It may provide symbols for rallying a group, broadcasting awareness of grievance and dramatizing challenge to the status quo. On the other hand, grievances may lose legitimacy, claims may be discouraged, and organizational capacity dissipated. The effects may be labeled *mobilization* and *demobilization.*

While supposition about the effects of litigation is abundant, serious studies of these effects are relatively rare. During the 1960s political scientists (chiefly) accumulated a body of findings on the impact of decisions of the United States Supreme Court (mostly) and other appellate courts, exploring the extent to which these decisions elicited compliance from the lower courts, school boards, police and other agencies they were designed to regulate. A critical survey of this literature concluded that:

> [T]he decisions of the Court, far from producing uniform impact or automatic compliance, have varying effects—from instances in which no action follows upon them to wide degrees of compliance (usually underreported), resistance, and evasion. These varying effects include increases in the level of political activity and activity within the judicial system itself and changes in governmental structure.... Important social interests, both economic and noneconomic, may be dislocated or legitimated, and the court's decisions also often perform an agenda-setting function for other political actors.

A new generation of "impact" research has widened its concerns from the United States Supreme Court to other courts, from public to private law, and from a focus on compliance with doctrinal pronouncements to ascertainment of a wider range of effects. Recent work includes studies tracing out the effects of specific tort cases. Thus Wiley found that a decision of the Supreme Court of Washington holding liable an ophthalmologist for failing to test a young patient for glaucoma did bring about an increase in the amount of testing for glaucoma in young patients. And Givelber, Bowers and Blitch found that a California decision [Tarasoff v. Regents of University of California, 17 Cal.3d 425, 131 Cal.Rptr. 14, 551 P.2d 334 (1976)], holding that therapists had a duty to exercise reasonable care to protect third parties from violence by their patients, had important effects nationwide. Eighteen months after its highly publicized original ruling that a therapist has a duty to warn the potential victim, the court, upon reconsideration, nullified its earlier opinion and modified the duty to one of exercising reasonable care to protect potential victims. The researchers found that the case was widely known by therapists throughout the nation, that observation of its ruling was felt to be obligatory by most even though technically it bound only those in California and "by and large the case appears to be misunderstood as involving and requiring the warning of potential victims" [i.e., in accordance with the withdrawn original opinion]—and to have influenced therapist responses to threatening behavior toward giving warnings, initiating involuntary hospitalizations and taking notes. The story is wonderfully complex. What happens is remote from a calculated intervention by the court designed to bring about these effects; and the therapists' response is more than a calculating re-estimation of costs and benefits.

In contrast to these studies focusing on the radiating effects of a single decision, other researchers have examined the way that an array of judicial decisions impinges on decision making by private actors. Thus a study of large manufacturers found that:

> [E]xcept for firms subject to the maximally intrusive regulation of such agencies as the Food and Drug and the General Aviation administrations, product liability is the most significant influence on product safety efforts. Product liability, however, conveys an indistinct signal. The long lags between the design decision and the final judgment on product liability claims (frequently five or more years), the inconsistent behavior of juries, and the rapid change in judicial doctrine in the area, all tended to muffle the signal.

*   *   *

A study of small manufacturers of agricultural implements in California found that 22% had dropped product lines out of fear of product liability suits.

I am not claiming that these effects are optimal or that the benefits they product outweigh all the costs or that existing litigation patterns represent the best way to achieve these benefits. But we should recognize that benefits are present and that any assessment of the social value of litigation must take account of them and must involve an attempt to estimate the *net* effects of present litigation patterns and the proposed or likely alternatives. These examples should also remind us that these effects are not ascertainable by supposition or by deduction.

NOTES AND QUESTIONS

1. Professor Galanter suggests that when courts decide cases by authoritatively stating generally applicable "rules," they strongly influence the primary conduct of all actors in our society. The courts convey information and warnings that are intended to bring private conduct into compliance with norms of appropriate behavior. In addition, the communication by courts of rules of decision plays a part in the process by which disputes are managed. Information disseminated in the form of "legal precedents" is used every day by individuals and their lawyers in routine decisions concerning which claims they should assert, and under what circumstances they should settle those claims. The pattern of decided cases thus helps provide a "blueprint" for settlement, a background against which settlement negotiations can take place. We will discuss this function later when we consider in some detail the dynamics of settlement. See also Galanter,

Justice in Many Rooms: Courts, Private Ordering, and Indigenous Law, 19
J.Legal Pluralism & Unofficial L. 1, 6–16 (1981).

2. Some information conveyed by courts is undoubtedly redundant, in the
sense that even without it the parties to a litigated case would already be
quite able to predict the outcome with some clarity. But if too many suits
are settled—if too many important cases are taken out of the judicial
system—is it possible that this function of courts in facilitating the settlement process might be impaired? "[I]n a world where all cases settle, it
may not even be possible to base settlements on the merits because lawyers
may not be able to make reliable estimates of expected trial outcomes. If
similar cases never go to trial, predictions of expected trial outcomes will
have no factual grounding. * * * [T]here is nothing to cast a shadow in
which the parties can bargain." Alexander, Do the Merits Matter? A Study
of Settlements in Securities Class Actions, 43 Stan.L.Rev. 497, 567 (1991).
What might be the ultimate effects of the resulting uncertainty? Might one
consequence—paradoxically—be a decrease in the rate of settlement? See
Richard Posner, Economic Analysis of Law 541–42 (4th ed. 1992); cf.
Coleman & Silver, Justice in Settlements, 4 Soc.Phil. & Pol. 102 (1986).

3. It has been suggested that one substantial obstacle to the ability of
litigation to generate information for future disputants is the "increased
variability of judges and juries," which "reduces the value of a litigation
outcome as an accurate guide to the resolution of later cases. If federal
juries increasingly vary in their evaluation of similar evidence, or federal
judges increasingly vary in their evaluation of legal issues, then the
presumptive value of the information lost on account of settlement is
reduced accordingly." Bundy, The Policy in Favor of Settlement in an
Adversary System, 44 Hastings L.J. 1, 54 (1992). What might account for
such "increased variability"?

The "Alternative Dispute Resolution" Movement

The notion that use of the official court system is only one among an
abundant variety of ways of solving disputes has flourished in recent years.
There has been an outpouring of scholarly work, creative proposals, and
practical experimentation. The "ADR movement" referred to by Fiss is one
reflection of that idea—an idea that is, in fact, one impetus for this book.
Indeed by 1990, as Laura Nader has written, ADR had "become a major
industry. * * * In some ways it was a rebellion against law and lawyers—
often by lawyers themselves."[1]

Although Fiss speaks of the ADR "movement" as if it were unified and
homogeneous, that is hardly the case. The proponents of alternatives to
litigation are of diverse backgrounds—from "elite" lawyers like corporate
counsel and luminaries such as former President Bok of Harvard and
former Chief Justice Burger, to the sponsors of neighborhood "community
justice centers." And in addition, each advocate of ADR is likely to have his

---

1. Laura Nader, Controlling Processes
in the Practice of Law: Hierarchy and Pacifi-
cation in the Movement to Re–Form Dispute
Ideology, 9 Ohio St. J. on Disp. Resol. 1
(1993).

or her own agenda. Encouragement of non-judicial means of dispute resolution may reflect different goals and the desire to promote widely differing values.

Thus one can identify in the ADR literature a "cool" theme—a theme that emphasizes "efficient institutional management: clearing dockets, reducing delay, eliminating expense, unburdening the courts."[2] For example, in a 1997 survey of corporate counsel of "Fortune 1000" companies, 90% of the respondents identified ADR as a "critical cost control technique."[3] And at the same time, one can identify a "warm" theme—in which the search is for higher *quality* solutions than may be available in the courts. The stress here may be on generating solutions that are more responsive than is litigation to the underlying needs and interests of the parties: "Freed from formal legal categories and procedures," alternative processes "could get at the heart of problems and actually solve them."[4] Or the focus may be on replacing adversary conflict with "reconciliation" of the parties—on finding processes that can restore mutual understanding and preserve ongoing relationships.[5] ADR processes may appear "more humanely 'real,' democratic, participatory, and cathartic than more formalized processes."[6]

Consider, for example, the "informality" that is often associated with processes like mediation and arbitration. "Informality" can hardly be an ultimate value in itself. "Informal" procedure may be valued by some who see in it merely a loosening of the rules, restrictions, and rituals of the judicial process. They praise it, then, for its potential for speedier and less expensive decisionmaking. But for others, "informality" may be understood primarily to involve "a more relaxed flow of procedure, to make parties more comfortable and decrease enmity and disaffection costs."[7] Under this

---

2. Marc Galanter, The Emergence of the Judge as a Mediator in Civil Cases 2 (1985).

3. See Rinat Fried, "Corporations Backing ADR, Study Says," The Recorder, April 29, 1997 at p. 4; David Lipsky & Ronald Seeber, In Search of Control: The Corporate Embrace of ADR, 1 U. Pa. J. Lab. & Employment L. 133 (1998) (the "competitive market pressure faced by American corporations" has led many to examine the costs associated with their legal affairs; some respondents "told us that the transaction costs associated with settling a dispute, including the costs of inside and outside legal counsel, * * * were often two to three time the amounts of the settlements themselves.")

4. Silbey & Sarat, Dispute Processing in Law and Legal Scholarship: From Institutional Critique to the Reconstruction of the Juridical Subject, 66 Denver U.L.Rev. 437, 453 (1989) (characterizing views of "quality proponents" of ADR).

5. See, e.g., Smith, A Warmer Way of Disputing: Mediation and Conciliation, 26 Am.J.Comp.L. (Supp.) 205 (1978) ("Therapy and catharsis, rather than an attempt to arrive at some 'truth,' becomes the goal of dispute settlement"); McThenia & Shaffer, For Reconciliation, 94 Yale L.J. 1660 (1985) ("[T]he religious tradition seeks not *resolution* (which connotes the sort of doctrinal integrity in the law that seems to us to be Fiss's highest priority) but *reconciliation* of brother to brother, sister to sister, sister to brother, child to parent, neighbor to neighbor, buyer to seller, defendant to plaintiff, *and judge to both.*").

6. Carrie Menkel–Meadow, Whose Dispute Is It Anyway?: A Philosophical and Democratic Defense of Settlement (In Some Cases), 83 Geo. L.J. 2663, 2692 (1995).

7. Bush, Dispute Resolution Alternatives and the Goals of Civil Justice: Jurisdictional Principles for Process Choice, 1984 Wisc.L.Rev. 893, 1006 n. 251.

view it may be valued because of its beneficial effects on the relationship, and on the level of trust, respect, and understanding between the parties. "Conversation and cooperation replace conflict; informality empowers."[8]

The goals that the various proponents of ADR seek to advance are not only diverse; in some cases they may actually be in conflict. Judge Harry Edwards has warned that

> Inexpensive, expeditious, and informal adjudication is not always synonymous with *fair* and *just* adjudication. The decisionmakers may not understand the values at stake and parties to disputes do not always possess equal power and resources. Sometimes because of this inequality and sometimes because of deficiencies in informal processes lacking procedural protections, the use of alternative mechanisms will produce nothing more than inexpensive and ill-informed decisions. And these decisions may merely legitimate decisions made by the existing power structure within society.[9]

Consider, for example, the case for "alternatives" made by former Chief Justice Burger:

> One reason our courts have become overburdened is that Americans are increasingly turning to the courts for relief from a range of personal distresses and anxieties.
>
> Remedies for personal wrongs that once were considered the responsibility of institutions other than the courts are now boldly asserted as legal "entitlements." The courts have been expected to fill the void created by the decline of church, family, and neighborhood unity.
>
> Possibly the increased litigiousness that court dockets reflect simply mirrors what is happening worldwide. The press, television, and radio for hours every day tell us of events in Asia, Africa, Europe, and Latin America where there is seething political, social, and economic turmoil. It is not surprising that our anxieties are aggravated.[10]

8. Resnik, Many Doors? Closing Doors? Alternative Dispute Resolution and Adjudication, 10 Ohio St.J.Disp.Res. 211, 249–50 (1995) (characterizing claims that alternative processes are "more congenial than adjudication"; by contrast adjudication "is seen as a process that often brings out the worst in its participants, either because it distorts their abilities to pursue self-interest or because it defines self-interest in such a fashion that requires inflicting losses, rather than maximizing gains").

9. Edwards, Alternative Dispute Resolution: Panacea or Anathema, 99 Harv.L.Rev. 668, 679 (1986). See also Lazerson, In the Halls of Justice, the Only Justice is in the Halls, in 1 Richard Abel (ed.), The Politics of Informal Justice 119 (1982) ("informaliza-tion" of New York City Housing Court—through introduction of hearing officers who encouraged "conciliation" in order to reduce court backlog—eroded the legal position of tenants in substandard housing); Anita Bernstein, Complaints, 32 McGeorge L. Rev. 37, 48 (2000) ("When he encounters ADR that he doesn't want, our complainant has reached another minefield: a consensus that certain types of grievances do not warrant the full attention of the law, even though longstanding legal rules cover them and even though a person has cried out to the law for justice").

10. Burger, Isn't There a Better Way?, ABA Journal, March 1982, pp. 274–275 (1982).

What seems to be the underlying message that is being conveyed here? It has been suggested that in some cases, the recent discovery of alternatives to courts may be a reaction to an increased consciousness of legal rights and an explosion of claims to "entitlements" on the part of consumers, users of substandard housing, victims of sexual and racial discrimination or of domestic violence, and other disadvantaged groups. The encouragement of alternatives may not proceed entirely from the desire to ensure these groups broader access to inexpensive and meaningful dispute resolution—it may proceed instead from a desire to relieve the courts from the pressures and problems posed by these cases, enabling judges to deal more efficiently with more "traditional" types of judicial business. "Elite lawyers want to conserve judicial resources for the resolution of business and commercial disputes and are willing to see other matters removed from courts if not from the legal field itself."[11] From this point of view ADR can indeed be seen (as Professor Fiss suggests) as subordinating legal rights and public values to accommodative bargaining, and justice to the single-minded objective of settling disputes. It has even been claimed that for some proponents, an enthusiastic support of non-judicial processes may be nothing more than "another form of the deregulation movement, one that permits private actors with powerful economic interests to pursue self-interest free of community norms."[12]

Many of the recent experiments with ADR have been designed to be separate from and independent of the courts. But an increasingly important phenomenon is the use of ADR processes that are closely linked to the judicial system. One impetus for such a development was the Civil Justice Reform Act of 1990, which required every federal district court to implement "a civil justice expense and delay reduction plan"; in drawing up such plans courts were instructed to consider a number of case management principles aimed at reducing cost and delay—including notably "authorization to refer appropriate cases to alternative dispute resolution programs that * * * the court may make available, including mediation, minitrial, and summary jury trial."[13] An even more significant piece of legislation is

11. Silbey & Sarat, supra n. 4 at 446.

12. McThenia & Shaffer, For Reconciliation, 94 Yale L.J. 1660, 1665 n. 33 (1985) (suggestion of Milner Ball). See also Provine, Justice a la Carte: On the Privatization of Dispute Resolution, 12B Studies in Law, Politics, and Society 345 (1992) ("the recent transformation of dispute resolution is part of a broader political movement to reduce the scope and power of government as a provider of services").

In Jansen v. Packaging Corp. of America, 123 F.3d 490 (7th Cir.1997), the court affirmed a grant of summary judgment in favor of an employer on an employee's Title VII retaliation claim. In Judge Coffey's concurring opinion, he "join[ed] with thousands of American citizens who are of the opinion that employers today are over-regulated and saddled with an increasingly burdensome, indeed an overwhelming, amount of litigation, including Title VII litigation (much of which, as we realize, often is without merit)." "Indeed," he went on, "the rising tide of employment-related litigation has prompted many firms to require * * * that employees agree to accept arbitration and forego their right to sue in court over employment-related disputes." 123 F.3d at 541; see Chapter V, Section C.4.b., infra.

13. 28 U.S.C.A. §§ 471, 473(a)(6). A district-by-district survey of ADR programs operating in federal courts is Elizabeth Plapinger & Donna Stienstra, ADR and Settle-the Alternative Dispute Resolution Act of 1998: ADR, Congress found, "has the potential" to provide "greater satisfaction of the parties, innovative methods of resolving disputes, and greater efficiency in achieving settlements"—as well as to reduce "the large backlog of cases now pending" in some federal courts, thus allowing courts "to process their remaining cases more efficiently." As a consequence each federal district court was instructed to provide litigants in all civil cases with "at least one alternative dispute resolution process," and was to "require" that litigants "consider the use of an alternative dispute resolution process at an appropriate stage in the litigation."[14]

Courts have in other ways, too, become more frequently and more visibly involved in the direct promotion of settlement. Recent amendments to the Federal Rules of Civil Procedure encourage judges at pretrial conferences to raise and take action on such subjects as "settlement and the use of special procedures to assist in resolving the dispute"; judges may also require that a party or its representative be present or available by telephone "in order to consider possible settlement of the dispute."[15] And in many jurisdictions courts have the authority, either at the request of a party or on their own initiative, to order the parties to engage in an ADR procedure prior to trial.[16] Some years ago a survey revealed that state courts have instituted ADR (mostly mediation) programs in all but seven states.[17] In short, judges have begun to "make ADR their own—either by sponsoring or by running it."[18]

These developments are explored in considerable detail in the chapters that follow. They have given rise to some concern that the ADR movement may now be in the process of being "captured" or "co-opted" by the very legal system to which it was supposed to be an "alternative." To some purists, the virtues of alternative processes may be lost where the parties have been coerced into participating.[19] And in the view of a number of critics, the growing institutionalization of ADR programs has inevitably led to their being "legalized"—with the danger that they may become "just

ment in the Federal District Courts: A Sourcebook for Judges & Lawyers (1996) ("In marked contrast to five years ago when only a few courts had court-based programs for mediation, over half of the ninety-four districts now offer—and in several instances, require—mediation"; "arbitration is the second most frequently authorized ADR program, but falls well short of mediation in the number of courts that have implemented it").

14. Public Law 105–315, 112 Stat. 2993; see 28 U.S.C. § 652.

15. FRCP Rule 16(c).

16. E.g., V.T.C.A., Civ.Prac. & Rem. Code § 154.021. The federal ADR Act of 1998 also provides that a district court may "elect

to require the use of [ADR] in certain cases" but, in the absence of the parties' consent, may do so only with respect to mediation and early neutral evaluation. 28 U.S.C. § 652(a).

17. See Richard Reuben, "The Lawyer Turns Peacemaker," ABA J., Aug.1996, at pp. 54, 56.

18. Resnik, Failing Faith: Adjudicatory Procedure in Decline, 53 U.Chi.L.Rev. 494, 536 (1986).

19. E.g., Katz, Compulsory Alternative Dispute Resolution and Voluntarism: Two–Headed Monster or Two Sides of the Coin?, 1993 J.Disp.Res. 1 ("voluntariness is consistent with the underlying philosophy of ADR").

another battleground for adversarial fighting" on the part of attorneys.[20] Perhaps the ultimate irony is that we are now witnessing the growth of a body of "law of ADR" in court-related processes that itself may be spawning considerable litigation.

C. THE CHOICE OF PROCESS

1. LAWYERS AND THE CHOICE OF PROCESS

As we have seen, the overwhelming majority of disputes—even when a lawsuit has been filed—terminate short of a trial. It may seem something of a paradox, then, to suggest that for the average member of the bar, awareness and acceptance of non-judicial processes of dispute resolution have been slow in coming. Even now, it seems, thinking about alternative processes—and making conscious choices among them—have not yet become habits that have penetrated very deeply into the everyday practice of law.

Some of the lingering indifference to ADR on the part of the bar might be attributed simply to unfamiliarity with the potential for alternative processes, and with the form they might take. This at least has certainly begun to change—as new generations of law students filter through the system, and as many more lawyers have the occasion to participate in court-mandated processes. In addition, some lack of enthusiasm can often be explained by simple self-interest. "Self-interest" is at least partly a matter of economics: Lawyers, especially those paid by the hour, are able to extract substantial fees from prolonged conflict, and may have an incentive to shape disputes in such a way as to maximize their benefits from them. Economic changes such as intensified business conflict—and above all heightened competition in an increasingly entrepreneurial legal profession—may also play a role in dampening interest in non-adversarial settlement.[1] And "self-interest" can have other, less tangible, aspects: Alternative processes often function in such a way as to transfer greater power and control over disputing to the parties themselves, or to other professionals (such as mediators) who may be involved in helping to resolve the dispute. To many lawyers, this may seem to threaten the attorney's exclusive control over dispute resolution—a feeling of dominance that only the judicial process can provide.

Still another explanation might be found in the education of attorneys. We have all gone through the most rigorous and stressful training, focusing almost exclusively on the virtues of "legal analysis" and argumentation—of "thinking like a lawyer." Carefully defining the issues, marshalling the

---

20. E.g., Menkel–Meadow, Pursuing Settlement in an Adversary Culture: A Tale of Innovation Co-opted or "The Law of ADR," 19 Fla.St.U.L.Rev. 1, 17 (1991).

1. See Bryant Garth, From Civil Litigation to Private Justice: Legal Practice at War with the Profession and Its Values, 59 Brooklyn L. Rev. 931, 938–45 (1993) (referring to a variety of "scorched earth litigation" tactics and other tactical innovations in high-stakes disputes, attributable to a search for competitive advantage within the profession).

arguments and counterarguments, manipulating the precedents—all in the interest of "zealous advocacy" in the assertion of one's legal "rights"—are made to seem the essence of the lawyer's craft. Having survived such a process, lawyers are likely to have an investment in the belief that this is the "natural" way for disputes in our society to be resolved. The role models and legendary cult figures held up to the admiration of law students are likely to be those who have proven themselves "toughest" as "hired guns" in the service of their clients' advantage. (You can readily think of examples.). This process of socialization reinforces the thrust of the curriculum, with its emphasis on formal court adjudication. The result, as suggested by the following excerpt, is that litigation and the adversary system tend to dominate the "mental landscape" of the lawyer and obscure other possibilities that may be in the background. "Lawyer and client are apt to agree that adversary combat in a judicial arena is the normal, socially acceptable, and psychologically satisfying method of resolving disputes."[2]

Robert Kagan, Do Lawyers Cause Adversarial Legalism? A Preliminary Inquiry

19 Law and Social Inquiry 1, 5, 25–26, 37–39, 61–62 (1994)

In a society pervaded by the threat of legal action, lawyers for business corporations, school boards, and other organizations undoubtedly prevent litigation simply by spreading the word about potential liabilities. In their everyday practice, corporate lawyers attempt in many ways to forfend litigation, drafting imaginative contractual provisions for resolving conflict in case business earnings decline or debts go unpaid. Many attorneys decline to advance claims or defenses that seem to them unjustified in law or in equity. Other lawyers, emphasizing the costliness of the adversarial process, push clients intent on moral vindication to accept financial compromise.

Some American lawyers go further, systematically trying to *reduce* the overall volume of adversarial legalism. Bar associations dominated by elite lawyers often have fought against "ambulance chasing" or increased litigation in hopes of enhancing the image of the profession. In some corporations, the general counsel has insisted on using private mediation firms, rather than litigation, to resolve entire categories of disputes; the leading mediation firms are run and staffed by lawyers and former judges. * * *

Consequently, one might argue that even if some members of the American legal profession consciously and on their own account work to amplify adversarial legalism, there are even more members of the profession who work to dampen it. * * *

---

2. Stephen Goldberg et al., Dispute Resolution 422 (2nd ed. 1992). See also Bush, Dispute Resolution Alternatives and the Goals of Civil Justice: Jurisdictional Principles for Process Choice, 1984 Wisc. L. Rev. 893, 995–1004.

Perhaps, but probably not. The dampeners undoubtedly reduce adversarial legalism below the level that would exist if they had instead become amplifiers. But the relative number of lawyers in each camp does not resolve the question. The burglary rate can go up even if most people try to deter burglary. Relatively small numbers of determined people can have a big impact. The fact remains that adversarial legalism, by most measures, has increased in the last quarter-century. The issue is whether the actions of lawyers—not all lawyers, but lawyers—have played a role in that net increase, even though many of their professional brothers and sisters may have prevented the increase from being greater.

* * *

Law Professors and the Culture of Adversarial Legalism

* * * Comparative observers often note that when contrasted with legal education in England and Western Europe, current day American law schools promote a remarkably activist, instrumentalist image of law and the role of lawyers and judges. * * * [W]hile English legal academics defer to barristers and judges in shaping law and legal culture, American law professors actively seek to shape legal culture, and through it, society, and have had a significant degree of success: "American law schools have been the source of the dominant general theory of law in America—'*instrumentalism*'—[which] conceives of law essentially as a pragmatic instrument of social improvement." Instrumentalism is embraced by many politically conservative as well as liberal professors, most prominently by adherents of the influential "law and economics" movement, who seek law reforms designed to enhance economic efficiency.

Whereas British law students are expected to learn the rules of rules as laid down in rather dogmatic textbooks, and Continental students are expected to learn and accept the theoretical underpinnings of their legal systems, American law students are taught to challenge or at least to question their country's law. They spend more time studying the most disputed cases than basic black letter doctrine. They are urged to analyze the merits of legal doctrines and judicial opinions in terms of the fairness, economic efficiency, or equality of their social consequences. They are prodded to formulate legal arguments that would support their gut feelings about what the results should be. The law reviews they edit bulge with articles calling for new legal rights and changes in old ones, along with essays stressing the indeterminacy of legal rules.

American law students are taught by their professors that judges often are incompetent or as apt to be influenced, by their political attitudes and allegiances as by the letter of the law. [And "[l]aw is treated as more malleable, open to parties' novel legal and policy arguments. In civil cases, lay jurors still play a large and normatively important role in the United States, which magnifies the importance of skillful legal advocacy and reduces legal certainty."] The legal system, many American law professors implicitly suggest, is a field of political struggle, shaped by the play of creative lawyering and argumentation (at best) and by raw economic and political power (at worst). So the lawyer's job is to pick her way through that uncertain mine field, striving for justice as best she can when she sees an opening, whether as lawyer or judge. Not surprisingly, that is the view of the system that American lawyers convey to their clients.

* * *

Constructing Lawyers' Ethics

In constructing rules of ethics for practitioners, a legal profession has a range of choices. It can stress the lawyer's duty to her client alone, zealously protecting and advocating the client's interests regardless of the costs or injustices to the rest of the world. Or legal ethics can enjoin attorneys to temper pursuit of clients' interests with concern for legitimate interests of third parties and society at large. The American legal profession long has stressed the ethic of zealous advocacy, in contrast to the legal professions of England and Western European nations, where the ethical rules of conduct set greater limits on the lawyer's duty to protect client loyalty and confidentiality in deference to larger societal and third party interests. * * *

Thus American lawyers have fought for rules of evidence that provide a broader and more absolute lawyer-client privilege than exists in most other countries. In contrast to most other legal professions, the American bar has endorsed contingency fees, justifying them on grounds that they facilitate litigation by the nonwealthy. American legal ethics endorse lawyers' practice of pretrial coaching of witnesses; German legal ethics strongly discourage it.

The American legal profession's endorsement of the lawyer's duty of zealous advocacy—as opposed to her duty to serve as "officer of the court"—encourages a more entrepreneurial form of legal practice than prevails in Europe. It authorizes lawyers to advance novel legal claims and claims and arguments, challenging or stretching existing, doctrine, and asserting that it is the court's job, not the lawyer's, to separate the wheat from the chaff.[130]

The adversarial ethic disseminated by the profession also has validated American trial lawyers' competition to develop ever more aggressive and costly techniques of litigation-dramatic "day-in-the-life" videos to illustrate the adverse effects of accidents; calculatedly burdensome pretrial discovery demands in high-stakes cases; extended voir dire of prospective jurors. Finally, the ethic of zealous advocacy encourages an aggressive style bounds of existing legal rules and institutions * * *.

---

130. [Mark J. Osiel, Lawyers as Monopolists and Entrepreneurs: Review of *Lawyers in Society,* 103 Harv. L. Rev. 2009, 2060 (1990)] argues, "The stringency of their ethical guidelines on matters of client loyalty impelled American lawyers toward the imaginative discovery of doctrinal ambiguity where such ambiguity would otherwise have remained merely latent. In particular, the view of legal expertise as the skillful exploitation of doctrinal uncertainty would not have become so central to the self-understanding of American attorney's had their ethical guidelines encouraged them to view themselves, like many lawyers elsewhere in the West primarily as 'officers of society.' "

Most attorneys, sociolegal studies indicate, serve as stolid gatekeepers for the courts. Hence, most day-to-day, non-law-reform litigation, we can safely assume, is stimulated not by lawyers but by clients or complainants. But surely that is not *always* the case. * * *

Well, how much legal contestation is lawyer-induced (as opposed to client-induced)? 10%? 15%? 20%? 2%? We don't know. Legal and scholars have had little to say on the subject, perhaps for fear of providing support to conservative lawyer bashers. But a great deal of anecdotal evidence, and limited systematic evidence, suggests that there is a significant amount of what we might call superaggressive lawyering, exacerbating the costs and delays of "adversarial legalism as practice." Quantitative measures are elusive. * * *

* * *

What if all the lawyers—or at least those who consciously work to extend and preserve adversarial legalism, or engage in superaggressive litigation—were suddenly banished to a reservation in central Nevada? It is hard to believe that the resulting change in the legal order would be truly massive in the long run. The social divisions, economic conflicts, political fragmentation, and popular beliefs that generate adversarial legalism surely would not disappear.

On the other hand, suppose American lawyers—not just a few but most of them—reconfigured legal ethics to discourage superaggressive litigation; and argued that social insurance was preferable to tort law for compensating injury; and insisted that judges should urge legislatures to reform the laws rather than doing it themselves; and lobbied for the creation of cheaper, less adversarial dispute-resolution forums; and fostered administrative law and conceptions of due process that sought to improve rather than subvert administrative authority? After all, that is not so different from the stance taken by the legal profession in other rich democracies. If the bulk of the legal profession did these things, it almost certainly would have some effect—probably a considerable effect—on the level of adversarial legalism. For what lawyers think and say, the legal culture they generate and the behaviors they exhibit, surely influence what clients, interest groups, legislators, journalists, and the general public think appropriate to demand of the legal order.

* * *

In the 1960s, the comedian Lenny Bruce used to say that in New York City, even the Gentiles were Jewish. In the law-saturated United States of today, he might say that even the laymen are lawyers. Or at least every politician, governmental official, and corporate executive, law-trained or not, thinks like a lawyer to a considerable extent. So if American lawyers are not the only force working to recreate adversarial legalism, it may be partly because they have trained their fellow citizens to do it too.

NOTES AND QUESTIONS

1.   Lawyers are increasingly coming into contact on a daily basis with non-judicial processes. But it should hardly be surprising, in light of the previous discussion, that even when they do so they may have a tendency to view these processes through the optic of litigation—that is, they may expect their experience to mirror or mimic what happens in court. We will see later that this is particularly noticeable in the attitude of some lawyers to negotiation and arbitration. These processes may be approached as if they were merely variants or extensions of the judicial, adversarial model which to so many lawyers is the paradigm of disputing. See, e.g., Susan Sturm, From Gladiators to Problem–Solvers: Connecting Conversations About Women, the Academy, and the Legal Profession, 4 Duke J. of Gender L. & Pol'y 119, 121–22 (1997) ("Even in more informal settings such as negotiations or in-house advising, lawyering often proceeds within the gladiator model"—a model that "celebrates analytical rigor, toughness, and quick thinking").

It is perhaps symptomatic of this attitude that a recent continuing legal education program promises to help attorneys to learn how they can "win at ADR." (JAMS/Endispute Workshop, "Effective Negotiation and Winning at ADR," [Boston, May 15, 1995]).

2.   The United States has many more lawyers than any other country—the number of lawyers per capita in the United States is roughly four times as great as it is in England, and ten times as great as it is in France. In contrast, the number of judges is relatively small, and the American ratio of lawyers to judges is one of the highest anywhere. Marc Galanter, Reading the Landscape of Disputes: What We Know and Don't Know (And Think We Know) About Our Allegedly Contentious and Litigious Society, 31 U.C.L.A. L.Rev. 4, 52, 55 (1983). In addition, we have seen in recent years an extraordinary growth in the number of large law firms: In 1993 the largest firm had 1662 lawyers, and 184 firms were larger than the largest law firm in 1968 (which then had "only" 169 lawyers). See Ronald Gilson & Robert Mnookin, Disputing through Agents: Cooperation and Conflict Between Lawyers in Litigation, 94 Colum. L. Rev. 509, 538 (1994).

How might these facts be relevant to Professor Kagan's discussion? See also John Setear, The Barrister and the Bomb: The Dynamics of Cooperation, Nuclear Deterrence, and Discovery Abuse, 69 B.U. L. Rev. 569 (1989).

3.   One empirical study of family and neighbor disputes in a small American city concluded that by the time a conflict has become serious enough to warrant an outsider's intervention, disputants simply "do not want what alternatives have to offer." At that point, they want "vindication, protection of his or her rights * * * an advocate to help in the battle, or a third party who will uncover the 'truth' and declare the other party wrong." "It is in precisely those cases which have developed to the point where they seem so unavoidable and principled that the grievant can justify going to an outside agency that she/he is least likely to be enthusiastic about the offer of an alternative dispute resolution process which removes the advocate and eliminates the third party who would make a definitive decision about right and wrong." Sally Engle Merry & Susan Silbey, What Do Plaintiffs Want? Reexamine the Concept of Dispute, 9 Justice System J. 151, 153–54 (1984). More generally, as Professor Kagan suggests, cultural attitudes concerning the centrality of the adversary process may routinely mold the assumptions of *clients* with respect to how disputes should normally be resolved, as well as the assumptions of lawyers. So the behavior of a lawyer may in fact often be a response to the desire or expectation of the *client* for a "valiant champion"—or, perhaps, an attempt to live up to what the lawyer *assumes* the client expects. See Riskin, Mediation and Lawyers, 43 Ohio St. L.J. 29, 49 (1982).

Is there any way to break out of this vicious circle? Can we envisage that there may be clients, or areas of the law, where an attorney's experience and talent in non-litigation processes may constitute a competitive advantage—even, indeed, a "marketing tool"? See Bryant Garth, From Civil Litigation to Private Justice: Legal Practice at War With the Profession and Its Values, 59 Brooklyn L. Rev. 931, 950–53 (1993).

4. The assumptions behind the "adversary model" are tested, in a rather unique context, by the Supreme Court's decision in the *Walters* case, which follows.

Walters v. National Association of Radiation Survivors

Supreme Court of the United States, 1985.
473 U.S. 305, 105 S.Ct. 3180, 87 L.Ed.2d 220.

■ JUSTICE REHNQUIST delivered the opinion of the Court.

* * *

Congress has by statute established an administrative system for granting service connected death or disability benefits to veterans. The amount of the benefit award is not based upon need, but upon service connection—that is, whether the disability is causally related to an injury sustained in the service—and the degree of incapacity caused by the disability. A detailed system has been established by statute and Veterans Administration (VA) regulation for determining a veteran's entitlement, with final authority resting with an administrative body known as the Board of Veterans' Appeals (BVA). Judicial review of VA decisions is precluded by statute. The controversy in this case centers on the opportunity for a benefit applicant or recipient to obtain legal counsel to aid in the presentation of his claim to the VA. [38 U.S.C. § 3404(c) limited to $10 the fee that may be paid an attorney or agent who represents a veteran seeking benefits for service-connected death or disability, and § 3405 imposed criminal penalties on anyone charging fees in excess of this $10 limitation.]

Appellees here are two veterans' organizations, three individual veterans, and a veteran's widow. The two veterans' organizations are the National Association of Radiation Survivors, an organization principally concerned with obtaining compensation for its members for injuries resulting from atomic bomb tests, and Swords to Plowshares Veterans Rights Organization, an organization particularly devoted to the concerns of Vietnam veterans. * * *

Appellees contended in the District Court that the fee limitation provision of § 3404 denied them any realistic opportunity to obtain legal representation in presenting their claims to the VA and hence violated their rights under the Due Process Clause of the Fifth Amendment and under the First Amendment. The District Court agreed with the appellees on both of these grounds, and entered a nationwide "preliminary injunction" barring appellants from enforcing the fee limitation. To understand fully the posture in which the case reaches us it is necessary to discuss the administrative scheme in some detail.

Congress began providing veterans pensions in early 1789, and after every conflict in which the Nation has been involved Congress has, in the words of Abraham Lincoln, "provided for him who has borne the battle, and his widow and his orphan." The VA was created by Congress in 1930, and since that time has been responsible for administering the congressional program for veterans benefits. In 1978, the year covered by the report of the Legal Services Corporation to Congress that was introduced into evidence in the District Court, approximately 800,000 claims for service-connected disability or death and pensions were decided by the 58 regional offices of the VA. Slightly more than half of these were claims for service-connected disability or death, and the remainder were pension claims. Of the 800,000 total claims in 1978, more than 400,000 were allowed, and some 379,000 were denied. Sixty-six thousand of these denials were contested at the regional level; about a quarter of these contests were dropped, 15% prevailed on reconsideration at the local level, and the remaining 36,000 were appealed to the BVA. At that level some 4,500, or 12%, prevailed, and another 13% won a remand for further proceedings. Although these figures are from 1978, the statistics in evidence indicate that the figures remain fairly constant from year to year.

As might be expected in a system which processes such a large number of claims each year, the process prescribed by Congress for obtaining disability benefits does not contemplate the adversary mode of dispute resolution utilized by courts in this country. It is commenced by the submission of a claim form to the local veterans agency, which form is provided by the VA either upon request or upon receipt of notice of the death of a veteran. Upon application a claim generally is first reviewed by a three-person "rating board" of the VA regional office—consisting of a medical specialist, a legal specialist, and an "occupational specialist." A claimant is "entitled to a hearing at any time on any issue involved in a claim...." Proceedings in front of the rating board "are ex parte in nature"; no Government official appears in opposition. The principal issues are the extent of the claimant's disability and whether it is service-connected. The panel is required by regulation "to assist a claimant in developing the facts pertinent to his claim," and to consider any evidence offered by the claimant. In deciding the claim the panel generally will request the applicant's Armed Service and medical records, and will order a medical examination by a VA hospital. Moreover, the board is directed by regulation to resolve all reasonable doubts in favor of the claimant.

After reviewing the evidence the board renders a decision either denying the claim or assigning a disability "rating" pursuant to detailed regulations developed for assessing various disabilities. Money benefits are calculated based on the rating. The claimant is notified of the board's decision and its reasons, and the claimant may then initiate an appeal by filing a "notice of disagreement" with the local agency. If the local agency adheres to its original decision it must then provide the claimant with a "statement of the case"—a written description of the facts and applicable law upon which the panel based its determination—so that the claimant may adequately present his appeal to the BVA. Hearings in front of the BVA are subject to the same rules as local agency hearings—they are ex parte, there is no formal questioning or cross-examination, and no formal rules of evidence apply. The BVA's decision is not subject to judicial review.

The process is designed to function throughout with a high degree of informality and solicitude for the claimant. There is no statute of limitations, and a denial of benefits has no formal res judicata effect; a claimant may resubmit as long as he presents new facts not previously forwarded. Although there are time limits for submitting a notice of disagreement and although a claimant may prejudice his opportunity to challenge factual or legal decisions by failing to challenge them in that notice, the time limit is quite liberal—up to one year—and the VA boards are instructed to read any submission in the light most favorable to the claimant. Perhaps more importantly for present purposes, however, various veterans' organizations across the country make available trained service agents, free of charge, to assist claimants in developing and presenting their claims. These service representatives are contemplated by the VA statute, and they are recognized as an important part of the administrative scheme. Appellees' counsel agreed at argument that a representative is available for any claimant who requests one, regardless of the claimant's affiliation with any particular veterans' group.[4]

* * *

In reaching its conclusions the court relied heavily on the problems presented by what it described as "complex cases"—a class of cases also focused on in the depositions. Though never expressly defined by the District Court, these cases apparently include those in which a disability is slow-developing and therefore difficult to find service-connected, such as the claims associated with exposure to radiation or harmful chemicals, as well as other cases identified by the deponents as involving difficult matters of medical judgment. Nowhere in the opinion of the District Court is there any estimate of what percentage of the annual VA caseload of 800,000 these

---

4. The VA statistics show that 86% of all claimants are represented by service representatives, 12% proceed pro se, and 2% are represented by lawyers. Counsel agreed at argument that the 12% who proceed pro se do so by their own choice.

cases comprise, nor is there any more precise description of the class. There is no question but what the three named plaintiffs and the plaintiff veteran's widow asserted such claims, and in addition there are declarations in the record from 12 other claimants who were asserting such claims. The evidence contained in the record, however, suggests that the sum total of such claims is extremely small; in 1982, for example, roughly 2% of the BVA caseload consisted of "agent orange" or "radiation" claims, and what evidence there is suggests that the percentage of such claims in the regional offices was even less—perhaps as little as 3 in 1,000.

With respect to the service representatives, the court again found the representation unsatisfactory. Although admitting that this was not due to any "lack of dedication," the court found that a heavy caseload and the lack of legal training combined to prevent service representatives from adequately researching a claim. Facts are not developed, and "it is standard practice for service organization representatives to submit merely a one to two page handwritten brief."

Based on the inability of the VA and service organizations to provide the full range of services that a retained attorney might, the court concluded that appellees had demonstrated a "high risk of erroneous deprivation" from the process as administered. The court then found that the Government had "failed to demonstrate that it would suffer any harm if the statutory fee limitation ... were lifted." The only Government interest suggested was the "paternalistic" assertion that the fee limitation is necessary to ensure that claimants do not turn substantial portions of their benefits over to unscrupulous lawyers. The court suggested that there were "less drastic means" to confront this problem.

* * *

Appellees' first claim, accepted by the District Court, is that the statutory fee limitation, as it bears on the administrative scheme in operation, deprives a rejected claimant or recipient of "life, liberty or property, without due process of law," by depriving him of representation by expert legal counsel. Our decisions establish that "due process" is a flexible concept—that the processes required by the Clause with respect to the termination of a protected interest will vary depending upon the importance attached to the interest and the particular circumstances under which the deprivation may occur. See *Mathews* [*v. Eldridge,* 424 U.S. 319 (1976)] at 334. In defining the process necessary to ensure "fundamental fairness" we have recognized that the Clause does not require that "the procedures used to guard against an erroneous deprivation ... be so comprehensive as to preclude any possibility of error," and in addition we have emphasized that the marginal gains from affording an additional procedural safeguard often may be outweighed by the societal cost of providing such a safeguard.

These general principles are reflected in the test set out in *Mathews,* which test the District Court purported to follow, and which requires a court to consider the private interest that will be affected by the official action, the risk of an erroneous deprivation of such interest through the procedures used, the probable value of additional or substitute procedural safeguards, and the government's interest in adhering to the existing system. In applying this test we must keep in mind, in addition to the deference owed to Congress, the fact that the very nature of the due process inquiry indicates that the fundamental fairness of a particular procedure does not turn on the result obtained in any individual case; rather, "procedural due process rules are shaped by the risk of error inherent in the truth-finding process as applied to the generality of cases, not the rare exceptions."

The government interest, which has been articulated in congressional debates since the fee limitation was first enacted in 1862 during the Civil War, has been this: that the system for administering benefits should be managed in a sufficiently informal way that there should be no need for the employment of an attorney to obtain benefits to which a claimant was entitled, so that the claimant would receive the entirety of the award without having to divide it with a lawyer. This purpose is reinforced by a similar absolute prohibition on compensation of any service organization representative.

* * *

There can be little doubt that invalidation of the fee limitation would seriously frustrate the oft-repeated congressional purpose for enacting it. Attorneys would be freely employable by claimants to veterans' benefits, and the claimant would as a result end up paying part of the award, or its equivalent, to an attorney. But this would not be the only consequence of striking down the fee limitation that would be deleterious to the congressional plan.

A necessary concomitant of Congress' desire that a veteran not need a representative to assist him in making his claim was that the system should be as informal and nonadversarial as possible. This is not to say that complicated factual inquiries may be rendered simple by the expedient of informality, but surely Congress desired that the proceedings be as informal and nonadversarial as possible. The regular introduction of lawyers into the proceedings would be quite unlikely to further this goal. Describing the prospective impact of lawyers in probation revocation proceedings, we said in *Gagnon v. Scarpelli,* 411 U.S. 778, 787–788 (1973):

> The introduction of counsel into a revocation proceeding will alter significantly the nature of the proceeding. If counsel is provided for the probationer or parolee, the State in turn will normally provide its own counsel; lawyers, by training and disposition, are advocates and bound by professional duty to present all available evidence and arguments in support of their clients' positions and to contest with vigor all adverse evidence and views. The role of the hearing body itself . . . may become more akin to that of a judge at a trial, and less attuned to the rehabilitative needs of the individual. . . . Certainly, the decisionmaking process will be prolonged, and the financial cost to the State—for

appointed counsel, ... a longer record, and the possibility of judicial review—will not be insubstantial.

* * *

Knowledgeable and thoughtful observers have made the same point in other language:

> To be sure, counsel can often perform useful functions even in welfare cases or other instances of mass justice; they may bring out facts ignored by or unknown to the authorities, or help to work out satisfactory compromises. But this is only one side of the coin. Under our adversary system the role of counsel is not to make sure the truth is ascertained but to advance his client's cause by any ethical means. Within the limits of professional propriety, causing delay and sowing confusion not only are his right but may be his duty. The appearance of counsel for the citizen is likely to lead the government to provide one—or at least to cause the government's representative to act like one. The result may be to turn what might have been a short conference leading to an amicable result into a protracted controversy.

> These problems concerning counsel and confrontation inevitably bring up the question whether we would not do better to abandon the adversary system in certain areas of mass justice.... While such an experiment would be a sharp break with our tradition of adversary process, that tradition ... was not formulated for a situation in which many thousands of hearings must be provided each month.

Friendly, "Some Kind of Hearing," 123 U.Pa.L.Rev. 1267, 1287–1290 (1975).

Thus, even apart from the frustration of Congress' principal goal of wanting the veteran to get the entirety of the award, the destruction of the fee limitation would bid fair to complicate a proceeding which Congress wished to keep as simple as possible. It is scarcely open to doubt that if claimants were permitted to retain compensated attorneys the day might come when it could be said that an attorney might indeed be necessary to present a claim properly in a system rendered more adversary and more complex by the very presence of lawyer representation. It is only a small step beyond that to the situation in which the claimant who has a factually simple and obviously deserving claim may nonetheless feel impelled to retain an attorney simply because so many other claimants retain attorneys. And this additional complexity will undoubtedly engender greater administrative costs, with the end result being that less Government money reaches its intended beneficiaries.

We accordingly conclude that under the *Mathews v. Eldridge* analysis great weight must be accorded to the Government interest at stake here. The flexibility of our approach in due process cases is intended in part to allow room for other forms of dispute resolution; with respect to the individual interests at stake here, legislatures are to be allowed considerable leeway to formulate such processes without being forced to conform to a rigid constitutional code of procedural necessities. It would take an extraor-

dinarily strong showing of probability of error under the present system—
and the probability that the presence of attorneys would sharply diminish
that possibility—to warrant a holding that the fee limitation denies claimants due process of law. We have no hesitation in deciding that no such
showing was made out on the record before the District Court.

* * *

Passing the problems with quantifying the likelihood of an erroneous
deprivation, however, under *Mathews* we must also ask what value the
proposed additional procedure may have in reducing such error. In this
case we are fortunate to have statistics that bear directly on this question,
which statistics were addressed by the District Court. These unchallenged
statistics chronicle the success rates before the BVA depending on the type
of representation of the claimant, and are summarized in the following
figures taken from the record.

**ULTIMATE SUCCESS RATES BEFORE THE BOARD OF VETER-
ANS APPEALS BY MODE OF REPRESENTATION**

American Legion	16.2%
American Red Cross	16.8%
Disabled American Veterans	16.6%
Veterans of Foreign Wars	16.7%
Other nonattorney	15.8%
No representation	15.2%
Attorney/Agent	18.3%

The District Court opined that these statistics were not helpful,
because in its view lawyers were retained so infrequently that no body of
lawyers with an expertise in VA practice had developed, and lawyers who
represented veterans regularly might do better than lawyers who represented them only pro bono on a sporadic basis. * * *

We think the District Court's analysis of this issue totally unconvinc-
ing, and quite lacking in the deference which ought to be shown by any
federal court in evaluating the constitutionality of an Act of Congress. We
have the most serious doubt whether a competent lawyer taking a veteran's
case on a pro bono basis would give less than his best effort, and we see no
reason why experience in developing facts as to causation in the numerous
other areas of the law where it is relevant would not be readily transferable
to proceedings before the VA. * * *

The District Court also concluded, apparently independently of its ill-
founded analysis of the claim statistics, (1) that the VA processes are
procedurally, factually, and legally complex, and (2) that the VA system
presently does not work as designed, particularly in terms of the representation afforded by VA personnel and service representatives, and that these
representatives are "unable to perform all of the services which might be
performed by a claimant's own paid attorney." Unfortunately the court's
findings on "complexity" are based almost entirely on a description of the
plan for administering benefits in the abstract, together with references to
"complex" cases involving exposure to radiation or agent orange, or post-

traumatic stress syndrome. The court did not attempt to state even approximately how often procedural or substantive complexities arise in the run-of-the-mill case, or even in the unusual case.

* * *

The District Court's treatment of the likely usefulness of attorneys is on the same plane with its efforts to quantify the likelihood of error under the present system. The court states several times in its opinion that lawyers could provide more services than claimants presently receive—a fact which may freely be conceded—but does not suggest how the availability of these services would reduce the likelihood of error in the run-of-the-mill case. Simple factual questions are capable of resolution in a nonadversarial context, and it is less than crystal clear why *lawyers* must be available to identify possible errors in *medical* judgment. The availability of particular lawyers' services in so-called "complex" cases might be more of a factor in preventing error in such cases, but on this record we simply do not know how those cases should be defined or what percentage of all of the cases before the VA they make up. Even if the showing in the District Court had been much more favorable, appellees still would confront the constitutional hurdle posed by the principle enunciated in cases such as *Mathews* to the effect that a process must be judged by the generality of cases to which it applies, and therefore a process which is sufficient for the large majority of a group of claims is by constitutional definition sufficient for all of them. But here appellees have failed to make the very difficult factual showing necessary.

* * *

We have in previous cases, of course, held not only that the Constitution permits retention of an attorney, but also that on occasion it requires the Government to provide the services of an attorney. The Sixth Amendment affords representation by counsel in all criminal proceedings * * *.

In cases such as *Gagnon v. Scarpelli,* 411 U.S. 778 (1973), we observed that counsel can aid in identifying legal questions and presenting arguments, and that one charged with probation violation may have a right to counsel because of the liberty interest involved. * * *

But where, as here, the only interest protected by the Due Process Clause is a property interest in the continued receipt of Government benefits, which interest is conferred and terminated in a nonadversary proceeding, these precedents are of only tangential relevance. Appellees rely on *Goldberg v. Kelly,* 397 U.S. 254 (1970), in which the Court held that a welfare recipient subject to possible termination of benefits was entitled to be represented by an attorney. The Court said that "counsel can help delineate the issues, present the factual contentions in an orderly manner, conduct cross-examination, and generally safeguard the interests of the recipient." But in defining the process required the Court also observed that "the crucial factor in this context . . . is that termination of aid pending resolution of a controversy over eligibility may deprive an *eligible* recipient of the very means by which to live while he waits. . . . His need to concentrate upon finding the means for daily subsistence, in turn, adversely affects his ability to seek redress from the welfare bureaucracy."

We think that the benefits at stake in VA proceedings, which are not granted on the basis of need, are more akin to the Social Security benefits involved in *Mathews* than they are to the welfare payments upon which the recipients in *Goldberg* depended for their daily subsistence. * * *

This case is further distinguishable from our prior decisions because the process here is not designed to operate adversarially. While counsel may well be needed to respond to opposing counsel or other forms of adversary in a trial-type proceeding, where as here no such adversary appears, and in addition a claimant or recipient is provided with substitute safeguards such as a competent representative, a decisionmaker whose duty it is to aid the claimant, and significant concessions with respect to the claimant's burden of proof, the need for counsel is considerably diminished. We have expressed similar concerns in other cases holding that counsel is not required in various proceedings that do not approximate trials, but instead are more informal and nonadversary. See *Parham v. J.R.*, 442 U.S., at 608–609; *Goss v. Lopez*, 419 U.S. 565, 583 (1975). *Wolff v. McDonnell*, 418 U.S., at 570.

* * *

■ JUSTICE O'CONNOR, with whom JUSTICE BLACKMUN joins, concurring.

I join the Court's opinion and its judgment because I agree that * * * the District Court abused its discretion in issuing a nationwide preliminary injunction against enforcement of the $10 fee limitation in 38 U.S.C. § 3404(c). I also agree that the record before us is insufficient to evaluate the claims of any individuals or identifiable groups. I write separately to note that such claims remain open on remand.

* * *

[I]t is my understanding that the Court, in reversing the lower court's preliminary injunction, does not determine the merits of the respondents' individual "as applied" claims. The complaint indicates that respondents challenged the fee limitation both on its face and as applied to them, and sought a ruling that they were entitled to a rehearing of claims processed without assistance of an attorney. Respondent Albert Maxwell, for example, alleges that his service representative retired and failed to notify him that he had dropped his case. Mr. Maxwell's records indicate that he suffers from the after effects of malaria contracted in the Bataan death march as well as from multiple myelomas allegedly a result of exposure to radiation when he was a prisoner of war detailed to remove atomic debris in Japan. Maxwell contends that his claims have failed because of lack of expert assistance in developing the medical and historical facts of his case. * * *

The merits of these claims are difficult to evaluate on the record of affidavits and depositions developed at the preliminary injunction stage. Though the Court concludes that denial of expert representation is not "per se unconstitutional," given the availability of service representatives to assist the veteran and the Veterans' Administration boards' emphasis on nonadversarial procedures, "[o]n remand, the District Court is free to and should consider any individual claims that [the procedures] did not meet the standards we have described in this opinion."

■ JUSTICE STEVENS, with whom JUSTICE BRENNAN and JUSTICE MARSHALL join, dissenting.

The Court does not appreciate the value of individual liberty. It may well be true that in the vast majority of cases a veteran does not need to employ a lawyer, and that the system of processing veterans benefit claims, by and large, functions fairly and effectively without the participation of retained counsel. Everyone agrees, however, that there are at least some complicated cases in which the services of a lawyer would be useful to the veteran and, indeed, would simplify the work of the agency by helping to organize the relevant facts and to identify the controlling issues. What is the reason for denying the veteran the right to counsel of his choice in such cases? The Court gives us two answers: First, the paternalistic interest in protecting the veteran from the consequences of his own improvidence; and second, the bureaucratic interest in minimizing the cost of administering the benefit program. I agree that both interests are legitimate, but neither provides an adequate justification for the restraint on liberty imposed by the $10–fee limitation.

* * *

The first fee limitation—$5 per claim—was enacted in 1862. That limitation was repealed two years later and replaced by the $10–fee limitation, which has survived ever since. The limitation was designed to protect the veteran from extortion or improvident bargains with unscrupulous lawyers. Obviously, it was believed that the number of scoundrels practicing law was large enough to justify a legislative prohibition against charging excessive fees.

At the time the $10–fee limitation was enacted, Congress presumably considered that fee reasonable. The legal work involved in preparing a veteran's claim consisted of little more than filling out an appropriate form, and, in terms of the average serviceman's base pay, a $10 fee then was roughly the equivalent of a $580 fee today. At its inception, therefore, the fee limitation had neither the purpose nor the effect of precluding the employment of reputable counsel by veterans. Indeed, the statute then, as now, expressly contemplated that claims for veterans' benefits could be processed by "agents or attorneys."

The fact that the statute was aimed at unscrupulous attorneys is confirmed by the provision for criminal penalties. Instead of just making an agreement to pay a greater fee unenforceable—as an anticipatory pledge of an interest in future pension benefits is unenforceable—the Act contains a flat prohibition against the direct or indirect collection of a greater fee, and provides that an attorney who charges more than $10 may be imprisoned for up to two years at hard labor. Thus, an unscrupulous moneylender or merchant who might try to take advantage of an improvident veteran might have difficulty collecting his bill, but the unscrupulous lawyer might go to jail.

* * * In today's market, the reasonable fee for even the briefest conference would surely exceed $10. Thus, the law that was enacted in 1864 to protect veterans from unscrupulous lawyers—those who charge excessive fees—effectively denies today's veteran access to all lawyers who charge reasonable fees for their services.

The Court's opinion blends its discussion of the paternalistic interest in protecting veterans from unscrupulous lawyers and the bureaucratic interest in minimizing the cost of administration in a way that implies that each interest reinforces the other. Actually the two interests are quite different and merit separate analysis.

In my opinion, the bureaucratic interest in minimizing the cost of administration is nothing but a red herring. Congress has not prohibited lawyers from participating in the processing of claims for benefits and there is no reason why it should. The complexity of the agency procedures can be regulated by limiting the number of hearings, the time for argument, the length of written submissions, and in other ways, but there is no reason to believe that the *agency's* cost of administration will be increased because a claimant is represented by counsel instead of appearing *pro se*. The informality that the Court emphasizes is desirable because it no doubt enables many veterans, or their lay representatives, to handle their claims without the assistance of counsel. But there is no reason to assume that lawyers would add confusion rather than clarity to the proceedings. As a profession, lawyers are skilled communicators dedicated to the service of their clients. Only if it is assumed that the average lawyer is incompetent or unscrupulous can one rationally conclude that the efficiency of the agency's work would be undermined by allowing counsel to participate whenever a veteran is willing to pay for his services. I categorically reject any such assumption.

* * *

The paternalistic interest in protecting the veteran from his own improvidence would unquestionably justify a rule that simply prevented lawyers from overcharging their clients. Most appropriately, such a rule might require agency approval, or perhaps judicial review, of counsel fees. It might also establish a reasonable ceiling, subject to exceptions for especially complicated cases. In fact, I assume that the $10–fee limitation was justified by this interest when it was first enacted in 1864. But time has brought changes in the value of the dollar, in the character of the legal profession, in agency procedures, and in the ability of the veteran to proceed without the assistance of counsel.

* * *

It is evident from what I have written that I regard the fee limitation as unwise and an insult to the legal profession. It does not follow, however, that it is unconstitutional. The Court correctly notes that the presumption of constitutionality that attaches to every Act of Congress requires the challenger to bear the burden of demonstrating its invalidity.

* * *

The Court recognizes that the Veterans' Administration's procedures must provide claimants with due process of law, but then concludes that the constitutional requirement is satisfied because the appellees have not proved that the "probability of error under the present system" is unacceptable. In short, if 80 or 90 percent of the cases are correctly decided, why worry about those individuals whose claims have been erroneously rejected and who might have prevailed if they had been represented by counsel?

The fundamental error in the Court's analysis is its assumption that the individual's right to employ counsel of his choice in a contest with his sovereign is a kind of second-class interest that can be assigned a material value and balanced on a utilitarian scale of costs and benefits. It is true that the veteran's right to benefits is a property right and that in fashioning the procedures for administering the benefit program, the Government may appropriately weigh the value of additional procedural safeguards against their pecuniary costs. It may, for example, properly decide not to provide free counsel to claimants. But we are not considering a procedural right that would involve any cost to the Government. We are concerned with the individual's right to spend his own money to obtain the advice and assistance of independent counsel in advancing his claim against the Government.

In all criminal proceedings, that right is expressly protected by the Sixth Amendment. As I have indicated, in civil disputes with the Government I believe that right is also protected by the Due Process Clause of the Fifth Amendment and by the First Amendment. If the Government, in the guise of a paternalistic interest in protecting the citizen from his own improvidence, can deny him access to independent counsel of his choice, it can change the character of our free society. Even though a dispute with the sovereign may only involve property rights, or as in this case a statutory entitlement, the citizen's right of access to the independent, private bar is itself an aspect of liberty that is of critical importance in our democracy. Just as I disagree with the present Court's crabbed view of the concept of "liberty," so do I reject its apparent unawareness of the function of the independent lawyer as a guardian of our freedom.[24]

In my view, regardless of the nature of the dispute between the sovereign and the citizen—whether it be a criminal trial, a proceeding to terminate parental rights, a claim for social security benefits, a dispute over welfare benefits, or a pension claim asserted by the widow of a soldier who

---

24. That function was, however, well understood by Jack Cade and his followers, characters who are often forgotten and whose most famous line is often misunderstood. Dick's statement ("The first thing we do, let's kill all the lawyers") was spoken by a rebel, not a friend of liberty. See W. Shakespeare, King Henry VI, pt. II, Act IV, scene 2, line 72. As a careful reading of that text will reveal, Shakespeare insightfully realized that disposing of lawyers is a step in the direction of a totalitarian form of government.

was killed on the battlefield—the citizen's right to consult an independent lawyer and to retain that lawyer to speak on his or her behalf is an aspect of liberty that is priceless. It should not be bargained away on the notion that a totalitarian appraisal of the mass of claims processed by the Veterans' Administration does not identify an especially high probability of error.

NOTES AND QUESTIONS

1. Precisely what does Justice Rehnquist mean when he describes the VA's claim procedure as "nonadversarial"?

2. Following the Supreme Court's decision, the plaintiffs in *Walters* amended their complaint to challenge the constitutionality of the fee limit "as applied to claimants with service-connected disability or death compensation claims based on exposure to ionizing radiation." See the concurring opinion of Justice O'Connor. A motion for class certification was granted, 111 F.R.D. 595 (N.D.Cal.1986). The district court ultimately found that the $10 fee limitation was a violation of the plaintiffs' rights under the due process clause and the First Amendment, because it deprived them "of a meaningful opportunity to present their claims to the VA and to petition the government":

> [P]reparation of ionizing radiation [IR] claims involves a wide variety of tasks for which attorneys are trained and particularly well suited. * * * Attorneys are skilled and experienced in working with experts in support of legal claims [and are] trained to be and are effective at framing the legally relevant issues for experts and at understanding the legal standards by which those issues will be judged. This training would contribute substantially to the work of medical and scientific experts in IR claims.
>
> * * * Attorneys are more likely to detect and respond to procedural violations by the VA and to ensure that the claimant effectively takes advantage of procedural protections such as the right to a hearing. Attorneys are better able to track down the relevant regulations, manual provisions and internal documents of the VA in order to muster support for their clients' IR claims and to interpret the myriad of complex regulations and rules relating to IR cases. Moreover, attorneys, because of their training, can more competently prepare briefs and appellate papers, conduct legal research, apply the law to the facts, and bring legal challenges to mistaken agency interpretations of regulations and statutes.

National Ass'n of Radiation Survivors v. Derwinski, 782 F.Supp. 1392, 1406 (N.D.Cal.1992). The Ninth Circuit, however, reversed, 994 F.2d 583 (9th Cir.1992) (accepting the government's argument that "the proper inquiry is whether lawyers are necessary to make the process fair, not whether lawyers are better able to pursue claims than non-lawyers").

3.   After the Supreme Court's decision in *Walters,* significant changes were made with respect to the adjudication of benefits claims before the VA (now the Department of Veterans Affairs). Under the Veterans' Judicial Review Act of 1988, decisions of the BVA may now be reviewed by a newly-created Article I court, the Court of Veterans' Appeals; further review on issues of law is possible by appeal to the Court of Appeals for the Federal Circuit. An attorney is still not permitted to charge a claimant any fee at all for services rendered "before the date on which the [BVA] first makes a final decision" on a claim. (By prohibiting an attorney from charging for services "until the VA affirms its decision to deny a claim, the [Act] intends to preserve as much of the informal and efficient means of claim adjudication as possible," H.R.Rep. 100–963, 1988 U.S.C.C.A.N. 5782, 5810–11). However, claimants may now agree to pay a lawyer for services rendered *after* that date—for example, in an appeal to the Court of Veterans' Appeals or in seeking to reopen a claim for further proceedings based on new evidence. Any fee agreement is subject to review by the BVA, which may order a reduction in a fee found to be "excessive or unreasonable." If the agreement provides for a contingent fee to be paid directly by the Department to the attorney out of any past-due benefits awarded, the fee may not exceed 20% of such benefits. See 38 U.S.C.A. § 5904(c), (d), § 7252, § 7263, § 7292.

4.   The new Court of Veterans' Appeals has consistently overturned more than 60% of the BVA decisions it reviews. In many of these cases, substantial recovery in the form of retroactive benefits is at stake, and in most successful appeals prosecuted by a lawyer, attorneys' fees are awarded. Nevertheless more than two-thirds of the nearly 20,000 veterans who have appealed to the Court have proceeded pro se. "Nobody knows how many others have chosen not to appeal or file a reopened claim due to lack of representation." The probable explanation for this dearth of willing lawyers "is an unfortunate legacy of the longstanding limit on attorney fees. This is an entirely new area of law for the private bar and the upfront costs of becoming proficient can seem daunting." See Barton Stichman, Veterans Benefits Law: A Wide–Open Area of Practice, 17 No. 5 GPSolo 47 (July/Aug. 2000); see also Lawrence Hagel & Michael Horan, Five Years Under the Veterans' Judicial Review Act, 46 Maine L. Rev. 43 (1994).

5.   Does the *Walters* case suggest that there is a necessary trade-off between an "efficiency" interest in the mass processing of claims and an interest in the quality of decision in the individual case? Does it suggest that the efficiency interest is necessarily impaired by an "adversarial" procedure and the presence of lawyers? Do you agree with these propositions? Are the concerns expressed by Professor Fiss relevant in helping to draw a proper balance between the two interests?

6.   Compare Justice Rehnquist's observations on the "informal" and "nonadversarial" nature of VA proceedings with these excerpts from an article by Professor Lon Fuller:

> What generally occurs in practice is that at some early point [in adjudication] a familiar pattern will seem to emerge from the evidence;

an accustomed label is wanting for the case and, without awaiting further proofs, this label is promptly assigned to it. It is a mistake to suppose that this premature cataloguing must necessarily result from impatience, prejudice or mental sloth. Often it proceeds from a very understandable desire to bring the hearing into some order and coherence, for without some tentative theory of the case there is no standard of relevance by which testimony may be measured. But what starts as a preliminary diagnosis designed to direct the inquiry tends, quickly and imperceptibly, to become a fixed conclusion, as all that confirms the diagnosis makes a strong imprint on the mind, while all that runs counter to it is received with diverted attention.

An adversary presentation seems the only effective means for combatting this natural human tendency to judge too swiftly in terms of the familiar that which is not yet fully known. The arguments of counsel hold the case, as it were, in suspension between two opposing interpretations of it. While the proper classification of the case is thus kept unresolved, there is time to explore all of its peculiarities and nuances.
* * *

These, then, are the reasons for believing that partisan advocacy plays a vital and essential role in one of the most fundamental procedures of a democratic society. * * * Viewed in this light, the role of the lawyer as a partisan advocate appears not as a regrettable necessity, but as an indispensable part of a larger ordering of affairs. The institution of advocacy is not a concession to the frailties of human nature, but an expression of human insight in the design of a social framework within which man's capacity for impartial judgment can attain its fullest realization.

Fuller, The Forms and Limits of Adjudication, 92 Harv.L.Rev. 353, 382–85 (1978).

7. One commentator has suggested that *lawyers* too may have an independent interest in having their "day in court," whether or not their clients need one. He argues that "lack of trial experience in a legal and ethical system premised on adjudication threatens the effective functioning" of litigators. For example, a movement towards increased reliance on settlement of litigation might impair attorney competence in forensic skills—and it might lead lawyers to seriously underestimate their chances of success at trial, out of a "fear of the unknown" or an unconscious attempt to avoid "embarrassment" from a "public display" of untested trial skills. All this may have a "demoralizing" impact on litigators. And litigators may also become "demoralized" because their "role and function are tied to the process and results of adjudication since the cardinal tenets of legal ethics are most often justified in terms of the function of the adversary system of adjudication": If adjudication becomes less frequent, "the value and justifications for lawyers become more attenuated," bringing "a lessening of the lawyer's ability to believe in the value of her own role."

Does any of this ring true? Or is it in effect an argument that we should burn down some perfectly good houses "in order to give the fire department the opportunity to improve its fire fighting skills"? See McMunigal, The Costs of Settlement: The Impact of Scarcity of Adjudication on Litigating Lawyers, 37 U.C.L.A. L.Rev. 833 (1990).

2. PROBLEM: SHERIDAN V. HOPEWELL COLLEGE[1]

You are practicing law in a large Dallas law firm. On several occasions in the past you have handled some litigation on behalf of your alma mater, Hopewell College. Hopewell is a small well-regarded liberal arts college located in the small North Texas town of Mt. Pleasant. The school was founded by the Lutheran Church in 1897 and is now coeducational (women were admitted for the first time in 1959).

You have just received a copy of a complaint in a lawsuit filed against the College by a former instructor in its Physical Education Department, Mary Kate Sheridan. The complaint alleges discrimination on the basis of sex in violation of Title VII of the Civil Rights Act, and names Hopewell, the College's President, and various other school officials as defendants. Hopewell's in-house counsel has very little trial experience and has been used mostly for routine legal problems. Your firm has therefore been asked to handle the defense of this suit.

After reviewing the complaint, you discussed the matter briefly with the College's counsel and have been able to obtain a certain amount of background information about the case. You gather that Sheridan was hired as an instructor in the Phys. Ed. Department eight years ago; she taught Modern Dance and Tap Dance, and was apparently a popular teacher. In her fifth and sixth years the Department put her name forward for promotion to Assistant Professor; despite favorable recommendations by the Faculty Personnel Committee, the President and the College Board of Trustees refused to promote her. Again the following year the Department recommended her for both promotion and tenure; again the FPC voted to approve the recommendation, and again the President and the Board refused. Last spring she was given a "terminal" contract for the current school year. (An "up or out" decision is required after seven years of teaching under the rules of both Hopewell and the American Association of University Professors.) Sheridan appealed to the elected "Faculty Board of Appeals," which unanimously voted that she be given tenure; this recommendation also was rejected. She filed suit against the College shortly after receiving a "right to sue" letter from the Equal Employment Opportunity Commission.

Ms. Sheridan received a Bachelor's degree 17 years ago, but has no higher degree. The Hopewell "faculty handbook" requires that before receiving tenure, a faculty member must hold a "terminal degree" (in Physical Education, this is a Master's) or its "scholarly equivalent." At Hopewell this requirement has traditionally been honored in the breach—

---

1. This problem draws on George La-Noue & Barbara Lee, Academics in Court: The Consequences of Faculty Discrimination Litigation (1987). See also Kunda v. Muhlenberg College, 621 F.2d 532 (3d Cir.1980).

the head of the Phys. Ed. Department, a full professor, has only a Bachelor's degree. However, the appointment six years ago of President Davies, who came to the job with a firm commitment to "upgrade the quality of the faculty," has led to the degree requirement being rigorously enforced.

Sheridan's complaint asks for $600,000 in compensatory and punitive damages, attorneys' fees, and reinstatement to her job with the rank of Associate Professor with tenure.

President Davies is concerned. The College has no liability insurance that will cover this kind of discrimination claim. Davies assures you that this is the first such complaint that has ever been made against the College. However, he has heard disquieting stories about the impact of discrimination suits on other educational institutions—in terms of the burden of litigation on the time and energy of school officials, of the divisiveness and harm to institutional morale, and of the difficulty thereafter in raising funds and recruiting talented new faculty:

> Administrators at large institutions who employ full-time counsel may regard litigation as simply another cost of doing business; that is, legal expenses may be considered a sunk cost. Nevertheless, institutions of higher learning rarely emerge from wrongful discharge and employment discrimination litigation unscathed. A race, sex, national origin, or other discrimination charge against a college or university is almost certain to generate media exposure. Students may hold public demonstrations to protest the termination, especially if the case involves a popular professor. Charges of racism, sexism, religious bias, or blatant disregard for a faculty member's career are likely to tarnish the liberal image of the institution and may make it more difficult for the school to attract high-quality students and faculty or to generate philanthropic support and research funds. University administrators who are named in an employment discrimination suit almost always have their personal integrity called into question and run the risk of suffering irreparable damage to their professional reputations. Faculty members in the department or college where the suit originated may split into factions, some of whom support the faculty member while others support the administration. Many cases involve comparisons between the qualifications of faculty who were promoted or tenured and those who were not. Counsel for the plaintiff may attempt to belittle the research and teaching accomplishments of the faculty who have been selected for comparison. When such attacks are made public, either through the press or during a grievance hearing or trial, the damage to interpersonal relationships in a department may be irreparable.[2]

At the same time, of course, the costs—social and psychological as well as financial—that such lawsuits can impose on the plaintiff faculty member can also be traumatic. You understand, by the way, that Sheridan would very much like to stay at Hopewell. She was born and raised in Mt.

2. Terry Leap, Tenure, Discrimination, and the Courts 16–17 (1993).

Pleasant, and her two young children are now in the local public schools. She continues to perform in her own physical fitness program that she developed some years ago and that is shown twice a week on the local television station. College officials have made a point of telling you that this show, along with sporadic employment as a substitute high-school teacher and manager of a health spa, has been her only source of income following her divorce.

Davies has asked your firm for a memorandum on the legal issues raised by Sheridan's claim. He has also asked you for advice as to what process should be used to resolve the problem in the best interests of the College. What do you tell him?

Your first reaction may be to focus on the relevant law invoked in the complaint: What elements does the plaintiff have to establish to make a prima facie case under Title VII? Where are the burdens of proof and of producing evidence? What remedies do courts impose for violations of Title VII? You will also of course want to ask a number of questions concerning the facts relevant to the merits of the claim: You may want to ask, for example, whether Sheridan's failure to achieve promotion or tenure might be due to reasons other than discrimination such as inadequate performance as an instructor. (The faculty "Board of Appeal" did note that it had "uncovered no statement about Mary Kate's contribution to the College that was less than enthusiastic." But of course, adverse tenure decisions may frequently be based on any number of other considerations including the College's future plans for the department, the number of tenured faculty already in the department, and the financial constraints both on the department and the College as a whole.) You would certainly also want to inquire into the College's practices with respect to promotion and tenure of male faculty. It appears that Davies has been adamant about uniformly requiring a "terminal" degree for tenure candidates, and that over the past five years no faculty member at Hopewell has been given tenure without such a degree. However, Sheridan claims that she had never been warned that any Master's degree requirement would be insisted on in her case—although male candidates had been advised of the requirement and encouraged to make progress towards the higher degree. You also understand that two male instructors who did not have a Master's were promoted to Assistant Professor without tenure four years ago, even though the faculty handbook states that a Master's is "normally" required even for promotion to that rank.

In addition to these issues of fact and law, it is clear that sustained attention will have to be given to the *process* by which you expect to help Hopewell resolve this problem. You will probably think of the litigation process first—if only because the opposing lawyer has already announced his intention to use the court system. In addition, you have to recognize that both Ms. Sheridan and the College might want or need vindication, in the form of an authoritative public decision that they are "in the right." But is litigation an inevitable process? Is it the best process for the College? What other processes might be useful, and how might opposing counsel be induced to participate in these processes? How do you evaluate and compare processes in terms of the best interests of the client?

Litigation is far from being the only process available in a situation like this. By filing a lawsuit, Sheridan's attorney has certainly gotten the College's attention. But he has hardly foreclosed the opportunity for negotiation and private settlement. You may have many opportunities to negotiate a voluntary settlement of the dispute, even though the suit has been filed—and indeed, this opportunity will persist even as discovery in the suit proceeds and even as the "trial" gets under way. Although lawyers are expected to understand and use the negotiation process, they usually have very little formal instruction in this part of their work. It is inevitable then that there will be wide variations in the skill which different lawyers bring to bear in negotiation and the energy with which they pursue a negotiated settlement.

You might also wish to explore other, alternative processes that might be appropriate in the Sheridan case. Some processes would bring in third parties to help the College and Ms. Sheridan reach a settlement of their dispute short of trial and with some privacy—such third parties might even have some special familiarity with the particular culture and problems of higher education. However, you are not entirely clear how such suitable persons might be chosen—or just what their role would be in the dispute: Is the third party expected merely to help facilitate the parties' own voluntary settlement by helping them bargain and communicate with each other? Or is she expected to render a "decision?" If the latter, is this decision intended to be binding on the parties or merely advisory? May the power of the state be harnessed to support this decision, and does the third party enjoy other sources of influence and authority? Is she expected to proceed by articulating and applying general "rules," or in a more ad hoc manner through compromise or persuasion?

Lawyers seldom use just one process to try to resolve a single dispute. They may combine two or more and work them simultaneously, playing one against the other, or they may try them in succession. The dynamics of this interactive use of process is a substantial part of a lawyer's practice and therefore an important focus of these materials. An equally important point is that processes like "negotiation," "mediation," and "arbitration" are ideal types; we use them primarily for purposes of organization. There are no sharp or clear distinctions between them, and the various techniques of dispute resolution represent points on a continuum rather than essentially distinct methods. There exist in fact any number of hybrid processes that reflect unique combinations of the primary forms—and only the limited creativity of the lawyers involved imposes any restrictions on the fashioning of new hybrid combinations. Moreover, our organization is not meant to imply that there is any fixed or rigid form which a particular process must inevitably take. The way a process works in practice will depend on the context and the personalities involved. Some "mediators" may be so active in devising solutions and so forceful in imposing them on the parties that it may in fact be hard to distinguish them from arbitrators.

The lawyer's search throughout is for the "appropriate process" to use in resolving the client's problem, and this, of course, becomes an important theme in these materials. There are many variables that will affect the choice of process; particular case factors, for example, may make a dispute more or less suitable for resolution by a particular process. One of the most important case-related factors centers on the relationship between the disputing parties: Is the relationship an ongoing one, which looms large in the life of both parties? Is there an expectation of frequent or valuable interaction in the future? This may be true, for example, not only in family and neighborhood disputes, but in employment, collective bargaining, and many business disputes as well. In such cases, the value of the continuing relationship may furnish an incentive for both parties to participate in an alternative dispute resolution process even though it lacks the coercive effects of the court system. Stated in another way, the prospect of damage to an ongoing relationship may constitute one sanction for failing to participate in the process or to comply with the result reached.

That a dispute arises in the context of a continuing relationship may have implications for the choice of process. When the potential benefits from future contacts (and the costs from disruption or termination) are great, a process that seeks to restore and maintain satisfying patterns of personal interaction seems called for. Such a process might be structured in such a way as to help the parties to reduce the causes of future conflict by helping them to deal with and work at the "real," underlying problems in their relationship. Merely getting the parties to understand and to talk directly to each other in an "atmosphere of mutual recognition and empathy"[3] may go a long way in this respect. Adjudication, by contrast,

3. Bush, Dispute Resolution Alternatives and the Goals of Civil Justice: Jurisdictional Principles for Process Choice, 1984 Wisc.L.Rev. 893, 982.

seems ill-suited to the task, since it can easily sour future relations by escalating conflict and focusing on symptoms rather than on underlying causes. Indeed in many cultures the very invocation of formal legal "rights" in the adversarial contest of litigation may be seen as a violation of the social norms governing a relationship.[4]

As Professor Auerbach has observed:

> Whether disputants ignore their differences, negotiate, submit to mediation or arbitration, or retain lawyers to litigate is a matter of significant choice. How people dispute is, after all, a function of how (and whether) they relate. In relationships that are intimate, caring, and mutual, disputants will behave quite differently from their counterparts who are strangers or competitors. Selfishness and aggression are not merely functions of individual personality; they are socially sanctioned—or discouraged. So is the decision to define a disputant as an adversary, and to struggle until there is a clear winner and loser; or, alternatively, to resolve conflict in a way that will preserve, rather than destroy, a relationship. In some cultures, the patterns of interaction suggest that those who participate in litigation may be psychologically deviant. Among Scandinavian fishermen and the Zapotec of Mexico, in Bavarian villages and certain African tribes, among the Sinai Bedouin and in Israeli *kibbutzim* * * *, the importance of enduring relations has made peace, harmony, and mediation preferable to conflict, victory, and litigation. But in the United States, a nation of competitive individuals and strangers, litigation is encouraged; here, the burden of psychological deviance falls upon those who find adversary relations to be a destructive form of human behavior.[5]

It is probably illusory to hope to be able to match particular processes of dispute resolution to particular types of disputes—to "fit the forum to the fuss"[6]—in any systematic way. Considerations are so diverse, and factual situations so fluid, that the choice may ultimately have to be made in a more intuitive fashion. But one threshold question might be, *from whose perspective* are we to engage in this task of evaluating processes?

4. See, e.g., Merry, Book Review, 100 Harv.L.Rev. 2057, 2061 (1987) (if murder occurred between two Nuer tribesmen and their kinsmen lived nearby and expected to see one another in the future, "they would mediate the dispute and pay bloodwealth in cattle"; however, if they lived further apart "they would refuse to pay damages and transform their relationship into a feud."). See also Robert Ellickson, Order without Law: How Neighbors Settle Disputes 62–64 (1991) (for the ranchers and farmers of Shasta County, California, the " 'natural working order' calls for two neighbors to work out their problems between themselves"; only deviants—termed "bad apples" or "odd ducks"—would turn to an attorney for help on a problem with a neighbor). Cf. Yngvesson, Re–Examining Continuing Relations and the Law, 1985 Wisc.L.Rev. 623 (courts and other official forums often resorted to in order to redefine and reshape terms of an ongoing relationship over the "long run").

5. Jerold S. Auerbach, Justice Without Law? 78 (1983).

6. See Sander & Goldberg, Fitting the Forum to the Fuss: A User–Friendly Guide to Selecting an ADR Procedure, Negotiation J., Jan. 1994 at p. 49.

Lawyers frequently tend to assume that all that matters for their clients is the size of the settlement and the speed of resolution—in this respect they regard "the psychology of client satisfaction as self-evident."[7] The underlying assumption is that the client has no serious independent concern with just *how* the problem has been resolved. But are these assumptions correct? A number of recent studies suggest that "non-outcome concerns"—like the ability to personally participate in the process or to have some "control over the processing or handling of the case," the opportunity to "express oneself and to have one's views considered by someone in power"—may be at least as important as the actual result in determining a disputant's satisfaction with a dispute-resolution process.[8] Other studies report a higher level of satisfaction and sense of fairness among those whose disputes were resolved in mediation as compared to those whose cases were litigated.[9] But on the other hand—even if we can identify such preferences—is disputant satisfaction truly a reliable indication of the quality of a dispute resolution process? After all, are not expressed "preferences" often a product of ignorance, of lack of awareness of alternatives, or of simple rationalization? "[A]n inexperienced litigant's preference for harmony may reflect ignorance of the pleasures of vindication and justice," or may reflect the fact that a litigant who has been the victim of injustice "may, as a means of reducing her unhappiness, have lost her taste for justice precisely because it seems unattainable."[10]

A related question is whether the choice of process is to be an entirely private matter: Are we to engage in this evaluation exclusively from the viewpoint of the lawyer with a client sitting in front of him? Or from that of the social engineer or philosopher-king, whose primary concern is the impact on the broader society? What role is there for public intervention and oversight of the decision on the basis of external social values? As Professor Menkel–Meadow has asked in a recent article, "Whose dispute is

---

7. Tyler, A Psychological Perspective on the Settlement of Mass Tort Claims, 53 Law & Contem.Probs. 199 (1990).

8. See E. Allan Lind & Tom R. Tyler, The Social Psychology of Procedural Justice 85–86, 94–106, 215–17 (1988); Lind et al., In the Eye of the Beholder: Tort Litigants' Evaluations of their Experiences in the Civil Justice System, 24 Law & Soc'y Rev. 953 (1990) (in small-dollar tort litigation, trial and arbitration were both perceived as fairer than judicial settlement conferences or bilateral settlement; "it is noteworthy that there was no substantial relationship between procedural fairness judgments and objective measures of outcome"); Lind et al., Decision Control and Process Control Effects on Procedural Fairness Judgments, 13 J.Applied Soc.Psych. 338 (1983) (judgments of procedural fairness are less influenced by control over the likely *outcome* of the dispute than by control over the *process;* the "general im-

plication [is] that procedural evaluations are less outcome-oriented and more process-and structure-oriented than had previously been thought").

9. See the review of the literature in Galanter & Cahill, "Most Cases Settle": Judicial Promotion and Regulation of Settlements, 46 Stan.L.Rev. 1339, 1355–57 (1994).

10. Bundy, The Policy in Favor of Settlement in an Adversary System, 44 Hastings L.J. 1, 16–17 (1992). See also Michele Hermann et al., University of New Mexico Center for the Study and Resolution of Disputes, The MetroCourt Project Final Report xi (1993). This study found that minority women reported the highest level of satisfaction with mediation—"[d]espite their tendency to achieve lower monetary awards as claimants and to pay more as respondents" compared with nonminorities.

it anyway?"[11] Should we aspire to replace our courthouses with "dispute resolution centers" where a "screening clerk" would "channel" parties to the process he considers "most appropriate" for the case?[12] Or could this "screening" function more appropriately be performed in the lawyer's office? These too are questions that you should be prepared to consider as we proceed through these materials.

11. See Menkel–Meadow, Whose Dispute Is It Anyway?: A Philosophical and Democratic Defense of Settlement (In Some Cases), 83 Georgetown L.J. 2663, 2669 (1995).

12. Cf. Sander, Varieties of Dispute Processing, 70 F.R.D. 111, 131 (1976); see also Ericka B. Gray, Multi–Door Courthouses (State Justice Institute 1993).

CHAPTER II

NEGOTIATION

We all negotiate every day. You may be buying or selling a car, working out the lease on an apartment or the closing terms for purchasing a house, starting or ending a business partnership, asking for a raise, or dealing with a contractor working on your home who is late or significantly over his bid price. You may negotiate with friends, family, or a spouse about seemingly simple personal issues like what movie to see, who should take the trash out, whether to spend holidays with your in-laws, or where to take a vacation. Any time your interests differ from or conflict with another person's and you actively attempt to persuade them or to resolve your differences, you are negotiating.[1] We have all been practicing the art of negotiation since we first learned as infants that crying induced someone to pick us up or to give us milk.

Attorneys also negotiate constantly. In transactions or "deal-making," a lawyer may bargain over the structure of a corporate merger, try to hammer out the details of a client's executive compensation agreement, or negotiate the terms of a real estate purchase and sale. In dispute resolution, an attorney may sit down with opposing counsel to discuss a divorce or separation agreement, debate the meaning of a disputed contract clause, plea bargain a client's criminal matter, contest the distribution of an estate, or seek payment for a client who has initiated a personal injury suit.

---

1. Lax and Sebenius define negotiation as "a process of potentially opportunistic interaction in which two or more parties, with some apparent conflict, seek to do better through jointly decided action than they could do otherwise." Lax and Sebenius, The Manager as Negotiator 11 (1986). Abhinay Muthoo defines bargaining as occurring in a situation where parties "can mutually benefit from reaching agreement on an outcome from a set of possible outcomes (that contains two or more elements), but have conflicting interests over the set of outcomes." Muthoo, Bargaining Theory with Applications 1–2 (1999). Melissa Nelken says, "Anytime you deal with someone else, seeking to reach agreement on some matter, you are involved in a negotiation." Nelken, Understanding Negotiation 1 (2001).

As we have already seen, the vast majority of disputes that involve legal issues—disputes that *could* be tried in a court of law—are settled through informal negotiation. Understanding the negotiation process and how best to approach bargaining opportunities is thus critically important for attorneys.

In this chapter we focus on the use of negotiation to resolve legal disputes. The chapter is divided into four parts. In Section A we first explore the basic structure of negotiation—the economic underpinnings of both single and multiple issue bargaining. This section investigates the distributive aspects of negotiation—who gets how much of whatever is in dispute—and the integrative or value-creating opportunities bargaining can present—how the two parties can "expand the pie" by finding mutually-beneficial trades. Section B then considers the problem of strategy—given that many disputes present both distributive issues and integrative opportunities, how should you negotiate? Should you bargain hard and press for every possible concession? Or work towards a fair resolution that satisfies both parties' interests? What are the advantages and disadvantages of different strategies? Section C explores several factors that can complicate legal negotiation. We examine certain cognitive and social psychological biases or heuristics that can act as a barrier to conflict resolution, and consider their implications for decision-making in the negotiation context. We also discuss the interpersonal skills needed to negotiate effectively, and the role of race, gender and cultural differences in negotiation. Finally, Section D considers the ethical and legal framework for settlement negotiations, including the ways in which litigation processes affect negotiation, the law governing negotiation behavior, and the judge's role in settlement discussions.

A.   THE STRUCTURE OF NEGOTIATION

1.   ONE ISSUE

It is easiest to analyze the structure of a simple negotiation between two parties with only one issue in dispute. Two neighbors might be negotiating over where to put the fence between their properties—each wants it to be farther onto the other's land. You might be trying to persuade a plumber to come fix your leaking kitchen sink—he wants to do the job tomorrow morning, you want him to come out to your apartment tonight. Often money is the issue in dispute and each party has the same goal: to maximize their own return by receiving more or paying less. If you are buying a used laptop computer from a stranger, bargaining with a mechanic over the price of his repairs to your car, or trying to secure a discount on your rent—and both sides focus solely on the single issue of money—then you want to pay less and the other side wants you to pay more. This sort of negotiation is often called "zero-sum," because a gain for one party means an equivalent loss for the other.

Imagine the following situation. Tammy Tompkins has brought a lawsuit against Dr. Sander alleging that the doctor negligently caused the death of Tammy's mother, Lyla.[2] Lyla died a year ago at age sixty-seven from complications related to a rare immunological disease called Pemphigus. This disease causes the body's immune system to malfunction and to begin to attack the afflicted patient's skin and tissues. If left untreated it causes painful skin lesions, hemorrhaging and deterioration of vital organ function. It also leaves its victim exposed to infection and all manner of diseases. In severe cases it can lead to death.

Lyla lived in a rural town in the Midwest and was caught completely by surprise when she became ill. She had no idea that she had Pemphigus. After unsuccessfully trying various remedies for Lyla's early symptoms, her local primary care physician referred her to Dr. Sander, an "expert" on skin disorders who practiced at a larger nearby hospital. Although Lyla visited Dr. Sander several times over a three-month period, he never diagnosed her accurately as having Pemphigus. Instead, he thought she was suffering from severe allergies. Lyla's medical records show that he prescribed several different steroids for Lyla in hopes of alleviating whatever allergic reaction was causing her such distress.

Just four months after her initial visit to Dr. Sander, Lyla died from a massive stroke. At first Tammy and the rest of Lyla's family assumed that the stroke was a random event, and they made no connection between the "allergies" that Lyla had complained about and her death. One day, however, Tammy mentioned Lyla's symptoms to a friend's father who was an immunologist. After hearing the list of Lyla's problems, this physician was sure that Lyla must have had Pemphigus, and he was shocked that Dr. Sander hadn't considered that possibility. At his urging, Tammy hired a lawyer who began investigating her mother's case.

The initial complaint that Tammy's lawyer filed in state court asked for $1 million from Dr. Sander (and his insurance company) for Lyla's death. Tammy alleges that Dr. Sander's negligent misdiagnosis caused her mother's premature death by delaying treatment and aggravating her condition through the prescription of steroids (which raised her blood pressure and made her symptoms worse, not better). The stroke, according to Tammy, was a direct result of this improper medical care. To date, Dr.

2. For a discussion of the law and economics of medical malpractice, see Bovbjerg, Medical Malpractice: Research and Reform, 79 Va.L.Rev. 2155 (1993); Frankel, Medical Malpractice Law and Health Care Cost Containment: Lessons for Reformers from the Clash of Cultures, 103 Yale L.J. 1297 (1994); Liang, Medical Malpractice: Do Physicians Have Knowledge of Legal Standards and Assess Cases as Juries Do?, 3 U.Chi.L.Sch. Roundtable 59 (1996); Silver, One Hundred Years of Harmful Error: The Historical Jurisprudence of Medical Malpractice, 1992 Wis. L.Rev. 1193.

Several legal scholars have written about medical malpractice and informal dispute resolution. See Farber and White, A Comparison of Formal and Informal Dispute Resolution in Medical Malpractice, 23 J.Leg.Stud. 777 (1994); Wheeler, Medical Malpractice Dispute Resolution: A Prescription for the New Millenium, 28 Cap.U.L.Rev. 249 (2000); Dauer, Marcus & Payne, Prometheus and the Litigators: A Mediation Odyssey, 21 J.Leg.Med. 159 (2000).

Sander has agreed to pay $30,000, which he says is a "good faith gesture" to settle the claim.

These wildly divergent initial positions are just part of the story. In addition to these initial offers or demands, each party also generally has (or should have) a *reservation value*—the point at which that party is indifferent between staying in the negotiation and walking away. Here, the reservation values are the minimum amount Tammy will accept to settle the claim and the maximum amount that Dr. Sander will pay. For example, if Tammy will accept $250,000 to drop her lawsuit, that is her reservation value. If offered less she will walk away rather than settle.

Although sometimes negotiators arbitrarily invent a "bottom line," reservation values should be tied to the parties' Best Alternative To a Negotiated Agreement (or *BATNA*), a term invented by Roger Fisher, William Ury and Bruce Patton. See Fisher, Ury and Patton, Getting to Yes 100 (2d ed., 1991). The set of a negotiator's alternatives is made up of all those actions that the negotiator can take away from the table if no agreement is reached. The BATNA is the best alternative in that set. For example, if you are choosing whether to leave your current job and accept an offer from another employer, the set of alternatives open to you consists of all of the offers you have so far received. Your BATNA is the offer that you would most likely take if you leave your current position—it is, in your estimation, the best of those available to you.

Your reservation price is not the same thing as your BATNA, but they are related. For example, imagine that your best alternative to your current job is to work for a competing company in another city. The competing company has offered you $100,000 per year, which is a substantial increase from your present salary. If you can't negotiate a raise from your current boss, you will take this job offer—it is your best alternative *away from the table* in your negotiation with your boss. What is your reservation value? In other words, how will you know when to walk away from your negotiations with your boss? You need to translate your BATNA into a reservation value that you can keep in mind while you negotiate. To do so, you must factor in any intangible costs associated with that BATNA. For example, perhaps staying in your current home and not being forced to transfer locations is worth something to you—for simplicity's sake, imagine that it is worth $10,000 to you *not* to have to move. If that is the only variable that affects your evaluation of your BATNA, then your reservation value in your negotiation with your boss is $90,000—so long as your boss offers $90,000 or greater, you would prefer to stay in your current job rather than walk to your BATNA.

The bargaining range is determined by these reservation values. In our medical example, imagine that Dr. Sander would be willing to pay up to $750,000 to settle Tammy's claim.[3] Because the parties' reservation values

3. In litigation, both parties usually share the same alternative to negotiating a resolution of their dispute: proceeding to court. Theoretically, then, their reservation values should be fairly close, adjusted for risk preferences and transaction costs. We discuss

overlap, there is a *zone of possible agreement* (or ZOPA for short) in this negotiation. We can illustrate this ZOPA using a simple diagram. (See Figure 1.)

how one analyzes a litigation alternative in section A(3)(b), below. In addition, we consider the subjective nature of analyzing one's BATNA or reservation value and the ways in which one's perspective or biases may influence this analysis.

Figure 1

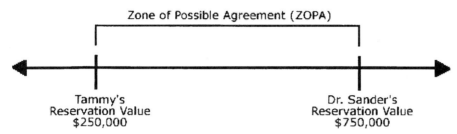

Zone of Possible Agreement (ZOPA)

Tammy's
Reservation Value
$250,000

Dr. Sander's
Reservation Value
$750,000

Assuming that Tammy and Dr. Sander focus solely on the single issue of money, they face a zero-sum negotiation in which all that they must decide is how to distribute the $500,000 ZOPA, or *surplus*, between them. Any settlement between their reservation values is better for each than refusing to settle, but of course not all agreements within the ZOPA are equally good for one party or the other. For example, if they ultimately settled for $700,000, Tammy would claim most of the surplus—she would get the better deal. If they settled for $300,000, Dr. Sander would claim the majority of the surplus. If they split the difference between their reservation values and reached agreement at $500,000, they would divide the surplus equally. They must negotiate over this *distributive issue* to resolve their dispute.

Of course, Tammy is unlikely to know the most that Dr. Sander will pay, and he is unlikely to tell her. Similarly, he will not know that Tammy would accept an offer of as little as $250,000. We will discuss strategy in Section B, but for now we can assume from their extreme initial positions—$1 million versus $30,000—that each is trying to claim as much value as he or she can in this distributive bargaining situation.

2. MULTIPLE ISSUES

Although the one-issue case is convenient as a starting point, many negotiations—perhaps most—involve more than one issue. If you are buying a house, most of the bargaining may focus on the sale price. But timing may be contested as well—you might prefer to close the deal quickly because your apartment lease is expiring, while the seller wants to delay until he closes on the new house he has purchased in another city. You might also bargain over the amount of the down payment, mortgage contingencies, who should pay for various improvements or repairs, or what fixtures to include in the sale. All of these variables may be in play simultaneously as you and the seller attempt to reach a deal.

If each issue is considered in isolation, the addition of these multiple variables merely complicates the distributive bargaining. You now not only want to secure the lowest possible price but also to push the seller as far as possible on timing, fixtures, financing and the other issues on the table.

Viewed separately, each new issue is simply another item to be bargained over.

Considered in combination, however, multiple issues can dramatically alter a negotiation by introducing the possibility of trade-offs *between* issues. For example, timing might be extremely important to you but only moderately important to the seller—he can stay with a friend for a few weeks quite easily if you move the closing date forward. Conversely, having a larger cash deposit might be extremely valuable to him—because he wants to ensure that you won't walk away from the deal—but relatively easy for you to provide because you have the cash on hand. You and the seller might be better off if your agreement takes advantage of these different priorities by providing for an early closing date in exchange for a large cash deposit. Each of you then captures value on the issue you care about, in return for sacrificing on an issue that is less important to you.

The possibility of such trade-offs between issues can transform a multiple issue negotiation from a zero-sum situation—in which when I gain, you lose—to a positive-sum bargain in which both parties can be made better off through trades. In economic terms, a negotiated agreement is *efficient* if the parties have captured all of the possible gains from trade. Finding such efficiencies is often called integrative, "win-win," positive-sum, joint gains, or value-creating negotiation. Regardless of the label we affix, the point is simple but powerful. In a multiple issue negotiation, the parties can "expand the pie," not merely slice it up.

a. PARETO OPTIMALITY

Returning to the example of Tammy and Dr. Sander, we can illustrate the concept of efficiency using a two-dimensional graph. Figure 2 shows Tammy's utility—the benefit she would receive from a given negotiated solution—on the vertical axis and Dr. Sander's utility on the horizontal axis.

Imagine that Solution I represents a simple compromise: Dr. Sander pays Tammy $500,000. Both Tammy and the defendant get some satisfaction from this agreement. It is certainly better for each than no agreement at all. But now add a second issue to the negotiation: whether Dr. Sander will agree to attend training about Pemphigus so that he will be less likely to make such a mistake in the future. Tammy and her family might get great benefit from knowing that Dr. Sander will attend such a training.

Imagine that Solution A represents a payment of $500,000 *plus* an agreement from Dr. Sander to attend a training session. This solution is better for Tammy than Solution I: she receives the same financial compensation plus the intangible benefits of having done something to help future patients. And Solution A is just as good for Dr. Sander as Solution I— imagine that the training is free and that the costs in terms of his time and

Figure 2

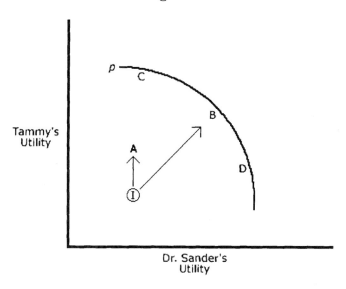

effort are balanced equally by the benefit he receives from learning more about this disease. So long as Dr. Sander is not envious of Tammy's improved position, he will be indifferent between Solution A and Solution I. Because Solution A is better for one party—Tammy—without being worse for another, we say that Solution A is *Pareto superior* to Solution I.[4]

Now consider incorporating a related issue into the negotiation: rather than merely attending a training session, what if Dr. Sander were to agree to implement a hospital-wide education campaign to inform his colleagues about Pemphigus? This campaign would cost Dr. Sander time, money and energy. Tammy and her family, however, would value this campaign even more than they value Dr. Sander attending an educational training session. This seems like a straight distributive issue—she wants him to do the campaign, he doesn't want to incur the costs.

But what if Tammy were willing to sacrifice on one issue—dollars—to trade for the educational campaign? Assume that the intangible, emotional benefit to Tammy of implementing such a program is worth $50,000. In other words, she would accept up to $50,000 less in return for an agreement that includes such programs. Similarly, assume that the cost to Dr. Sander of implementing an educational campaign is roughly $20,000. Clearly, the value of such measures to Tammy is significantly greater than the cost to Dr. Sander. Assuming they started from Solution I—the simple compromise at $500,000—*both would be better off* by moving to Solution B—an agreement that includes $475,000, the training and an educational campaign.[5] All else being equal, both would prefer Solution B to Solution I.

---

4. Vilfredo Pareto was a 19th century economist who is credited with proposing this definition of efficiency.

5. Tammy would be better off because she receives the equivalent of $525,000 in value ($475,000 plus the educational programs that she values at $50,000). Dr. Sand-

These parties might find a variety of other issues that they could also work into value-creating trades. They might jointly contribute to a national Pemphigus foundation. Tammy might be involved with Dr. Sander's educational campaign. Over time, Tammy might find it extremely beneficial to receive recent articles and information about Pemphigus from medical journals and sources. It might be easy for Dr. Sander to provide her with such reference materials, and extremely difficult or costly for her to gain access to them on her own. Finally, an apology might also create value in this negotiation. It may be relatively easy for Dr. Sander to apologize, and it may be of great benefit to Tammy and her family.[6]

If Solutions C and D in Figure 2 represent some of these other value-creating agreements that Tammy and Dr. Sander could explore, then Line *p*—connecting Solutions C, B and D—represents what economists call the *Pareto frontier* or the *efficiency frontier*. See Raiffa, The Art and Science of Negotiation 139 (1982). This frontier is made up of all of the *Pareto optimal* solutions in a negotiation. A solution is Pareto optimal if there is no other solution that can make one party better off without making the other party worse off. In other words, the parties have exploited all of the achievable joint gains—there are no solutions Pareto superior to a Pareto optimal one.

Two points about the efficiency frontier deserve mention. First, the frontier is finite—there is only so much value that the parties can create in a given interaction. Second, as between possible agreements *along* the frontier—as between Solutions B, C, or D, for example—the parties face a distributive negotiation. Although each solution on the frontier is efficient or value-creating vis-à-vis other, less efficient solutions (such as I or A), each solution on the frontier will be better for one party or the other. Both parties, for example, would prefer Solution C to Solution A, but choosing Solution *B* over Solution C would make Dr. Sander better off but Tammy worse off. Thus, even in multiple issue negotiations where the parties can exploit joint gains, certain distributive issues remain.

b. SOURCES OF VALUE

In a real negotiation, of course, neither party is likely to know all of the possible solutions nor the priorities and preferences that suggest trade-offs between different agreements. In our Section B on "Strategy" we turn to the strategies and tactics that negotiators can use to try to find efficient outcomes and expand the pie—*how* to engage in value-creating or integrative negotiation. First, however, we explore the sources of value-creating solutions—*what* value-creating trades are economically based on.

Shared interests or preferences are the first and most intuitive source of value-creating agreements. If we both like pizza, it makes sense to

er would be better off because he pays only $495,000 instead of $500,000 ($475,000 plus the educational programs that cost him only $20,000).

6. For a discussion of apology in litigation, see Cohen, Apology and Organizations: Exploring an Example from Medical Practice, 27 Fordham Urban L.J. 1447 (2000); Cohen, Advising Clients to Apologize, 72 S.Cal.L.Rev. 1009 (1999).

choose that for dinner rather than to go to a burger joint. We will both be better off. Similarly, both parties may wish to benefit a third party—if two divorcing parents both care deeply about the well-being of their children, they will want to craft custodial and visitation arrangements that are in their kids' best interests. Creating workable terms on this issue will make both better off than they would be if conflict permeated their future relationship. Conversely, two parties may be able to maximize their joint utility at the expense of a third party: disputants might share an interest in minimizing the tax consequences of their settlement agreement, for example (at the expense of the government). If two parties can find such non-competitive similarities, they can create value. See Mnookin, Peppet, and Tulumello, Beyond Winning: Negotiating to Create Value in Deals and Disputes 16 (2000).

In addition to shared interests, *differences* between the parties are a major source of value-creating trades. Although the parties' stated positions may seem to conflict, sometimes their interests are merely different, not opposed. In the 1920s, Mary Parker Follett, a pioneer in conflict and management studies, described a now classic example:

> [W]hen two desires are integrated, that means that a solution has been found in which both desires have found a place, that neither has had to sacrifice anything. Let us take some very simple illustration. In the Harvard Library one day, in one of the smaller rooms, someone wanted the window open, I wanted it shut. We opened the window in the next room, where no one was sitting. This was not a compromise, because there was no curtailing of desire; we both got what we really wanted. For I did not want a closed room, I simply did not want the North wind to blow directly on me; likewise the other occupant did not want that particular window open, he merely wanted more air in the room.

Follett, Constructive Conflict (1925), in Graham (ed.), Follett: Prophet of Management 69 (1995). See also Kolb, The Love for Three Oranges, or What Did We Miss about Ms Follett in the Library?, 11 Neg.J. (1995).

The following two excerpts explore the ways in which differences can generate integrative bargaining solutions.

David Lax and James Sebenius, The Manager as Negotiator

90–102 (1986).

Gain from negotiation often exists because negotiators *differ* from one another. Since they are not identical—in tastes, forecasts, endowments, capabilities, or in other ways—they each have something to offer that is relatively less valuable to them than to those with whom they are bargaining. * * *

* * *

That differences lie at the heart of many joint gains follows readily from the fact that two utterly identical individuals may have no basis for any negotiation: neither has or wants anything that the other does not. If differences are admitted among many dimensions, however, negotiation opens up the prospect of joint gains. For example, gains may arise from differences in interests, in possessions, in forecasts, in aversion to risk, in attitudes toward the passage of time, in capabilities, in access to technology, and in other areas.

Since joint gains often derive from such differences, a primary orientation of managers, negotiators, and mediators should be toward discovering and dovetailing them. In line with this observation, this section will argue on behalf of two broad prescriptions:

1. When contemplating the potential gains from agreement, begin with a careful inventory of all the ways that the parties differ from one another—not how they are alike.

2. The basic principle underlying the realization of joint gains from differences is to match what one side finds or expects to be relatively costless with what the other finds or expects to be most valuable, and vice versa.

* * *

DIFFERENCES OF INTEREST IMPLY EXCHANGES

If a vegetarian with some meat bargains with a carnivore who owns some vegetables, it is precisely the *difference* in their known preferences that can facilitate reaching an agreement. No one would counsel the vegetarian to persuade the carnivore of the zucchini's succulent taste. More complicated negotiations may concern several items. Although the parties may have opposing preferences on the settlement of each issue, they may feel most strongly about different issues. An overall agreement can reflect these different preferences by resolving the issues of relatively greater importance to one side more in favor of that side. A package or "horse trade" can be constructed this way so that, as a whole, all prefer it to no agreement.

* * * This theory applies not only to trading discrete things but also to constructing agreements that respond to different underlying interests. One party may primarily fear the precedential effects of a settlement; another may care about the particulars of the current question; thus, both might profit by contriving a unique-looking agreement on the immediate issue. One side may be keen on a political "victory"; the other may want quiet accommodation for a particular constituency. Whether the differences are between vegetables and meat, form and substance, ideology and practice, reputation and results, or the intrinsic versus the instrumental qualities of a settlement, cleverly crafted agreements can often dovetail differences into joint gains.

From an economic viewpoint, then, differences in relative valuation can lead to the possibility of gain from exchange and thus can improve the likelihood of reaching agreement. This contention is consistent with the proposition of the noted analyst of social behavior, George Homans: "The more the items at stake can be divided into goods valued more by one party than they cost to the first, the greater the chances of a successful outcome."

* * *

[Consider the example of a] midwestern utility that wanted to build a dam. The company had become embroiled in a dispute with farmers about downstream water flow and with conservationists worried about the effects of water diversion on the downstream habitat of the endangered whooping crane. After years of wrangling, the utility offered to guarantee downstream waterflow and to pay $7.5 million to purchase additional water rights or otherwise to protect the whooping crane habitat. Although both the utility and the conservationists saw the offer on the issue of financial compensation as generous, the utility was surprised that the conservationists rejected it.

After much more discussion, the utility came to understand that the conservationists' personal control over the money might make it appear as if they were being paid off and reduce their credibility with conservationist groups. An acceptable settlement had to unbundle the issue of financial compensation in a way that separated compensation and control. So, the parties created a $7.5 million trust fund to protect the whooping crane with a strict covenant that limited its trustees' control over the fund. To reach agreement, the parties needed to learn a great deal about the others' real interests. They had to identify differentially valued interests that were unnecessarily bundled. Then, they needed to invent ways to modify the issues and unbundled the interests to permit joint gains.

* * *

PROBABILITY DIFFERENCE SUGGEST CONTINGENT ARRANGEMENTS

At the heart of the sale of an investment property may be the buyer's belief that its price will rise and the seller's conviction that it will drop. The deal is facilitated by differences in belief about what will happen. * * *

Probability assessments of uncertain events derive from the combination of prior beliefs and observed evidence; discrepancies in either of these factors may form the basis for contingent agreements. We have already observed that value differences can lead to horse trades. Analogously, for probabilities, Mark Twain noted that "it is difference of opinion that makes horse races." Two classes of situations suggest themselves in which contingent agreements based on different expectations may produce joint gains.

Issues Subject to Different Odds. In the first case, outcomes of the event under discussion may be uncertain and subject to different probability estimates. * * * For example, an engineering firm had completed plans for a plant designed to burn garbage, to produce steam, and to convert it into electricity. The firm was negotiating with a medium-sized southern city over the sale of this electricity to the city. The city wanted to pay a lower price; the company insisted on a much higher one. As the discussions proceeded and then stalled, it became clear that the city representatives expected an oil glut and hence a drop in the price of the fuel most important to its electrical generation. The company believed that an oil price rise was much more likely. After protracted talks, the two sides could not agree on a set price for the sale of the plant's electricity to the city. Finally, however, they agreed to tie that price to the future cost of oil. Thus, the city expected to pay a lower price while the company expected to receive a higher price. While they also negotiated an upper and lower cap on the range of acceptable fluctuations, both sides could live with either outcome, and the plant went forward.

* * *

Different Assessments of the Attractiveness of Proposed Procedures. Contingent agreements may be employed in a second common class of situations where the parties believe that they can positively affect the chances for favorable outcome of an uncertain event. Consider the voluntary submission of a dispute to arbitration. Firmly believing the persuasiveness of its position and highly confident in the quality of its representation before the tribunal, each side may feel that its chances of obtaining the desired outcome are very good. * * *

* * *

DIFFERENCES IN RISK AVERSION LEAD TO RISK–SHARING SCHEMES

Suppose that two people agree on the probabilities of an uncertain prospect. Even so, they may still react differently to taking the risks involved. In such cases, they may devise a variety of ways to share the risk. In general, such mechanisms should shift more of the risk to the party who is less risk-averse than the other. For example, suppose that Mr. Broussard, a single, fairly wealthy, middle-aged accountant, and Ms. Armitage, a younger, less-well-off lawyer with significant family responsibilities, are planning to buy and operate a business together. The younger, more risk-averse Ms. Armitage may prefer to take a larger but fixed salary while Mr. Broussard may prefer a smaller set salary but much larger share of any profits. Though they may expect the same total amount of money to be paid in compensation, both parties are better off than had they, say, both chosen either fixed salaries or larger contingent payments.

* * *

DIFFERENCES IN TIME PREFERENCES SUGGEST ALTERED PAYMENT PATTERNS

People may value the same event quite differently, depending on when it occurs. If one side is relatively less impatient than the other, mechanisms for optimally sharing the consequences over time may be devised.

* * * Consider a highly stylized example. Suppose that Ms. Kanwate has a 10 percent discount rate, that Mr. Hurree's rate is 20 percent, and that each party cares about the present value of income.[8] Ms. Kanwate will receive $100 next year; Mr. Hurree is slated to receive $100 the year afterward. Thus the present value of her income is about $91 and his is $69.[9] The two could engineer a variety of profitable trades to dovetail this difference. Because Mr. Hurree values early income relatively more than does Mr. Kanwate, though, he should get the first year's $100. If, in the second year, Ms. Kanwate gets $100 plus $20 from him, the present value of her income rises from $91 in the original division to $99. The present value of Mr. Hurree's income stream (+ $100 in a year,—$20 in two years) remains at about $69. If he gave $10 to Ms. Kanwate in the second period, she could have the same present value as in the original division ($91), while the present value of his income would be $76 instead of the original $69. Any outcome in which he gets the first $100 and she gets between $110 and $120 in the second period is as good as or better than the original division for both parties.

Max H. Bazerman and James J. Gillespie, Betting on the Future: The Virtues of Contingent Contracts

Harvard Bus.Rev. 155, 156–160 (Sept.–Oct. 1999).

It used to be assumed that differences were always a source of contention in negotiations, limiting the parties' ability to reach an agreement. But in recent years, negotiation scholars have shown that differences are often constructive. They provide the basis for tradeoffs that can pave the way to mutually beneficial agreements. When the differences have to do with uncertain future events that are critically important to both parties, however, trade-offs become very difficult to make. By making the differences the basis for a bet that offers potential gains to both parties, contingent contracts enable negotiators to avoid long, costly, and often futile arguments. * * *

Consider how a contingent contract might have changed the course of one of the century's most famous (and fruitless) antitrust cases. In 1969, the U.S. Department of Justice filed suit against IBM, alleging monopolistic behavior. More than a decade later, the case was still bogged down in litigation. Some 65 million pages of documents had been produced, and

---

8. The "future value" of a present amount of money reflects the compounding of interest forward over time. The "present value" of a future amount of money reverses this process, "discounting" it back to the present amount that, if compounded forward at the same interest (or discount) rate, would just equal the future amount.

9. That is, because Ms. Kanwate has alternative investment possibilities that re-

turn 10 percent, her getting $100 in a year is equivalent to placing $91 now in the alternative investment and taking out the $100 it will produce a year later. Similarly, for Mr. Hurree, getting $100 in two years is equivalent to putting $69 now in an investment that returns 20 percent and, two years hence, drawing the $100 produced by the investment.

each side had spent millions of dollars in legal expenses. The DOJ finally dropped the case in 1982, when it was clear that IBM's once-dominant share of the computer market was eroding rapidly.

During the case's 13 years, IBM and the DOJ had essentially been arguing over differences in expectations. IBM assumed that its market share would decrease in coming years as competition in the lucrative computer market increased. The DOJ assumed that IBM, as a monopolist, would hold its dominant market share for the foreseeable future. Because neither felt the other's view was valid, neither would compromise.

A contingent contract would have been an efficient and rational way to settle this dispute. IBM and the government might have agreed, for example, that if by 1975 IBM still held at least 70% of the market—its share in 1969—it would pay a set fine and divest itself of certain businesses. If, however, its market share had dropped to 50% or lower, the government would not pursue antitrust actions. If its share fell somewhere between 50% and 70%, another contingency plan would be executed.

Constructing such a contract would not have been easy. There were, after all, an infinite number of feasible permutations, and many details would have had to have been hammered out. But it would have been far more rational—and far cheaper—to have lawyers from both sides devote a few weeks to arguing over how to structure a contingent contract than it was for them to spend years filing motions, taking depositions, and reviewing documents. We would suggest, parenthetically, that a similar course might have been taken in the dispute between Microsoft and the U.S. government.

* * *

While we believe that contingent contracts are valuable in many kinds of business negotiations, they're not right in every situation. [Negotiators] should keep three points in mind:

First, contingent contracts require *continuing interaction* between the parties. After all, the final outcome of the contract will not be determined until sometime after the initial agreement is signed. Therefore, negotiators need to consider the nature of their future relationship with the other party. If the parties are seeking a spot transaction, or if there's outright ill will between the two, they should probably not enter into a contingent contract.

Second, negotiators need to think about the *enforceability* of a contract. Under a contingent contract, it is probable that one or more of the parties will not receive its full value up front. In some cases, the deferred value may represent a significant portion of the overall value. What if the loser of the bet refuses to pay up? What should the winner do? There are many ways to solve such issues—placing the money in escrow, for instance. Our main message is, don't bet if you can't collect.

Third, contingent contracts require *transparency*. The future event the parties bet on must be one that both sides can observe and measure and that neither side can covertly manipulate. Vague bets set the stage for different interpretations later. The terms of the bet should be clearly delineated by the contract.

NOTES AND QUESTIONS

1. George Bernard Shaw stated the basic principle behind trading on differences when he said, "It is unwise to do unto others as you would have them do unto you. Their tastes may not be the same." Although negotiators often assume that reaching agreement requires uncovering *similarities*, mining differences for mutually-beneficial trades is often most rewarding. As a thought experiment, consider the ways in which you might create value through trading on differences in the following examples. For each example, identify whether you would be trading on differences in resources or capabilities, relative valuations, predictions about the future (probabilities), risk preferences, or timing preferences.

a. You are buying a used car from a dealer but worry that the new clutch the dealer installed may be a lemon. The dealer has mechanics in his shop that could easily repair the clutch if it breaks. What might you do to create value in this negotiation?

b. You are negotiating an executive compensation agreement for a client who is becoming Chief Financial Officer at BigCorp. Your client fears that a change in corporate control is imminent if BigCorp. gets taken over by a competitor, and in that event he might lose he new job. He initially demands a $1 million signing bonus to protect himself against that imminent possibility. BigCorp.'s lawyer refuses, insisting that the company is not a likely takeover candidate. What might you do?

c. You represent a client in a negotiation over the division of a family estate. Your client has one sibling, and they are the only two heirs. There are five items in dispute: a beautiful antique grandfather clock (worth $120,000), a small painting by Picasso ($50,000), a photo album with rare pictures of the sibling's now deceased parents and grandparents (worth $200), a small silver brooch often worn by their mother (worth $6,500), and a baby grand piano (value unknown). The siblings live far from each other and will be unable, and unwilling, to share the items over time. Assuming that the two siblings have intangible interests—such as emotional attachment—in addition to their desire for financial gain, how will you ensure that the estate division is most efficient, in the sense that it allocates the five items to create the most value possible? Will an efficient division necessarily be "fair?"[7]

---

7. For an innovative and useful discussion of decision-making procedures that can be useful in crafting efficient outcomes in such circumstances, see Brams and Taylor, The Win–Win Solution (1999).

2. In addition to exploiting shared interests and the categories of differences that Lax and Sebenius describe, negotiators can create value by generating *economies of scale*. If two people carpool to work it is significantly cheaper than if they drive separately. Similarly, it is less expensive for a couple to live together—and share a stereo, appliances, heat, etc.—than to maintain separate residences. As we consume together, the individual cost of consumption drops. Finding such efficiencies is another way to create value in negotiations. See Lax and Sebenius, The Manager as Negotiator 90–102 (1986); Mnookin, Peppet and Tulumello, Beyond Winning: Negotiating To Create Value in Deals and Disputes 16 (2000).

3. Value-creating trades are the foundation of most economic exchange. You can easily discover opportunities for such trades. Try this simple exercise with another student in your class or with a friend or neighbor. Take two minutes together—time yourselves—and try to find ways that you could trade to make one or both of you better off. Perhaps you each subscribe to a magazine that the other would like to read? After finishing reading your magazine you could swap each month to get a chance to enjoy the other's subscription. Maybe you know how to ski and she knows how to set up a computer? You could take your friend for a daylong skiing lesson in exchange for her setting up your printer and explaining how to back up your computer files. Look for trades in goods, capabilities or services, timing, or risk-preferences. Also look for shared interests and for economies of scale.

4. Finding value-creating opportunities can require in-depth understanding of the economics and trade-offs in a given context. Experienced negotiators sometimes don't even realize they are "expanding the pie"—they just know how the various issues connect in their context and where trades are typically found. The following description from David Falk, a sports agent and attorney, illustrates that finding trade-offs can be central to a negotiator's task:

> * * * Every deal has trade-offs; they are the essence of the bargaining process. You can call it bargaining, negotiating, or horse-trading. There are some basic trade-offs I use when I am negotiating a deal. The first is the length of the contract. You must understand the needs and goals of your client. Does he want security? Does he want to maximize the amount of dollars protected in case he fails to reach an expected level of performance? Or does he want flexibility, so if the market changes substantially in the first two or three years of his contract, he has the ability to renegotiate as a free agent? * * * [Consider] the case of Stanley Roberts, * * * the twenty-third pick in the 1991 [NBA] draft. * * * Most general managers thought that he was overweight, was not a very hard worker, and therefore was a risky pick. Roberts averaged ten points and six rebounds a game as a rookie. But he was a center, and centers are extremely hard to obtain in the NBA. As a result, at the conclusion of his one-year contract, four or five teams bid for him. He signed a contract averaging in excess of $3 million a year. Had he come out of school and signed a great contract

for the twenty-third pick, let's say $1 million a year, but locked himself up for five years, he would have cost himself a tremendous amount of money. Because he was in a position to get only a one-year deal, it ended up working to his benefit. The decision whether to sign long-term or short-term is a critical one that demands full discussion with your client. You cannot make judgments *for* your client. You have to make judgments *with* your client. You have to point out the benefits of security and the detriments of locking him in for a long period of time and having to renegotiate a contract when you do not have a lot of leverage.

The second trade-off is guarantees. In basketball, eighty-three percent of all contracts are guaranteed for either skill or injury. This means that if the club terminates the contract, it remains obligated to pay the player. In football, a very small percentage of contracts are guaranteed. Since guarantees provide security, teams will often pay a player more dollars if he will take fewer guarantees. Conversely, teams may propose that the player sacrifice dollars in order to get the entire contract guaranteed.

The third trade-off is current cash dollars versus deferred money. * * *

* * *

Another area of trade-offs is incentive bonuses. * * * [W]hen you are negotiating a contract and you are apart in your positions, one area available to you to close the deal is incentive bonuses. * * * When you have "maxed out" guaranteed cash, but you have not closed the deal, bonuses are a creative trade-off in closing the gap.

Falk, The Art of Contract Negotiation, 3 Marquette Sports L.J. 1, 12–14 (1992).

5. Some commentators have tried to clarify what exactly constitutes win-win or integrative bargaining and what distinguishes it from distributive negotiation. Gerald Wetlaufer makes the following distinctions between what he calls Form I, II and III value creation:

For purposes of clarification, I will distinguish three forms of value creation, only one of which constitutes an opportunity for integrative or win-win bargaining. The first of these forms is found where the pie can be made larger only in the sense that is true of all bargaining including bargaining that is merely distributive. In such circumstances, there is a zone of agreement * * * within which both parties will be better off than they would have been in the absence of the agreement. Thus, in this minimal sense, purely distributive bargaining can be said to "create value" or "expand the pie." I shall call this "Form I" value creation. * * *

* * * Form II value creation is possible when there is one issue (e.g., the amount of money to be paid for some product), and one party cares more about that issue than does the other. This is a situation in

which, assuming there is a range of possible agreements that would leave both parties better off, there is an opportunity for Form I value creation in that the aggregate benefits to the parties will vary depending on whether or not they can reach agreement. Also, and this is what distinguishes Form II value creation, this is a situation in which the aggregate benefits to the parties, the size of the pie, will vary across the range of possible agreements. Thus, the total value created by the agreement will be relatively large if most of that over which the parties are negotiating (e.g., surplus as measured in dollars) is captured by the party who cares more about that issue. Similarly, the total value created by the agreement will be relatively small if most of the surplus is captured by the party who cares less about that issue.

An opportunity for Form II value creation is not an opportunity for integrative bargaining because the possible agreements are arrayed along a single continuum such that any possible agreement is, in its relationship to any other, better for one party but worse for the other. One cannot move from any one possible agreement to any other possible agreement in such a way that both parties are made better off by the move. Nor can one even move from one possible agreement to another in such a way that one party is better off and the other is no worse off. Thus Form II value creation, like Form I, does not involve integrative bargaining.

Only what I shall call "Form III" value creation offers an opportunity for integrative or win-win bargaining. Unlike Forms I and II, Form III value creation involves that kind of pie-expansion or value creation in which the parties can reach a range of different agreements, in which the size of the pie will vary across the range of possible agreements (also true of Form II), but in which some of those agreements leave both parties better off than do others. If there are some possible agreements that both parties would regard as better than others, then the size of the pie created by the agreements depends both upon the parties' ability to reach some agreement (Form I value creation) and upon their wit and ability to arrive at one of the better agreements. It is in this sense that a situation presenting an opportunity for Form III value creation is a non-zero sum game and an opportunity for integrative or win-win bargaining.

Wetlaufer, The Limits of Integrative Bargaining, 85 Georgetown L.J. 369, 374–375 (1996).

Review the discussion of possible trades in Tammy and Dr. Sander's negotiation. Are those Form I, II, or III value creation, according to Wetlaufer's scheme? What about the example earlier in this section having to do with the purchase of a house—and trades based on closing date and the down payment amount? Does Wetlaufer's distinction make a difference? Why or why not?

3. THE ROLE OF INFORMATION

As this discussion of single-issue and multiple-issue bargaining shows, information plays a critical role in both distributive and integrative negotiation. To create value, each side must know its own interests, preferences and priorities—as well as something about the other side's—to be able to find trades. To approach distributive issues, each party must at least know its own best alternative and reservation value *and* try to estimate the other side's.

In legal disputes, attorneys are often at the table negotiating on behalf of their clients, who may or may not be present for the actual bargaining. A lawyer, therefore, must prepare herself for a negotiation by uncovering the information she will need to conduct that negotiation successfully. What information should an attorney search for in advance of a negotiation? What does she need to know to be able to create value-creating trades? To resolve distributive issues? How much of that information should she try to learn from her client before (and during) her negotiation, and how much will she have to find elsewhere? And what will she need to tell her client both before and during the negotiation?

Here we explore the role of information and the lawyer's role as gatherer and organizer of that information. To begin, we consider the information that a lawyer must learn in order to find integrative solutions to a client's problem. We then turn to the problem of estimating the value of a client's best alternative in a legal dispute.

a.   INTERESTS, RESOURCES AND PREFERENCES

If a lawyer is "in the middle" between her client and the other side, that lawyer must be prepared to find value-creating trades if such trades are possible. This requires that an attorney discover her client's interests, resources and preferences in order to be able to base deals upon them. Are lawyers well suited to this task? In the following excerpt, noted bargaining scholar Carrie Menkel–Meadow argues that they are not. Instead, she claims, lawyers are more prone to "narrowing" a dispute—not broadening it to find creative, integrative solutions.

Carrie Menkel–Meadow, The Transformation of Disputes by Lawyers: What the Dispute Paradigm Does and Does Not Tell Us

J. of Disp.Res. 25, 31–33 (1985).

The literature on lawyer transformation of disputes is rather accusatory. In general, if the *who* of dispute processing is a lawyer one may assume that the lawyer will make the dispute worse, much as medical treatment may make the illness worse. Lawyers are said to exacerbate disputes by increasing the demands and conflicts and narrow disputes by translating into limited legal categories what might have been broader and more general. * * *

For Mather & Yngvesson, the principal transformation of disputes occurs in their *rephrasing*, that is, "some kind of reformulation into a public discourse." Thus, the grievant tells a story of felt or perceived wrong to a third party (the lawyer) and the lawyer transforms the dispute by imposing "categories" on "events and relationships" which redefine the subject matter of the dispute in ways "which make it amenable to conventional management procedures." This process of "narrowing" disputes occurs at various stages in lawyer-client interactions * * * First, the lawyer may begin to narrow the dispute in the initial client interview. By asking questions which derive from the lawyer's repertoire of what is likely to be legally relevant, the lawyer defines the situation from the very beginning. Rather than permitting the client to tell a story freely to define what the dispute consists of, the lawyer begins to categorize the case as a "tort," "contract," or "property" dispute so that questions may be asked for legal saliency. This may narrow the context of a dispute which has more complicated fact patterns and may involve some mix of legal and non-legal categories of dispute. A classic example of such a mixed dispute is a landlord-tenant case in which relationship issues and political issues (such as in rent control areas) intermingle with strictly legal issues of rent obligation, maintenance obligation, and nuisance. Thus, during the initial contact the lawyer narrows what is "wrong" by trying to place the dispute in a legal context which the lawyer feels he can handle.

Even if the client is allowed to tell his lawyer a broader story, the lawyer will narrow or rephrase the story in his efforts to seek remediation. Beginning with an effort to negotiate with the other side, the lawyer will construct a story which is recognizable to the other lawyer so that he can demand a stock remedial solution. In recent social, psychological, and legal literature this process has been called the telling of "stock stories." The "stock stories" can be likened to a legal cause of action with prescribed elements which must be pleaded in a particular way in the legal system to state a "claim for which relief can be granted." If pre-litigation negotiation fails and the lawyer begins to craft a lawsuit, the dispute will be further narrowed by the special language requirements of the substantive law, pleading rules, and the rules of procedure. * * *

Once negotiation commences the dispute is further narrowed, the issues become stylized, and statements of what is disputed become ritualized because of the very process and constraints of litigation. In negotiation, lawyers begin to demand what they will ask the court to do if the case goes to trial. Lawyers are told to plan "minimum disposition," "target," and "reservation" points that are based on an analysis of what would happen if the case went to trial. Because a court resolution of the problem will result in a binary win/loss ruling, lawyers begin to conceive of the negotiation process as simply an earlier version of court adjudication. Thus, lawyers seek to persuade each other, using many of the same principles and normative entreaties that they will use in court, that they are right and ought to prevail now, before either party suffers further monetary or temporal loss. The remedies lawyers seek from each other may be sharply limited to what they think would be possible in a court case considering the court's remedial powers. Thus, most negotiations, like most lawsuits, are converted into linear, zero-sum games about money, where money serves as the proxy for a host of other needs and potential solutions such as apologies or substitute goods. Negotiated solutions become compromises in which each side concedes something to the other to avoid the harshness of a binary solution. The compromise, which by definition forces each side to give up something, may be unnecessary and fail to meet the real needs of the parties. * * *

* * *

In counseling clients lawyers may tell them what remedies are legally possible (money or an injunction) and thus preclude inquiry into alternatives which the client might prefer or which might be easier to obtain from the other party. [S]ome disputants prefer an acknowledgement that wrong has been done to them to receiving money. Once lawyers are engaged and the legal system, even if only informally, has been mobilized, the adversarial structure * * * forces polarization and routinization of demands and stifles a host of possible solutions.

NOTES AND QUESTIONS

1. Do you agree with Menkel–Meadow's assessment that a lawyer can disserve his client by narrowing a dispute and focusing too much on the categories of information with which the lawyer is already familiar and comfortable? Assuming this tendency exists, what are its advantages? Disadvantages?

2. It seems reasonable to assume that many lawyers *do* focus on the legal aspects of a dispute—on the information that might prove or disprove a client's legal claim, for example, instead of on the client's broader interests, needs, concerns and priorities. This is, of course, important: as we'll see below, part of a lawyer's job is determining whether a client has a case and how strong that case may be. At the same time, lawyers and clients will almost certainly be better served if a lawyer also prepares to search for value-creating trades when he goes to negotiate with the other side. What information does he need to do so?

Consider the example of Tammy and Dr. Sander. Imagine that you are Tammy's lawyer and that you have not yet begun to negotiate with Dr. Sander's attorney. You are about to meet with Tammy to discuss the upcoming negotiation. You know that the settlement amount in dollars is most likely going to be the primary distributive issue to be negotiated. At the same time, you are concerned that you could miss value-creating opportunities if you and Dr. Sander's attorney merely spend your time trading offers and counteroffers. You have even thought about the possibility that Tammy might be interested in some creative options like asking Dr. Sander to educate his peers or to apologize to Tammy and her family. Yet you aren't sure whether Tammy would go along with such a trade, nor how valuable it would be to her.

In preparation for a meeting with Tammy, make a list of the information you would like to learn from her. Then add to that a list of the questions that you can imagine asking her to learn that information.

Review the Lax and Sebenius excerpt in Section A(2)(b) above. Are your questions likely to prepare you to find value-creating trades based on the parties' differences, as Lax and Sebenius discuss?

3. Not all disputes are created equal. Some offer a wide variety of integrative opportunities, even if at first glance they appear to be primarily distributive. Disputes in which the parties have had (or could have) an ongoing relationship, there are various intangible interests at stake in addition to money, there are interests that extend over time, and there are many issues on the table are more likely to present value-creating opportunities. Other disputes—such as a very simple personal injury case in which the plaintiff and defendant have no long-term relationship and few interests on the table other than receiving or avoiding compensation—are more like the single-issue distributive example that we explored earlier.

Think about the following types of disputes: (1) divorce litigation; (2) personal injury litigation; (3) medical malpractice; (4) family estate litigation; (5) disputes over commercial contracts; (6) intellectual property litigation over copyright infringement; (7) dissolution of a business partnership or joint venture; (8) employee discrimination litigation; (9) securities class actions; (10) a mass tort class action against the maker of an allegedly defective product.

Which of these are likely to be primarily distributive? Which will have integrative possibilities (and what might those be)? If there is a spectrum—with "mostly distributive" at one end and "mostly integrative" at the other—where do these types of disputes fall upon it? See Mnookin, Peppet and Tulumello, Beyond Winning: How to Create Value in Deals and Disputes 43 (2000).

b. ALTERNATIVES: USING LITIGATION ANALYSIS

We have seen that searching for value-creating trades requires information about interests, resources, preferences and priorities, that clients are most often likely to possess such information, and that lawyers must therefore prepare carefully *with* their clients to enable themselves to find such trades. We have also seen, however, that a negotiator must know the value of her best alternative to a negotiated agreement so that she knows when and whether to walk away from the negotiating table. Such information allows you to compare any proposed settlement agreement against the value of your BATNA.

Parties in a legal dispute generally share the same best alternative: proceeding to court. In the words of Professors Mnookin and Kornhauser, they "bargain in the shadow of the law." See Mnookin and Kornhauser, Bargaining in the Shadow of the Law: The Case of Divorce, 88 Yale L.J. 950 (1979). Their private negotiations are—and should be—shaped by the public rights, duties and norms that a court would apply if their bargaining fails. If Tammy or Dr. Sander doesn't like the deal they arrive at through negotiation, either could walk away and continue with their litigation. This should, in theory, make matters simple. If both sides have the same

BATNA, then the parties should be able to determine what going to court would be worth and settle for that amount, thereby saving the transaction costs (in time, money, aggravation, etc.) that they would spend fighting it out before a judge.[8]

Reality is rarely so simple.

First, the lawyers might face a great deal of *uncertainty* about what the court outcome would be. Perhaps the facts in dispute are still unclear, either because discovery has not yet occurred or because it has failed to reveal a "smoking gun" that makes one side's story a slam-dunk. Perhaps the substantive law governing their dispute is novel or unsettled. Perhaps the judge presiding over their litigation is difficult to read or seems equivocal. Regardless, sometimes litigants are extremely uncertain about what outcome they face if they walk away from their negotiation.

Second, there can be *strategic temptations* to exaggerate, argue about, or try to influence the other side's perception of the value of continuing litigation. Each lawyer may posture and advocate to try to influence the other side's perceptions of its legal case. After all, if I can persuade you that your case is weak, then you may be willing to pay more or accept less. At the same time, my attempts to do so may undermine our ability to work constructively together to resolve our clients' differences. "Our case is a sure winner; your case is lousy." "Your client will never get a penny out of a jury for such a flimsy claim." "Do you *really* want to put your client on the stand?" The lawyers (or the parties) in litigation may be unable to discuss the likely court outcome without escalating their dispute and derailing their negotiations.

Third, lawyers and clients often struggle with *communication problems* when discussing the litigation alternative. When the lawyer says "you have a strong case," the client may think it's a sure winner. The lawyer, however, may only mean that there is a better than average chance of success—a fifty-fifty situation. Studies show that lawyers and clients experience difficulty communicating about such probabilities.[9] Such communication failures can lead to unmatched expectations and poor decision-making. For example, a lawyer may not understand why her client is holding out for more rather than accepting the other side's settlement offer, while the client simultaneously wonders why the lawyer is "suddenly" sounding so pessimistic about the case and pressuring him to agree to such a poor offer. They may fail to realize that their initial communications about the value of the litigation alternative left them with widely divergent understandings about expectations of success.

---

8. See Gross and Syverud, Getting to No: A Study of Settlement Negotiations and the Selection of Cases for Trial, 90 Mich. L.Rev. 319 (1991); Priest and Klein, The Selection of Disputes for Litigation, 13 J.Leg. Stud 1 (1984); Mnookin and Kornhauser, Bargaining in the Shadow of the Law: The Case of Divorce, 88 Yale L.J. 950, 973–77 (1979).

9. See e.g. Lerman, Lying to Clients, 138 U.Pa.L.Rev. 659, 734 (1990).

Litigation analysis can be a useful tool for a lawyer struggling with such complications.[10] By breaking down a client's legal dispute, analyzing the uncertainties and attempting to quantify—as much as possible—the value of the dispute's component parts, an attorney can sometimes make more precise and accurate estimations of the value of proceeding with litigation *and* more skillfully communicate those estimations to her client or the other side.

To illustrate, begin with the simple example of a coin toss. I am about to flip a dollar coin. If it lands heads, you win the dollar. If it lands tails, you win nothing. If I were to charge you some fixed amount to allow you to play my coin-toss game, and if you were risk neutral, what would you be willing to pay to take this bet?

The answer is any amount up to or equal to fifty cents. Although the outcome of any given coin toss is uncertain, we know that there is a fifty percent probability of heads and a fifty percent probability of tails. We also know the payoff associated with each possibility: you win one dollar if it lands heads, and nothing if tails. The *expected value* of this coin toss—the average value of betting on the toss many times—is thus fifty cents. This does not mean, of course, that you will win fifty cents on any given toss: it's an all or nothing game. Nevertheless, the law of averages tells us that if we toss the coin one hundred times, it will likely come up heads fifty of those one hundred. To compute the expected value of the coin toss you must merely multiply the probabilities by their associated outcomes and then add the results. (E.g., (.50 x $1.00) + (.50 x $0) = $.50)

Litigation analysis offers a similar way to model the decision of whether to settle or litigate. Assuming no transaction costs, the expected value of proceeding with a lawsuit equals the value of winning (say, $100,000) multiplied by the probability of winning (say, 30 percent) plus the value of losing ($0) multiplied by the probability of losing. In this simple example, of course, the expected value is $30,000. A risk-neutral plaintiff should take any settlement offer greater than $30,000 rather than gamble on going to court.

You can arrange this information in a decision tree—a graphical representation of a decision showing its *ultimate issues* and *influencing factors*. In dispute settlement, ultimate issues are those on which the outcome of the legal case turns. For example, will the jury find that the defendant was negligent? Influencing factors are uncertainties that will impact a given ultimate issue. For example, whether the jury finds the

---

10. Commentators use various terms to describe the process of breaking down and attempting to quantify the decision to sue or settle, including decision analysis, litigation risk analysis, BATNA-analysis, strategic choice analysis and decision tree analysis. Although decision analysis has a long history, particularly in management circles, and decision trees are a useful means of structuring such analysis, we use the term "litigation analysis" because it both refers specifically to the subject to which decision analysis is applied in this context and because it is slightly more broad than "BATNA-analysis" or "decision tree analysis," allowing that some techniques other than decision trees may be employed.

defendant negligent may depend on whether the judge rules that the plaintiff can discover the hospital's internal peer review reports related to the incident.

Decision trees are traditionally diagrammed in a fairly formal way to make them easier to chart and to read. *Decision nodes*, which identify an uncertainty that is completely within your control, are generally represented by a small square box. *Chance nodes*, which identify an uncertainty that is not within your control, are identified with a circle. In most legal disputes, the primary decision node represents a litigant's choice to litigate or settle. The branches following the choice to litigate will represent the various ultimate issues and influencing factors that could impact the litigation.

We can use Tammy's litigation against Dr. Sander to illustrate the process of creating a decision tree. Remember that Tammy's reservation value was $250,000—that was the least amount that she thought she should accept to settle the case. How did Tammy's attorney determine this reservation value? How could we use litigation analysis to calculate the expected value of her litigation alternative?

First, Tammy's lawyer must create the tree's structure by diagramming the basic issues that will have to be decided in court. Tammy's attorney tells her that she must overcome two hurdles: the possibility that the jury will find that Dr. Sander did not breach the standard of care (e.g., was not negligent) and the possibility that the jury will find that Dr. Sander's negligence did not cause Lyla's death. In addition, uncertainty exists about what amount of damages the jury might award. Tammy's lawyer believes the jury will choose between the maximum amount of $1,000,000, a "compromise" amount of $500,000, or a minimum amount representing medical costs of $200,000. Each of these three basic issues can be represented with a chance node. (See Figure 3.)

Figure 3

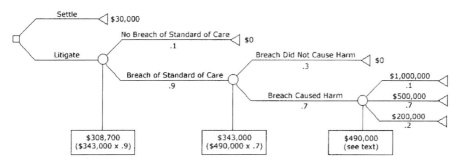

Next, Tammy's lawyer must attach probabilities to each of these chance nodes. Based on the best information he has available about the law, the facts, and the decision-makers, her attorney estimates a ninety percent chance of proving a breach of the standard of care and a seventy percent chance of then prevailing in convincing a jury that Dr. Sander's actions caused Lyla harm. He believes that there is only a ten percent chance that the jury would award $1,000,000 in damages, a similarly small chance of a small verdict of $200,000, and a seventy percent chance of a middle-of-the-road verdict of $500,000.

To calculate the expected value, one starts at the *right* of the tree and "rolls back" towards the decision node. Here the expected value of the jury's damages determination is $490,000: ($1,000,000 x .10 = $100,000) + ($500,000 x .70 = $350,000) + ($200,000 x .20 = $40,000) = $490,000. This is the expected value if Dr. Sander is found to have negligently caused Lyla harm, but he may not be. This $490,000 amount is multiplied by the probability of a causation determination (.70) to find that the expected value of the case upon the finding of negligence: $343,000. We continue to move towards the left, "rolling back" the tree, by multiplying this value of $343,000 by the probability that the jury *will* find Dr. Sander negligent (.90), for an expected value of litigation of $308,700.[11]

In addition, Tammy must adjust this expected value to account for her preferences regarding risk. A litigating party may be risk neutral, risk averse or risk preferring. Describing Tammy as risk neutral simply means that she is indifferent between accepting a fixed amount of money and taking a gamble that has the same expected value. For example, if Tammy is risk neutral she might be indifferent between accepting a cash payment of $308,700 and proceeding with litigation. But Tammy may be risk averse. She may be willing to pay a premium to avoid the risk inherent in gambling on litigation. For example, if Tammy is risk averse—she would rather have cash in hand than gamble—she might willingly accept *less* than $308,700 to reduce her uncertainty. Imagine that Tammy says she'd take $250,000 in cash rather than a chance at more, even though the expected value of the gamble is $308,700. In that case, we say that Tammy is willing to pay a $58,700 *risk premium*—$308,700 minus $250,000—to avoid the risk of losing in court. (If Tammy were risk *preferring*, she might demand *additional* compensation to give up the opportunity to gamble.) See D'Amato, Legal Uncertainty, 71 Calif.L.Rev. 1, 15 (1983).

This quick analysis shows how Tammy's lawyer can use litigation analysis to assist in valuing her litigation alternative. Her reservation value of $250,000 is tied to her best assessment of what will happen if she goes to court. By analyzing the structure of her case and the chances of succeeding at the various junctions that will determine its outcome, her lawyer can help her set a reservation value for her negotiations.

We must note, however, that this discussion of litigation analysis is not meant to suggest that a lawyer can or should determine the value of her

11. One can also perform sensitivity analysis to determine how sensitive the expected value is to changes in the probabilities associated with any given chance node. For example, instead of assuming a ninety percent chance that a judge will deny summary judgment, you might substitute a range of probabilities (from a 10 percent chance up to a ninety percent chance). You could then recalculate the tree to see the effects of changing that value. See Hoffer, Decision Analysis as a Mediator's Tool, 1 Harv. Neg.L.Rev. 113, 118–119 (1996).

client's litigation alternative once and for all. The litigation game is fluid, not static. While negotiating with the other party, a lawyer may be simultaneously filing pre-trial motions, searching for new evidence, deposing the other side's witnesses, and researching novel legal theories in order to better her own case and worsen her opponent's. Events may take place that change the bargaining range because they change the expected outcome of the litigation—should the case go to trial. A new decision may come down from a higher court that will influence how a judge applies the law to the facts in dispute. A key witness may die or move away. One litigant may run out of money and be unable to continue the fight. Through various moves *away from the negotiating table*, a disputant or his lawyer may be able to change the game *at the table*.

NOTES AND QUESTIONS

1. There are various advantages to using a decision tree to model litigation. It can aid lawyer-client communication, making it easier for an attorney to explain the value of her client's case and its strengths and weaknesses. It can force attorneys or their clients to attain a more balanced perspective on a case than they might otherwise. It can promote earlier settlement by permitting negotiation to continue even in the face of uncertainty. Finally, it may help to persuade the other side to settle by making it easier to reach consensus on the value of litigation. The two sides might jointly create a decision tree, discovering along the way where their points of disagreement lie.

Obviously, however, one should not pretend that a decision tree gives a completely objective or reliable estimate of the expected value of litigation. Although litigation analysis may look scientific, it depends completely upon the probability assessments and damages estimates that a lawyer uses. As one text states, decision analysis is subject to the principle of "garbage in, garbage out." See Mnookin, Peppet and Tulumello, Beyond Winning: Negotiating To Create Value in Deals and Disputes 238 (2000).

Lax and Sebenius warn of the dangers of inflating your perception of your alternative:

A negotiator's evaluation of alternatives is inherently subjective and, thus, depends on perceptions. Analysts and practitioners should, therefore, be sensitive to different possible perceptions of the same alternative. In an experiment at Harvard, the findings of which have been replicated in many contexts with students and executives, players were given detailed information about the history of an out-of-court negotiation over insurance claims arising from a personal injury case. They were not told whether the negotiators settled or if the case went into court. Each player was assigned to the role of either the insurance company or the [plaintiff]. After reading the case file, the players were privately asked to give their true probability estimates that the plaintiff would win the case and, given a win, the expected amount of the ultimate judgment. Systematically, those assigned the role of the plaintiff estimated the chances of winning and the expected amount of winning as much higher than those assigned the role of the insurance company defendant. Players who were not assigned a role prior to reading the case gave private estimates that generally fell between those of the advocates for each position. Similar results have been found in cases involving the worth of a company that is up for sale. Even given identical business information, balance sheets, income statements, and the like, those assigned to buy the company typically rate its true value as low, while those assigned to sell it give much higher best estimates. Neutral observers ranked the potential someplace in between.

These results, in combination with many other negotiation experiences, suggest that advocates tend to overestimate the attractiveness of their alternatives to negotiated agreement. If each side has an inflated expectation of its alternatives, no zone of possible agreement for negotiation may exist. Awareness of this common bias dictates a conscious attempt to be more realistic about one's own case, not to "believe one's own line" too much, and to be aware and seek to alter counterparts' estimates of their alternatives. * * *

Lax and Sebenius, The Power of Alternatives or the Limits of Negotiation, 1 Neg.J. 163, 169–170 (1985).

Despite the subjectivity of decision analysis, it can help litigants to think clearly about their disputes. Litigation analysis can help to reduce uncertainties, force clear thinking about a complex decision and initiate discussion about the strengths and weaknesses of one's case. By asking basic questions—Does the tree include all of the ultimate issues that may impact the outcome of the litigation? Are all the influencing factors represented? Do the probabilities seem reasonable?—a lawyer can test whether her decision tree is sound.

2.   As the example of Tammy's litigation illustrates, a party's risk preferences can greatly influence the decision to settle. In general, do you think plaintiffs or defendants are more likely to exhibit risk aversion—to be willing to settle for a sure amount rather than gamble on the prospect of gaining a greater (or paying a lesser) amount? Why?

As we explore in Section C, below, psychological research has shown that people seem prone to take a sure gain over a gamble but to be risk preferring when trying to avoid a sure loss. This effect can have profound implications for dispute resolution. Professor Jeff Rachlinski, for example, tested the effect using the following hypotheticals. How would you behave in each of these two situations?

Version 1:

Imagine you are the plaintiff in a copyright infringement lawsuit. You are suing for the $400,000 that the defendant allegedly earned by violating the copyright. Trial is in two days and the defendant has offered to pay $200,000 as a final settlement. If you turn it down, you believe that you will face a trial where you have a 50% chance of winning a $400,000 award.

Do you accept the settlement?

Version 2:

>   Imagine you are the defendant in a copyright infringement lawsuit. You are being sued for the $400,000 that you allegedly earned by violating the copyright. Trial is in two days and the plaintiff has offered to accept $200,000 as a final settlement. If you turn it down, you believe that you will face a trial where you have a 50% chance of losing a $400,000 award.

Do you agree to pay the settlement?

Rachlinski, Gains, Losses, and the Psychology of Litigation, 70 S.Cal.L.Rev. 113, 127–128 (1996). See also Kahneman and Tversky, Choices, Values, and Frames, 39 Am. Psychologist 341, 342–344 (1984); Kahneman and Tversky, Prospect Theory: An Analysis of Decision Under Risk, 47 Econometrica 263, 268–269 (1979); Tversky and Kahneman, The Framing of Decisions and the Psychology of Choice, 211 Sci. 453 (1981).

These two hypotheticals are economically identical—in each, the expected value of proceeding to court is $200,000. Both the plaintiff and the defendant must choose between gambling on winning (or not losing) the $400,000 and walking away with a sure $200,000.

Yet when Rachlinski ran these hypotheticals with first-year Cornell Law School students, he found that 77% of the plaintiffs (Version 1) chose to settle while only 31% of the defendants (Version 2) settled. Psychological "framing effects" most likely account for the difference: plaintiffs frame their choice as between a sure gain and a gamble on a larger gain (and are risk averse and prone to take the sure gain), whereas defendants frame their choice as between a sure loss and a gamble on avoiding loss (and are risk seeking in hoping to avoid the sure loss). For further variations on this theme, see Korobkin and Guthrie, Psychological Barriers to Litigation Settlement: An Experimental Approach, 93 Mich.L.Rev. 107, 133 (1994).

Defendants' actual litigation behavior seems to follow the predictions of this theory. Rachlinsky notes that a study of litigation behavior found that defendants' final offer of settlement was consistently below the ultimate jury award. This is what we would expect given framing effects: risk-seeking defendants trying to avoid sure losses are likely to be reluctant to settle and therefore offer less than the expected value of litigation. See Rachlinski, Gains, Losses, and the Psychology of Litigation, 70 S.Cal.L.Rev. 113, 149–150 (1996). See also Gross and Syverud, Getting to No: A Study of Settlement Negotiations and the Selection of Cases for Trial, 90 Mich. L.Rev. 319 (1991).

3. A litigant should factor several additional considerations into her litigation analysis. Transaction costs such as attorney's fees, court costs and emotional strain will reduce the value of any award secured through litigation. In addition, a litigant must consider the time value of money in comparing a settlement offer to the promise of a litigated victory. A dollar received today is worth more than a dollar received a year from now, because with prudent investment you can earn returns on the dollar over the course of the year. Thus, the expected value of litigation must be converted into a present value. To do so requires first determining the *discount rate*—the annual rate of interest you assume you could earn on the money were it received today. The present value is then calculated with the following formula: Present Value = Future Value / $(1+r)^n$, where r = rate expressed as a decimal and n = number of periods. For example, if Tammy's case would take three years to litigate, her expected value is $308,700 (not considering risk preferences), and her discount rate is ten percent, the present value of her expected return from her litigation alternative is roughly $232,000.[12] If she invested $232,000 today she would have $308,000 in three years. This is a dramatic difference, and must be taken into account when comparing any settlement offer to the possibility of continuing with litigation.[13]

Because the time value of money can so change the present value of a decision to continue litigation, whether a damage award may include pre-judgment interest can be extremely important. Courts generally award pre-judgment interest in contract cases, and, in some jurisdictions, in non-contract cases involving wrongful death, personal injury, or property damage. Pre-judgment interest awards are usually based solely on pecuniary or compensatory damages, not punitive or other non-compensatory damages. Without the threat of a pre-judgment interest award, of course, a defendant has a great incentive not to settle: the interest-free use of the defendant's money during the litigation. If pre-judgment interest is available, however, and if the pre-judgment interest rate equals the actual interest rate in the marketplace, a plaintiff should not need to discount his or her expected value of settlement to account for the time value of money. This obviously can have a great effect on the settlement decision. But see Bernstein, Understanding the Limits of Court–Connected ADR: A Critique of Federal Court–Annexed Arbitration Programs, 141 U.Pa.L.Rev. 2169 n.231 (1993) (noting that courts often award pre-judgment interest at below market rates, benefiting defendants).

4. What would the decision tree in Tammy's litigation look like if you added the following issue to it? Assuming the probability estimates given are accurate, what is the expected value of Tammy's case when you take this additional issues into account?

Tammy's lawyer intends to file a discovery motion seeking access to the hospital's internal peer review board records regarding Tammy's case. This is a fairly controversial legal question in many states. On the one hand, the medical profession insists that internal peer review documents should be confidential to permit doctors to critique and learn from each

---

12. $308,700 / (1 + .10)^3 = $232,000.

13. It can sometimes be helpful to be able to calculate the *future* value of a present settlement offer. The formula for future value is simply: Future Value = Present Value x $(1 + r)^n$.

other without the threat of their communications surfacing in a later lawsuit. On the other hand, plaintiffs insist that society will most benefit if doctors feel pressure to change their ways from outside, not merely inside, their profession. Tammy's attorney believes that she is forty percent likely to win this motion (and sixty percent likely to lose). If the discovery motion is granted, however, Tammy's attorney believes that the likelihood of establishing that Dr. Sander's negligence caused Lyla harm will rise to ninety percent instead of seventy percent. If the motion is denied, the probability of establishing causation remains seventy percent, as shown in Figure 3.

5. For more in-depth discussion of decision trees and litigation analysis, see Victor, Litigation Risk Analysis and ADR, in ADR Practice Book 308 (1990); Aaron and Hoffer, Decision Analysis as a Method of Evaluating the Trial Alternative, in Mediating Legal Disputes 307 (1996); Hoffer, Decision Analysis as a Mediator's Tool, 1 Harv.Neg.L.Rev. 113 (1996); Victor, The Proper Use of Decision Analysis to Assist Litigation Strategy, 40 Bus.Law 617 (1984); Raiffa, The Art and Science of Negotiation 30 (1982).

B. STRATEGY

That negotiations can have value-creating opportunities or integrative potential in addition to distributive issues explains their underlying economic structure, but does not necessarily dictate the choice of strategy. Negotiators must constantly choose how to approach a given bargaining situation. All things being equal, most of us prefer more money (or whatever else is in dispute) rather than less; negotiators generally seek the best deal they can for themselves. The constant question, then, is whether trying to find integrative trades—expanding the pie—will lead you to a bigger slice, or whether bargaining hard from the outset will maximize your return in a given negotiation. Here we explore three common negotiation approaches: hard or competitive positional bargaining, "soft" or compromising positional bargaining, and problem-solving.

1. POSITIONAL BARGAINING

Roger Fisher, William Ury and Bruce Patton's negotiation text Getting to Yes labeled as "positional bargaining" the traditional haggling that most people associate with negotiation.

Roger Fisher, William Ury and Bruce Patton, Getting to Yes

3–4 (2d ed. 1991).

Whether a negotiation concerns a contract, a family quarrel, or a peace settlement among nations, people routinely engage in positional bargaining. Each side takes a position, argues for it, and makes concessions to reach a compromise. The classic example of this negotiating minuet is the haggling that takes place between a customer and the proprietor of a secondhand store:

Customer	Shopkeeper
How much do you want for this brass dish?	
	That is a beautiful antique, isn't it? I guess I could let it go for $75.
Oh come on, it's dented. I'll give you $15.	
	Really! I might consider a serious offer, but $15 certainly isn't serious.
Well, I could go to $20, but I would never pay anything like $75. Quote me a realistic price.	
	You drive a hard bargain, young lady. $60 cash, right now.
$25.	
	It cost me a great deal more than that. Make me a *serious* offer.
$37.50. That's the highest I will go.	
	Have you noticed the engraving on that dish? Next year pieces like that will be worth twice what you pay today.

And so it goes, on and on. * * *

a.   HARD POSITIONAL BARGAINING

We first explore "hard" or competitive positional bargaining. A negotiator employing this strategy stakes out a position and demands concessions. Usually the negotiator starts with an extreme position and concedes slowly. He may make threats to walk away from the negotiation or use commitment tactics to pressure the other side. The following excerpts explore the tactics and mindset associated with this approach.

Donald G. Gifford, A Context–Based Theory of Strategy Selection in Legal Negotiation

46 Ohio St.L.J. 41, 48–52 (1985).

* * * The basic premise underlying the competitive strategy is that all gains for one's own client are obtained at the expense of the other party.

The strategy aims to convince the opposing party that her settlement alternative is not as advantageous as she previously thought. Competitive tactics are designed to lessen the opponent's confidence in her case, thereby inducing her to settle for less than she originally asked. The competitive negotiator moves "psychologically against the other person," with behavior designed to unnerve the opponent. Competitive negotiators expect similar behavior from their opponents and therefore mistrust them. In undermining their opponents' confidence, competitive negotiators employ a strategy which often includes the following tactics:

1. a high initial demand;

2. limited disclosure of information regarding facts and one's own preferences;

3. few and small concessions;

4. threats and arguments; and

5. apparent commitment to positions during the negotiation process.

A negotiator who utilizes the competitive strategy begins with a high initial demand. Empirical research repeatedly demonstrates a significant positive relationship between a negotiator's original demand and his payoff. A high initial demand conceals the negotiator's minimum settlement point and allows the negotiator to grant concessions during the negotiation process and still achieve a favorable result. The negotiator's opening position may also include a false issue—a demand that the negotiator does not really care about, but one that can be traded for concessions from the opponent during the negotiation. Generally, the more that the negotiator insists upon a particular demand early in the negotiation, the larger the concession that ultimately will be obtained from the opponent in exchange for dropping that demand. In addition, the opponent may have evaluated the negotiator's case more favorably than the negotiator has; a high demand protects the negotiator from quickly agreeing to a less favorable settlement than that which he might later obtain. If the demand is high but credible, the opponent's response to the demand may also educate the negotiator about how the opponent evaluates her own case.

The competitive negotiator selectively and strategically shares information with his opponent. He does not disclose the least favorable terms to which his client would agree, that is, his minimum reservation point. * * * Conversely, the competitive negotiator selectively discloses information which strengthens his case and which undermines the opponent's case.

* * * The competitive negotiator makes concessions reluctantly, because concessions may weaken one's position through both "position loss" and "image loss." Position loss occurs because in most negotiations a norm exists against withdrawing a concession. Further, an early concession results in an opportunity loss for something that might have been extracted in exchange for the concession later in the negotiation process. Image loss occurs because after a concession, the opponent perceives that the negotiator is flexible; in the opponent's mind this may suggest that further

concessions can be obtained. * * * When possible, the competitive negotiator seeks to create the illusion in his opponent's eye that he is making a concession without diminishing his own satisfaction. This is done by either conceding on an issue the negotiator does not care about or appearing to make a concession without really making one.

The competitive negotiator obviously strives to force his opponent into making as many and as large concessions as possible while he makes few concessions, small in degree. To force concessions from his opponent, he employs both arguments and threats. In negotiations, arguments are communications intended to persuade the opponent to draw logical inferences from known data. For example, a plaintiff's attorney might describe a favorable eyewitness account of a collision and ask the defense counsel to infer the probability that her client will be found liable. * * * A threat, on the other hand, is a communication intended to inform the opponent that unless she agrees to a settlement acceptable to the negotiator, the negotiator or his client will act to the opponent's detriment. For example, a union negotiator might threaten that the union will strike if management refuses to make wage concessions.

* * * To the extent that the success of a negotiation strategy is measured by the payoff in a single negotiation involving the division of limited resources between two parties, studies of simulated negotiations suggest that the competitive strategy yields better results than other strategies for the negotiator. However, the competitive strategy suffers severe disadvantages. The likelihood of impasse is much greater for negotiators who employ the competitive strategy than for those who use other approaches. Competitive tactics engender tension and mistrust between the parties, which can give the appearance that the parties are farther apart than they really are. These negative attitudes may carry over into matters other than the current negotiation and may make continuing relationships difficult.

Gary Goodpaster, A Primer on Competitive Bargaining
J. of Disp.Res. 325, 346–348 (1996).

Generally, the competitive negotiator seeks to persuade the other party that she will not agree to or settle above or below a certain point. In devising a negotiating strategy, the competitor uses some general approaches and rules of thumb. These are:

Negotiation is an information game. The competitor treats negotiation as a game in which the party with the most accurate information wins. Thus, the competitor either seeks to gather as much information as possible while giving away as little as possible or gives and manipulates information in such a way that the other party is led indirectly to draw conclusions the competitor wishes it to draw. Realizing that the other party will decide what to do on the basis of what he or she thinks and believes, the competitor seeks to shape, manage, and manipulate the other party's perceptions of the situation and that party's available choices.

Take an opening position at the margin (high or low openers). The negotiator who opens with a high or low offer and makes few and small concessions generally has the most success in negotiation. As used here, "opens high" or "opens low" means at the extreme or far end of the potential bargaining range but sufficiently within the range to retain credibility. The competitive negotiator prepares an opening position by first estimating her best possible deal and then staking out an initial position considerably beyond that estimate while developing justifications for the latter position.

Treat concessions as a way to gain and disclose information. Concessions convey information about what a party wants and values, about the party's preferences and intentions, and about the party's perception of the other party. The skillful, competitive negotiator "reads" concessions to infer this information and plans her own concessions to give the other party only those impressions she wants it to have. Concessions are not only, and perhaps are not even principally, a way to give something to the other party to narrow differences, but are also a way to gain advantage. A skillful competitor crafts concessions to shape the perceptions and expectations of the other party.

Hang tough on concessions; do not make concessions one-for-one nor trade concessions equally. Concessions seem to beget concessions. In general, an expectation exists in bargaining that when one party makes a concession, then the other party will also make a concession in return. * * * Notwithstanding this expectation, it is not *always* necessary to give a concession in exchange for receiving one. * * *

* * *

Make small, infrequent, and declining concessions. As a corollary to the foregoing, the competitive negotiator makes it a practice to make small concessions and force the other party to work hard to gain any concessions. The aim is to send the message that there is not much to give: if there is to be a bargain, the other party will have to move much further than the competitor. The competitive negotiator also makes concessions in declining increments in order to suggest a convergence on his apparent bottom line. * * *

One effect of "hanging tough" and making small concessions is to shape or alter the other party's expectations or aspirations about what it can get out of the negotiation. Treating a negotiator's concessions as information about what can be achieved, the other party may alter its expectations in a way favorable to the negotiator.

Select an opening position by reference to the mid-point rule. Once two settlement offers are on the table, the natural settling point is the mid-point. This rule of thumb, while not always true, is true often enough that competitive negotiators can use it to good effect. Typically, the competitive negotiator will allow, or more likely, *get* the other party to make the first offer. This allows the competitor to set his or her offer at the most advantageous point, given the likelihood that once both offers are out, the negotiators will settle in the middle. Alternatively, a competitive negotiator simply starts with an extreme offer, hoping that the other party is either innocent or will overvalue the item being negotiated and will open with an offer more favorable to the competitor. In effect, the competitor's high opener draws the other party's opener in its direction. * * *

Link positions and concessions to convincing justifications or rationales. Experienced competitive negotiators know that they may not be able to persuade the other party to agree to settle at any particular point in the perceived bargaining range simply by hanging tough. * * * In bargaining situations, people want justifications for positions taken. Understanding this, in preparing for a negotiation, the competitor picks positions on the bargaining continuum that he can defend with some plausible justification. * * *

Thomas C. Schelling, An Essay on Bargaining

in Thomas C. Schelling, The Strategy of Conflict 22–28 (1960).

"Bargaining power," "bargaining strength," "bargaining skill" suggest that the advantage goes to the powerful, the strong, or the skillful. It does, of course, if those qualities are defined to mean only that negotiations are won by those who win. But, if the terms imply that it is an advantage to be more intelligent or more skillful in debate, or to have more financial resources, more physical strength, more military potency, or more ability to withstand losses, then the term does a disservice. These qualities are by no means universal advantages in bargaining situations; they often have a contrary value.

The sophisticated negotiator may find it difficult to seem as obstinate as a truly obstinate man. If a man knocks at your door and says that he will stab himself on the porch unless given $10, he is more likely to get the $10 if his eyes are bloodshot. The threat of mutual destruction cannot be used to deter an adversary who is too unintelligent to comprehend it or too weak to enforce his will on those he represents. * * *

Bargaining power has also been described as the power to fool and bluff, "the ability to set the best price for yourself and fool the other man into thinking this was your maximum offer." Fooling and bluffing are certainly involved; but there are two kinds of fooling. One is deceiving about the facts; a buyer may lie about his income or misrepresent the size of his family. The other is purely tactical. Suppose each knows everything about the other, and each knows what the other knows. What is there to fool about? The buyer may say that, though he'd really pay up to twenty and the seller knows it, he is firmly resolved as a tactical matter not to budge above sixteen. If the seller capitulates, was he fooled? Or was he convinced of the truth? Or did the buyer really not know what he would do next if the tactic failed? If the buyer really "feels" himself firmly resolved, and bases his resolve on the conviction that the seller will capitulate, and the seller does, the buyer may say afterwards that he was "not fooling."

Whatever has occurred, it is not adequately conveyed by the notion of bluffing and fooling.

How does one person make another believe something? The answer depends importantly on the factual question, "Is it true?" It is easier to prove the truth of something that is true than of something false. To prove the truth about our health we can call on a reputable doctor; to prove the truth about our costs or income we may let the person look at books that have been audited by a reputable firm or the Bureau of Internal Revenue. But to persuade him of something false we may have no such convincing evidence.

When one wishes to persuade someone that he would not pay more than $16,000 for a house that is really worth $20,000 to him, what can he do to take advantage of the usually superior credibility of the truth over a false assertion? Answer: make it true. How can a buyer make it true? If he likes the house because it is near his business, he might move his business, persuading the seller that the house is really now worth only $16,000 to him. This would be unprofitable; he is no better off than if he had paid the higher price.

But suppose the buyer could make an irrevocable and enforceable bet with some third party, duly recorded and certified, according to which he would pay for the house no more than $16,000, or forfeit $5,000. The seller has lost; the buyer need simply present the truth. Unless the seller is enraged and withholds the house in sheer spite, the situation has been rigged against him; the "objective" situation—the buyer's true incentive— has been voluntarily, conspicuously, and irreversibly changed. The seller can take it or leave it. This example demonstrates that if the buyer can accept an irrevocable *commitment* in a way that is unambiguously visible to the seller, he can squeeze the range of indeterminacy down to the point most favorable to him. It also suggests, by its artificiality, that the tactic is one that may or may not be available; whether the buyer can find an effective device for committing himself may depend on who he is, who the seller is, where they live, and a number of legal and institutional arrangements (including, in our artificial example, whether bets are legally enforceable).

If both men live in a culture where "cross my heart" is universally accepted as potent, all the buyer has to do is allege that he will pay no more than $16,000, using this invocation of penalty, and he wins—or at least he wins if the seller does not beat him to it by shouting "$19,000, cross my heart." If the buyer is an agent authorized by a board of directors to buy at $16,000 but not a cent more, and the directors cannot constitutionally meet again for several months and the buyer cannot exceed his authority, and if all this can be made known to the seller, then the buyer "wins"—if, again, the seller has not tied himself up with a commitment to $19,000. Or, if the buyer can assert that he will pay no more than $16,000 so firmly that he would suffer intolerable loss of personal prestige or bargaining reputation by paying more, and if the fact of his paying more would necessarily be known, and if the seller appreciates all this, then a loud declaration by itself may provide the commitment. The device, of course, is a needless surrender of flexibility unless it can be made fully evident and understandable to the seller.

* * *

Some examples may suggest the relevance of the tactic, although an observer can seldom distinguish with confidence the consciously logical, the intuitive, or the inadvertent use of a visible tactic. First, it has not been uncommon for union officials to stir up excitement and determination on the part of the membership during or prior to a wage negotiation. If the union is going to insist on $2 and expects the management to counter with $1.60, an effort is made to persuade the membership not only that the management could pay $2 but even perhaps that the negotiators themselves are incompetent if they fail to obtain close to $2. The purpose—or, rather, a plausible purpose suggested by our analysis—is to make clear to the management that the negotiators could not accept less than $2 *even if they wished to* because they no longer control the members or because they would lose their own positions if they tried. In other words, the negotiators reduce the scope of their own authority and confront the management with the threat of a strike that the union itself cannot avert, even though it was the union's own action that eliminated its power to prevent the strike.

Something similar occurs when the United States Government negotiates with other governments on, say, the uses to which foreign assistance will be put, or tariff reduction. If the executive branch is free to negotiate the best arrangement it can, it may be unable to make any position stick and may end by conceding controversial points because its partners know, or believe obstinately, that the United States would rather concede than terminate the negotiations. But, if the executive branch negotiates under legislative authority, with its position constrained by law, and it is evident that Congress will not be reconvened to change the law within the necessary time period, then the executive branch has a firm position that is visible to its negotiating partners.

When national representatives go to international negotiations knowing that there is a wide range of potential agreement within which the outcome will depend on bargaining, they often seem to create a bargaining position by public statements, statements calculated to arouse a public opinion that permits no concessions to be made. If a binding public opinion can be cultivated and made evident to the other side, the initial position can thereby be made visibly "final."

These examples have certain characteristics in common. First, they clearly depend not only on incurring a commitment but on communicating it persuasively to the other party. Second, it is by no means easy to establish the commitment, nor is it entirely clear to either of the parties concerned just how strong the commitment is. Third, similar activity may be available to the parties on both sides. Fourth, the possibility of commitment, though perhaps available to both sides, is by no means equally available; the ability of a democratic government to get itself tied by public opinion may be different from the ability of a totalitarian government to incur such a commitment. Fifth, they all run the risk of establishing an immovable position that goes beyond the ability of the other to concede, and thereby provoke the likelihood of stalemate or breakdown.

NOTES AND QUESTIONS

1. Many negotiation analysts have described the various tactics that hard positional bargainers employ. See Churchman, Negotiation: Process, Tactics, Theory (1995) (describing fifty negotiation tactics); Genn, Hard Bargaining: Out of Court Settlement in Personal Injury Actions 134–139 (1987) (discussing hard bargaining in the litigation context); Reitz (ed.), Negotiation: Theory and Practice 49–67 (1985) (discussing aggressive and coercive tactics); Pruitt, Negotiation Behavior 72–76 (1981).

Roger Volkema lists eight common difficult tactics: an exaggerated first offer, speed-ups (setting false deadlines to impose time pressure), delays, drawing artificial bottom lines, exaggerating your BATNA, making false concessions to coax someone into reciprocating, inducing the other to invest time and effort—so that they'll then keep bargaining, and false authority limits. See Volkema, The Negotiation Toolkit 78–91 (1999). Mnookin, Peppet and Tulumello list ten: extreme claims followed by small, slow concessions, commitment tactics, take-it-or-leave-it offers, inviting unreciprocated offers, pushing until the other side "flinches," personal insults and feather ruffling, bluffing and lying, threats, belittling the other side's alternatives, and playing good cop, bad cop. See Mnookin, Peppet and Tulumello, Beyond Winning: Negotiating to Create Value in Deals and Disputes 24–25 (2000).

What "hard" positional tactics have you seen? Which do you most fear? Which have you used yourself? What are the advantages of a hard positional strategy? The disadvantages? In what contexts, about what subjects and with what people is this approach suitable? Does a positional strategy lead to fair agreements? To efficient, value-creating or integrative agreements? What different characteristics of a bargaining situation make it easier or more difficult to succeed in using this approach?

2. A hard positional bargainer often attempts to influence the other party's subjective understanding of the bargaining situation. Indeed, the positional strategy can seem like a game of illusions—each side starts with an extreme position and concedes slowly in an attempt to signal to the other that their reservation value is more extreme than it is in reality. The bluffs, threats and positioning characteristic of this approach can be purely arbitrary. I might say that I will take no less than $200,000 for my house, but we both know that I could be lying—I might willingly accept $150,000. See Lax and Sebenius, The Manager as Negotiator 119–121 (1986).

Some tactics, however, aim not at the other side's subjective *perceptions* of the bargaining situation but instead at the negotiation's actual structure. In other words, they attempt to alter the parties' actual reservation values. The Schelling excerpt on commitment tactics illustrates that sometimes limiting one's freedom of action can be of great benefit in negotiations. His example of a house purchase illustrates this counterintuitive notion. By committing to a third party, the house buyer constrains his freedom—because he commits to forfeiting a penalty if he pays more than $16,000—but simultaneously changes his own reservation value and thus the zone of possible agreement. Assuming his third-party commitment really is irrevocable, this tactic is not smoke and mirrors: he has altered the negotiation structure, not merely influenced the other side's perception of it.

When are such tactics commonly used? When are they appropriate or inappropriate?

b.   SOFT POSITIONAL BARGAINING

Although positional bargaining is most often associated with extreme offers, threats, commitment tactics and other attempts to pressure one's opponent to submit, we must note that sometimes negotiators engage in a softer version of the same basic approach to negotiation. That is, they continue to trade offers and concessions—arguing between competing positions—but they do so in a more conciliatory way. Roger Fisher and his co-authors explain this in Getting to Yes:

> Many people recognize the high costs of hard positional bargaining, particularly on the parties and their relationship. They hope to avoid them by following a more gentle style of negotiation. Instead of seeing the other side as adversaries, they prefer to see them as friends. Rather than emphasizing a goal of victory, they emphasize the necessity of reaching agreement. In a soft negotiating game the standard moves are to make offers and concessions, to trust the other side, to be friendly, and to yield as necessary to avoid confrontation.

> * * *

> The soft negotiating game emphasizes the importance of building and maintaining a relationship. Within families and among friends much negotiation takes place in this way. The process tends to be efficient, at least to the extent of producing results quickly. As each party competes with the other in being more generous and more forthcoming, an agreement becomes highly likely. But it may not be a wise one. * * * [A]ny negotiation primarily concerned with the relationship runs the risk of producing a sloppy [e.g., economically inefficient] agreement.

> More seriously, pursuing a soft and friendly form of positional bargaining makes you vulnerable to someone who plays a hard game of positional bargaining. In positional bargaining, a hard game dominates a soft one. If the hard bargainer insists on concessions and makes threats while the soft bargainer yields in order to avoid confrontation and insists on agreement, the negotiating game is biased in favor of the hard player. The process will produce an agreement, although it may not be a wise one. It will certainly be more favorable to the hard

positional bargainer than to the soft one. If your response to sustained, hard positional bargaining is soft positional bargaining, you will probably lose your shirt.

Fisher, Ury and Patton, Getting to Yes 7–9 (2d ed. 1991).

A soft positional bargainer may start reasonably, concede generously and act pleasantly. He may avoid threats and try not to discuss his BATNA—which can sometimes seem threatening to the other side. He may make concessions to preserve his relationship with the other side.

We have all used this approach, and sometimes it has great advantages. If you are negotiating with a friend about where to go for dinner you may simply concede to her wishes rather than hold out for your first choice. Getting your way may not be worth it. The disadvantages, however, are obvious. You may get exploited. And, as with insisting on your position through hard positional bargaining, you may arrive at an inefficient agreement if you merely accept the other person's position rather than probing for integrative possibilities. Perhaps your friend wants Chinese and you want to go to your favorite Italian restaurant. Giving in and going for Chinese doesn't create the most possible value if another option could better meet both of your interests. Perhaps your friend really just wants to eat somewhere nearby because she is tired and doesn't feel like walking far. Maybe you want Italian because you prefer somewhere quiet where you can talk together, and your friend's proposed Chinese restaurant tends to be loud. A third option—the local hamburger joint—may meet these interests and create value. In terms of efficiency, giving in may be no better than holding out.

c. THE FIRST OFFER PROBLEM

A positional strategy—hard or soft—inevitably gives rise to a common negotiation dilemma: who should make the first offer or demand? Imagine responding to an advertisement in your local paper: "Used 27-inch Sony television set for sale. Two years old, good condition. Best offer." You call the owner and talk briefly about the set and its features. But then you hesitate. Should you make an offer? Or wait until the seller states an asking price? What are the advantages and disadvantages of each approach?

Making the first offer can confer several benefits. First, you may be able to anchor the bargaining around your first offer or demand. If you start low—"I'll give you $5 for the television"—your negotiation may center on that starting point and you may get a better price. Conversely, if the seller started high—"I want $150 for the TV, no less"—you might be inclined to revise your expectations upwards and make a counter-offer much closer to his starting point. "Research has shown that individuals often use a salient piece of information as an anchor on which to base their future judgments. Regardless of the level of the anchor, adjustments tend to be insufficient. Thus, different opening offers (anchors) will result in final outcomes which are biased in the direction of that offer." Weingart,

Thompson, Bazerman and Carroll, Tactical Behavior and Negotiation Outcomes, 1 Intl.J. of Conflict Mgt. 7, 9–10 (1990).

The disadvantage with making the first offer is obvious, however. If you offer too much or demand too little, you may exceed the other side's expectation of what is possible in your negotiation. For example, you might offer $50 for the television thinking that you were low-balling, but the other side's reservation value might be only $10. In trying to take advantage of the first offer, you instead give up more than you need to.

Allowing—or requiring—the other person to "go first" thus has advantages. They might similarly "over-offer" and exceed your expectations. And both sides know this. As a result, negotiations sometimes turn comical as each side tries to persuade the other to make the first move. Like two wrestlers circling in a ring, neither negotiator wants to jump first for fear that the other side will exploit their volunteerism.

Consider the following excerpts.

Harry Edwards and James J. White, The Lawyer as Negotiator
115–116 (1977).

Almost without exception it is desirable to cause the opposing party in a negotiation to make the first realistic offer. If one has made a serious miscalculation about his position, the opponent's first offer may save a considerable sum. Assume for example that a new and totally inexperienced law school graduate is seeking a job in a middle-sized city. From his very limited perspective he believes that the yearly wage for beginning lawyers in that town is $10,000. He is pleasantly surprised therefore when his prospective employer offers him $17,000 to begin. If the employee had made the first offer, it would have cost him $7,000 and perhaps more. Thus, causing the opponent to make the first realistic offer is most helpful in circumstances in which one regards his opponent's case as stronger than the opponent regards it.

A standard defense to an opponent's demand for a first offer is to give him a large demand. Thus, if convention calls for one party to make the first move, he may choose to make that move by giving an outrageous demand simply to get the negotiation underway. Such an exchange is commonplace in the negotiation of personal injury cases in which the plaintiff's lawyer will often start with the demand far in excess of anything he thinks the defense will grant him. In fact such a demand is not a first offer at all but simply a way of instituting negotiation without having to set the level at the outset.

In contexts other than personal injury such as commercial litigation and the purchase or sale of goods or land, the large demand rule is not widely used. One who makes an outrageous demand in such circumstances may find that he has killed the deal entirely by signaling to the other party that he is not truly interested. For that reason it is more important in those situations that one concentrate on getting the first offer from the opponent.

The challenging question is not why one wants the first offer, but how he procures that offer from his opponent. In some situations one can rely upon the customary practice to require the other side to make the first offer. For example it is customary practice in the employment field for the employer to commence with an offer. Usually the employee is not expected to come up with an initial request of a specific dollar figure. There are similar customs in other areas.

Of course the simplest method of procuring the first offer in contexts in which there is no convention is simply to ask the opponent to state his price. An experienced negotiator is likely to reply that he is willing to offer, "Whatever you think it is worth," but the inexperienced negotiator may simply respond with a realistic first offer.

David Lax & James Sebenius, The Manager as Negotiator
132–134 (1986).

One common school of thought on how to choose offers is nicely expressed by Henry Kissinger:

> If agreement is usually found between two starting positions, there is no point in making moderate offers. Good bargaining technique would suggest a point of departure far more extreme than what one is willing to accept. The more outrageous the initial proposition the better is the prospect that what one "really" wants will be considered a compromise.

But, beyond the risk of souring the atmosphere, such tactics may stimulate equally extreme counteroffers that may simply cancel the intended effects and increase the chances of impasse. If one invests an extreme offer with a great deal of credibility, eventual movement may damage the credibility of subsequent "firm" stands.

If this is so and Kissinger's advice need not always apply, is there anything to guide the choice of offers?

CHOOSING OPENING OFFERS

* * *

The choice of an effective opening offer and even the decision whether or not to make the first offer should also reflect a negotiator's perceptions about the counterpart's reservation value. When quite uncertain about the counterpart's reservation value, the negotiator may be better off letting the counterpart make the initial offer. Why? First, the negotiator hopes to gain information about the bargaining range from the offer. Second, the uncertainty inherently implies that there is a good chance a "moderate" opening offer would be too high or too low. An offer much worse than the counterpart's reservation value may provoke anger, sour the atmosphere, and raise questions of seriousness or good faith. For example, if [a] building owner's reservation value were much higher than [a buyer's] $320,000 offer, he might be offended by it and feel that the offering group is not really serious. Yet offering too high a price, say $550,000, runs the opposite risk: if the owner would have accepted $450,000, the buyers would have overpaid by $100,000. Thus, by refraining from making a first offer, a negotiator who is quite uncertain about the counterpart's reservation value avoids giving too much away and offering insultingly little.

But, the negotiator who defers when uncertain about the counterpart's reservation value bears another risk: his perceptions of the bargaining set may be manipulated by the opening offer. Thus, in this situation, many buyers make very low offers but try to make them seem soft or flexible. They hope to substantially reduce the counterpart's aspirations without being insulting, without unnecessarily giving up value, or risking committing to an unrealistic point.

By contrast, if the negotiator becomes fairly confident that the counterpart's reservation value lies in a small range, than he may clearly be best off making the opening offer. In this case, he does not expect to gain much information about the bargaining set from his counterpart's initial offer. Moreover, he is not likely to run the risks of either an insultingly low offer or an overly generous opening. For example, if the [buyer] attempting to buy the building were fairly confident, after studying the market and the actual competing potential buyers, that the owner's reservation value was between $425,000 and $475,000, the firm might offer something below this range. For example, the firm might offer $400,000, which it feels has a 90 percent chance of being below the owner's reservation value; or it might go lower still. Given the [buyer's] assessment, such an offer is likely to be outside the bargaining set, is unlikely to leave much profit for the owner, is close enough to entice him to bargain, and is chosen to guide the final agreement to a point just above the owner's reservation value.

Experimental results in distributive bargaining suggest that, within limits, the higher the opening offer, the better the outcome. But, what is acceptably high and what is insultingly extreme depends on the assumed norms. When making an offer to another member of the diamond industry in Switzerland, being 2 percent below the asking price might be insulting; when buying a used car in the United States, offers 20 to 40 percent below the asking price can be reasonable. Couching potentially extreme offers in "reasonable" trappings by appeal to "fair" principles and presenting them in a low-key manner may help mitigate the risk of adverse reaction. Finally, what is "high" depends on the degree of uncertainty about the counterpart's reservation value. Thus, a seller might choose an offer she thinks is 90 to 95 percent likely to be above the buyer's reservation value. The offer is likely to be much higher when she is more uncertain than when she is fairly confident.

ANCHORING

People often deal poorly with uncertainty. * * * When many people assess an uncertain quantity, they tend to jump to a point estimate of it and then adjust a bit around it to account for the uncertainty. By influencing a counterpart's point estimate of the quantity, a negotiator can locate where the small range of uncertainty will lie. One can thus "anchor" another's beliefs about the quantity in a way favorable to one's bargaining position.

For example, in one experiment, groups of college students were asked to name the percentage of the countries in the United Nations that are African. Before answering the question, a roulette wheel (modified to have the numbers one through one hundred) was spun in front of the students. For one typical group, the wheel stopped at 10 percent; for another group it landed at 65 percent. The first group was asked if the percentage of U.N. nations that are African was higher or lower than 10 percent (the number chosen by the spin of the wheel); the other group was asked whether the percentage was higher or lower than 65 percent. Then discussion was allowed to take place. In all other ways the groups were treated identically. Surprisingly, the first group's estimates were strikingly lower than those of the second: the mean of the first group's estimates was 24 percent while the mean of the second group's estimate was 45 percent! Thus, the clearly irrelevant piece of information—a randomly chosen starting point of 10 percent versus 65 percent—seemed strongly to anchor their perceptions about the proportion of U.N. member nations that are African.

A negotiator is typically uncertain about his counterpart's reservation value and aspirations. His own aspirations follow, in part, from these uncertain perceptions. And * * * social psychological experiments on "limits" (bottom lines or reservation values) suggest that [bargainers will often change their reservation value in the face of new information.]

When there is considerable uncertainty, a strong opening offer can sharply anchor perceptions of the bargaining set and aspirations. Prenegotiation tactics, initial discussions, and opening offers by the counterparts can favorably anchor a negotiator's perception of these values, cause him to reduce his own aspirations, and alter his reservation value. The building owner who demands $600,000, argues forcefully that this price is fair and reasonable, refuses for weeks to listen to other offers, and keeps returning discussions to his $600,000 price may strongly anchor toward $600,000 potential buyers' perceptions of what the owner will accept. Their original aspiration to pay much less will also likely be revised.

NOTES AND QUESTIONS

1. Do you agree with Edwards and White that making the first offer is a disadvantage best avoided? Or with Lax and Sebenius that it can confer benefits? Which makes you most comfortable? Does your answer depend on factors such as what issue is under negotiation or with whom you are negotiating?

2. Lax and Sebenius describe the anchoring effect that a first offer can have on subsequent negotiations. One study in the legal context found that subjects were nearly twice as likely to accept a settlement offer of $12,000 in a hypothetical product defect case if the offeror initially offered $2,000 (and then increased his offer to $12,000) than if the offeror initially offered $10,000 (and then increased his offer to $12,000). The researchers argue that the $2,000 initial offer anchors the plaintiff-offeree's expectations at a low figure, making the subsequent large increase seem like a major concession. See Korobkin and Guthrie, Opening Offers and Out of Court Settlement: A Little Moderation Might Not Go a Long Way, 10 Ohio St. J.Disp.Res. 1 (1994).

3. As we've seen, bargaining over a single issue—such as money—is difficult in part because every move you make sends signals to the other side about what your next move may be. If you make too generous an offer up front, for example, the other side will realize that you're willing to pay more than they expected and may try to take advantage of you. If you're too stingy, however, the other side may perceive you as overly zealous, not serious about settling, or personally offensive, and may stop negotiating with you. Thus, the very act of trying to settle may make settlement more difficult.

Professors Gertner and Miller have argued that using "settlement escrows" can help to overcome such strategic difficulties and to promote settlement. To create a settlement escrow one would simply appoint a mediator or agent to accept cash settlement offers from both parties to a lawsuit. If the offers did not "cross," the neutral would indicate that there was no settlement but would not disclose the amounts of the offers. If the offers crossed, the neutral would impose a settlement at the midpoint of the two offers. See Gertner and Miller, Settlement Escrows, 24 J. Leg.Stud. 87 (1995).

Not surprisingly, several Internet services now offer systems that operate much like these settlement escrows. The most common are online blind bidding mechanisms. When two disputing parties sign on to use one of these services, each is typically instructed to submit, in private, their offer or demand. The system's computer then compares these submissions and informs the parties either that their figures overlap—in which case the case is settled—or that the figures do not overlap—in which case the parties may have an opportunity to try again.

On www.clicknsettle.com, for example, the system settles a case in one of two ways. First, if a plaintiff's demand is lower than the defendant's offer, the case is settled for the plaintiff's demand. Second, if at any time the plaintiff's demand comes within 30 percent of the defendant's offer, the computer splits the difference between demand and offer and settles the case at that mid-point. The bidding process is blind; at no point does the computer reveal to you what your opponent has bid. Bids need not proceed in fixed rounds. Instead, a plaintiff could, for example, lower her demand several times unilaterally before getting a response from the defendant. On clicknsettle.com, offers must increase (and demands decrease) in no less than 5 percent increments.

Another site, www.cybersettle.com, is designed to aid settlement of insurance-related claims. The insurance carrier initiates the process by submitting claim information and three offers—one for each round of a blind three-round bidding process. The service then notifies the plaintiff's attorney, who may log on and make an online demand. If the insurance carrier's offer is greater than 85 percent of the plaintiff's demand, the case is automatically settled for the average of that amount (85 percent of the demand) and the offer. For example, if the carrier offered $90,000 and the plaintiff demanded $100,000, the case would settle because the offer is greater than $85,000 (85 percent of $100,000). The settlement amount would be $87,500 (the average of $90,000 and $85,000).

For a sample of such services, see www.clicknsettle.com; www.cybersettle.com; www.ussettle.com. Some sites assist users by offering free, secure, online communication services so that parties may negotiate directly. If parties fail to reach agreement, the site may refer them to a mediator. See www.squaretrade.com. For an overview of online systems, see Katsh and Rifkin, Online Dispute Resolution: Resolving Conflicts in Cyberspace (2001); Hang, Online Dispute Resolution Systems: The Future of Cyberspace Law, 41 Santa Clara L.Rev. 837 (2001).

4. This first offer problem is one of the reasons that negotiators often adopt a hard positional strategy and begin with *extreme* first offers. After all, starting with a reasonable position may just allow the other side to take advantage of you. Rather than fretting about how much to offer, however, or about whether to move first or not, Roger Fisher recommends changing the game completely—not engaging in a positional strategy (soft or hard) to begin with:

> There is little doubt that if both parties are playing the haggling game of positional bargaining, the best position to start with is often an extreme one. Rather than denying that statement, we question whether haggling is the best game to play.
>
> *Getting to YES* probably overstates the case against positional bargaining. The New York Stock Exchange demonstrates that thousands of transactions a day can successfully be concluded without discussing interests and with little concern for ongoing relationships. Yet most cases of what we all think of as negotiations involve more than one issue and also involve ongoing matters of implementation or future dealing. In such cases, I would suggest that taking an extreme position is rarely the best first move. Coming up with an extreme and unilaterally determined answer before understanding the other side's perception of the problem involves risks to one's credibility, to a cooperative problem-solving relationship, and to the efficient reaching of an agreement.

Fisher, Beyond *YES*, 1 Neg.J. 67, 67 (1985). In the next section we turn to an alternative to positional negotiation: a problem-solving strategy.

2.   PROBLEM-SOLVING

Whereas negotiations typically focus on the parties' positions, offers and counteroffers, a problem-solving strategy centers more on the parties' underlying interests. The goal is to search for trades and creative agreements that can create value and to deal with distributive issues as amicably and efficiently as possible. This strategy does not *depend* upon there being integrative possibilities to create value, but it certainly is well suited to such negotiations. In this section we explore the basic components of a problem-solving approach.

a.   THE BASICS OF A PROBLEM-SOLVING APPROACH

Roger Fisher, William Ury and Bruce Patton, Getting to Yes

40–50 (2d ed. 1991).

For a wise solution reconcile interests, not positions

* * * Since the parties' problem appears to be a conflict of positions, and since their goal is to agree on a position, they naturally tend to think and talk about positions—and in the process often reach an impasse.

Interests define the problem. The basic problem in a negotiation lies not in conflicting positions, but in the conflict between each side's needs, desires, concerns, and fears. The parties may say: "I am trying to get him to stop that real estate development next door."

Or "We disagree. He wants $100,000 for the house. I won't pay a penny more than $95,000."

But on a more basic level the problem is: "He needs the cash; I want peace and quiet."

Or "He needs at least $100,000 to settle with he ex-wife. I told my family that I wouldn't pay more than $95,000 for a house."

Such desires and concerns are *interests*. Interests motivate people; they are the silent movers behind the hubbub of positions. Your position is something you have decided upon. Your interests are what caused you to so decide.

The Egyptian–Israeli peace treaty blocked out at Camp David in 1978 demonstrates the usefulness of looking behind positions. Israel had occupied the Egyptian Sinai Peninsula since the Six Day War of 1967. When Egypt and Israel sat down together in 1978 to negotiate a peace, their positions were incompatible. Israel insisted on keeping some of the Sinai. Egypt, on the other hand, insisted that every inch of the Sinai be returned to Egyptian sovereignty. Time and again, people drew maps showing possible boundary lines that would divide the Sinai between Egypt and Israel. Compromising in this way was wholly unacceptable to Egypt. To go back to the situation as it was in 1967 was equally unacceptable to Israel.

Looking at their interests instead of their positions made it possible to develop a solution. Israel's interest lay in security; they did not want Egyptian tanks poised on their border ready to roll across at any time. Egypt's interest lay in sovereignty; the Sinai had been part of Egypt since the time of the Pharaohs. After centuries of domination by Greeks, Romans, Turks, French, and British, Egypt had only recently regained full sovereignty and was not about to cede territory to another foreign conqueror.

At Camp David, President Sadat of Egypt and Prime Minister Begin of Israel agreed to a plan that would return the Sinai to complete Egyptian sovereignty and, by demilitarizing large areas, would still assure Israeli security. The Egyptian flag would fly everywhere, but Egyptian tanks would be nowhere near Israel.

Reconciling interests rather than positions works for two reasons. First, for every interest there usually exist several possible positions that could satisfy it. All too often people simply adopt the most obvious position, as Israel did, for example, in announcing that they intended to keep part of the Sinai. When you do look behind opposed positions for the motivating interests, you can often find an alternative position which meets not only your interests but theirs as well. * * *

* * *

[Second, in] many negotiations * * * a close examination of the underlying interests will reveal the existence of many more interests that are shared or compatible than ones that are opposed.

* * *

Agreement is often made possible precisely because interests differ. You and a shoe-seller may both like money and shoes. Relatively, his interest in the fifty dollars exceeds his interest in the shoes. For you, the situation is reversed: you like the shoes better than the fifty dollars. Hence the deal. Shared interests and differing but complementary interests can both serve as the building blocks for a wise agreement.

How do you identify interests?

The benefit of looking behind positions for interests is clear. * * * How do you go about understanding the interests involved in a negotiation, remembering that figuring out *their* interests will be at least as important as figuring out *yours*?

Ask "Why?" One basic technique is to put yourself in their shoes. Examine each position they take, and ask yourself "Why?" * * *

Ask "Why not?" Think about their choice. One of the most useful ways to uncover interests is first to identify the basic decision that those on the other side probably see you asking them for, and then to ask yourself why they have not made that decision. What interests of theirs stand in the way? If you are trying to change their minds, the starting point is to figure out where their minds are now.

* * *

The most powerful interests are basic human needs. In searching for the basic interests behind a declared position, look particularly for those bedrock concerns which motivate all people. If you can take care of such basic needs, you increase the chance both of reaching agreement and, if an agreement is reached, of the other side's keeping to it. Basic human needs include:

— security

— economic well-being

— a sense of belonging

— recognition

— control over one's life

As fundamental as they are, basic human needs are easy to overlook. In many negotiations, we tend to think that the only interest involved is money. Yet even in a negotiation over a monetary figure, such as the amount of alimony to be specified in a separation agreement, much more can be involved. What does a wife really want in asking for $500 a week in alimony? Certainly she is interested in her economic well-being, but what else? Possibly she wants the money in order to feel psychologically secure. She may also want it for recognition: to feel that she is treated fairly and as an equal. Perhaps the husband can ill afford to pay $500 a week, and perhaps his wife does not need that much, yet she will likely accept less only if her needs for security and recognition are met in other ways.

Carrie J. Menkel–Meadow, When Winning Isn't Everything: The Lawyer as Problem–Solver

28 Hofstra L.Rev. 905, 915–918 (2000).

A good problem solver must take the problem, transaction, or matter presented by the client, analyze what the problem or situation requires, and then use creative abilities to solve, resolve, arrange, structure, or transform the situation so it is made better for the client, not worse. To do this, the lawyer must also take account of the other side, not as someone to be "bested" or beaten, but as someone with needs, interests, and goals as well. How can both or all parties (including the state and the defendant in a criminal case, the plaintiff-victim and the tortfeasor, the breaching contractors, buyer-sellers, the regulated and private industry, and the many responsible parties in a clean-up site in an environmental case) attempt to structure their negotiations so that they learn what they want to do and what they can do?

Here, the important observation of social psychologist George Homans is significant: people often have complementary interests. Individuals do not always value things exactly the same way—[I like] icing and my brother like[s] cake. By having many issues and many different preferences, individuals actually increase the possibility of reaching an agreement, whether it is settling a case or arranging a transaction. It may be useful if judges and litigators narrow the issues for trial, but it is detrimental to the settlement process to narrow issues. The more issues, the more likely trades or "log-rolls," as the legislators call them, will be possible. Therefore, seeing many issues and parties and all organizational needs and preferences is essential to good problem solving.

Before one starts to compete with the other side, it is useful to see if the pie for which one is fighting can be expanded, before one divides it, if one must. This is what negotiation theorists call "expanding the pie" or "value creation," before one gets to the nasty "value claiming" or pie-dividing stages. * * * So, one should always ask the journalist's basic questions of every matter: 1) What (What is at stake? What is the "res" of the dispute? Can it be changed, expanded or traded?); 2) When (Must one resolve this now? Are installments possible? Are there any tax consequences or contingency arrangements? What risk allocation and sharing is involved?); 3) Where (Where can something be moved or transferred? Can a change of forum or process be effected?); 4) Who (Who are all the relevant parties here? Can one add some people or entities with resources and the power to do things?); 5) How (What means may be used to solve the problem: money, land, or an apology?); and finally, 6) Why (Why are the parties here? What are the underlying reasons, motivations, or interests in this matter? Can one reconstruct the reasons for being here and look for new ways to resolve the issues?). Answering these questions often, not always, provides new insights and new resources for solving problems.

One still needs law and a lot of other knowledge to solve problems and structure transactions. As Gary Klein's work indicates, "pattern recognition" helps those with experience quickly analyze and diagnose a problem and select a single solution, which is abandoned if it does not work. Lawyers need life experiences and they need to be generalists who can recognize many different kinds of patterns. Specialization may be increasing because of a perception or belief that individuals can only recognize a limited number of "patterns" in their experiences. I want to suggest that good legal problem solving, however, also requires the cross-fertilization of solving problems across fields. Individuals develop creativity by translating from one realm to another * * * The cost sharing of clean-up sites in environmental law is related to market share settlement grids in mass torts. The "structured settlement" or annuity in tort can work in installment payments for other damages or employment settlements. * * * So, in this sense, problem solving is analytic, rigorous, intellectual, interdisciplinary, and certainly more than doctrinal learning. Lawyers must learn to think of themselves in terms of experts in problem solving who draw on a wide range of disciplines. Lawyers are intelligent; they work with words and concepts ("linguistic intelligence"). They must learn to be facile with more systems of thought, as well as with the experiences on the ground * * * of the people they serve.

Finally, and perhaps most important * * * is the recognition that professionals solve human and legal problems by working with others. We need to, as my third grade report card said: "Work and play well with others." The emphasis on argument, debate, issue spotting, moot courts, and trials does, I think, encourage a culture of acrimony, or as author Deborah Tannen calls it, "The Argument Culture." As problem solvers, lawyers must learn to be more effective interpersonally. Their work is with words and concepts, but it is used with people who will sometimes agree with them and sometimes not. * * *

Howard Raiffa, Post–Settlement Settlements

1 Neg.J. 9–12 (1985).

"It's all very well to talk about collegial, joint problem-solving negotiation processes, but my opponent has unreasonable aspirations and I'm not going to weaken my just claim by trying to be a nice guy. I'm going to bargain tough, for myself, by myself." No matter how much we might bemoan this state of affairs, we must recognize that a lot of disputes are settled by hard-nosed, positional bargaining. Settled, yes. But efficiently settled? Often not. Both sides are often so intent on justifying their individual claims that not much time is spent on creating gains to be shared. They quibble about sharing a small pie and often fail to realize that perhaps the pie can be jointly enlarged. Even where there is a modicum of civility and some cooperative behavior on the part of the negotiators, it is not easy to squeeze out joint gains.

Here's one suggestion for how such intransigent negotiators might be helped. Let them negotiate as they will. Let them arrive at a settlement, or let a judge or jury impose a settlement on them. Mr. Jones, one protagonist, might feel happy about the outcome—he got more than he expected—but Ms. Spencer, the other protagonist, is unhappy—she did not realize her just aspirations. But even in this case the negotiators might not have squeezed out the full potential gains. There may be another carefully crafted settlement that both Jones and Spencer might prefer to the settlement they actually achieved.

Now let's imagine that along comes an intervenor * * * and he asks Jones and Spencer after they have achieved their settlement if they would be willing to let him try to sweeten the contract for each. The intervenor carefully explains to Jones that he will have the security of the outcome level he has already achieved but that he (Jones) may have the opportunity to do still better. The intervenor proposes that after some analysis he will suggest an alternate settlement—a *post-settlement settlement*, if you will— that would replace the original settlement only on the condition that both parties agree to the change; and of course they would only do this if each prefers the new settlement proposal to the old one.

Is this pie in the sky? Can the intervenor deliver the goods? Not always, but then Spencer and Jones would not have lost anything in trying, except perhaps their time. But it is my contention that in really complex negotiations where a lot of issues are at stake, where uncertainties are involved, or where settlements could involve transactions and payments over time, jointly desirable post-settlement settlements more often than not could be achieved by an analytical intervenor. If successful, the intervenor would add a surplus value to each side, and he might be recompensed for his effort by getting a small proportional slice of this surplus (if there is such a surplus) from each of the protagonists. So everybody would be happy.

NOTES AND QUESTIONS

1. The search for integrative or value-creating agreements is central to the problem-solving strategy. Obviously this search requires seeking out information about the other side's preferences, priorities and interests. Problem-solving then requires creating possible agreements and testing for optimality. Fisher, Ury and Patton recommend "brainstorming" about possible options before choosing one agreement. This changes the typical positional pattern of proposing two opposed agreements and battling between them—instead, negotiators are urged to propose many possibilities before evaluating their merits. See Fisher, Ury and Patton, Getting to Yes (2d ed. 1991).

In the legal context, Mnookin, Peppet and Tulumello recommend separating negotiations over a legal dispute into "two tables"—one focused on estimating the expected value of the case (using decision analysis) and the other focused on discovering the parties' interests and coming up with joint gain solutions. See Mnookin, Peppet and Tulumello, Beyond Winning: Negotiating to Create Value in Deals and Disputes 226–227 (2000). Whereas lawyers may be more involved at the first "table," clients or principals may be more involved in the interest-based negotiations.

Raiffa's post-settlement settlement is another possible approach. Although he calls for a third-party intervenor, two parties can theoretically use the approach by simply reaching an initial agreement and then trying to improve upon it. Some suggest that parties can, and do, engage in such modification, and that it is essential in problem-solving negotiation. See Bazerman, Russ, and Yakura, Post–Settlement Settlements in Two–Party Negotiations, 3 Neg.J. 283–292 (1987).

2. Information sharing is at the heart of a problem-solving approach to negotiation. Without information about the other side's interests, preferences, priorities and resources, finding value-creating trades is unlikely. Not surprisingly, increased information exchange has been shown to lead to improved negotiation performance. See Thompson, Peterson and Brodt, Team Negotiation: An Examination of Integrative and Distributive Bargaining, 70 J. of Personality & Soc.Psychol. 66–78 (1996). And lack of information exchange is a constant problem. After conducting a meta-analysis of 32 negotiation experiments, Thompson and Hrebec conclude, "Remarkably few people provided or sought information about the other party's interests during negotiations (about 20% and 7%, respectively), even though they had ample opportunity and there were no obvious costs of information exchange." Thompson and Hrebec, Lose–Lose Agreements in Interdependent Decision–Making, 120 Psychol.Bull. 396–409 (1996).

Why don't parties seek out their counterparts' interests in negotiation? One answer is that sharing information in an attempt to collaborate may risk exploitation. This "negotiator's dilemma," which we explore in more detail below, derives from the possibility that if I tell you my interests and needs in an attempt to facilitate value-creating trades, you may instead use that information to capture a greater amount of the surplus for yourself. The more you know about what I want, the easier it is to hold that information hostage and demand concessions from me on those issues I care about.

Another answer is what some researchers have called the "fixed pie bias." Negotiators tend to assume that they face a zero-sum situation, not a positive-sum or integrative opportunity:

> The fixed-pie assumption * * * represents a fundamental bias in human judgment. That is, negotiators have a systematic intuitive bias that distorts their behavior: They assume that their interests directly conflict with the other party's interests. The fundamental assumption of a fixed-pie probably results from a competitive society that creates the belief in a win-lose situation. This win-lose orientation is manifested objectively in our society in athletic competition, admission to academic programs, industrial promotion systems, and so on. Individuals tend to generalize from these objective win-lose situations and apply their experience to situations that are not objectively fixed-pies. Faced with a mixed-motive situation requiring both cooperation and competition, it is the competitive aspect that becomes salient—resulting in a win-lose orientation and a distributive approach to bargaining. This in turn results in the development of a strategy for obtaining the largest share possible of the perceived fixed-pie. Such a focus inhibits the creativity and problem-solving necessary for the development of integrative solutions.

Bazerman, Negotiator Judgment: A Critical Look at the Rationality Assumption 27 Am.Behavioral Sci. 211 (1983).

In one study, for example, Thompson and Hastie found that sixty-eight percent of negotiators assumed that there would be no opportunities for mutual gains or value-creating. See Thompson and Hastie, Social Perception in Negotiation, 47 Org. Behavior & Human Dec.Processes 98–123 (1990). Fixed-pie assumptions can be self-fulfilling. Studies have shown that negotiators who assume there will be value-creating opportunities are more likely to use strategies to identify an opponent's preferences and interests. See Pinkley, Griffith, and Northcraft, Fixed Pie A La Mode: Information Availability, Information Processing, and the Negotiation of Suboptimal Agreements, 62 Org. Behavior & Human Dec.Processes 101–112 (1995). Conversely, the fixed-pie assumption can lead negotiators to ignore information that would disprove their expectations. In one study, for example, Pinkley et al. found that twenty-five percent of experts and forty percent of beginners failed to identify their negotiating counterpart's interests and preferences *even when told those preferences in advance.* See id.

What causes the fixed-pie bias? As Professor Max Bazerman notes above, researchers have suggested that perhaps we have a cultural norm of competition that people erroneously generalize to negotiation situations. See also Bottom and Paese, False Consensus, Stereotypic Cues, and the Perception of Integrative Potential in Negotiation, 27 J. Applied Soc.Psychol. 21 1919, 1920 (1997); Dieffenbach, Psychology, Society and the Development of the Adversarial Posture, 16 J. Legal Prof. 205 (1991). Do you agree? Is our culture so competitive that we assume that our interests are opposed to—rather than merely different from—others'?

3. Just as computers have become useful tools in resolving distributive issues by facilitating structured positional negotiations, some negotiation support systems (NSS) are designed to assist negotiators in analyzing a negotiation problem and finding joint gains. Some systems help bargainers prepare for a negotiation. Others structure the bargaining process in ways that promote finding efficient outcomes. For example, one system, called NEGOTIATION ASSISTANT, helps parties to disaggregate their preferences and priorities by answering a series of questions in preparation for a negotiation. This, in turn, facilitates finding trades and packages that create value. In addition, the system allows for "post-settlement settlements"—finding Pareto-superior settlements to whatever deal the parties reached. Early studies suggest that using such computerized tools can lead to more efficient negotiated outcomes. See Rangaswamy and Shell, Using Computers to Realize Joint Gains in Negotiations: Toward an "Electronic Bargaining Table," 43 Mgt. Sci. 1147 (1997). See also Yuan, Rose and Archer, A Web–Based Negotiation Support System, 8 Elec.Mkts. 13 (1998).

b. FAIRNESS AND NORMS

It is important to note that problem-solving is not limited to the integrative aspects of bargaining. Problem-solving skills are also helpful in resolving the distributive issues present in any negotiation. Consider the following excerpt from Roger Fisher, author of Getting to Yes:

> The guts of the negotiation problem, in my view, is not who gets the last dollar, but what is the best process for resolving that issue. It is certainly a mistake to assume that the only process available for resolving distributional questions is hard bargaining over positions. In my judgment it is also a mistake to assume that such hard bargaining is the best process for resolving differences efficiently and in the long-term interest of either side.

> Two men in a lifeboat quarreling over limited rations have a distributional problem. One approach to resolving that problem is to engage in hard bargaining. *A* can insist that he will sink the boat unless he gets 60 percent of the rations. *B* can insist that he will sink the boat unless he gets 80 percent of the rations. But *A*'s and *B*'s

shared problem is not just how to divide the rations; rather it is how to divide the rations without tipping over the boat and while getting the boat to safer waters. In my view, to treat the distributional issue as a shared problem is a better approach than to treat it as a contest of will in which a more deceptive, more stubborn, and less rational negotiator will tend to fare better. Treating the distributional issue as a problem to be solved ("How about dividing the rations in proportion to our respective weights?" or "How about a fixed portion of the rations for each hour that one of us rows?") is likely to be better for both than a contest over who is more willing to sink the boat.

* * * It is precisely in deciding such distributional issues that objective criteria can play their most useful role. * * *

* * *

Two negotiators can be compared with two judges, trying to decide a case. There won't be a decision unless they agree. It is perfectly possible for fellow negotiators, despite their self-interest, to behave like fellow judges, in that they advance reasoned arguments seriously, and are open to persuasion by better arguments. They need not advance standards simply as rationalizations for positions, but as providing a genuine basis for joint decision.

Fisher, Comment, 34 J. of Leg.Educ. 120, 121 (1984).

A central aspect of problem-solving is using norms or standards of fairness to resolve or diminish distributive conflicts. As the following excerpts demonstrate, research has shown that fairness is an important concern for most people. At the same time, many commentators have debated both the efficacy and availability of "objective criteria" in negotiation, and have questioned how useful norms are in resolving conflict.

Max H. Bazerman, Robert Gibbons, Leigh Thompson, and Kathleen L. Valley, Can Negotiators Outperform Game Theory?

in Debating Rationality: Nonrational Aspects of Organizational Decision Making 78 (1998).

* * * Substantial evidence exists that individuals place utility on fairness in ways that are inconsistent with the self-interest assumption. In a provocative set of experiments, Kahneman, Knetsch, and Thaler asked subjects to evaluate the fairness of the action in the following situation:

A hardware store has been selling snow shovels for $15. The morning after a large snowstorm, the store raises the price to $20. Please rate this action as:

Completely Fair—Acceptable—Unfair—Very Unfair

The two favorable and the two unfavorable categories were combined to indicate the proportion of respondents who judged the action acceptable or unfair. Despite the (short-run) economic rationality of raising the prices on the snow shovels, 82 percent of the respondents considered this action unfair. * * *

Fairness issues also arise in ultimatum games. [In an ultimatum game, one person—the offeror—is given a certain sum of money by the experimenter. The offeror must then make an offer to divide that sum of money with the offeree. If the offeree accepts the offer, then the money is in fact divided and both keep their sum. If the offeree rejects the offer, however, then the experimenter keeps the sum and neither subject receives anything.] A number of researchers have methodically studied how people respond to ultimatums. [G]ame theory predicts that player 1 will offer player 2 only slightly more than zero, and that player 2 will accept any offer greater than zero. Empirical observation suggests, however, that individuals incorporate fairness considerations into their choices. Player 1 demands less than 70 percent of the funds on average, while individuals in the role of player 2 sometimes reject profitable but unequal offers, and accept zero only 20 percent of the time it is offered. * * *

In recent work, Straub and Murnighan manipulated knowledge of the size of the pie in ultimatum games. When player 1 knew the size of the pie but player 2 did not, player 2s accepted lower offers and player 1s made lower offers. The latter evidence suggests that it is 1's evaluation of 2's requirement of fairness that drives 1's observed behavior when the size of the pie is common knowledge, rather than any absolute preference for fairness on the part of player 1. * * *

Fairness considerations may be so powerful that players will be willing to pay to punish their opponent if their opponent asks for too much. In two-stage, alternating-offer bargaining games, Ochs and Roth found that 81 percent of rejected offers were followed by disadvantageous counteroffers, where the party who rejected the initial offer demanded less than he or she had just been offered. Ochs and Roth argue that the players' utility for fairness may explain the results. * * * [P]arties realize that the other side may very well refuse offers perceived as unfair, despite the economic rationality of accepting them. * * *

Russell Korobkin, A Positive Theory of Legal Negotiation

88 Georgetown L.J. 1789, 1821–1829 (2000).

Many common negotiating tactics are best understood as attempts to establish a procedure that the other party will view as "fair" for agreeing on a deal point within the bargaining zone. In employing such tactics, the negotiator may have either of two motives. He might believe that the procedure is equitable to both parties, and the resulting deal point will thus create a mutually beneficial transaction in which neither side gets the better of the other. Alternatively, he might attempt to establish a procedure that will lead to an agreement that benefits him or his client substantially more than it benefits the other negotiator. Whether the negotiator's motives are communitarian or individualistic, however, the procedures must have the appearance of equity in order to win acceptance.

1. The Reciprocity Norm: Exchanging Concessions

Perhaps the most common behavioral norm invoked in the negotiation process is reciprocity. When one person takes some action on behalf of another, it is assumed that the favor will be returned. The person who fails to reciprocate commits a social faux pas, which can lead to social ostracism and derision.

* * *

The reciprocity norm is a fundamental element of the negotiation process as well. When one party makes a concession, the other finds himself under a social obligation to do likewise. If Esau offers $150,000 for Jacob's catering business, and Jacob counters with $200,000, Esau might increase his offer to $160,000 for the primary purpose of obligating Jacob to make a reciprocal concession. Even if Jacob believes that his original $200,000 demand is below Esau's [reservation price,] meaning that Esau could pay that amount and still be made better off by completing the transaction, Jacob will find himself under immense pressure to lower his demand in the interest of fairness.

* * *

The failure of negotiators to reciprocate in some fashion when an opponent makes a concession will almost certainly increase the likelihood that bargaining will end in impasse. The reciprocity norm is so strong that most commentators strongly warn against negotiators making single, take-it-or-leave-it offers, often called "Boulwarism" after a famous negotiator known for this tactic. Boulwarism can be successful, but only if the offeror is able to justify her offer as consistent with another procedural or substantive fairness norm.

2. Procedural Equity: "Splitting the Difference"

Absent situation-specific reasons to think that a particular substantive division of the bargaining zone is the most fair, negotiators often assume that an equal division, or "parity," is consistent with fairness norms. Consequently, splitting the difference between the parties' [reservation prices] is often perceived as a fair procedure for reaching a deal point. * * *

Of course, while each party can estimate the other's [reservation price,] in most cases neither will know the other's [reservation price] precisely. Consequently, they may invoke the norm of strict procedural equality by agreeing to split the difference between the two initial offers, two later offers (after reciprocal concessions have been made), or what each party represents to be his [reservation price.] One problem with each of these shortcuts, however, is that a party who presents the more extreme offer or is more dishonest about his [reservation price] will succeed in capturing the majority of the cooperative surplus. * * *

3.   Focal Points

* * * Deal points within the bargaining zone can be called "focal points" if they have some special salience, or prominence, to the negotiating parties, compared to other possible deal points. Focal points can strike negotiators as neutral deal points, and thus, their selection often meets the parties' expectations of procedural fairness.

When negotiations are denominated in currency, round numbers are often natural focal points. Consider the following simple empirical demonstration. J. Keith Murnighan told students that a woman found a car she wished to buy with a sticker price of either $10,650, $2,650, or $2,450, and asked what they thought the exact final sales price would be. The dominant responses were $10,000, $2,500, and $2,000 respectively—all very round numbers. Since most car dealers bargain over the price of their wares, the reciprocity norm suggests that it is fair to expect they will offer some sort of discount off the sticker price in return for concessions made by the purchaser. What price would be a fair deal point resulting from reciprocal concessions? In the absence of a good reason to choose a different deal point, one that stands out from the others often seems about as neutral—and thus fair—a point as any.

* * *

C.   SUBSTANTIVE FAIRNESS: SEEKING NEUTRAL DEAL POINTS

Singling out a deal point requires the parties to agree on what is fair. In many negotiations, agreement is achieved by the parties acting consistently with procedural norms of bargaining behavior such as reciprocity, splitting the difference, and selection of prominent focal points. The deal point that emerges from a procedurally fair process is accepted by the parties as itself fair, assuming it lies within the bargaining zone. In other negotiations, the parties instead negotiate over what specific deal point would be most substantively fair.

In the best-selling book, Getting to Yes, Fisher and his co-authors urge negotiators to "insist on using objective criteria," which might include such benchmarks as market price, historic price, historic profit level, or some conception of merit. In other words, the authors present a normative case for agreeing on a deal point via negotiations over the most substantively fair way to divide the cooperative surplus, which they can create by reaching an agreement. Calling such criteria "objective" is a misnomer because (1) any such criteria will benefit one party over the other as opposed to a different criteria and (2) none can be conclusively established by logical argument to be justifiable ways to divide the cooperative surplus. Nonetheless, they are critical concepts in legal negotiation because they facilitate the parties' agreement on a single deal point that both can perceive as fair.

1.   Market Standards

Negotiating parties often justify the proposal of a specific deal point within a larger bargaining zone by reference to the market price of the good in question. * * * This price might be determined by averaging the sales prices of similar companies sold recently, by an independent appraiser's examination, or in some other generally accepted way.

* * *

2. Other Reference Transactions

A significant amount of research suggests that individuals make fairness judgments about a particular transaction based on other "reference transactions." When past transactions are used as reference points, proposed transactions are perceived as fair to the extent that they are consistent with the reference transactions. Fairness is based on the normalcy of the proposed transaction relative to its antecedents, not on the intrinsic justice of the referent. * * *

* * * Parties who have done business together in the past might contend that their past dealings are a natural reference point, and that a proposed transaction ought to take place on the past terms—possibly with an allowance for inflation—rather than current market prices. A seller might defend a proposed price on the ground that it provides him with a certain percentage profit, implicitly arguing the seller's cost is a fair reference point. A commercial buyer might ask a seller for terms embodied in an industry association's form contract on the grounds that trade custom is the appropriate reference point for the transaction.

* * *

3. Merits and Morals

When negotiating parties rely on procedural fairness norms to settle on a deal point, they implicitly agree that neither has a stronger claim to the cooperative surplus that their deal will create on the basis of merit or morality. But often times negotiators argue that fairness requires an unequal distribution of that surplus or, in other words, that to preserve equity in the relationship between the parties, one must be allocated the lion's share of the gains from trade.

Hoffman and Spitzer found that when one subject was given a unilateral right to receive $12—leaving the other subject with nothing—unless the subjects could agree on a method to divide $14 between them, the first subject bargained for a far larger share of the $14 stake when he "earned" the dominant role by beating the other subject in a simple game than when he won the role in a coin flip. Subjects, it seems, believe that unequal divisions are fair if one party is more deserving in some way external to the experiment, but not if one party merely has the good luck of being randomly assigned the role with more power.

Those results and others similar to them suggest that individuals often equate fairness with the "contribution principle": the allocation of the cooperative surplus proportional to contributions or "inputs" to the surplus. * * *

As an alternative to the contribution principle, either party might lay moral claim to the cooperative surplus by demonstrating relative poverty or need, such that an unequal division is necessary to ensure equal—or close to equal—outcomes. * * *

Leigh Thompson and Janice Nadler, Judgmental Biases In Conflict Resolution and How to Overcome Them

in Morton Deutsch and Peter T. Coleman (eds.), The Handbook of Conflict Resolution: Theory and Practice 213, 224–225 (2000).

Although people generally want what is fair, their assessments of fairness are often self-serving. Moreover, the fact that we have little or no self-awareness of this influence on our otherwise sound judgment heightens the intransigence of our views. Suppose you have worked for seven hours and have been paid $25. Another person has worked for ten hours doing the same work. How much do you think the other person should get paid? If you're like most people, you believe the other person should get paid more for doing more work—about $30, on average. This is hardly a self-serving response. Now, consider the reverse situation: the other person has worked for seven hours and been paid $25. You have worked for ten hours. What is a fair wage for you to be paid? Messick and Sentis found the average response to be about $35. The difference * * * illustrates the phenomenon of egocentric bias: people pay themselves substantially more than they are willing to pay others for doing the same task.

Consider another example. You are told about an accident in which a motorcyclist was injured after being hit by a car. After learning all the facts, you are asked to make a judgment of how much money you think is a fair settlement to compensate the motorcyclist for his injuries. Then, you are asked to play the role of either the injured motorcyclist or the driver of the car and to negotiate a settlement. Most of the time, people in this situation have no trouble coming to an agreement.

Now imagine doing the same thing, except that your role assignment comes first. That is, first you are asked to play the role of the motorcyclist or the driver, and then you learn all the facts, decide on a fair settlement, and finally negotiate. In this situation, the only thing that changes is that you learn the facts and make a fair settlement judgment through the eyes of one of the parties, instead of from the standpoint of a neutral observer. As it turns out, this difference is crucial. Instead of having no trouble coming to an agreement * * * people who know their roles from the beginning have a very difficult time coming to an agreement. The high impasse rate * * * is linked to self-serving judgments of fairness. The more biased the prenegotiation fair-settlement judgment, the more likely the later negotiation will result in impasse. * * *

In conflict situations, there are often as many proposed solutions as there are parties. Each party sincerely believes its own proposed outcome is fair for everyone. At the same time, each party's conception of fairness is tainted by self-interest, so that each solution is most favorable to the party proposing it.

NOTES AND QUESTIONS

1. Experimental research, particularly on ultimatum games, shows that people are often willing to sacrifice in the name of fairness. In other words, most individuals would rather take a worse outcome than a slightly better agreement that they see as unfair. See e.g., Fehr and Gachter, Fairness and Retaliation: The Economics of Reciprocity, 14 J.Econ. Perspectives 159 (2000). For a discussion of ultimatum games and their use by game theorists, see Kramer, Shah and Woerner, Why Ultimatums Fail: Social Identity and Moralistic Aggression, in Coercive Bargaining in Negotiation as a Social Process 288–289 (1995).

This suggests that a skilled negotiator should consider whether others will likely see her proposals as fair, regardless of whether that negotiator actually cares about fairness as a social or moral good in itself. Fairness, in short, is effective. Are you willing to accept an "unfair" agreement just because it is better than your best alternative to negotiation? Or do you turn down such agreements if they seem unfair? What standard should you use to judge the fairness of a proposed agreement?

2. Thompson and Nadler point out that our judgments of fairness can be biased, and Korobkin notes that "objective criteria" are rarely truly objective. Given that the parties to a dispute will often disagree about what's fair and may seek to apply different (and self-serving) standards of fairness, are appeals to fairness helpful in negotiation?

In many transactions such standards or focal points may be obvious. If you are purchasing a used car, for example, the "blue book" will approximate the car's value. If you are buying a house, you might look at other recent sales in the neighborhood, the average price per square foot in your town, or what the house sold for most recently. Yet, what focal points, market standards, or reference transactions are likely to be available in most legal disputes? For example, what standards of fairness might you turn to in a medical malpractice litigation? In a product liability case? In a commercial contract litigation? For each of these examples, what types of information would you like to have to judge the fairness of the other side's proposed agreement? Is that information likely to be available?

3. Although appealing to fairness is a common problem-solving approach to resolving distributive issues, pursuing fair agreements can sometimes conflict with another central goal of problem-solving: seeking integrative or efficient solutions.[14] If you and I are negotiating over who should keep a

---

14. Social theorists, philosophers and economists have long debated whether Pareto efficiency is compatible with fundamental notions of fairness. See Sen, The Impossibility of a Paretian Liberal, 78 J.Pol.Econ. 152 (1970); Kaplow and Shavell, Any Non–Welfarist Method of Policy Assessment Violates the Pareto Principle, 109 J.Pol. Econ. (2001); Kaplow and Shavell, The Conflict Between Notions of Fairness and the Pareto Principle,

fossil that we found while hiking, several "fair" solutions might not be the most value-creating. We could split the fossil in two, each keeping an equal half. Although this might be fair, it is obviously inefficient. Neither gets what we really want. If we draw straws, our process might be fair but the outcome might be inefficient: I might get the fossil even if you value it more.

The basic point is that the choice of a division process to manage the distributive issues in a negotiation can make that division inefficient. For example, imagine that Sarah and Ned are divorcing and that they have six items to try to divide fairly (E.g., a car, their house, etc.). What should they do? One option is to flip a coin to see who goes first and then alternate. This may seem fair, but it may not be. If Sarah chooses first, she may come out ahead if Ned and Sarah value the items similarly. In addition, alternating may not produce an efficient allocation. If Ned thinks the six items are all equally valuable but Sarah finds two items valuable and six worthless, *both* would prefer to give Sarah her two valuable items (and Ned the other four items) than to alternate Sarah–Ned–Sarah–Ned–Sarah–Ned. The non-alternating solution gives Sarah one hundred percent of her total value (because she gets both of her valuable items) and Ned approximately sixty-seven percent of his total value (because he gets four items, which he values equally). In the pure alternating scheme, Sarah and Ned each receive only approximately fifty percent of their respective value. Thus, in some circumstances alternation can lead to an inefficient outcome—there is a division that would leave at least one party better off without leaving the other worse off. See Brams and Taylor, The Win–Win Solution: Guaranteeing Fair Shares to Everybody 26 (1999).

Another option is "divide and choose"—flip a coin to see who divides, and then that person creates two piles of items. The other person then gets to pick which pile he or she keeps and which pile the divider keeps. From an efficiency standpoint the problem is that the divider may not know the chooser's preferences. For example, imagine that Sarah and Ned were each given 100 points to distribute (in secret) among the six items to be divided. For example, if Sarah really wanted their Mercedes she could place fifty points on it in her list. (This would indicate that she thought the Mercedes was worth fifty percent of the total value of all the items, given that she put half of her points on that item.) Now imagine that Sarah tries to divide the items into two roughly equivalent piles. She places the Mercedes in one pile (because to her it is worth fifty points) and the other five items in the other pile (also worth fifty points). But Ned's perspective is quite different. He has allocated his points according to his preferences, and he doesn't much want the Mercedes. In his opinion, the piles are worth 10 points (for the car) versus 90 points. He'll obviously take the second pile, but this allocation may be inefficient. Imagine that two of the items Ned has received (a stereo and a painting) are worth nothing to Ned. Sarah, however, placed 10 points on each. If she got those items she would receive

1 Am.L. & Econ.Rev. 63 (1999); Chang, A Liberal Theory of Social Welfare: Fairness, Utility, and the Pareto Principle, 110 Yale L.J. 173 (2000).

70 points and Ned would still receive 90. The divide and choose method, although it can seem fair, may not have produced an optimal outcome.

A third procedure is often referred to as "adjusted winner." In adjusted winner, each person again allocates 100 points to the items in question. Each person is then given those items on which he or she has placed more points. Thus, if Sarah put fifty points on the Mercedes but Ned allocated only 10 to it, Sarah would get the car. This initial distribution is efficient—each item goes to the person who most values it. When all of the items were distributed, Sarah and Ned could adjust the final distribution somewhat to make it more fair. For example, Sarah might have ended up with items equaling a total of 70 of her points, whereas Ned received a total of only 55 of his points. Sarah would then transfer items to Ned to even out the distribution. See id. at 69. See also Brams and Taylor, Fair Division: From Cake–Cutting to Dispute Resolution (1996); Brams and Taylor, A Procedure for Divorce Settlements, 13 Mediation Q. 191 (1996); Raiffa, Lectures on Negotiation Analysis (1996).

No approach is perfect. The point is that fairness, although helpful and important in deciding distributive issues, can create problems in terms of value creation or efficiency.

3.   Choosing an Approach

Imagine that you are preparing for a negotiation that you believe will involve both value-creating opportunities and, inevitably, distributive issues. You have a choice: bargain hard for distributive advantage, thereby perhaps sacrificing some undiscovered gains from trade if the negotiation fails to explore adequately the parties' interests and potential solutions, or attempt to set a more collaborative, problem-solving tone, thereby increasing your chances of enlarging the pie but perhaps simultaneously exposing yourself to an increased risk of exploitation. What should you do? Here we explore different perspectives on how to choose a negotiation strategy.

a.   THE NEGOTIATOR'S DILEMMA

Unfortunately, the choice between strategies is not a simple one. On the one hand, the possibility of creating value may lead you to favor a problem-solving approach in which you share information and search for trades. On the other hand, adopting this collaborative stance may leave you vulnerable to exploitation. The very steps needed to expand the pie—in particular the sharing of information—may be disadvantageous when it comes time to carve the pie up. Consider the following description of this "negotiator's dilemma."

Robert H. Mnookin and Lee Ross, Barriers to Conflict Resolution: Introduction

in Arrow et al., eds., Barriers to Conflict Resolution 7–8 (1995).

Self-interested actors may fail to achieve efficient outcomes because their rational calculations induce them to adopt strategies and tactics that preclude such efficiency. Negotiators characteristically face a dilemma arising from the inherent tension between two different goals. The first goal consists of maximizing the joint value of the settlement—that is, the pool of benefits or size of the "pie" to be divided. The second goal consists of maximizing their own share of the benefit pool—that is, the size and attractiveness of their particular "slice" of the pie. Disputants * * * can affect the size of the pie and of their own slice in several ways; but often the strategies and tactics that maximize the size of the pie compromise their ability to achieve the largest possible slice. Conversely, negotiation ploys designed to increase the size of their own slice tend to stand in the way of maximizing, and may even shrink, the size of the pie.

* * *

The "negotiators' dilemma" that we have described is particularly clear with respect to the question of revealing versus concealing interests. Clearly, the parties have a strong incentive to ascertain each other's true interests. Accurate information about goals, priorities, preferences, resources, and opportunities is essential for the principals (or those negotiating on their behalf) to frame agreements that offer optimal "gain of trade"—that is, agreement tailored to take full advantage of asymmetries of interests. Such information may even allow the parties to create additional value, that is, to contribute complementary skills or resources that combine synergistically to offer the parties "win-win" opportunities that might not heretofore have been apparent.

At the same time, parties have a clear incentive to conceal their true interests and priorities—or even to mislead the other side about them. By feigning attachment to whatever resources they are ready to give up in trade, and feigning relative indifference to whatever resources they seek to gain (while concealing opportunities and plans for utilization of those resources), each party seeks to win the best possible terms of trade for itself. In other words, total frankness and "full disclosure"—or simply greater frankness and fuller disclosure than that practiced by the other side in a negotiation—leave one vulnerable in the distributive aspects of bargaining. Accordingly, the sharp bargainer is tempted, and may rationally deem it advantageous—to practice secrecy and deception.

Such tactics, however, can lead to unnecessary deadlocks and costly delays, or, more fundamentally, to failures to discover the most efficient trades or outcomes. A simple example illustrates the dilemma facing negotiators, and the barrier imposed by the strategic concealment or misrepresentation of information. Suppose Bob has ten apples and no oranges, while Lee has ten oranges and no apples. Suppose further that, unbeknownst to Lee, Bob loves oranges and hates apples, while Lee, unbeknownst to Bob, likes them both equally well. Bob, in service of his current resources and preferences, suggests to Lee that they might both be made better off through a trade.

Now, if Bob discloses to Lee that he loves oranges and doesn't eat apples, Lee might "strategically" but deceptively insist that he shares Bob's preferences and, accordingly, propose that Bob give him nine apples (which he says have relatively little value to him) in exchange for one of his "very valuable" oranges. Bob might even agree, and thus sell his apples more cheaply than he could have sold them if he had concealed his taste for oranges and suggested a trade of five oranges for five apples (on the grounds that they "both might enjoy a little variety in their diet").

Note, however, that such an "even trade," while more equitable, would not really be efficient, because it fails to take full advantage of the differing tastes of the two parties. That is, a more efficient trade would be accomplished by an exchange of Bob's ten apples for Lee's ten oranges, perhaps with some "side payment" to sweeten the deal for Lee, or better still, with linkage to some other efficient trade—one in which it was Bob who, at little or no cost to himself, accommodated Lee's particular needs or tastes.

NOTES AND QUESTIONS

1. The "negotiator's dilemma" that Mnookin and Ross discuss was first articulated by Walton and McKersie in their early treatment of labor negotiations. See Walton and McKersie, A Behavioral Theory of Labor Negotiations (1965). See also Kelley, A Classroom Study of the Dilemmas in Interpersonal Negotiation, in Archibald (ed.), Strategic Interaction and Conflict (1966); Lax and Sebenius, The Manager as Negotiator (1986). For an in-depth discussion of the tension between creating and distributing value, see Mnookin, Peppet and Tulumello, Beyond Winning: Negotiating to Create Value in Deals and Disputes (2000).

2. Research suggests that negotiating parties often do *not* reach efficient agreements—they "leave value on the table" by settling on sub-optimal solutions to their conflicts. See Raiffa, The Art and Science of Negotiation 139 (1982); Bazerman, Magliozzi, and Neale, Integrative Bargaining in a Competitive Market, 34 Org. Behavior & Human Performance 294–313 (1985); Bazerman, Negotiator Judgment: A Critical Look at the Rationality Assumption, 27 Am.Behavioral Sci. 618–634 (1983). Why might this be? The negotiator's dilemma suggests one possible answer: strategic interaction prevents value-creation by inhibiting the exchange of information needed to find integrative trades. Because parties fear exploitation, they hold their cards close to their chest and therefore cannot exploit differences in resources and interests, relative valuations, forecasts, and time and risk preferences.

3. Despite the logic of the negotiator's dilemma, some studies show that it may not accurately portray bargaining. One study, for example, found that although "[i]nformation exchange appears to lead to a problem-solving atmosphere which allows negotiators to make tradeoffs," disclosing information did *not* affect the negotiators' distributive outcomes. "Although information sharing affected the integrativeness of the solution, the difference between the amount of information provided by each party did not impact the distribution of outcomes. * * * This suggests that negotiators should engage in information sharing without being overly concerned about being put at a disadvantage." Weingart, Thompson, Bazerman and Carroll, Tactical Behavior and Negotiation Outcomes, 1 Intl.J. of Conflict Mgt. 7, 27, 28 (1990). Have you found that this dilemma pervades your negotiations? What factors seem to exacerbate the tension, and what seems to ameliorate it? Are you personally more inclined towards seeking to create value through integrative trades or to try to claim more value in the distributive aspects of bargaining? In what situations, or with what sorts of people, do you tend towards—or should you tend towards—one sort of negotiation or the other?

b. SELF–INTEREST AND THE PRISONER'S DILEMMA ANALOGY

In 1984, a political scientist named Robert Axelrod published a seminal book titled *The Evolution of Cooperation*. In it he presented the results of computerized "tournaments" in which various human participants submitted computer programs designed to play repeated Prisoner's Dilemma games. Axelrod paired these programs off against each other in order to determine what program—or strategy—would most succeed in a repeat-play series of games.

Luce and Raiffa set out the classic definition of a Prisoner's Dilemma:

> Two suspects are taken into custody and separated. The district attorney is certain that they are guilty of a specific crime, but he does not have adequate evidence to convict them at a trial. He points out to each prisoner that each has two alternatives: to confess to the crime, or not to confess. If they both do not confess, then the district attorney states he will book them on some minor trumped-up charge such as petty larceny or illegal possession of a weapon, and they both will receive minor punishment. If they both confess they will be prosecuted, but he will recommend less than the most severe sentence; but if one confesses and the other does not, then the confessor will receive lenient treatment for turning state's evidence whereas the latter will get "the book" slapped at him. * * *

Luce and Raiffa, Games and Decisions 95 (1957).

In a Prisoner's Dilemma game, two players must simultaneously choose, without communicating, whether to "cooperate" or "defect." To simplify, imagine that if both players cooperate, each receives three points. If player A cooperates and B defects, B gets five points and A gets nothing. (Or, if B cooperates and A defects, A gets five points and B gets nothing.) If both defect, each gets one point. (See Figure 4.) The dilemma is that while mutual cooperation may be attractive, the temptation to defect—and the *fear* that the other player will succumb to that temptation—may lead to mutual defection and relatively low payoffs.

Economists assume that if two people are playing a prisoner's dilemma game only once, the optimal strategy for either player is to defect. Although mutual cooperation would be nice, each player will reason that the other is

Figure 4

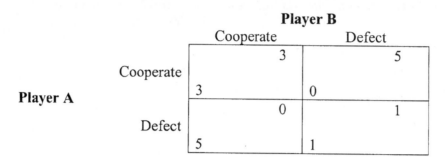

going to defect, and thus each will defect. Although this produces a collectively sub-optimal result, it is individually rational.

The analogy to negotiation is fairly obvious. In a given negotiation, we may both do better by cooperating—by adopting a problem-solving approach. But if you adopt such an approach and I "defect" or bargain hard, I may be able to exploit you and receive a bigger slice of the pie. Unfortunately, if we both defect and adopt a hard bargaining strategy we may each end up with a poor payoff. Our negotiation may stalemate, we may damage our relationship, and we may fail to find value-creating options. See Gilson and Mnookin, Disputing Through Agents: Cooperation and Conflict Between Lawyers in Litigation, 94 Colum.L.Rev. 509, 514–15 (1994).[15]

The game becomes more interesting, however, if played many times. David Lax and James Sebenius explain Axelrod's results:

> Axelrod's striking results have received widespread notice and scientific praise. * * * Axelrod asked a number of specialists from a broad sweep of related disciplines to submit computer programs to participate in a tournament of repeated plays of the Prisoner's Dilemma. Each program would be pitted against every other program for a large number of plays of the Prisoner's Dilemma; each program of "strategy" would be rated according to the total number of points obtained against the strategies of all its opponents. The strategies range from the simple—RANDOM which flipped a coin to decide whether to cooperate or defect and TIT–FOR–TAT which cooperated on the first play and in subsequent rounds merely repeated its opponent's immediately previous move—to many devilishly exploitative schemes, including some that calculated the rate at which the opponent defected and then defected just a little bit more frequently.

15. Negotiations over a legal dispute may be analogous to a repeat-play Prisoner's Dilemma in one of two ways. First, you might think of each communication or interaction between the parties as a choice point in which each can decide either to defect or to cooperate. Thus, over the course of a single piece of litigation the parties may interact many times, perhaps establishing a cooperative equilibrium over time. Second, you can treat a given litigation or negotiation as one "round" of the iterated Prisoner's Dilemma game, and assume that the potential benefits of repeat play arise only if the parties will negotiate together again in the future.

Axelrod's synthesis of his results is intriguing. First, the strategies that did well were "nice," they did not defect first. Second, they were "provocable" in that they punished a defection by defecting, at least on the next round. Third, they were "forgiving" in that after punishing a defection they gave the opponent the opportunity to resume cooperation. Thus, unlike other strategies that were less nice or forgiving, they did not become locked, after a defection, in a long series of mutual recriminations. Fourth, they were clear or "not too clever." Eliciting continued cooperation is sufficiently tricky that moves whose intentions were difficult to decipher tended to result in unproductive defections. Such strategies performed well because they were able to elicit cooperation and avoid gross exploitation. We call these strategies "conditionally open." The simplest of the submitted conditionally open strategies, TIT–FOR–TAT, actually won the tournament.

After disseminating these results, Axelrod ran a second tournament with a much larger number of participants. With TIT–FOR–TAT and other "nice" strategies as the contenders to beat, the second tournament brought forth a flood of even more clever, even more fiendish schemes. And, perhaps surprisingly, the best-performing strategies were conditionally open, and again, TIT–FOR–TAT won the tournament. The conclusions of these studies are of course only suggestive. The success of particular strategies depends on the population of submitted strategies. Yet, the studies imply that being open in each round to cooperation conditional on an opponent's openness elicits payoffs from cooperation sufficient to offset the costs of occasional defections.

Axelrod's results suggest the elements of a strategy for managing the tension between creating and claiming value. A negotiator can attempt to divide the process into a number of small steps and to view each step as a round in a repeated Prisoner's Dilemma. He can attempt to be conditionally open, warily seeking mutual cooperation, ready to punish or claim value when his counterpart does so, but ultimately forgiving transgressions. The attempt to create value is linked to an implicit threat to claim vigorously if the counterpart does, but also to the assurance that a repentant claimer will be allowed to return to good graces. Thus, both can avoid condemnation to endless mutual recriminations. Throughout the process, the negotiator may be better off if his moves are not mysterious.

Lax and Sebenius, The Manager as Negotiator: Bargaining for Cooperation and Competitive Gain 157–60 (1986). See also Axelrod, The Evolution of Cooperation (1984); Axelrod, The Complexity of Cooperation: Agent–Based Models of Competition and Collaboration (1997).

NOTES AND QUESTIONS

1. The Prisoner's Dilemma game has been used to analyze various litigation issues, including the problem of discovery abuse and the advantages of hiring a lawyer. See Setear, The Barrister and the Bomb: The dynamics of Cooperation, Nuclear Deterrence, and Discovery Abuse, 69 B.U.L.Rev. 569 (1989); Gilson and Mnookin, Disputing Through Agents: Cooperation and Conflict Between Lawyers in Litigation, 94 Colum.L.Rev. 509, 520–522 (1994). In the discovery context, for example, we might both be better off if we keep costs down by cooperating in exchanging information rather than waging a discovery battle with expensive depositions and document requests. At the same time, however, I may realize that by "defecting"—by holding back information or by imposing costs on you—I can gain advantage (if you do not reciprocate). Like a Prisoner's Dilemma, we may thus both "defect," allowing individually rational behavior to lead to a collectively irrational outcome.

Is the Prisoner's Dilemma a helpful metaphor for the negotiation process? In bargaining, unlike in a Prisoner's Dilemma game, the parties can communicate normally and are not confined to merely communicating by submitting a "cooperate" or "defect" bid. Their interaction may be face-to-face, whereas in a Prisoner's Dilemma game the interaction is usually handled through an intermediary. And in negotiation, the parties must bargain within a social and cultural context that may lead them to cooperate (or defect) more often than they would in a pure Prisoner's Dilemma. Such social influences can be extremely important. For example, in one experiment two sets of subjects played the same Prisoner's Dilemma game, with the same instructions, incentives, and opportunities to cooperate or defect. One group, however, was told that it was playing "The Community Game," while the other group was told that it was "The Wall Street Game." As you might expect, this social cue led to a higher rate of defection in the latter game than in the former. See Samuels and Ross, Reputations Versus Labels: The Power of Situational Effects in the Prisoner's Dilemma Game (unpublished manuscript, 1993).

Given such differences, how useful is the Prisoner's Dilemma in thinking about the choice between negotiation strategies?

2. Although Axelrod's analysis suggests that starting with an open, "nice" strategy can most often lead to a mutually-beneficial interaction, you may intuit that starting tough can reap benefits—if the other side is exploitable. Your approach, therefore, may be to try to claim value early in order to test the other side's mettle. If they give in, you walk away with the lion's share. If they don't, you can always switch to a more problem-solving approach.

Some fear that this strategy merely leads to mutual escalation and stalemate. Consider the following example: "In July, 1964, Undersecretary of State George Ball tried to dissuade Lyndon Johnson from sending U.S. ground forces to Vietnam en masse. Johnson intended to pressure the North Vietnamese to end the war on his terms, but Ball feared that escalation would become an autonomous force, impelling both sides to higher and higher levels of violence. 'Once on a tiger's back,' his memo argued, 'we cannot be sure of picking a place to dismount.'" O'Neill, Conflictual Moves in Bargaining: Warnings, Threats, Escalations, and Ultimatums, in Young (ed.), Negotiation Analysis 87 (1991).

Others, however, see this as a viable approach. Dean Pruitt, for example, argues that scholars have over-emphasized the risks of bargaining hard initially:

> While supported by certain lines of evidence, this indictment of contentious behavior seems overdrawn. Negotiations that reach reasonable agreements often go through an initial contentious stage followed by a later stage of joint problem solving. Furthermore, it can be argued that contending is often a necessary precursor to successful problem solving. Negotiators commonly start out with aspirations that greatly outstrip the integrative potential. In other words, their aspirations are so high that no degree of problem solving can yield a solution. Under such conditions, they are likely to engage in initial contentious behavior. During this stage, however, both parties often become more realistic about what aspirations can be sustained. If their actions have not produced too much antagonism, they can then enter a stage of joint problem solving that has prospects of yielding agreement because of their reduced aspirations.

Pruitt, Strategic Choice in Negotiation, 27 Am. Behavioral Sci. 167–194 (1983).

3. As Axelrod might predict, and as you might expect, research has shown that friends—who are by definition engaged in a long-term, repeat-play relationship—are more likely than strangers to manage conflict constructively. See Shah and Jehn, Do Friends Perform Better than Acquaintances? The Interaction of Friendship, Conflict and Task, Group Decision & Negot., 2, 149–165 (1993). Similarly, there is some evidence that small-town lawyers—who must interact repeatedly with each other and with those in their community—are less likely to engage in hostile or extremely competitive litigation. See Dieffenbach, Psychology, Society and the Development of the Adversarial Posture, 16 J.Leg.Prof. 205, 219–220 (1991) (discussing results of a study by Donald Landon).

More surprisingly, general studies of lawyer-negotiators lend some support to the notion that cooperation may be able to evolve and survive even in a largely adversarial environment, just as Axelrod showed in the Prisoner's Dilemma context:

> A study of American lawyer-negotiators reported by Professor Gerald R. Williams revealed that roughly 65 percent of a sample of attorneys from two major U.S. cities exhibited a consistently cooperative style of negotiation, whereas only 24 percent were truly competitive in their orientation. (11 percent defied categorization using these two labels). Roughly half of the sample was rated as ''effective'' negotiators by their peers. Most interesting, more than 75 percent of the ''effective'' group were cooperative types and only 12 percent were competitive. The remaining effective negotiators came from the pool of mixed strategy negotiators.

> In contrast to the stereotypes, this study suggests that a cooperative orientation is more common than a competitive orientation within

at least one sample of professional negotiators in the United States. Moreover, it appears to be easier to gain a reputation for being effective (at least as rated by peers) by using a cooperative approach rather than using a competitive one.

The second study was conducted over a period of nine years by Neil Rackham and John Carlisle in England. Rackham and Carlisle observed the behavior of forty-nine professional labor and contract negotiators in real transactions. * * * The most effective of them displayed distinctly cooperative traits.

For example, the study examined the use of what the researchers called irritators at the negotiating table. Irritators are such things as self-serving descriptions of one's offer, gratuitous insults, and direct attacks on the other side's proposal—typical competitive tactics. The average negotiator used 10.8 irritators per hour of negotiating time; the more skilled negotiators used an average of only 2.3 irritators per hour.

In addition, skilled negotiators avoided what the researchers called defend/attack spirals, cycles of emotion-laden comments assigning blame or disclaiming fault. Only 1.9 percent of the skilled negotiators' comments at the table fell into this category, whereas the average negotiators triggered or gave momentum to defend/attack spirals with 6.3 percent of their comments. The profile of the effective negotiator that emerges from this study seems to reflect a distinct set of cooperative, as opposed to stereotypically competitive, traits.

Shell, Bargaining for Advantage: Negotiation Strategies for Reasonable People 12–14 (1999).

The Williams study has been repeated and expanded by Professor Andrea Schneider. She asked lawyers to rate the last attorney against whom they had negotiated. She found that lawyers thought that 54 percent of their "problem-solving" peers were "effective," whereas only 9 percent of their "adversarial" peers were effective. See Schneider, An Empirical Study of Negotiation Skills, 6 Dispute Resolution Magazine (Summer 2000).

These studies suggest that adversarial negotiators, although certainly prevalent, do not totally dominate the landscape in legal disputes and are not seen as being particularly effective. Other research, however, suggests that adversarial bargaining *is* most common. One study of civil litigation in New Jersey found that litigators thought that "positional" bargaining was used in 71 percent of the cases and problem-solving in approximately 16 percent. (Respondents indicated that both approaches were used together roughly 17 percent of the time.) See Heumann and Hyman, Negotiation Methods and Litigation Settlement Methods in New Jersey: "You Can't Always Get What You Want," 12 Ohio St.J.Disp.Resol. 253, 255 (1997).

What negotiation approach do you think is most common in legal disputes? On what do you base that assumption? How is legal negotiation commonly portrayed in films or television? In the press? Are such depictions accurate? At a more general level, do you believe that cooperation can evolve and flourish in a competitive world? Under what conditions?

4. Although Axelrod's work focused on repeat-play or iterated Prisoner's Dilemma games, some researchers have found that subjects cooperate even in one-shot games.

> How can cooperation in PD games be explained? In repeated games, the players have an ongoing relationship, so the decision to cooperate may reflect an attempt to influence the other player—by cultivating a reputation, by inducing reciprocity, and so forth. Cooperation can be explained as a social influence strategy that serves a player's long-run self-interest. The conditions under which a cooperative strategy optimizes a player's outcome have been explored analytically and empirically. In one-shot games, however, there is no ongoing relationship between players. Because social influence is impossible, cooperation is always suboptimal in terms of an individual's outcome. Nonetheless, subjects act as if social influence were possible: The rate of cooperation is as high as in repeated games. The explanation may be that subjects take the same approach to one-shot games as to repeated games: They follow rules of thumb learned through their experiences of interdependent decision making in everyday social contexts. That is, decision makers simplify dilemmas by introducing tacit assumptions about social relations—they respond to uncertainty by automatically drawing on mental representations of typical social contexts. In short, the explanation may be that you can take the decision maker out of a social context, but you can't take the social context out of the decision maker. * * *

> Ethical principles vary greatly across individuals and cultures, but a few that serve basic social functions are widely shared. One of these, reciprocity, has been called a "cement of society" because it leads to behaviors that hold together social organizations. Essentially, this norm obligates a person to match what another person has provided. It can be seen in interpersonal exchanges ranging from the explicit give-and-take of concessions in negotiation to the implicit turn taking of self-disclosure in conversation. A reciprocity norm benefits society by ensuring rewards for those who initiate exchanges of goods and services. It fosters trade, the formation of interpersonal interdependencies, and ultimately the establishment of stable social organizations. * * *

See Morris, Sim, & Girotto, Time of Decision, Ethical Obligation, and Causal Illusion: Temporal Cues and Social Heuristics in the Prisoner's Dilemma, in Kramer & Messick (eds.), Negotiation as a Social Process 210–213 (1995).

5. The tendency to defect in a one-shot Prisoner's Dilemma game may also be constrained by the possibility of distinguishing between "cooperators" and "defectors"—types of players. In experimental studies, subjects given only a short amount of time to interact with other subjects have been able to predict with both accuracy and confidence the likelihood that others will either cooperate or defect in a Prisoner's Dilemma game. If you can distinguish one type of player from another with even modest accuracy and modest effort, "the population settles at a stable mix of cooperators and defectors, one in which members of both groups have the same average payoff and are therefore equally likely to survive. There is a stable ecological niche, in other words, for both cooperators and defectors. This result stands in stark contrast to the traditional sociobiological prediction of universal defection in one-shot prisoner's dilemmas played by nonrelatives." Frank, Gilovich, and Regan, The Evolution of One–Shot Cooperation: An Experiment, 14 Ethology & Sociobiology 247–256 (1993).

Should this research influence your choice of strategies? Do you believe that you can accurately predict how a negotiating counterpart is going to behave? Although potentially accurate (and helpful), such predictions can be risky. Sometimes you may incorrectly assume that your counterpart is going to defect or be a hard bargainer. This may then become self-fulfilling, making it difficult or impossible in hindsight to determine who initiated the hard bargaining. As Morton Deutsch explains, "[s]elf-fulfilling prophecies are those wherein you engage in hostile behavior toward another because of a false assumption that the other has done or is preparing to do something harmful to you; your false assumption comes true when it leads you to engage in hostile behavior that then provokes the other to react in a hostile manner to you. The dynamics of an escalating, destructive conflict have the inherent quality of a *folie a deux* in which the self-fulfilling prophecies of each side mutually reinforce one another. As a result, both sides are right to think that the other is provocative, untrustworthy, and malevolent. Each side, however, tends to be blind to how it as well as the other have contributed to this malignant process." Deutsch, Cooperation and Competition, in Deutsch & Coleman, eds., The Handbook of Conflict Resolution: Theory and Practice (2000).

6.   Research suggests that when people choose *not* to cooperate—choose to defect in a Prisoner's Dilemma game or perhaps, by analogy, to "bargain hard" rather than problem-solve—they are likely to rationalize that choice by denigrating their belief in their own self-efficacy. In other words, an individual may tell himself that there was "nothing he could have done to make a difference anyway" rather than believing that he walked away from a genuine chance to promote cooperation. See Kerr and Kaufman–Gilliland, "... and besides, I probably couldn't have made a difference anyway": Justification of Social Dilemma Defection via Perceived Self–Inefficacy, 33 J. of Experimental Soc.Psychol. 211–230 (1997). Have you ever found yourself explaining your behavior in this way? For example, if you've bargained hard—perhaps too hard—have you ever justified your actions by saying "there was nothing else I could do" or "they made me do it?" Is such reasoning justified?

7.   The Prisoner's Dilemma may not be a perfect metaphor for negotiation because many disputes involve more than two parties . Multiparty disputes create the possibility of coalitions, in which two parties may join forces against a third. Such coalitions may shift, break apart, and re-form, and are notoriously difficult to model or predict. We do not focus on multiparty disputes here, but see Raiffa, The Art and Science of Negotiation (1982); Watkins and Rosegrant, Sources of Power in Coalition Building, 12 Neg.J. 47 (1996); Sebenius, Dealing with Blocking Coalitions and Related Barriers to Agreement: Lessons from Negotiations on the Oceans, the Ozone, and the Climate, in Barriers to Conflict Resolution 151 (Arrow et al., eds.,1995); Goodpaster, Coalitions and Representative Bargaining, 9 Ohio St.J. on Disp.Res. 243 (1994); Lax and Sebenius, Thinking Coalitionally: Party Arithmetic, Process Opportunism, and Strategic Sequencing, in Young, Negotiation Analysis 154 (1991); Touval, Multilateral Negotiation: An Analytic Approach, 5 Neg.J. 159 (1989).

8. What variables should influence your choice between strategies? Lax and Sebenius suggest a conditionally open strategy—start a negotiation willing to problem-solve but defend against exploitation if the other side bargains hard. When would this be good advice, and when might it be unwise? Consider how the following variables might influence your choice of approach:

- Is the negotiation a one-shot transaction, or will there be future dealings over time?

- Is it a single issue, primarily distributive negotiation, or are there multiple issues with integrative potential?

- Are the stakes high or low?

- How is the other side likely to act? Do they have a reputation for being a hard bargainer? Have you seen them negotiate in similar situations? What would *you* do if you were in their shoes?

- What are the negotiation norms in your community? Is problem-solving more common or is a hard, adversarial strategy the norm?

- What strategy does your client prefer?

- What strategy is more in line with your own personal style as a person or as an attorney? What strategy are you more skilled at?

c. WILL PROBLEM–SOLVING SACRIFICE MY CLIENT'S INTERESTS?

Many lawyers fear that adopting a problem-solving strategy will sacrifice their clients' interests in the name of cooperation. In a study of litigators in New Jersey, for example, Milton Heumann and Jonathan Hyman found that although litigators believed that problem-solving was used only 16 percent of the time, 61 percent thought that it should be used more. These lawyers, however, feared for their clients' interests. The following excerpt contains some of the lawyers' explanations of why positional hard bargaining seemed necessary, as well as the authors' explanation of the confusion that often exists between problem-solving, on the one hand, and "soft" positional bargaining in which one unilaterally over-discloses information, on the other.

Milton Heumann and Jonathan M. Hyman, Negotiation Methods and Litigation Settlement Methods in New Jersey: "You Can't Always Get What You Want"

12 Ohio St.J.Disp.Resol. 253, 262–265 (1997).

In their interviews, the litigators gave us vivid examples of how they act against their own preferences because they want to protect themselves against the positional excesses of the other side. Although they dislike it, they told us they must play a highly positional game of concealing their settlement positions. Candor about settlement positions is rarely the best policy. Lawyers learn that they must exaggerate demands and understate offers as part of the settlement ritual. Even when requested to divulge what they "really" want or what they "really" can offer, they learned that their "real" position only became the next starting point for another round of offers and demands. If they were honest about stating their positions and insisted on not budging once they had revealed what they would settle for, they came to be seen as inflexible and as an impediment to realistic settlement of the case.

* * *

We have set out several interview excerpts to illustrate the almost painful way attorneys learn that strategic bargaining is generally linked to some misrepresentation about true bargaining positions. We also include some excerpts from attorneys who found that the adversarial posture itself forced a sort of personal compromise with their own sense of truthful representation and required a slanting of issues with which they were not always comfortable.

[The practice of law] means never telling the truth; it means using tricks and scams. * * * The instinct [of a new attorney] to be honest is a disadvantage. I had to resort to lying.

* * *

[I learned to be an advocate, which means] learning to see with blinders. You learn to cloud weak things. * * *

* * *

[With experience] you become less naïve, learn the system. I try to be honest and straightforward, but I've learned that in certain circumstances you can't do that. [For example,] my firm [the insurance company he was representing] asked me to get a demand. I got a letter asking for $750,000, but I valued the case at $500,000 or less, the insurance company told me to go for a structured settlement of $400,000 or less but that they could go up to $500,000. I wrote a letter [to plaintiff's attorney] saying $100,000 up front, plus $100,000 structured. The plaintiff's attorney called me and said: "The offer is ridiculous. We won't consider it." I told him his 750 was high, and I asked him: "What do you really need?" His answer was "750, my client wants to net half a million and I need $250,000." I responded: "Let's avoid the game, cut through this nonsense, what do you really need." The attorney called me back and said: "Our rock bottom is half a million." I figured now we could settle, since I knew I had this amount. But when I called the insurance company, they now said they didn't want to pay it. Their feeling was that "if he says half a million, he'll take less." * * * [The attorney concluded by observing how] honesty can work against you. People expect you to play the game and if you don't . . .

* * *

As suggestive as these examples are, however, we do not think they confirm the working assumption that positional bargaining overwhelms problem-solving whenever the two meet. The lawyers in these excerpts are not describing a conflict between positional and problem-solving methods of negotiation. Instead, they are only describing a tension that inheres in the positional method of negotiating. The concealment or disclosure of settlement positions is a key issue—perhaps the key issue—of positional negotiation strategy, entirely independent of problem-solving strategies. Positional bargaining depends on each side eventually disclosing its settlement position, but it equally depends on each side initially concealing its true settlement positions and disclosing misleading settlement positions instead. Through misleading disclosures, each side tries to convince the other side that there is little left to give and that it would be better to settle for the proposed terms. But the concealment or disclosure of settlement positions forms only a minor sideshow for problem-solving negotiation. In contrast to advancing and defending settlement positions, the key to problem-solving methods of negotiation is maintaining focus on the underlying interests of the parties. At most, the stories we heard describe a conflict that arises within the four corners of the positional bargaining method. They do not describe the exploration of underlying interests or the crafting of mutually satisfactory agreements from those interests.

Robert Mnookin, Scott Peppet & Andrew Tulumello, Beyond Winning: Negotiating to Create Value in Deals and Disputes

321–322 (2000).

Will the client always be better off if a skilled lawyer adopts a problem-solving orientation rather than taking a more traditional adversarial approach? Our answer is straightforward: Usually, but not always.

The outcome of any negotiation depends on the behavior of the parties on both sides. Consider the following thought experiment. Imagine two lawyers—equally skilled—asked to represent the same client. One lawyer has a problem-solving orientation; the other is a hard bargainer. Each lawyer will represent this client in a series of negotiations where there is a random spread of lawyers and clients on the other side. In our view, clients do better, certainly in the long run, when represented by lawyers who have a problem-solving orientation. But common sense and anecdotal observation suggest that in *some* cases a competitive hard bargainer will achieve a better result for a client than a problem-solver—*if* the other side is represented by ineffective counsel so eager to settle the dispute or make a deal that he simply offers concession after concession. Adopting a problem-solving stance toward negotiations probably gives up some opportunities to fish for suckers who can be exploited with hard-bargaining tactics. But in large part, how you see this cost of problem-solving will depend on how likely you believe it is that those you negotiate against will be less skilled, intelligent, or sophisticated than you are. Assuming that more often than not those on the other side will be competent, then on average fishing for suckers may have a negative return.

Negotiators also fear that by adopting a collaborative posture their clients may be exploited. If I try to lead the way toward problem-solving, will my client be hurt? We think not. With an understanding of hard-bargaining tactics and how they work, an effective problem-solver can defend his client's interests. Will there be *any* cost of trying to lead with a problem-solving approach? Perhaps. But in most situations it's not so hard to change course quickly and take a defensive posture if necessary.

At the same time, if two problem-solving lawyers work together on opposite sides of the table, sometimes they will be able to create tremendous value for their clients and find outcomes that would simply be unimaginable using a traditional adversarial posture. Two companies in a dispute may realize that they can make millions doing a joint venture. * * * Even in contentious disputes, problem-solving lawyers may design creative processes to save their clients time and money. While there may be some downside risk to problem-solving, the upside benefit can be well worth it.

In short, if there is a sucker on the other side and future relationships don't matter very much, adopting a highly adversarial strategy * * * may sometimes lead to a higher pay-off. More often, it will lead to retaliation, and the net result may be no deal at all or simply much higher transaction costs.

NOTES AND QUESTIONS

1. Professor Robert Condlin suggests that lawyers have a "duty to compete" that may run counter to the problem-solving strategy:

> * * * While lawyers may not take action that is frivolous (i.e., primarily to harass or maliciously to injure) or prohibited by law, they must use any legally available move or procedure helpful to a client's bargaining position. Among other things, this means that all forms of leverage must be exploited, inflated demands made, and private information obtained and used whenever any of these actions would advance the client's stated objectives, even if such action would jeopardize a lawyer's long-term, working relationship with her bargaining counterpart.
>
> Lawyers also must show enthusiasm for the bargaining task. Once described as the obligation of zealous representation, and now ex-

pressed as the duty of diligence, this duty requires lawyers to act with "commitment and dedication to the interests of the client," and to "carry to a conclusion all matters undertaken" on the client's behalf. Lawyer bargainers, in other words, must develop and play out client-bargaining hands with energy and believability, and not undercut those efforts with a tone or attitude which indicates that their hearts are not in it, or that they do not believe what they say. Plausibility and sincerity are the most important attributes of effective bargaining maneuvers; the duty of competence requires the first, and the duty of diligence the second.

Condlin, Bargaining in the Dark: The Normative Incoherence of Lawyer Dispute Bargaining Role, 51 Md.L.Rev. 1, 71–72 (1992). Do you agree?

Although the Model Rules of Professional Conduct do not require "zealous advocacy" per se, Model Rule 1.3 does require "reasonable diligence" on behalf of a client. The earlier Canon 7 of the Model Code of Professional Responsibility stated that "a lawyer should represent a client zealously within the bounds of the law." And the even older Canon 15 of the ABA Canons of Professional Ethics stated that "[t]he lawyer owes 'entire devotion to the interest of the client, warm zeal in the maintenance and defense of his rights and the exertion of utmost learning and ability,' to the end that nothing be taken or be withheld from him, save by the rules of law, legally applied."

Does problem-solving square with these requirements? Given that problem-solving generally requires consideration of the other side's interests and concerns, and tailoring of agreements to dovetail your own client's needs with the other side's to create value, is a lawyer who pursues this approach letting down her client? When Mnookin, Peppet and Tulumello suggest that on *average* "fishing for suckers" will have a negative return, they implicitly admit that occasionally it may succeed in a given negotiation. Should a lawyer play the averages, or must she always seek to exploit the other side if that might be in her individual client's interests?

2. What should an attorney do if her client wants to adopt a hard bargaining strategy but she feels this is not necessarily in the client's best interest? Should she acquiesce? Try to persuade the client to change strategies? Withdraw from the representation? How clear must a lawyer be at the *start* of representation if she wants to take a problem-solving approach to the client's legal dispute? As a thought experiment, try writing down how you would explain to a new potential client that you preferred problem-solving to an adversarial strategy. What main points would you cover? How would you explain what "problem-solving" meant? What questions would your client likely have about your proposed approach?

C. PSYCHOLOGICAL AND SOCIAL ASPECTS OF BARGAINING

Choosing and executing a strategy may be complicated by a variety of psychological and social aspects of bargaining. In this Section we first explore several psychological barriers to negotiating the resolution of legal disputes. We then turn to the problem of interpersonal style—what mix of interpersonal skills a negotiator should employ to be effective in dealing with her own client and the other side. Finally, we examine the role of race, gender, culture and stereotyping in the negotiation process.

1.   PSYCHOLOGICAL BARRIERS TO CONFLICT RESOLUTION

Psychological aspects of bargaining were woven throughout Sections A and B. We have already seen, for example, that the fixed pie bias can diminish prospects for integrative bargaining, that negotiators are likely to have biased constructions of what should count as a fair outcome in a given dispute, and that anchoring effects can greatly increase the power of a first offer. Negotiation analysts, economists and legal scholars increasingly debate and explore the ways in which such psychological phenomena affect bargaining, litigation behavior and the legal system generally. See e.g., Sunstein, Behavioral Law and Economics (2000); Korobkin and Ulen, Law and Behavioral Science: Removing the Rationality Assumption from Law and Economics, 88 Cal.L.Rev. 1051 (2000); Jolls, Sunstein and Thaler, A Behavioral Approach to Law and Economics, 50 Stan.L.Rev. 1471 (1998); Mnookin, Why Negotiations Fail: An Exploration of Barriers to the Resolution of Conflict, 8 Ohio St.J. on Dis.Res. 235, 238–247 (1993).

a.   COGNITION, PERCEPTION AND RECALL

The following excerpt reviews several additional psychological barriers to conflict resolution and offers remedial prescriptions to help lawyers overcome them. It is structured around several central questions that lawyers and clients must answer in a negotiation, including "How much is this case worth?", "How likely am I to win if this case goes to trial?", "How should I frame my offer?" and "How should I evaluate their offers?"

Richard Birke and Craig R. Fox, Psychological Principles in Negotiating Civil Settlements

4 Harv.Neg.L.Rev. 1, 7–12, 14–20, 42–47, 48–51 (1999).

Question 1: How much is the case worth?

* * *

1.   *Psychology Relating to Preliminary Valuation: The Availability and Anchoring Heuristics*

Consider the following question: are there more male or female lawyers in America? To answer this question with complete accuracy would require demographic professional data. However, people render judgments on such matters all the time based on their own experience and intuition. In this case, for example, most people consult their memory and conclude that because it is easier to recall examples of male lawyers than female lawyers, the former are probably more common than the latter. They are using a mental short cut or heuristic to solve the problem. In this case, people automatically assume that when it is easier to recall examples of something, it tends to be more common. In the example of male and female attorneys, such reasoning provides the correct answer.

Now consider a different question: are there more murders or suicides each year in America? If you answered "murders," you might be surprised to learn that, in fact, suicides are much more common. In this second instance, the "availability heuristic"[27] fails because one's memories do not reflect a representative sampling of what exists in the world. Memories are often biased by vivid, extreme events that tend to receive extensive media coverage. Movies, television dramas, and news reports tend to make murder seem much more common than suicide.

There are many instances of such distortions. For example, people typically think that there is a higher percentage of African–American citizens in Los Angeles than African–American officers on the L.A. police force, that a higher proportion of top Hollywood actors than U.S. Congressmen are homosexual, and that it rains more in Seattle than it does in Northern Georgia. None of these apparent "facts" is true, but because it is easier to conjure images of African–American Los Angelinos than it is to conjure images of African–American L.A. police officers, openly gay actors than openly gay politicians, and rainy scenes of Seattle than rainy scenes of Georgia, most people automatically deem the former more common than the latter.

Media reporting facilitates availability distortions of legal matters as well. When people think of a tort case in contemporary society, they are likely to think of McDonald's coffee or Dow Corning breast implants. When thinking of a murder trial, O.J. Simpson may come to mind first. * * * Although people may be aware that these cases are atypical, their sensational portrayal by the media renders them readily available to memory. In fact, these cases are newsworthy precisely because they are not typical. However, when making predictions, people often fail to compensate for the gap between what is memorable and what is typical. If a lawyer knows that the upper end of jury awards in sexual harassment claims is 7.2 million dollars, she may realize that her case is worth less, but the fact that it is so easy to recall such notable cases * * * makes an extreme award seem possible.

This bias may be reinforced by a second psychological phenomenon: the tendency to anchor on a salient number and make insufficient adjustments in response to individuating details of the case at hand. For example, if a recent court award for a similar case comes to mind, people may be unduly influenced by this value in their assessment of the present case.

---

27. For a more detailed account of the psychology of the availability heuristic, see Amos Tversky & Daniel Kahneman, *Availability: A Heuristic for Judging Frequency and Probability*, 5 COGNITIVE PSYCHOL. 207 (1973). For an accessible introduction to different judgmental heuristics and associated biases, see Amos Tversky & Daniel Kahneman, *Judgment under Uncertainty, Heuristics and Biases*, 185 SCIENCE 1124 (1974).

Research shows that even when a focal number is not particularly relevant, it can exert a bias on judgment under uncertainty. * * *

People are especially susceptible to anchoring bias when they have little relevant experience or knowledge. However, expertise alone fails to provide protection from this tendency. In one study, several experienced real estate brokers were asked to provide information they used to appraise a piece of residential real estate and to estimate how accurately agents could appraise its value when given that information.[42] The brokers responded that the information should support an agent's estimate within five percent of the true value. Other groups of agents were given packets of information on a home that included a bogus listing price that was eleven percent above the true listing price or eleven percent below the true listing price. These two groups were asked to estimate the appraised value of the home. Although the agents explicitly denied that listing price affected their appraisals significantly, the manipulation of the bogus listing price led to a substantial difference in these values between the groups.

* * *

2. *Remediation*

To guard against bias when valuing a case, attorneys should research compiled statistics on outcomes of similar cases rather than relying exclusively on intuitive judgments which may be skewed by media reports of sensational cases. A thoughtful look at the class of comparable cases provides a reasonable starting point. Of course, the individuating circumstances of the present case are relevant considerations, but that judgment should be anchored on the average award in similar cases rather than on the outcomes of cases that happen to come to mind for idiosyncratic reasons. Psychological research in judgment under uncertainty suggests that people tend to undervalue base rates in their judgments of the case at hand. A modest investment of time researching comparable cases can help insulate against costly errors in valuation.

Question 2: How likely am I to win if this case goes to trial?

* * *

1. *Psychological Biases*

a. *Perspective Biases*

In general, people have great difficulty divorcing themselves from their idiosyncratic role sufficiently to take an objective view of disputes in which they are involved. In one study, researchers provided four groups of respondents with summary information pertaining to legal disputes.[57] In

---

42. *See* Gregory B. Northcraft & Margaret Neale, *Experts, Amateurs, and Real Estate: An Anchoring-and-Adjustment Perspective on Property Pricing Decisions*, 39 ORGANIZATIONAL BEHAV. & HUM. DECISION PROCESSES 84 (1987).

57. Lyle A. Brenner et al., *On the Evaluation of One–Sided Evidence*, 9 J. BEHAV.

the partisan conditions, respondents were given background information and either the plaintiff's or the defendant's arguments, but not both. In the neutral conditions, respondents were given either background information only or background information and both the plaintiff's and defendant's arguments. Participants in all conditions were asked to predict how many of twenty jurors would find for the plaintiff. Participants in the plaintiff condition predicted that a significantly higher proportion of jurors would find for the plaintiff than did participants in the defendant condition, despite the fact that both sides were aware that they were not provided with the other side's arguments. Participants in the neutral conditions (background only, or background and both sides' arguments) had a more balanced view than did participants in either of the partisan conditions.

Even when negotiators possess complete and shared information, they tend to assess the strength of their case in a self-interested (or "egocentric") manner. In one study, participants were randomly assigned to roles in a negotiation simulation involving a wage dispute between labor and management.[58] Both groups were given identical background information and asked to negotiate under the threat that a costly strike would occur if they failed to reach an agreement. Prior to negotiating, both groups were asked what they thought was a fair wage from the vantage point of a neutral third party. Despite the fact that both groups had been provided identical information, participants tended to be biased in a self-interested direction; that is, they tended to think a neutral third party would favor their side. Moreover, when members of a pair were farther apart in their predictions regarding the judgment of a third party, they tended to strike for longer periods of time. A similar pattern has been replicated with real money at stake in a simulated legal dispute negotiated under a regime of escalating legal fees.[59]

b. *Positive Illusions*

Egocentric biases are reinforced by so-called "positive illusions," which include unrealistic optimism, exaggerated perceptions of personal control, and inflated positive views of the self. For example, people tend to overestimate the probability that their predictions and answers to trivia questions are correct, at least for items of moderate to extreme difficulty. Overconfidence can inhibit negotiated settlements because if parties are overoptimistic about their ability to secure favorable litigated outcomes, they may set extreme reservation points. Indeed, one study found that overconfident negotiators were less concessionary and completed fewer deals than well-calibrated negotiators.[63] Also, in studies of final-offer arbitration, negoti-

---

Decision Making 59 (1996).

58. Leigh Thompson & George Loewenstein, *Egocentric Interpretations of Fairness and Interpersonal Conflict*, 51 Org. Behav. & Hum. Decision Proc. 176 (1992).

59. *See* Linda Babcock et al., *Biased Judgments of Fairness in Bargaining*, 85 Am. Econ. Rev. 1337 (1995); George Loewenstein et al., *Self-Serving Assessments of Fairness and Pretrial Bargaining*, 22 J. Legal Stud. 135 (1993). * * *

63. *See* Margaret A. Neale & Max H. Bazerman, *The Effects of Framing and Negotiator Overconfidence on Bargaining Behaviors and Outcomes*, 28 Acad. Mgmt. J. 34 (1985).

ators on average overestimated the probability that their offers would be favored by the arbitrator. Presumably, these negotiators would have turned down settlement offers that, ex post, would have yielded more on average than did the arbitration.

Overconfidence stems, in part, from pervasive biases in the ways people pursue and evaluate evidence. Psychological studies have shown that people are more likely to seek information that confirms rather than discredits their hypotheses, and they tend to assimilate data in ways that are consistent with their prior views. In discovery, for example, attorneys are more likely to seek information that supports their viewpoint than they are to seek information that supports their opponents' cases. They work on "their side" of a case, and tend to construe the information that they find in a way that confirms their pre-existing beliefs about their odds of prevailing.

A second positive illusion is people's tendency to overestimate their ability to control outcomes that are determined by factors outside of their control. In one classic study by psychologist Ellen Langer, subjects bet more on a game of pure chance when they competed against a shy, awkward, poorly dressed individual than when they competed against a confident, outgoing, well-dressed person.[69] In a second study, subjects were offered one-dollar tickets to an office lottery. Each ticket consisted of two pictures of a famous football player, one of which was put into the box from which the winning ticket would be drawn. When participants were asked later at what price they would be willing to sell their ticket, those who had chosen the ticket for themselves demanded $6.87 on average, whereas those who had been assigned a ticket at random demanded only $1.96 on average. On the basis of these studies and other literature, Langer concludes:

> Whether it is seen as a need for competence, an instinct to master, a striving for superiority, or a striving for personal causation, most social scientists agree that there is a motivation to master one's environment, and a complete mastery would include the ability to "beat the odds," that is, to control chance events.[70]

When lawyers try to anticipate the outcome of a trial or a motion, there are many factors outside of their control. For example, appellate case law may change during the pendency of a case; or, the trial judge may recuse herself, become sick, or be elevated to a higher court. Witnesses may fail to appear or may be distracted by other events in their lives and be unable to prepare effectively or testify forcefully. Nevertheless, the lawyers may overestimate their ability to control a trial's outcome, and in turn, overvalue the claim.

A third variety of positive illusion is the tendency to hold overly positive views of one's own attributes and motives. For example, most people think that they are more intelligent and fair minded than average.

---

69. Ellen J. Langer, *The Illusion of Control*, 32 J. PERSONALITY & SOC. PSYCHOL. 311 (1975).

70. *Id.* at 323 (internal citations omitted).

Ninety-four percent of university professors believe that they do a better job than their colleagues. More to the point, most negotiators believe themselves to be more flexible, more purposeful, more fair, more competent, more honest, and more cooperative than their counterparts.[74]

In a negotiation, this self-enhancing bias may lead an attorney to believe that she should hold out for a favorable settlement, because she is a more skilled attorney. Although skill among attorneys varies and it is rational to take skill into account when evaluating the worth of a case, lawyers at all skill levels are very likely to overestimate their abilities relative to those of their peers. This self-confidence may prove to be an effective bargaining tool to the extent that it sends a signal to her counterpart that the attorney is committed to seeing the case through to trial if necessary. However, if both sides overestimate their chances of prevailing in court, this bias will lead to excessive and costly discovery and litigation.

In sum, most people tend to make unrealistically optimistic forecasts regarding their own future outcomes. For example, an attorney may know that only twenty percent of appealed decisions in a particular practice area are overturned but nevertheless maintain that her odds of overturning an adverse ruling are higher—at least one in four, perhaps one in two. This perspective could eliminate the possibility of settlement in a case in which both sides agree on the value of a plaintiff's verdict and differ only in their assessment of the probability of a defense verdict. If the plaintiff feels that there is a forty percent chance that the verdict will be overturned and the defendant espouses the true base rate of twenty percent, the parties may not achieve a settlement that could have left them both better off than litigating through verdict.

2. Remediation

What can be done to circumvent these biases? Research suggests that egocentric biases may be very difficult to eliminate. It may be useful to actively anticipate arguments in favor of the opponent's case, but at least one study suggests that this tactic is not sufficient—perhaps because advocates easily generate counterarguments. However, this same study showed that egocentric bias was significantly mitigated when participants were asked to explicitly list weaknesses in their own case. Hence, to achieve a more balanced view of one's prospects, it is essential to make a concerted and sincere effort to play devil's advocate. Many experts recommend the use of test juries to perform this function.

As for optimistic overconfidence, experts suggest that this bias can be mitigated if lawyers take pains to adopt an outsider's perspective by seeking base rate statistics on cases that are similar in relevant respects to the present case, rather than relying solely on an insider's perspective that typically entails an analysis of plans and scenarios concerning the case at

---

74. *See* Roderick M. Kramer et al., *Self-Enhancement Biases and Negotiator Judgment: Effects of Self–Esteem and Mood*, 56 Org. Behav. & Hum. Decision Processes 110 (1993).

hand. For example, a plaintiff's lawyer in a routine tort case might normally form an opinion of the probability of a jury verdict in his client's favor by assessing the credibility of each of his witnesses and the persuasive value of each piece of evidence he intends to offer. We suggest that this estimate would profit from a perusal of the local statistics about plaintiffs winning in similar cases. Of course, some further adjustment might be called for to account for cases that were too weak to withstand pretrial motions to dismiss.

Self-enhancing bias is arguably both a strength and a weakness. Many clients want to be represented by a counselor brimming with confidence— they may find this reassuring and also expect rosy prophesies to be self-fulfilling. On the other hand, if each attorney believes himself to be more honest, intelligent, and capable than the other, such tendencies can be counterproductive because they undermine incentives to settle. A little defensive humility is in order. Recognition of this pervasive tendency may allow attorneys to temper their expectations slightly and provide clients with more realistic assessments.

* * *

Question 8: How should I frame the offer?

* * *

Traditional economic analysis suggests that people should be sensitive to the impact of offers on final states of wealth, and that the particulars of how those offers are communicated should not matter.[173] Empirical studies of attorneys suggest that describing an offer in terms of gains versus losses can affect a lawyer's willingness to accept the offer. Certainly, lawyers choose words carefully, and this tendency extends to the crafting and communication of offers. However, for the most part, attorneys use this skill to avoid admitting or denying liability, or to avoid the accidental creation of exploitable weaknesses in their cases. Less thought goes into the question of how to frame an offer so that it is most likely to be accepted.

1. *The Psychology of Value and Framing*

Behavioral decision theorists have documented systematic violations of the standard economic assumption that people evaluate options in terms of their impact on one's final state of wealth. In particular, prospect theory assumes that people adapt to their present state of wealth and are sensitive to changes with respect to that endowment.[176]

173. *See, e.g.,* Amos Tversky, *Contrasting Rational and Psychological Principles of Choices, in* Wise Choices: Decisions, Games, and Negotiations 5 (Richard J. Zeckhauser, et al. eds. 1996).

176. Daniel Kahneman & Amos Tversky, *Prospect Theory: An Analysis of Decision*

under Risk, 47 Econometrica 263 (1979); Amos Tversky & Daniel Kahneman, *Advances in Prospect Theory: Cumulative Representations of Uncertainty,* 5 J. Risk & Uncertainty 297 (1992).

Second, people exhibit diminishing sensitivity to increasing gains and losses. For example, increasing an award from zero to $1000 is more pleasurable than increasing an award from $1000 to $2000; increasing an award from $2000 to $3000 is even less pleasurable, and so forth. Similarly, increasing a payment from zero to $1000 is more painful than increasing a payment from $1000 to $2000, and so on. One key implication of this pattern is that people's willingness to take risks differs for losses versus gains. For example, because $1000 is more than half as attractive as $2000, people typically prefer to receive $1,000 for sure than face a fifty-fifty chance of receiving $2,000 or nothing (i.e., they are "risk-averse" for medium probability gains). In contrast, because losing $1000 is more than half as painful as losing $2000, people typically prefer to risk a 50–50 chance of losing $2,000 or losing nothing to losing $1,000 for sure (i.e., they are "risk-seeking" for medium probability losses).

Third, prospect theory asserts that losses have more impact on choices than do equivalent gains. For example, most people do not think that a fifty percent chance of gaining $100 is sufficient to compensate a fifty percent chance of losing $100. In fact, people typically require a 50% chance of gaining as much as $200 or $300 to offset a 50% chance of losing $100.

Taken together, the way in which a problem is framed in terms of losses or gains can have a substantial impact on behavior in negotiations. First, loss aversion contributes to a bias in favor of the status quo because relative disadvantages of alternative outcomes loom larger than relative advantages. Hence, negotiators are often reluctant to make the tradeoffs necessary for them to achieve joint gains.[179] To illustrate, consider the case of two partners in a failing consulting firm. The joint office space and secretarial support costs are unduly burdensome, and each could operate productively out of their homes with minimal overhead costs. If they could divide their territory and agree not to compete, each could have a profitable career—but each would have to agree to give up half the firm's client base. Each partner may view the territory they retain as a gain that doesn't compensate adequately for the territory they must relinquish. Yet failure to make such a split consigns them to continuation in a losing venture.

Second, both loss aversion and the pattern of risk seeking for losses may lead to more aggressive bargaining when the task is viewed as minimizing losses rather than maximizing gains. Indeed, in laboratory studies, negotiators whose payoffs are framed in terms of gains (e.g., they were instructed to maximize revenues) tended to be more risk-averse than those whose payoffs are framed in terms of losses (e.g., they were instructed to minimize costs): the first group tended to be more concessionary but completed more transactions. Recently, Professor Rachlinski documented greater willingness to accept settlement offers in legal contexts when the offer is perceived as a gain compared to when it is perceived as a loss.

---

179. *See* William Samuelson & Richard Zeckhauser, *Status Quo Bias in Decision Making*, 1 J. Risk & Uncertainty 7 (1988). The authors also attribute status quo bias to * * * psychological commitments motivated by misperceptions of sunk costs, regret avoidance, or a drive for consistency.

Third, the attractiveness of potential agreements may be influenced by the way in which gains and losses are packaged and described. In particular, if a negotiator wants to present a proposal in its best possible light to a counterpart, he or she should attempt to integrate each aspect of the agreement on which the counterpart stands to lose (in order to exploit the fact that people experience diminishing sensitivity to each additional loss) and segregate each aspect of the agreement on which the counterpart stands to gain (in order to avoid the tendency of people to experience diminishing sensitivity to each additional gain). For instance, in the partnership dissolution example, it would be most effective to describe the territory forgone as a single unit (e.g., "everything west of highway 6 is mine") and the territory obtained in component parts (e.g., "and you will have the Heights neighborhood, the eastern section of downtown, everything north of there to the river, South Village, etc."), and least effective to describe the territory foregone in component parts (e.g. "I keep the west side of downtown, the riverfront, North Village, and everything between downtown and Ballard Square . . .") and the territory obtained as a single unit (e.g., "everything east of highway 6 is yours").

2.   *Remediation: Protecting Against Framing Effects*

Knowledge of the psychology of value can help a negotiator make offers appear more desirable to her counterpart, as described above. As for defending against inconsistency or manipulations by others, a negotiator should be aware that aspirations, past history, or previous offers may influence the frame of reference against which a negotiator perceives losses and gains; as a result, risk attitudes may be influenced by these transitory perceptions, which in turn influence how aggressively a negotiator bargains. Furthermore, negotiators must consciously overcome their natural reluctance to make concessions in order to exploit opportunities for trades that make both sides better off. Finally, in order to protect against mental accounting manipulations by others, a negotiator might develop a scoring system for each of the issues under consideration or translate everything into a unified dollar metric. By adding up points or dollars across all issues, the negotiator can focus on the value of the aggregate outcome to her client, rather than a piecemeal melange of incremental gains and losses that may have been creatively framed by her counterpart.

* * *

Question 9: How should I evaluate their offers?

* * *

When an attorney receives an offer from the other side, he is ethically obligated to transmit that offer to his client. He is not obligated to show the client a letter or play a voice-mail message or recite verbatim the offer with appropriate inflections. As the lawyer communicates the offer, the lawyer inevitably, if unwittingly, introduces a spin on the offer that may influence the client to consider it favorably or unfavorably. Usually the attorney's impression (and indeed, the client's) of the offer will be influenced to some degree by the identity of the offeror. In particular, if the attorney's dealings with the other side have been rancorous, the attorney may view any offer with a great deal of suspicion. Sometimes the relationship impedes impartial evaluation of an offer, causing a negotiator to reject an offer from an adversary that he should have accepted.

1. *Psychology of Reactive Devaluation*

Fixed-pie bias (i.e., the assumption that what is good for my counterpart must be bad for me) may contribute to *reactive devaluation*, which is a tendency to evaluate proposals less favorably after they have been offered by one's adversary.[186] In one classic study conducted during the days of Apartheid, researchers solicited students' evaluations of two university plans for divestment from South Africa. The first plan called for partial divestment, and the second increased investments in companies that had left South Africa. Both plans, which fell short of the students' demand for full divestment, were rated before and after the university announced that it would adopt the partial divestment plan. The results were dramatic: students rated the university plan less positively after it was announced by the university and the alternative plan more positively.

We hasten to note that the source of an offer may be diagnostic of its quality. It may be reasonable to view an offer more critically when the source is one's opponent, particularly if there is an unpleasant history between the parties. However, evidence from the aforementioned studies suggests that people tend to experience a knee-jerk overreaction to the source of the offer. If negotiators routinely undervalue concessions made by their counterparts, it will inhibit their ability to exploit tradeoffs that might result in more valuable agreements.

Consider an example of how reactive devaluation might manifest itself in a negotiation between lawyers. Imagine a simplified environmental cleanup action in which the parties are a governmental enforcement agency (represented by a single person) and a single responsible polluter. There may be two solutions to their problem. In one, the government effectuates the cleanup and sends a bill to the polluter. In the second, the polluter does the cleanup and the government inspects. Perhaps solution one meets more of the polluters' interests than solution two. One might suppose that the polluter would prefer this solution regardless of how it emerges as the agreed method. However, studies of reactive devaluation suggest that once the government tentatively agrees to that particular solution, the polluter may view the alternative solution more favorably. The apparent thought process is "if they held it back, it must be worse for them and therefore better for me than the one offered." The polluter may irrationally reorder her priorities and reject a deal simply because it was offered freely by an opponent.

---

186. *See* Lee Ross and Constance Stillinger, *Barriers to Conflict Resolution*, 7 NE- GOTIATION J. 389, 394–95 (1991) * * *

2. *Remediation*

Resisting the destructive effects of reactive devaluation will require negotiators to unlearn a pervasive assumption that most people carry with them. Negotiations are rarely fixed-sum and it is simply not true that what is good for one side is necessarily bad for the other. As mentioned above, both parties often have congruent interests or a mutual interest in exploiting tradeoffs on issues that they prioritize differently. To resist reactive devaluation, one must short-circuit a deeply ingrained habit. It is natural to react against freedom to choose, and when an opponent holds back one offer in favor of another, it's natural to yearn for the alternative option. However, it would be wise to critically examine this natural impulse and ask if this impulse is a rational response to a truly inferior offer or an emotional reaction against the other side's initiative.

Even if a lawyer can restrain herself from reactive devaluation, it may be very difficult to buffer this response in [her] counterpart. Certainly, it first may help to cultivate a cordial relationship with one's counterpart to the extent that this is possible, so that offers are regarded with less suspicion. Second, it may be helpful to ask a mutually trusted intermediary to convey a proposal. Some commentators have suggested that reactive devaluation can be overcome with the help of a mediator. Finally, if a party crafts a settlement package that would be mutually beneficial, it may be helpful to work with opposing counsel to make them feel as if the solution was jointly initiated or even that it was the opposing counsel's idea.

NOTES AND QUESTIONS

1. Some of the psychological phenomena described by Birke and Fox are heuristic in nature—they are mental shortcuts to simplify the process of making meaning out of our experiences. Such shortcuts can have great benefit—the availability heuristic described first, for example, obviously makes it much easier to make quick judgments without having to assess a situation completely. In conflict, however, as the old saying goes, sometimes a shortcut ends up being the longest way around. When coupled with the tendency to perceive a situation in a self-serving light, for example, simplifying one's perceptions may lead to intractable differences:

> [T]he need to simplify a conflict situation can lead to faulty perception about cause-and-effect relationships. People may falsely infer a relationship where none exists, or they may assume that a given action by one person results in an action by the other person. This effect, known as the "biased punctuation of conflict," occurs when people interpret interaction with their adversaries in other-derogating terms. Actor A perceives the history of conflict with another actor, B, as a sequence of B–A, B–A, B–A, in which the initial hostile or aggressive move was always made by B, obliging A to engage in defensive and legitimate retaliatory action. Actor B punctuates the same history of interaction as A–B, A–B, A–B, however, reversing the roles of aggressor and defender. Disagreement about how to punctuate

a sequence of events in a conflict relationship is at the root of many disputes. * * *

Thompson and Nadler, Judgmental Biases in Conflict Resolution and How to Overcome Them in The Handbook of Conflict Resolution: Theory and Practice 213, 214–219 (2000).

2. Birke and Fox discuss the importance of prospect theory and its implications for framing effects and risk aversion. As we saw in Section A, prospect theory can explain why plaintiffs are often risk averse and defendants risk-preferring. In most cases, if a defendant sees her choice as between a sure loss through settlement or a chance of avoiding loss through further litigation, the defendant may be prone to gamble to try to avoid the loss. Conversely, plaintiffs are often likely to take a sure gain through settlement rather than gamble on the possibility of greater gain through litigation.

Professor Chris Guthrie has also applied prospect theory to explain so-called frivolous litigation. Research has shown that "[w]hen choosing between low-probability gains and losses with equal expected values, ... individuals make risk-seeking choices when selecting between gains and risk-averse choices when selecting between losses." Guthrie, Framing Frivolous Litigation: A Psychological Theory, 67 U.Chi.L.Rev. 163, 167 (2000). In other words, although normally a plaintiff may be risk-averse, when facing a low-probability of success, a plaintiff may be risk-preferring. For example, a plaintiff is more likely to choose to continue litigation and gamble on a five percent chance of a $1 million recovery than to accept a $50,000 settlement for that litigation, whereas a defendant will likely be risk-averse as between the same two choices and agree to settle. This may partly explain why plaintiffs pursue low-probability litigation so aggressively and why defendants may be willing to settle such claims.

3. Another psychological bias, called the "endowment effect," can also influence bargainers. The endowment effect is simple: people overvalue items they own as compared to items they don't. Individuals will demand more in compensation to give up something they already possess than they will offer as a payment to purchase the same item.

Many experiments have demonstrated this effect. In one classic study, experimenters gave some subjects a coffee mug and then offered them the choice to keep the mug or to sell it for an unspecified but predetermined price. These subjects had to write down the price at which they would sell their mug. Another group didn't receive mugs. Instead, they had to write down how much they were willing to spend to buy one. The researchers found that the median asking price for sellers was $7.12, whereas the median offer from buyers was $2.88. See Kahneman, Knetsch and Thaler, Experimental Tests of the Endowment Effect and the Coase Theorem, 98 J.Pol.Econ. 1325 (1990).

The endowment effect is related to loss aversion—those with a mug demand extra compensation to overcome what they perceive as a loss. Can you imagine ways in which the endowment effect may influence settlement negotiations in a legal dispute? When might a plaintiff, or a defendant, feel reluctant to give up something that they feel is already their entitlement or endowment?

For an argument that the behavior described as the endowment effect is not actually a cognitive error but instead can be explained in terms of self-interested "signaling," see Fremling and Posner, Market Signaling of Personal Characteristics 26–27 (U.Chi. Working Paper in L. & Econ.).

4. Birke and Fox briefly discuss the problem of overconfidence in negotiation-related judgments. Much research demonstrates that bargainers make self-serving and overconfident assessments, with obvious consequences:

> Conflicts and disputes are characterized by the presence of asymmetric information. In general, each side knows a great deal about the evidence and arguments that support its position and much less about those that support the position of the other side. The difficulty of making proper allowance for missing information * * * entails a bias that is likely to hinder successful negotiation. Each side will tend to overestimate its chances of success, as well as its ability to impose a solution on the other side and to prevent such an attempt by an opponent. Many years ago, we suggested that participants in a conflict are susceptible to a fallacy of initiative—a tendency to attribute less initiative and less imagination to the opponent than to oneself. The difficulty of adopting the opponent's view of the chessboard or of the battlefield may help explain why people often discover many new moves when they switch sides in a game. A related phenomenon has been observed in the response to mock trials that are sometimes conducted when a party to a dispute considers the possibility of litigation. Observers of mock trials have noted that the would-be litigators are often surprised and dismayed by the strength of the position put forth by their mock opponent. In the absence of such a vivid demonstration of their bias, disputants are likely to hold an overly optimistic assessment of their chances in court. More generally, a tendency to underestimate the strength of the opponent's position could make negotiators less likely to make concessions and thereby reduce the chances of a negotiated settlement. Neale and Bazerman (1983) illustrated this effect in the context of a final arbitration procedure, in which the parties submit final offers, one of which is selected by the arbitrator. Negotiators overestimated (by more than 15 percent, on the average) the chance that their offer would be chosen. In this situation, a more realistic appraisal would probably result in more conciliatory final offers.

Kahneman and Tversky, Conflict Resolution: A Cognitive Perspective, in Barriers to Conflict Resolution 47 (1995).

If you have ever been in the middle of a dispute—between two friends, two litigating parties, or two business partners, for example—you may have experienced such overconfidence effects first-hand. Both sides may seem supremely confident, so much so that to a third party their behavior and judgments seem almost comical. But when *you* are party to a dispute it is much more difficult to assess accurately your chances of success.

Reconsider the discussion of litigation analysis and decision trees in Section A. Is such analysis rendered worthless by the overconfidence bias? Or is litigation analysis a useful antidote to such psychological effects?

5. The phenomenon of reactive devaluation, covered at the end of the Birke and Fox excerpt, could theoretically have serious consequences for dispute resolution. If a party is likely to devalue an offer from the other side *merely because it comes from the other side*, finding solutions of any sort to a dispute may be jeopardized. Although the causes of this psychological effect are not entirely clear, the following excerpt summarizes two possibilities:

> One set of underlying processes involves changes in *perception, interpretation, or inference*, either about individual elements in a proposal or about the overall valence of that proposal. To the extent that the other side's initiative seems inconsistent with our understanding of their interests and/or past negotiation behavior, we are apt, perhaps even logically obliged, to scrutinize their offer rather carefully. That is, we are inclined to look for ambiguities, omissions, or "fine print" that might render the terms of that proposal more advantageous to the other side, and perhaps less advantageous to our side, than we had assumed them to be (or would have assumed them to be, had the question been asked) prior to their being offered. The results of such skeptical scrutiny—especially if the terms in question are unclear, complex, or imperfectly specified, and especially if trust vis-à-vis implementation of these terms is called for—are apt to be a revised assessment of what we stand to gain, both in absolute terms and relative to what we believe the other side stands to gain, from acceptance of the relevant proposal.
>
> This process of inference and deduction, as psychologists would be quick to note, could be even simpler and less cognitively demanding. Several theories of psychological consistency hold that any relevant object of judgment (including, presumably, a concession offer or a negotiation proposal) will be evaluated more negatively as a consequence of its linkage to a negative source (including, presumably, an enemy or adversary). In other words, no reinterpretation, in fact no consideration of content at all, need take place for devaluation to occur. One might simply reason that if "they" are offering a proposal it must be good for them; and if it is good for them (especially if "they" are adversaries who wish us harm) it must be bad for "us." Once again, although it is difficult to criticize such inferential leaps on purely normative grounds, the danger should be obvious. One can be led to conclude that any proposal offered by the "other side"—especially if that other side has long been perceived as an enemy—*must* be to our side's disadvantage, or else it would not have been offered. Such an inferential process, however, assumes a perfect opposition of interests, or in other words, a true "zero-sum" game, when such is rarely the

case in real-world negotiations between parties whose needs, goals, and opportunities are inevitably complex and varied.

The second type of underlying process or mechanism, suggested by demonstrations of the devaluation phenomenon in the Stanford divestment studies in which the source of the devalued proposal was not really an enemy of the recipient, is very different. This mechanism involves neither mindful nor mindless changes in interpretation, but rather changes in underlying *preferences*. Human beings, at least in some circumstances, may be inclined to reject or devalue whatever is freely available to them, and to covet and strive for whatever is denied them. Moreover, they may be inclined to do so even when no hostility is perceived on the part of the individual or institution determining what will or will not be made available. The familiar aphorism that "the grass is always greener on the other side of the fence" captures this source of human unhappiness and frustration very well, and it is easy to think of anecdotal examples in which children or adults, rather than "counting their blessings," seem to place inordinately high value on whatever commodity or opportunity is denied them.

* * *

The preceding discussion of the reactive devaluation phenomenon, and of the various processes that might underlie it, has some implication for those who seek to resolve disputes. Foremost, of course, is the likelihood that compromise proposals or concessions designed to demonstrate goodwill and prompt reciprocation will fail in their objectives. All too often, they will be dismissed as trivial and token, or received with coolness and expressions of distrust that serve to thwart the goal of negotiated agreement and to weaken rather than strengthen the hand of those who urge conciliation. Furthermore, such public dismissals or cool receptions are themselves apt to be misattributed—to be seen as the product of calculated strategy rather than genuine sentiment, or to be taken as evidence of a lack of good faith and seriousness in the pursuit of agreement. * * *

Two strategies for reducing reactive devaluation follow rather directly. Both are designed to discourage the recipients of a concession or compromise proposal from reinterpreting its terms or reordering their own preferences in ways that make the proposal seem less advantageous to them. The first strategy involves explicitly eliciting the potential recipients' values and preferences before making any concessionary proposal, and then explicitly linking the content of the subsequent proposal to those expressed values and preferences. * * *

A related strategy * * * would be for one side simply to offer the other a "menu" of unilateral concessions that it is willing to make as a gesture to initiate a cycle of future *reciprocal* concessions; and then to invite that other side to select the "pump-priming" concession of its choice.

Ross, Reactive Devaluation in Negotiation and Conflict Resolution, in Barriers to Conflict Resolution 34–40 (1995).

Do these ways to overcome reactive devaluation seem plausible? What of those suggested by Birke and Fox?

b. THE ROLE OF EMOTION

In addition to these cognitive and social psychological effects, the emotions play a critical role in disputes and in negotiation. The legal academy has become increasingly interested in the role of emotions in the law. See Bandes, The Passions of the Law (1999); Law, Psychology, and the Emotions, Symposium Issue, 74 Chi.–Kent L.Rev. 1423 (2000). The next two excerpts explore the role of attributions in creating and sustaining emotions in conflict and the steps a negotiator can take to deal with emotions in a dispute.

Keith G. Allred, Anger and Retaliation in Conflict: The Role of Attribution

in Morton Deutsch and Peter T. Coleman (eds.), The Handbook of Conflict Resolution: Theory and Practice 236, 243–244 (2000).

* * * Anger-driven conflict is often maladaptive in at least two respects. First, it is particularly destructive because, once angered at each other, parties in a conflict become less effective at solving the problems between them. One study found that negotiators who held each other responsible for harmful behavior in a previous interaction felt greater anger and less compassion toward each other than those who did not hold each other responsible for the same harmful behavior. Consequently, the angry negotiators had less positive regard for each other's interests in the negotiation. As a result, the negotiators who were angry with each other discovered fewer mutually beneficial solutions than the participants who were not angry with each other.

A second reason that angry, retaliatory conflicts are especially maladaptive is because they are frequently rooted in misperceptions that tend to escalate the conflict. Research on the actor-observer bias seems to suggest that a harmdoer attributes his or her behavior to external causes while the harmed party attributes the behavior to a disposition of the harmdoer. However, most actor-observer bias research has not examined situations in which the actor's behavior has a direct and negative impact on the observer. For example, many actor-observer bias studies investigate situations in which one person observes another in conversation or offering an opinion on a topic, rather than the situation [in which another's] behaviors have direct and negative impact * * *

A recent study investigated these situations in which the actor's behavior negatively affects the observer. * * * The results of the study indicated the presence of an *accuser bias*, the tendency for an observer negatively affected by an actor's behavior to attribute the behavior to causes under the control of the actor. For example, [if] Margaret is negatively affected by Robin's request that she come to work on Saturday, she is more likely to attribute the request to Robin's lack of organization than to her daughter's asthma attack. Consequently, Margaret is likely to feel greater anger and a stronger impulse to retaliate than she otherwise would. The accuser bias thus tends to make anger-driven conflict especially destructive because such conflicts are often rooted in exaggerated judgments of responsibility that lead to excessive anger and retaliation.

The destructive effects of the accuser bias are greatly exacerbated because the person who acts negatively falls victim to the opposite bias. The study documenting the accuser bias also revealed a *bias of the accused*, a tendency to attribute one's own harmful behavior to circumstances beyond one's control. In our example, Robin is likely to overattribute her need to have Margaret come in to her daughter's asthma attack, and underattribute it to her own lack of organization.

* * * The point of the research on the accuser bias and the bias of the accused is that, of the contributing causes of a harmful behavior, the accused tends to focus on those beyond her control, while the accuser focuses on those within the control of the accused. Consequently, the accuser holds the accused more responsible for the harmful behavior than the accused holds herself accountable.

* * *

In fact, research suggests that once these mutually derogating attributional patterns give rise to such dynamics they can become so entrenched that they define not only a unique and especially destructive type of conflict but an especially destructive type of relationship as well. * * * [D]ozens of studies investigating differences in attributional patterns among people in close relationships, mostly marital couples, have found similar results. In stressed or dissatisfied relationships, the parties consistently attributed each other's negative behavior to internal, controllable causes and attributed each other's positive behavior to external, uncontrollable causes. Consequently, people in stressed relationships felt negative emotions toward each other and had difficulty solving the problems that arose between them.

People in satisfied relationships, by contrast, tended to exhibit no such derogating pattern of attribution. In fact, people in some satisfied relationships exhibited a reversal of typical derogating attribution, attributing each other's negative behavior to external, uncontrollable causes and positive behavior to internal, controllable causes. * * *

Once established, both the stressed and satisfied marital patterns are self-fulfilling and self-perpetuating. That is, at some point the bias actually becomes an accurate perception. In a distressed relationship, the parties purposely behave negatively toward each other, although each sees his or her own negative behavior as the other person's just desserts for a prior negative act by that person. In a satisfied relationship, the parties intentionally act kindly toward each other. Nevertheless, * * * evidence suggests that attributional bias is the ultimate causal agent. In other words, the pattern is largely set in motion in the first place by the difference in attributional pattern. The research * * * thus suggests that once [two people] begin to exchange angry, retaliatory behavior—fueled by offsetting biases in judging how responsible each is for these behaviors—they face more than simply the destructiveness of a single angry conflict. They also run the risk of transforming their relationship into one characterized by chronic angry conflict.

Robert S. Adler, Benson Rosen, and Elliot M. Silverstein, Emotions in Negotiation: How to Manage Fear and Anger

14 Neg.J. 161, 167–177 (1998).

Anger in Negotiations

Two millennia ago, poet and satirist Horace wrote *Ira furor brevis est*—anger is a short madness. When we become truly furious, we may act in an utterly irrational way for a period of time. Although a temper tantrum may relieve pent-up feelings for a moment, we often find regret and negative recriminations following such displays. On this point, Queen Elizabeth I reportedly observed, "anger makes dull men witty, but it also keeps them poor."

Anger springs from many sources. On one hand, it may arise from the perception that someone has violated written or unwritten rules of behavior. In chimpanzee society, De Waal notes that members of a group exhibit what he terms *moralistic aggression*, that is, chimps perceived as stingy and unsharing are more likely to be attacked and refused favors than those that act in a more generous spirit. On a human level, someone who rudely breaks in line or recklessly cuts us off in traffic will likely ignite fires of indignation if we are the victims of these transgressions.

Anger also arises when one encounters snubs, rudeness, or anything that provokes a feeling of being unfairly diminished—we get angry because we feel vulnerable and exposed. In similar fashion, shame may trigger anger. If our egos are bruised in a manner that makes us feel small, we react defensively, and often in anger. The evolutionary basis for anger seems clear: anger motivates us to retaliate when we are attacked and to defend ourselves against those whom we believe are doing us harm. As with other emotions, what one feels at any given moment is both physical and situational. Fear may prompt a chimpanzee to flee from a more powerful lion, but anger will drive it to lash out at a weaker chimp who snatches a piece of food that it was about to eat.

In the negotiation context, a host of factors can contribute to anger and aggression. Citing a variety of studies, Barry and Oliver suggest the following examples where these negative emotions can arise in dyadic negotiations: where bargainers are accountable to angry constituents; where bargainers face time pressures; where they perceive the situation as win-lose with divergent goals between the parties; or, generally, where the parties are otherwise unconcerned with protecting a working relationship. In a study of anger in mergers and acquisitions, Daly found the following types of behavior likely to trigger anger: misrepresentation; making excessive demands; overstepping one's authority; showing personal animosity; questioning a representative's authority to negotiate; seeking to undermine a representative's authority by "going over his head"; and dwelling on unimportant details.

* * *

Dealing With Your Anger

The critical need for self-awareness. Virtually all researchers and commentators on emotions and negotiations insist that the first step necessary in controlling anger is self-awareness. If we cannot sense when our anger has been aroused, we will miss an opportunity to control it. Anger typically has physical manifestations, such as a rapid heartbeat, muscle tensing, increased sweating, or flushed face.

* * *

Determine situations that trigger inappropriate anger. In some cases, anger is an appropriate response to a provocative situation. At other times, we may instantly, and inappropriately, ignite in circumstances that most other bargainers would not find provocative. For example, some people react furiously to meetings that start a few minutes late. Others become livid at real or imagined slights to their dignity. Anger at these moments generally serves no useful purpose. Determining those things that trigger inappropriate anger may permit us to take steps to avoid them or to take preventative measures to control anger.

Decide whether to display anger. Recognizing how and why our anger arises does not mean that we should always avoid angry feelings or never display anger. But, if one can recognize the onset of anger, one can decide how best to deal with it. In some cases, we should reveal our feelings. For example, if a fellow negotiator has just falsely accused us of lying, we might want to demonstrate extreme displeasure in a way that persuades the other side that such charges are false and will not be tolerated. The trick is to do so in a manner that makes the point, but does not undermine the negotiation. This requires a careful assessment of the circumstances and of our opponent's reaction to our anger, and a measured approach to expressing our feelings.

* * *

Dealing With Your Opponent's Anger

Just as we need to develop a good instinct for determining when we become angry; we also need to be able to read our opponents' moods, particularly those involving frustration and anger. Here are some techniques that may be useful:

Defuse heated emotional buildups. Every good negotiator seeks to remain alert to the mood of a negotiation at all times. One should always seek to monitor opponents for anger. If one senses a rising temper on the other side, it may help to ask directly: "Mary, is something bothering you?" or "Tom, did my comment about the necessity of meeting deadlines disturb you?" or "Regina, you look angry. Are you?"

Assess the significance of angry displays. When an opponent erupts in anger, one should assess as carefully as possible the significance of the anger. Does it seem calculated? Can the person regain composure? In some cases, the other side may try to convey anger as a strategic maneuver to dislodge us from a firmly-held position. Dealing with such an approach calls for a different response than dealing with a truly lost temper. Trying to placate someone who is using anger strategically to gain concessions may well lead us to make overly generous offers.

Address an opponent's anger. In some cases, you may need to say something like, "Irv, I'm sure you're going to rethink the comments you've just made. I hope that you realize they were inappropriate. In the meantime, you've made me angry, so I need a break before we resume bargaining." It rarely hurts to acknowledge an opponent's anger even when one disagrees that it is justified. In some cases, an apology—even one felt to be undeserved—will help smooth the course of a negotiation. You should not apologize, however, in a way that leads an opponent to conclude that you have conceded a point that remains in dispute or that you are a weak negotiator. Thus, instead of offering a personal apology, you can—as easily and as effectively—simply apologize for the "bad situation."

* * *

Help an angry opponent save face. Perhaps the biggest deal breaker in negotiations is "face loss." Where parties feel they will lose face if they agree to an opponent's demands, they are likely to derail the negotiation even if it is not in their interest to do so. So critical is "face" to a negotiation that parties will hold to untenable positions that will cost them money or even provoke wars—Schoonmaker cites the example of two Latin American countries that fought a war because of angry feelings over a soccer match. Accordingly, one should always try to help an angry opponent save face especially if lost face is what triggered the outburst in the first place. * * *

NOTES AND QUESTIONS

1. Allred points out that the emotions are not wholly distinct from cognition and perception. If you think you've seen a coiled snake on the path, you're likely to jump in fear. But when you realize that it was merely a pile of old rope, your emotions calm, your heart rate may decrease, and you will experience the situation quite differently.

The actor-observer and accuser biases Allred discusses derive from what is known as the fundamental attribution error. We tend to assume that when others act in ways we dislike they do so because of their internal motivations, beliefs, or desires, whereas when *we* do something that others may dislike we attribute our own actions to circumstantial causes. You may, for example, assume that someone else is late because they're lazy; when you're late you know it's because your car broke down.

The angry emotions created by these misattributions can make negotiation much more difficult. The more anger and less compassion negotiators feel toward each other, the less willing they generally are to work together in the future. Similarly, high degrees of anger may make negotiators less likely to discover available joint gains. See Allred, Mallozzi, Matsui, and Raia, The Influence of Anger and Compassion on Negotiation Performance, 70 Org.Behav. & Human Dec. Proceses 175–187 (1997). However, anger does *not* seem to help negotiators claim more value for themselves. Id.

2. A dispute can become more emotional as the lawyers and clients involved negotiate about it. The other side's bargaining behavior may make you angry; their threats, bluffs, lying, delays, or other tactics may cause your blood to boil. Such behavior, and the emotion it engenders, may make you resist collaborating with the other side.

Adler, Rosen and Silverstein mention that "saving face" can be an important interest for many negotiators, and that loss of "face" can lead to angry reactions. Affronts to status are one way in which even seemingly innocent bargaining moves may generate an emotional reaction:

> [S]tudies indicate that bargainers whose social face has been affronted may resist making concessions, may fail to reach an agreement advantageous to them, and may engage in costly retaliation. These responses can be viewed as alternative ways of regaining self-esteem and social esteem.
>
> The affront to social face posed by an invalidation of a bargainer's position may be greatly reduced if the negotiator is able to assure the bargainer that he has not appeared personally weak and incapable. High-status bargainers whose position has been rejected and have no direct information concerning whether they have appeared effective as persons or not may try to assert that they are strong persons by resisting compromising.

Tjosvold and Huston, Social Face and Resistance to Compromise in Bargaining, 104 J. of Soc.Psychol. 57, 59 (1978).

3. Adler, Rosen and Silverstein suggest a fairly rational or cognitive approach to thinking through an emotional negotiation. First, they suggest thinking carefully about your own anger and whether displaying anger will be useful and appropriate. Second, they advise a negotiator to analyze an opponent's angry display and determine the best way to respond. Other commentators have likewise suggested that one should "think through" one's feelings in conflict situations rather than merely responding emotionally. See e.g., Stone, Patton and Heen, Difficult Conversations: How to Discuss What Matters Most 91–105 (1999). What are the advantages and disadvantages of such an approach? Will it work?

2. Interpersonal Style and Skill

These psychological barriers to dispute resolution affect the ways in which we think about and react to conflict. You may be unaware of their influence and yet subject to it. In addition to such psychological and emotional aspects of bargaining, however, we must consider the more social domain—the ways in which bargaining is an interpersonal event and is shaped by your interpersonal style and skills.

We each have different tendencies and our own style when faced with conflict. One's style differs from one's strategy:

> In settlement negotiation, it is not enough to say that one wants to negotiate "amicably" or "cooperatively." These words do not by themselves mean that someone wants to negotiate in a problem-solving manner. The words are as applicable to positional negotiation as they are to the problem-solving kind. For instance, one can negotiate positionally by using a pleasant, amicable outward "style" while still using a highly positional "strategy" of making and holding to settlement positions. Being cooperative might mean no more than making concessions to the bargaining positions taken by the other side. Not only is this an entirely positional kind of procedure, but it is also an ineffectual one. * * *

Heumann and Hyman, Negotiation Methods and Litigation Settlement Methods in New Jersey: "You Can't Always Get What You Want", 12 Ohio St.J. of Dis.Res. 253, 279–282 (1997).

In this Section we consider the different interpersonal skills needed to negotiate effectively.

Donald G. Gifford, Legal Negotiation: Theory and Applications

21 (1989).

It is important for the lawyer to distinguish style from strategy in a * * * negotiation for two reasons. First, many of the disadvantages of *competitive tactics*—the possibilities of deadlock and a premature breakdown of negotiation, and of generating ill-will and distrust with the other party—can be mitigated if the *style* of the negotiator is cooperative. Even when the substance being communicated to the other negotiator is very demanding and competitive, friendliness, courtesy and politeness help to preserve a positive working relationship.

Conversely, [a] lawyer needs to be able to identify *competitive tactics* even when the style of the negotiator is *cooperative*. Often, lawyers will be misled by the polite and friendly style of the other lawyer and assume that he is using *cooperative tactics, i.e.,* that his goals include a fair and just agreement and a positive, trusting working relationship between the parties. To the extent that the negotiator confuses cooperative style for cooperative substance, she may be inclined to reciprocate, and the resulting agreement will disadvantage her client.

Admittedly, the personal *style* of the negotiator often is intertwined with the negotiation strategy she is using in a specific negotiation or that she prefers to use. A negotiator who has an aggressive and forceful personal style frequently will succeed in causing the other negotiator to lose confidence in himself or his case, thereby inducing him to settle for less than he initially expected, a goal of the competitive strategy. In other instances, however, a negotiator who is courteous, personable and friendly may, through competitive strategic moves such as extreme opening demands and infrequent concessions, be even more successful in destroying the other party's confidence in his case and inducing unilateral concessions from him. Although a negotiator's personal style of interaction positively correlates with her preferred negotiating strategy, separating personal style from negotiation strategies and techniques yields new flexibility for the negotiator. It is possible for the negotiator with a *cooperative* personal *style* to adopt *competitive tactics* when it is advantageous, and naturally *competitive* individuals can adopt *cooperative tactics*.

Robert H. Mnookin, Scott R. Peppet and Andrew S. Tulumello, The Tension Between Empathy and Assertiveness

12 Neg.J. 217, 218–226 (1996).

* * * We propose that negotiation behavior can be conceptualized along two dimensions—*assertiveness* and *empathy*. By assertiveness, we mean the capacity to express and advocate for one's own interests. By empathy, we mean the capacity to demonstrate an accurate, non-judgmental understanding of another person's concerns and perspective.

Empathy and assertiveness are in "tension" because many negotiators implicitly assume that these two sets of skills represent polar opposites along a single continuum and that each is incompatible with the other. Some worry, for example, that to listen or empathize too much signals weakness or agreement; they perceive empathy to be incompatible with assertion. Others are concerned that if they advocate too strongly they will upset or anger their counterpart; they believe that assertion undermines empathy. Many negotiators fall somewhere in between. Not needing to dominate but preferring not to surrender control, they are unsure how much to assert. Or, open to understanding the other side but also wanting to secure the best possible outcome, they do not know how much to empathize. In short, many negotiators feel stuck. * * *

* * *

Our claim that empathy and assertiveness represent different dimensions [of negotiation behavior] can be illuminated by considering three common negotiation "styles." These are *competing*, *accommodating* and *avoiding*, each of which represents a different suboptimal combination of empathy and assertiveness. * * *

Competing

A competitive style consists of substantial assertion but little empathy. A competitor wants to experience "winning" and enjoys feeling purposeful and in control. Competitive negotiators exude eagerness, enthusiasm, and impatience. Because conflict does not make them feel uncomfortable, they enjoy being partisans. Competitive negotiators typically seek to control the agenda and frame the issues. They can stake out an ambitious position and stick to it, and they fight back in the face of bullying or intimidation.

The advantages of this style flow directly from this characterization. Competitors are not afraid to articulate and push for their point of view. With respect to distributive bargaining, they fight hard to get the biggest slice of any pie.

But this tendency also has disadvantages. Competitive negotiators risk provoking the other side and incur a high risk of escalation or stalemate. In addition, because competitive negotiators are often not good listeners, they have difficulty developing collaborative relationships that allow both sides to explore value-creating opportunities. They may also pay a high price in their relationships, as others, perceiving them as arrogant, untrustworthy, or controlling, avoid them. * * *

* * *

Accommodating

Accommodating consists of substantial empathy but little assertion. An accommodator prizes good relationships and wants to feel liked. Accommodators exude concern, compassion, and understanding. Concerned that conflict will disrupt relationships, they negotiate in "smoothing" ways to resolve difference quickly. Accommodators typically listen well and are quick to second-guess their own interests.

This style has straightforward advantages. Negotiators concerned with good relationships on balance probably do have better relationships, or at least fewer relationships marked by open conflict. Because they listen well, others may see them as trustworthy. Similarly, they are adept at creating a less stressful atmosphere for the negotiation.

One disadvantage of this tendency is that it can be exploited. Hard bargainers may extract concessions by implicitly or explicitly threatening to disrupt or terminate the relationship. Another disadvantage may be that accommodators pay insufficient attention to the substance of the dispute because they are unduly concerned about disturbing a relationship. Accommodators, therefore, can feel frustrated dealing with both substantive and interpersonal issues.

Avoiding

An avoiding style consists of low levels of empathy and assertiveness. Avoiders believe that conflict is unproductive, and they feel uncomfortable with explicit, especially emotional, disagreement. When faced with conflict, avoiders disengage. They tend not to seek control of the agenda or to frame the issues. Rather, they deflect efforts to focus on solutions, appearing detached, unenthusiastic, or uninterested.

At times, avoidance can have substantial advantages. Some disputes are successfully avoided. In other cases, avoiders may create a "chasing" dynamic in which the other side does all the work * * * Because they appear aloof, avoiders can have more persuasive impact when they do speak up. In addition, their reserve and cool-headedness makes it difficult for others to know their true interests and intentions.

The greatest disadvantage of this tendency is that avoiders miss opportunities to use conflict to solve problems. Avoiders often disengage without knowing whether obscured interests might make joint gains possible—they rarely have the experience of walking away from an apparent conflict feeling better off. Even when they do negotiate, avoiders leave value on the table because they refrain from asserting their own interests or flushing out the other side's. Avoiders fare poorly in the distributive aspects of bargaining.

* * *

* * * [W]e believe that a negotiator is most effective if she leads the way by successfully combining empathy and assertiveness. The normative task is to manage the tension between empathy and assertiveness by * * * helping design a process that permits the other side to do so as well. This often means agreeing to listen and empathize for a period on the condition that the other side agrees to try to do so later in the negotiation, and also discussing explicitly that a demonstrated understanding of the other's views should not be interpreted as agreement. In this way, a negotiation can sometimes evolve toward problem-solving even if it begins less productively.

Keith G. Allred, Distinguishing Best and Strategic Practices: A Framework for Managing the Dilemma Between Creating and Claiming Value
Neg. J. 387, 388–390 (2000).

This essay outlines a prescriptive framework for managing negotiation dilemmas * * * The prescriptive advice is based on drawing a distinction between "best practices" and "strategic practices." Best practices are defined as those that work well in terms of one or more dimensions of negotiation performance without diminishing one's performance on the other dimensions. For example, listening may be a practice that helps a negotiator create value and maintain the relationship with the other party without posing much risk to that negotiator's efforts to claim value. These are practices that pose no real dilemma. They tend to work well in most situations, regardless of what the other party does. The prescriptive advice is simply to use these practices in virtually all situations, even though there may be a tendency not to use them in certain situations. For instance, one may tend to listen less to an irritating and competitive other party, even though some situations could be handled more effectively by listening.

Strategic practices are defined as those that tend to work well in terms of one or more dimensions of negotiation performance, but that also tend to diminish one's performance on other dimensions. These are the practices, such as sharing information, that pose classic negotiation dilemmas. For example, full and truthful information sharing increases the chances of discovering an agreement that creates value and tends to enhance the relationship, but that information may also be exploited by the other party to gain a claiming-value advantage.

Accordingly, these practices work well in some situations and poorly in others. The key to generating prescriptive advice regarding strategic practices is to specify the conditions in which negotiators should use such practices more and those in which they should use them less. For example, a negotiator should probably share more information the more cooperative and trustworthy the other party is and the more significant and long-term the relationship is.

* * *

Asserting Facet

With respect to the asserting facet, the framework specifies three best practices and two strategic practices * * * The first best practice derives from prior work suggesting that working to develop and improve one's best alternative to a negotiated agreement (BATNA) is a practice that is effective in claiming-value terms without harming one in terms of creating value or maintaining the relationship. The second asserting best practice is based on research * * * indicating that effective professional negotiators * * * typically use a few of the most persuasive arguments available in support of the positions they advocate rather than diluting their persuasion efforts with a number of additional but weaker arguments. The third asserting best practice is derived logically. A minimally assertive practice of working to see that, where possible, one's own needs and interests are met would seem to present claiming-value advantages at little cost in terms of creating value or maintaining the relationship.

The first strategic asserting practice draws on research indicating that asserting practices such as taking extreme opening positions and being slow to make concessions can be used to gain a claiming-value advantage. A second strategic asserting practice that is similar is using one's power and authority to win a favorable outcome. While these practices can be effective in claiming-value terms, they can also compromise a negotiator's ability to create value and maintain the relationship. Accordingly, negotiators should be less willing to use them the more important, cooperative, trusting, and long-term the relationship with the other party is and the less important the interests the negotiator has at stake are.

Accommodating Facet

The framework identifies four best and one strategic practice with regard to accommodating * * * The accommodating best practices tend to involve accommodations in terms of the negotiation process rather than concessions on substantive issues. The first accommodating best practice draws on research on procedural and interactional justice suggesting that treating the other party with consideration and respect, even if one does not agree with the other party, will do a great deal to enhance the relationship without costing one anything in terms of substantive concessions. In fact, justice research suggests that such procedural and interactional accommodations will, in many ways, do more to prime the pump of trusting, cooperative interactions than will accommodation in the form of substantive concessions. Negotiators can provide the other party with a sense of procedural and interactional fairness through such actions as listening and seeking to understand and appreciate the other party's perspective.

The second accommodating best practice is drawn from research on attributional biases and anger in negotiation and conflict situations. This practice involves resisting the tendency to hold others more responsible for problems that arise than one holds oneself and resisting the tendency to retaliate angrily when one holds the other party responsible for problems.

The third and fourth best accommodating practices are based on * * * research on effective professional negotiators. That research indicated that effective negotiators do not use positive words such as "reasonable" and "generous" to describe their own proposals. The same research also indicated that effective negotiators do not immediately respond to the other party's proposal with a counterproposal.

Accommodation that takes the form of substantive concessions rather than process or interaction accommodations, logic would suggest, should be designated as strategic practices. While such substantive accommodations can help maintain the ongoing relationship, they clearly come at a claiming-value, and even a creating-value, cost. Negotiators should therefore be more willing to make such substantive concessions to the extent that the interests they have at stake are of limited importance and the relationship with the other party is important, cooperative, trusting, and ongoing.

Integrating Facet

Regarding the integrating facet, the framework specifies three best practices and two strategic practices * * * The first integrating best practice is based on research on logrolling that suggest that one should be willing to compromise on something of lesser importance in order to gain something of greater importance. The second integrating best practice is based on Pruitt's work suggesting that one should be firm in insisting that one's own interests and needs be fulfilled and flexible regarding the means by which those interests and needs are fulfilled. The third integrating best practice is based on Fisher, Ury, and Patton's work indicating that one should engage in collaborative consideration of how to fulfill both parties' underlying interests rather than engaging in positional bargaining.

The two strategic integrating practices involve the dilemmas of information exchange * * * Full, honest information exchange can facilitate the discovery of mutually satisfying solutions. However, information exchange can be exploited by the other party to gain a claiming-value advantage. Accordingly, two integrating practices regarding information exchange are strategic practices. First, one should be more willing to trust what the other party communicates the more cooperative and trustworthy the other party is and the more important and long-term the relationship is. Second, the more cooperative and trustworthy the other party is, and the longer and more important the relationship * * * the more willing negotiators should be to divulge their true interests, preferences, and alternatives to the other party.

Douglas Stone, Bruce Patton and Sheila Heen, Difficult Conversations

37–40, 167–168 (1999).

There's only one way to come to understand the other person's story, and that's by being curious. Instead of asking yourself, "How can they think that?!" ask yourself, "I wonder what information they have that I don't?" Instead of asking, "How can they be so irrational?" ask, "How might they see the world such that their view makes sense?" Certainty locks us out of their story; curiosity lets us in.

* * *

It can be awfully hard to stay curious about another person's story when you have your own story to tell, especially if you're thinking that only one story can really be right. After all, your story is so different from theirs, and makes so much sense to you. Part of the stress of staying curious can be relieved by adopting what we call the "And Stance."

We usually assume that we must either accept or reject the other person's story, and that if we accept theirs, we must abandon our own. [But who's] right between a person who likes to sleep with the window open and another who prefers the window closed?

The answer is that the question makes no sense. Don't choose between the stories; embrace both. That's the And Stance.

The suggestion to embrace both stories can sound like double-talk. It can be heard as "Pretend both of your stories are right." But in fact, it suggests something quite different. Don't pretend anything. Don't worry about accepting or rejecting the other person's story. First work to understand it. The mere act of understanding someone else's story doesn't require you to give up your own. The And Stance allows you to recognize that how you *each* see things matters, that how you each feel matters.

Regardless of what you end up doing, regardless of whether your story influences theirs or theirs yours, both stories matter.

The And Stance is based on the assumption that the world is complex, that you can feel hurt, angry, and wronged, *and* they can feel just as hurt, angry, and wronged. They can be doing their best, *and* you can think that it's not good enough. You may have done something stupid, *and* they will have contributed in important ways to the problem as well. You can feel furious with them, *and* you can also feel love and appreciation for them.

The And Stance gives you a place from which to assert the full strength of your views and feelings without having to diminish the views and feelings of someone else. Likewise, you don't need to give up anything to hear how someone else feels or sees things differently. Because you may have different information or different interpretations, both stories can make sense at the same time.

* * *

Scores of workshops and books on "active listening" teach you what you should *do* to be a good listener. Their advice is relatively similar—ask questions, paraphrase back what the other person has said, acknowledge their view, sit attentively and look them in the eye—all good advice. You emerge from these courses eager to try out your new skills, only to become discouraged when your friends or colleagues complain that you sound phony or mechanical. "Don't use that active listening stuff on me," they say.

The problem is this: you are taught what to say and how to sit, but the heart of good listening is authenticity. People "read" not only your words and posture, but what's going on inside of you. If your "stance" isn't genuine, the words won't matter. What will be communicated almost invariably is whether you are genuinely curious, whether you genuinely care about the other person. If your intentions are false, no amount of careful wording or good posture will help. If your intentions are good, even clumsy language won't hinder you.

Listening is only powerful and effective if it is authentic. Authenticity means that you are listening because you are curious and because you care, not just because you are supposed to. The issue, then, is this: Are you curious? Do you care?

NOTES AND QUESTIONS

1. Each of these excerpts stresses the importance of empathy and listening in negotiation. Empathy and listening have long been recognized as critically important skills in the resolution of conflict. The psychologist Carl Rogers used a simple rule to encourage his patients to demonstrate empathy for others: "Each person can speak up for himself only *after* he has first restated the ideas and feelings of the previous speaker accurately, and to that speaker's satisfaction." Rogers, On Becoming A Person 332 (1961). For an overview of current empathy-related research, see Duan and Hill,

The Current State of Empathy Research, 43 J. Counseling Psych. 261 (1996).

Empathy can help to overcome one of the causes of protracted conflict: mis-attributions about others' intentions and behavior. As we've seen, negotiators tend to assume that another's behavior was caused by that person's internal characteristics, and to under-attribute that behavior to external circumstances beyond the person's control. See Watson, The Actor and the Observer: How are Their Perceptions of Causality Divergent?, 92 Psychol.Bull. 682–700 (1982). This is particularly true in conflict situations. Are empathy and listening an effective antidote to these problems?

Listening and engaging in genuine dialogue has other obvious benefits. First, you may simply discover what the other person cares about—you may get to the heart of the matter. This may allow you to find a solution you would otherwise miss. Second, empathy may build respect and trust between the parties. Third, by demonstrating understanding of the other side's perspective and concerns you may defuse tensions and avoid polarization and escalation. Finally, your effective use of these interpersonal skills may build a context for collaboration or problem-solving. See Littlejohn and Domenici, Engaging Communication in Conflict 48–49 (2001).

2. For a discussion of the stages that children go through in developing empathy, see Hoffman, Empathy and Moral Development: Implications for Caring and Justice (2000) (exploring the reactive cry of the newborn on hearing other infants cry; "egocentric empathic distress," in which a small child seeks comfort upon seeing another person in distress; "quasi-egocentric distress," in which a toddler begins to try to help others but does so as *she* would like to be helped—patting, kissing, etc.—rather than in victim-appropriate ways; "sympathetic distress," in which a child understands that another's inner state differs from her own and offers more appropriate help; and "empathic distress," in which the suffering of others generates genuine empathy).

3. Stone, Patton and Heen suggest that empathy and listening will only be effective if they are genuine—if they reflect curiosity and concern on the part of the listener. Otherwise, they fear, the "listener" will simply be using tricks or techniques to try to accommodate the talker, and the talker will likely see through those techniques and spot the listener's disingenuousness. Do you agree? Can you "fake" listening? If not, how does one negotiate oneself into a stance of curiosity—particularly in a real conflict in which you disagree strongly with the other side?

4. Some claim that empathy may be dangerous to your negotiating position. One professional negotiator advises that you should "Put yourself in the shoes of your opponent, but do not remain there too long." He worries that empathy can lead a negotiator to sacrifice her own interests:

> The good negotiator feels the necessity to put himself or herself into the situation of the other side. This feeling is a natural byproduct of the negotiating process itself. Negotiation involves personal contact, communication, and interaction. The two parties are watching each

other like two boxing champions in the ring. They continually watch for signs that give insight into the other champion's mind. Very often, one negotiator openly invites the other to understand his or her situation. * * * You cannot reach an agreement without knowing as the Germans say, *wo die Schuh drückt*—where the shoe hurts.

* * *

Here lies the danger: Having put oneself in the shoes of the other fellow can lead to the road on which those shoes were marching—that is, seeking solutions which risk being beneficial to the other party alone. The right attitude in such a situation is to find answers that alleviate the burden of the other party while also providing satisfaction for yourself. Therefore, the more willing a negotiator is to assimilate, to feel the problems of the other side, the more that negotiator has to bear in mind the self-interested goals.

Nyerges, Ten Commandments for a Negotiator, 3 Neg.J. 21 (1987).

Do you agree with Nyerges? Are Mnookin, Peppet and Tulumello unrealistic when they counsel that empathy is a critical skill for lawyers in dispute resolution? One danger of demonstrating empathy for the other side's perspective is that your client may see you as disloyal—if you can understand their position it means you don't care enough about the client's. Does demonstrating empathy square with a lawyer's professional responsibilities to her client?

5. Not all assertions are created equal. Linguistic anthropologists have identified a variety of "powerless" speech patterns. These include:

Hedges: language that reduces the force of an assertion by allowing for exceptions or by avoiding commitments, such as "sort of," "a little," and "kind of"

Intensifiers: language that increases or emphasizes the force of an assertion, such as "very," "definitely," "very definitely," and "surely"

Hesitations: "meaningless" expressions, such as "oh, well," "let's see," "so, you see," "uh," "um," and "you know"

Questioning forms: use of rising question intonation at the end of what would otherwise normally be declarative sentences, such as "I weigh 125?" or "Definitely we could do that?"

Fairhurst and Sarr, The Art of Framing: Managing the Language of Leadership 175 (1996).

Research shows that use of these speech forms diminishes persuasive effect. "In one study, males and females heard the testimony of either a male or female witness who used either the powerful or powerless style to deliver the same substantive evidence. Regardless of whether the testimony was presented in transcript or through audiotape, and regardless of whether the witness or the rating audience was male or female, the powerful style resulted in greater perceived credibility of the witness." Id. at 176.

6. The therapeutic justice movement argues that as part of preparing for a negotiation, lawyers should identify with their clients' emotional concerns as well as typically legal and financial ones. See Kupfer Schneider, The Intersection of Therapeutic Jurisprudence, Preventative Law, and Alternative Dispute Resolution, 5 Psychol.Pub.Pol. & L. 1084, 1091 (1999). This requires that a lawyer demonstrate empathy for his client, listen carefully, and be willing to discuss or at least acknowledge the client's emotional state. Is this too much to ask of lawyers? Does it turn lawyers into therapists? How should a lawyer react to a very emotional or distraught client in a divorce case, for example, or in a corporate takeover situation? What is the lawyer's role in such moments?

3. Gender, Race, Culture and Stereotyping

Many have tried to determine whether men and women bargain differently. Some studies suggest that women consider competitiveness less desirable than do men, see Lipman–Blumen, Connective Leadership: Female Leadership Styles in the 21st-Century Workplace, 35 Soc.Persp. 183, 200–201 (1992), and that they settle more frequently. See Kennard, Lawyers, Sex, and Marriage: Factors Empirically Correlated with the Decision to Settle, 2 Harv.Neg.L.Rev. 149, 149 (1997). Others suggest that women place a higher value on empathetic reasoning. See Jack and Jack, Moral Vision and Professional Decisions: The Changing Values of Women and Men Lawyers 56–58 (1989); Burton et al., Feminist Theory, Professional Ethics, and Gender–Related Distinctions in Attorney Negotiating Styles, 1991 J.Dis.Resol. 199, 200–203; Menkel–Meadow, Portia in a Different Voice: Speculations on a Women's Lawyering Process, 1 Berkeley Women's L.J. 39, 55 (1985). Some have found that women are more likely than men to be client-oriented in their practice. See Maiman et al., Gender and Specialization in the Practice of Divorce Law, 44 Me.L.Rev. 39, 51 (1992). And, perhaps most intriguingly, some have claimed that men tend to compete in conflict situations whereas women tend to compromise or cooperate. See Cahn, Styles of Lawyering, 43 Hastings L.J. 1039, 1045 (1992); Berryman–Fink and Brunner, The Effects of Sex of Source and Target on Interpersonal Conflict Management Styles, 53 S. Speech Comm.J. 38, 44 (1987); Komorita, Cooperative Choice in a Prisoner's Dilemma Game, 2 J. Personality & Soc.Psych. 741, 744 (1965); Rose, Bargaining and Gender, 18 Harv.J.L. & Pub.Pol. 547, 550 (1995).

Other scholars, however, have rejected both the empirical results and theoretical underpinnings of this pursuit. Many studies, for example, have failed to find significant gender-related differences in competition and cooperation in Prisoner's Dilemma games. See Craver and Barnes, Gender, Risk Taking, and Negotiation Performance, 5 Mich.J. Gender & L. 299, 318, 347 (1999) (citing studies and arguing that there is "no factual basis for assuming that women are weaker or less capable negotiators"); Burton, Farmer, Gee, Johnson and Williams, Gender–Related Distinctions in Attorney Negotiating Styles, 1991 J.Disp.Res. 199. And scholars have argued that seeking such differences is itself suspect:

We are hopefully past the days of the simplest gender stereotyping—men are competitive, women are cooperative; men talk and interrupt more, women use tentative language and seek to please the other; men threaten and assert; women seek to please and concede too much, although as the recent research * * * suggests, there may be some truth in some of the stereotypes, at least *under certain conditions*. If we have learned anything from the hundreds of studies conducted on gender and negotiation, it is that in negotiation gender (though a constant for the individual negotiator) is dynamic and interactive—that is, its significance and expression varies under different conditions and in different situations.

* * *

* * * The empirical results are all over the map. For every study which seems to suggest some gender difference (women are more cooperative; men are more competitive), there is another that finds no statistically significant difference in negotiation performance, whether measured by integrative and joint gain outcomes or by more competitive outcomes. Some of the studies have pointed to the situational or "moderating factor" complexity (such as one study which demonstrates that overly cooperative women may actually achieve poorer joint gain solutions because they "settle" too early, do not probe for more information, or fail to hold on to their own interests), but this is consistent with research that finds similar results for friends or others in close relationships who bargain with each other.

Menkel–Meadow, Teaching about Gender and Negotiation: Sex, Truths, and Videotape, Neg.J. 357, 358–359, 364 (2000). Deborah Rhode argues similarly:

The celebration of gender difference risks not only oversimplifying, but also overclaiming. Recent research raises substantial questions about how different women's voice in fact is. Psychological surveys generally find few attributes on which the sexes consistently vary. Even for these attributes, gender typically accounts for only about five percent of the variance. The similarities between men and women are far greater than the disparities, and small statistical distinctions do not support sweeping sex-based dichotomies. Most empirical studies of moral development or altruistic behavior do not find significant gender distinctions. Nor does related research on managerial behavior reveal the consistent sex-linked variations that relational feminism would suggest.

Rhode, Gender and Professional Roles, 63 Fordham L.Rev. 39, 42–43 (1994).

The following excerpts consider three quite different perspectives. The first examines gender and ethnic bargaining patterns. The second argues that *power*, not gender, accounts for any observable behavioral differences in negotiation. The last excerpt considers the effects of culture and stereotyping.

Christine Rack, Negotiated Justice: Gender and Ethnic Minority Bargaining Patterns in the Metro Court Study

20 Hamline J.Pub.L. & Pol. 211, 222–236 (1999).

2. Culture & Gender Negotiation Differences: Soft & Firm Bargaining

Gender and cultural theories, supported by self-report empirical findings, suggest that individuals socialized into collectivist and female social patterns would be more likely to have enhanced concern for the other party and would concede more readily.

In comparison to U.S. culture, Latin American cultural norms are described as "collectivist," oriented toward shared benefit outcomes. Persons from collectivist cultures theoretically hold a greater concern for the other party when he or she is an in-group member as opposed to an out-group member. In addition, Latin American cultures are theoretically more willing to view unequal power relations as legitimate. United States acculturation on the same scales is likely to encourage high self-concern, a willingness to challenge superiors, and a lack of in-group preference. Indeed, cross national studies using scenario techniques have consistently found that people from collectivist cultures are more apt than those from individualistic cultures to report themselves as conciliatory (compromising and obliging) in conflict situations if they do not avoid the conflict altogether.

Virtually all studies report significant gender effects, with women reporting that they are more likely to conciliate than men. In survey and scenario research, women within the United States and cross-nationally self-report a greater likelihood and/or preference for using collaborative strategies in conflict situations. However, the logical consequences of women's theoretical constructions as being more relational, particularistic, and giving are questionable. Research has found complications in outcomes, process, and perceptual distortions.

3. Bargaining Variables & Culture–Gender Differences

Cultural and gender differences are likely in all three variables that are known to affect negotiations: fairness rules, power differences, and the positivity or negativity of relationships.

a. Fairness or Distributional Norms

Shared fairness norms facilitate resolutions. Pruitt and Carnevale argue that shared fairness rules provide the basis for tacit bargaining leading to a rapid resolution. However, when disputants do not share a fairness rule, research and theoretical speculation suggest divergent probabilities; if they point in opposite directions, agreements reached by lengthy and complex bargaining might be truly balanced and integrative. Because fairness is at the heart of justice claims, however, divergent fairness rules might also narrow negotiations through positional rigidity.

Fairness rules, the "normative" expectations that structure exchange behavior and justice perceptions, are culturally learned and situationally evoked. Theory from Weber, Piaget and Ricoeur synthesized with anthropological research demonstrate four identifiable and inherent patterns of relational exchange called "structures," which could also be called distributional norms. These are normative expectations based on the primacy of need, authority, reciprocity, and modern market valuations.

The first, "communal sharing," is archetypally feminine and premodern. It is a need-based distributional norm similar to the exchange relationship found in the family, "primordial" collectivism, traditional and gift-based economies. Fiske's second exchange structure, "authority-ranking," is consistent with Latin American cultural generalizations suggesting a more ready acceptance of authority in hierarchical orders. It is a status-based distribution norm in which the unequal exchange favoring the superior is usually accepted as a legitimate inequality by the subordinate. It underlies the notion of judicial decisionmaking and public compliance based on status deference. Fiske's third exchange pattern, "equality matching," is a more masculine pattern of exchange, if only because men tend to have greater physical power and the willingness to use it. It is a reciprocity-based distribution norm involving strictly in-kind reciprocity. Finally, Fiske described the fourth model, "market pricing," as the market-based equity exchange model in modern capitalist society, wherein rewards are distributed according to input, and the input is valued in accordance with a market metric.

In addition to cultural learning, Fiske specifies that situational salience will determine which exchange norm or fairness rule will be applied. The question is whether the mediation situation suggested to nondominant parties that alternative norms should be applied.

b.   Power Differences

Power differences between the parties have been closely studied in negotiation. As noted above, stronger parties tend to be advantaged in negotiations, an outcome achieved by higher claiming and undermatching concessions. The measure of greater power is the positive alternatives (court outcomes primarily) and the relative dependency of the weaker party on agreement. Corporate parties tend to have better court outcomes because the laws have been structured to affirm their rights according to rules they knew beforehand. In addition, previous experience can lead to greater power gained by developing strategic bargaining skills.

However, greater power, even when buttressed by weaker party dependence, does not immediately translate into dominance. Exchange researchers argue that normative constraints, including culturally-shaped justice norms and reciprocity, intervene between capacity and power use. Moreover, stronger parties are dependent on the other disputant for compliance with agreements they might make.

c. Positive & Negative Relationships

Trust and distrust, like the positive and negative relationships with which they are associated, tend both to be matched and to persist over time. Pruitt and Carnevale speculate that trusters tend to worry less about looking like suckers and would be more likely to make concessions and fill the gap produced by the other party's failure to concede at a deadline. Distrust is central to negative negotiating relationships, where bargainers tend to match contentious strategies (i.e., bargaining resistance and threats). In the absence of data, Pruitt and Carnevale theorized that past competition would result in less negativity if the competition was kept within normative boundaries rather than appearing as though the other party appeared to be trying to gain an unfair advantage, i.e., exploiting his or her bargaining partner.

d. Culture, Gender & Bargaining Variables

Theoretical and empirical arguments based on cultural and gender categorizations would suggest that Latinos and women might differ from dominant court players in all of the domains, fairness norms, power differences, and trust. Non-dominant groups may hold different fairness values, hold unequal power in negotiations with more dominant parties, and accept disadvantaged outcomes. Ridgeway explains that those who are traditionally perceived as less competent continue to be perceived that way persistently so that hierarchies are recreated through a process of self-fulfilling prophecy. Attempts to break free of others' expectations are often negatively misperceived and actively discouraged until less privileged actors retreat from trying.

Trust is particularly at issue for ethnic minorities because trust can be considered analogous to collectivist cultural patterns. But the trend of the predictions turns on the difference between outsiders and insiders. On the one hand, collectivist cultures might have distinct expressive motives in bargaining situations that appear as trusting but might be due to "face needs." Furthermore, collectivist identities would also, theoretically, be motivated to maintain the positive face of other parties, that is, to not subject them to shame. On the other hand, Hispanos have ample reason to distrust Anglos due to the historical memory of Anglo exploitation. Thus, past exploitation might establish Anglos as an outsider relation. The present bargaining situation is analyzed to more clearly indicate not only whether minorities did seem trusting toward Anglos, but also whether trust or distrust was warranted.

* * *

5. Summary

Cultural and gender theories suggest that minority and female disputants, who are more often socialized into collectivistic and relational patterns, will be soft bargainers. As a style, they will concede or conciliate more readily. But the empirical, historical, and theoretical specifics are contradictory, both for each group and in their relations with other parties.

* * *

Empirical research has failed to consistently support differences that are theorized for collectivistic culture groups. For example, although a collectivistic propensity for equality-based distribution norms was noted in scenario research, research has more consistently found a greater reported tendency for "lumping it" (i.e., conciliation and avoidance of overt conflict) among individuals socialized in nations considered collectivist.

Although women self-report that they would rather cooperate than compete, research has consistently shown status differences in which women seem to be more competitive when they held higher status positions and to be misperceived by others. Unlike cultural theories, gender theories based on relational psychology and particularistic moral reasoning have not been theorized to show an insider dynamic. Feminist theory, however, has focused on a fundamentally exploitative relationship between genders similar to the critical race theory applied to majority-minority ethnic relations. Predictions stemming from this theoretical orientation would suggest that men might more often exploit this relatively static "other-concern" or ethic of care.

Carol Watson, Gender Versus Power as a Predictor of Negotiation Behavior and Outcomes

10 Neg.J. 117, 119 (1994).[1]

Over the past ten to fifteen years, psychologists and sociologists have mounted a frontal assault on th[e] long-standing "different and inferior" assumption [about women] in many domains. Their work has shown the assumption to be frequently inaccurate. Recent literature reviews show, for example, that there are not clear gender differences in verbal ability, math ability, or spatial ability. Nor do there appear to be gender differences in more abstract characteristics or abilities such as moral reasoning or leadership. Nevertheless, the belief in significant, innate, gender differences refuses to die.

The probable reason for the durability of this belief is that, on a day-in, day-out basis, men and women *do* differ in countless ways that are apparent to each of us, researchers and members of the general public alike. One response to the dilemmas these differences have posed for women is advanced by the "cultural feminists" who have sought to fight society's inherent sexism by celebrating women as different from but superior to men. While such theories may be appealing because they highlight women's special qualities and help women feel good about themselves (rather than inferior or deficient), the "different-but-superior" argu-

---

1. This article is based on an earlier version. See Watson, Gender Differences in Negotiating Behavior and Outcomes: Fact or Artifact?, in Conflict and Gender 191 (1994).

ment does not hold up to the rigorous scrutiny of careful empirical investigation any better than does the more prevalent "different-and-inferior" argument.

An alternative perspective, offered in this article, is that gender differences do exist, but that those of significance relate to contextual rather than to innate personality factors. Contextual factors consist first and most obviously of the immediate situation and its particular demands. More broadly, however, the context of an individual's life includes all aspects in the environment of that individual's life—such as work, family, class, culture, etc.

Contextual factors have often been found to supplant personality factors in determining behavior * * * Nevertheless, researchers and the general public continue to make what psychologists have dubbed the "fundamental attribution error." This error consists of assuming that others behave the way they do because of internal personality characteristics rather than because of external situational demands.

Cooperative Women, Competitive Men?

* * * Early research suggested that women are "softer" negotiators than men, that they prefer an accommodating style, are generous, and are more concerned that all parties be treated fairly than they are about gaining positive substantive outcomes for themselves. These early studies also showed that men are "tough" negotiators who make many demands and few concessions, and that they are more concerned about winning positive substantive outcomes for themselves than about how the other party fares. Men were also found to be more flexible negotiators than women in that they seemed to use a tit-for-tat strategy more often, and were better at finding rational strategies that allowed them to maximize gains.

Although Rubin and Brown showed that these supposed gender differences in bargaining and negotiating were not consistently supported by research, there tends to be a continuing expectation that women will negotiate and bargain more cooperatively than men. Nevertheless, a few researchers have reached more negative conclusions. For instance, women have sometimes been found to lock into an unrelenting competitive stance when their partners refuse to cooperate, and this behavior has been construed by some as vindictive. * * *

The fact that negotiation researchers have often depicted women as cooperative might be construed to mean that the cultural feminist perspective (i.e., that women are different but superior) has predominated in the negotiation literature. This would be an incorrect assumption, however, because women's cooperativeness has generally been equated with weakness and ineffectiveness. * * * Thus, women have frequently been portrayed as "nicer" negotiators than men; and, since niceness does not help one to win, men have typically been credited with being more effective negotiators than women. * * *

* * *

* * * Interestingly, the literature on disputing shows differences in the behavior of high-and low-power negotiators that mirror the most commonly assumed gender differences in negotiator behavior and outcomes. That is, high-power negotiators tend to compete whereas low-power negotiators tend to cooperate. I am suggesting, then, that because women in American society are more likely to be found in low-power positions and occupations than men, we may have been misled into assuming that observed differences in the way men and women negotiate are due to gender when, in fact, they result from status and power differences.

* * *

Power generally leads to greater dominance, competitiveness, and success for both genders. On the one hand, this indicates that women are not softer or less effective negotiators * * * Given a reasonable degree of situational power, women are likely to be just as oriented toward beating their opponents as men are, and just as successful at doing so. Thus, there is no reason to mistrust women's negotiation abilities. * * *

On the other hand, this finding also implies that women are not nicer negotiators than men are. Women are not necessarily any more fair-minded or compassionate, despite what earlier research and some current feminist writers would have us believe. * * *

Jeffrey Z. Rubin and Frank E.A. Sander, Culture, Negotiation, and The Eye of The Beholder

7 Neg.J. 249 (1991).

To understand why culture should be so powerful in organizing stimulus, it is first necessary to understand the contributing role of labeling and stereotyping in our interpersonal perceptions. Social psychologists have observed that although we typically dismiss labeling (and the stereotyping to which it leads) as problematic, stereotyping has several apparent "benefits": First, it allows the perceiver to reduce a world of enormous cognitive complexity into terms of black v. white, good v. evil, friend v. enemy—thereby making it easier to code the things and people one sees. Second, armed with stereotypes, it becomes far easier to communicate in shorthand fashion with others, who we suspect share our views; "He's such a boy" conveys lots of (stereotypic) information very, very quickly, as does the time-worn phrase, "ugly American."

* * *

Robert Rosenthal and his colleagues have demonstrated the power of expectations and labels in an important series of experimental studies. In one of these experiments, teachers were told that some of the children in their elementary school classes had been identified as "intellectual bloomers," children who were likely to grow and develop substantially in the coming year. About other children (who had been privately matched with the "bloomers" in terms of measured aptitude) nothing was said. When an achievement test was administered at the end of the academic year, a shocking and important discovery was made: those children who had been labeled as intellectual bloomers scored significantly higher than those with whom they had been matched. In explanation, the researchers hypothesized that children who were expected to do very, very well were given more attention by their teachers; this increased attention, organized by a hypothesis that the child in question was a talented individual, created a self-fulfilling prophecy.

The label of culture may have an effect very similar to that of gender or intellectual aptitude; it is a "hook" that makes it easy for one negotiator (the perceiver) to organize what he or she sees emanating from that "different person" seated at the other side of the table. To understand how culture may function as a label, consider the following teaching exercise, used during a two-week session on negotiation conducted with a multinational, multicultural gathering. During one class session, the fifty or so participants were formed into rough national groups, and were asked to characterize their national negotiating style—as seen by others. That is, the task was *not* to describe true differences that may be attributable to culture or nationality, but to characterize the stereotypic perceptions that others typically carry around in their heads.

This exercise yielded a set of very powerful, albeit contradictory, stereotypic descriptions of different nationalities. To give a couple of examples, British participants characterized others' stereotypic characterizations of the British as "reserved, arrogant, old fashioned, eccentric, fair, and self-deprecating." A cluster of Arab participants from several Middle East nations characterized a "Levantine" negotiating style as "inclined to violence, aggressive, incohesive, indecisive, irrational, temperamental, emotional, impulsive, and romantic." The Irish self-characterization included such adjectives as "good social grease, people-oriented, fast-talking, good for a laugh, passionate but not serious, provincial, inefficient and undisciplined, unreliable and simple but shrewd." And a cluster of Central Americans listed other's stereotypes of them as negotiators as "idealistic, impractical, disorganized, unprepared, stubborn in arguments, and flowery in style."

Now imagine that you have begun to negotiate with someone from another culture, who at some point in the proceedings simply insists that he or she can go no further, and is prepared to conclude without agreement if necessary; in effect, says this individual, his BATNA has been reached, and he can do just as well by walking away from the table. How should you interpret such an assertion? If you share the general cluster of stereotypes described by the students, your interpretation will probably depend on the other person's culture or nationality. Thus, if the other negotiator is British, and (among other things) you regard the British as "fair," you may interpret this person's refusal to concede further as an honest statement of principle. The same behavior issuing from a Central American, however (someone you suspect of being "stubborn in arguments"), may lead you to suspect your counterpart of being stubborn and perhaps deceitful. Wouldn't you therefore be more likely to strike an agreement with a British than a Central American negotiator—despite the fact that each has behaved in the identical way?

If there is any truth to our surmise, you can see how powerful the effects of culture may prove to be, leading us (even before we have had a chance to gather information about our counterpart) to hold a set of expectations that guide and inform our judgments. Moreover, once our "hypotheses" about others are in place, it becomes very difficult to disprove them. We tend to gather interpersonal information in such a way that we pay attention only to the "facts" that support our preconceived ideas, ignoring or dismissing disconfirming data.

For example, if I believe that you are a defensive person, and then proceed to ask you why you are so defensive, I can be guaranteed of support for my hypothesis regardless of what you say * * *

What, then, are some implications of this brief essay for more effective negotiation across cultural/national boundaries? First, while cultural/national differences do exist, much of what passes for such differences may well be the result of expectations and perceptions which, when acted upon, help to bring about a form of self-fulfilling prophecy. Perhaps the best way to combat such expectations is to go out of one's way to acquire as much information as one can beforehand about the way people in other cultures view the kind of problem under consideration. Thus, if we are negotiating with a German about a health care contract, we should try to find out whatever we can about how Germans tend to view health care. Of course, in large countries, there may be regional variations that also need to be taken into account.

NOTES AND QUESTIONS

1.   Do you believe that gender- and culture-based differences in negotiation behavior play a part in bargaining? Or do you agree with Watson, who suggests that power, not gender, is the actual driver of negotiation behavior? How would you test your views of whether such differences exist?

2.   Like Rubin and Sander's excerpt on culture, many scholars now focus less on whether actual gender-based behavioral differences exist than on the different *perceptions* that negotiators have of each other because on gender, race or cultural difference. See Burrell et al., Gender–Based Perceptual Biases in Mediation, 15 Comm.Res. 447, 453 (1988). As Carol Rose puts it, "It is not as important that a gendered difference in tastes for cooperation actually exists, as that people simply think it exists." Rose, Bargaining and Gender, 18 Harv.J.L. & Pub.Pol. 547, 555 (1994). Are you persuaded by the argument that claims of gender- or culture-based difference are mostly stereotyping?

Consider the following five types of perceptual errors that may cause stereotyping. Do they seem likely to influence the negotiation process?

* * * Five major perceptual errors are typical: stereotyping, halo effects, selective perceptions, projections, and perpetual defenses. The first two—stereotyping and halo effects—are examples of perceptual distortion by *generalization*—small amounts of perceptual information are used to draw large conclusions about individuals. The last three—selective perception, projection, and perpetual defense—are examples of perceptual distortion by the *anticipation* of encountering another whom we believe to have certain attributes and qualities.

Stereotyping is a very common perceptual process. Stereotyping occurs when attributes are assigned to people solely on the basis of their membership in a particular social or demographic group. * * *

Halo effects in perception are similar to stereotypes. Rather than using a target individual's group membership as a basis for classification, halo effects occur when one attribute of an individual allows the perceiver to generalize about a wide variety of other attributes. A smiling person is judged to be more honest than a frowning or scowling person, even though there is no necessary relationship between a smile and honesty. * * *

Halo effects are likely to be as common as stereotypes in negotiation; we are likely to form rapid impressions of new opponents based on very limited initial information, such as their appearance or initial statements. We also maintain these judgments as we get to know people better, fitting each piece of "new" information into some consistent pattern. * * *

Selective perception occurs when the perceiver singles out certain information which supports or reinforces a prior belief, and filters out information which may not confirm that belief. Thus selective perception has the effect of perpetuating stereotypes or halo effects—quick judgments are formed about individuals on the basis of limited information, while any further evidence that might disconfirm the judgment is "filtered out" by attending only to the confirming information. An initial smile from the opponent, which leads the perceiver to believe that the opponent is honest, might also lead the perceiver to ignore statements by the opponent that he intends to be competitive and aggressive. The same smile, interpreted by the perceiver as a smirk, similarly leads the perceiver to ignore other information that the target wants to establish and honest and cooperative relationship. In both cases, the perceiver's own biases—predisposition to be cooperative or competitive—are likely to affect how the other's cues are selected and interpreted.

Projection occurs when an individual ascribes to others characteristics or feelings he possesses himself. * * * In negotiation, for example, it is extremely common for negotiators to claim that they want to be cooperative and to develop a positive relationship with the other negotiator, but that it is the opponent who is behaving uncooperatively and untrustingly. Such assertions often mask the negotiator's ability to

admit to himself that he really wants to be deceptive and dishonest.
* * *

Perpetual defense is the result of the same instinct for self-projection, and helps our perceptual apparatus defend us by "screening out," distorting, or ignoring information which is threatening or unacceptable to us. Information about ourselves or others which doesn't "fit" our self image, or the image of others, is likely to be denied, modified, distorted, or redefined to bring it into line with earlier judgments. * * *

It cannot be stated strongly enough that these perceptual distortions are frequently at the heart of breakdowns in communication between conflicting individuals. Perceptual biases tend to cast one's own position and behavior in more favorable terms, and to cast the other person ("the opponent") in more negative terms. These biases will affect the expectations that one has for his opponent, and lead to assumptions about the opponent: the position he is likely to take, his willingness to cooperate or make concessions, etc. Finally, these negative assumptions are likely to influence the party to assume a competitive, defensive stance in their initial negotiations. The tragic fallacy in this process is that if his assumptions are incorrect, there may be no way for the actor to discover it! By the time he is in a position to accurately judge the predisposition of his opponent, his own competitive mood and defensive posture have been interpreted by the opponent as offensive and antagonistic.

Lewicki and Litterer, Negotiation 166–169 (1985).

3. That others may stereotype you because of your gender may not be surprising, but research shows that gender may correlate with varied self-perceptions and self-confidence as well. In one study, researchers tested first-year law students for gender differences in their negotiation behavior and negotiated outcomes in a simulated negotiation. In addition, however, the students were asked to fill out questionnaires about their self-confidence and to assess their own negotiation abilities. Although ultimately the outcomes negotiated by men and women were very similar, women rated their abilities lower than men. See Farber and Rickenberg, Under–Confident Women and Over–Confident Men: Gender and Competence in a Simulated Negotiation, 11 Yale J.L. & Feminism 271, 291 (1999).

4. Regardless of whether gender, race and culture actually impact bargaining behavior, it is clear that some people may *treat* minorities and women differently in negotiations. For example, several studies by Ian Ayres of the Yale Law School have attempted to determine whether and why retail salespeople might discriminate in how they negotiate with minority and female car buyers. Ayres sent testers of different races and sexes to randomly selected car dealerships in the Chicago area to negotiate the purchase price of a given car model. The testers dressed similarly, arrived at their respective dealerships driving similar rented cars, and followed pre-arranged "scripts" so that all testers presented themselves to the dealerships in the same way.

The results were striking. Dealers offered white male testers lower initial and final offers than any other type of tester. Black male testers fared the worst, paying on average an extra $962 over white males on initial offers and an extra $1132 on final offers. See Ayres, Further Evidence of Discrimination in New Car Negotiations and Estimates of Its Cause, 94 Mich.L.Rev. 109, 116 (1995). Black females fared slightly better, paying approximately $470 more than white males on initial offers and $446 on final offers, and white females paid roughly $200 more than white males on both offers. In fact, "[t]he initial offer white male testers received was lower than the *final* offer 43.5 percent of nonwhite males received." Id. at 119. See also Ayres, Fair Driving: Gender and Race Discrimination in Retail Car Negotiations, 104 Harv.L.Rev. 817 (1991).

By comparing game theoretic models with the empirical data generated by his studies, Ayres tested several possible hypotheses regarding *why* car dealers might vary their offers depending on the race or gender of the potential buyer:

> [D]ifferent explanations of discrimination cause the dealer's choice of an initial offer, the size of concessions, and the speed of concessions, to vary. For example, sellers might offer a higher initial price to a black customer if they believe that black customers are averse to bargaining or if the sellers have a particular desire to disadvantage black customers. But game theory suggests that these two causes of discrimination will give rise to different concession rates: in particular, a desire to disadvantage blacks will cause sellers to hold out longer for a high price, implying a lower concession rate than a belief that black consumers are averse to bargaining. Our evidence of the dealers' initial offers and willingness to make concessions can thus be used to distinguish among competing causal theories

Ayres, Further Evidence of Discrimination in New Car Negotiations and Estimates of Its Cause, 94 Mich.L.Rev. 109, 120 (1995).

Ayres tested four reasons that sellers might offer higher prices to certain types of buyers: (1) sellers may have higher costs of bargaining with a disfavored group—if, for example, a male seller dislikes spending time with female buyers; (2) sellers may desire to disadvantage a disfavored group—the seller may feel a benefit from seeing that group pay higher prices; (3) sellers may believe that the disfavored group will pay more because it has higher costs of bargaining; or (4) sellers may believe that a disfavored group has a different (and higher) distribution of reservation prices than white males—that some black customers, for example, are "suckers" who are willing to pay more than most whites for a given car, perhaps because of a lack of information about the car's value. See id. at 124.

Of these possible explanations, Ayres argues that the second and fourth are the most robust. Sellers' offers and concession rates suggested a desire to disadvantage blacks and women. Indeed, "the seller's slow and small concessions to black males are consistent with the hypothesis that sellers enjoyed extracting dollars from black males *twice as much* as extracting dollars from white males." Id. at 132–133 (emphasis added). In addition, the data suggest that dealers believed that black males were willing to pay the most, and white males the least. Although the *average* black male is likely to be poorer than the average white male, dealers seemed to believe either that black males might pay more because they knew less about the car's value or because they knew less about the possibility of bargaining for a better price. See id. at 139–141.

D. PROFESSIONAL AND LEGAL FRAMEWORK FOR NEGOTIATION

1. CONSTRAINTS ON NEGOTIATION BEHAVIOR

In this section we consider various constraints on the negotiation behavior of a lawyer or her client. We begin with the constraints imposed by contract and tort law—constraints that apply equally to lawyers and clients. We then turn to the professional ethics codes that govern lawyers during bargaining and the possibility of post-settlement malpractice.

a. FRAUD, DURESS AND OTHER LIMITS ON BARGAINING

The bargaining behavior of lawyers and their clients is governed by tort, contract and agency law, as well as by specific statutes and regulations. The following excerpt considers various constraints, particularly in the context of unequal bargaining power.

Robert S. Adler & Elliot M. Silverstein, When David Meets Goliath: Dealing With Power Differentials in Negotiations

5 Harv.Neg.L.Rev. 1, 29–48 (2000).

* * * We now turn to an exploration of legal protections that apply in negotiation situations involving power imbalances.

Although the superior bargaining power of one party, standing alone, does not generally provide the basis for invalidating an agreement, the law does set limits within which bargainers must operate. These limits apply both with respect to the terms that can be negotiated and to the methods one can use to influence an opponent to agree to the terms. They are premised on the assumption that at some point in the bargaining process, power advantages can produce inequities so pronounced that the law must step in to protect the weak. In negotiations involving power imbalances, most abuses arise when the stronger party, either through threats or other overt displays of power, intimidates the other into entering an agreement so one-sided that it offends reasonable sensibilities. Of course, not all bargaining abuses result from overt power displays. Some arise from shifting the balance of power by exploiting trust or employing deceit.

Depending on the nature of the abuse, the law may take different approaches—regulating modestly where "arm's length" conditions exist or expansively where a "special relationship" requires protection for particularly vulnerable individuals. Where special relationships exist, special protections apply.

A. *Undue Influence*

When a relationship of trust and dependency between two or more parties exists, the law typically polices the relationship closely and imposes especially stringent duties on the dominant parties. * * *

Contract law imposes similar duties in the case of agreements involving undue influence in special relationships. Where one party—because of family position, business connection, legal authority or other circumstances—gains extraordinary trust from another party, the courts will scrutinize any agreements between them with great care to ensure fairness. Common examples of special relationships include guardian-ward, trustee-beneficiary, agent-principal, spouses, parent-child, attorney-client, physician-patient, and clergy-parishioner. To treat negotiations in these settings as arm's length interactions would invite "unfair persuasion" by the dominant parties either through threats, deception, or misplaced trust. Accordingly, the law imposes special obligations on those who play the dominant role in such relationships, requiring them to exercise good faith and to make full disclosure of all critical facts when negotiating agreements with dependent parties. In determining whether a dominant party in a special relationship exerted undue influence, the courts generally look to the fairness of the contract, the availability of independent advice, and the vulnerability of the dependent party. An agreement entered into as a result of undue influence is voidable by the victim.

B. *Protections in Arm's Length Transactions*

Under the "bargain theory" of contracts, parties negotiate at arm's length to exchange consideration. An arm's length transaction is one in which the parties stand in no special relationship with each other, owe each other no special duties, and each acts in his or her own interest. * * * This is not to suggest that parties are free to operate without rules, but it does mean that they are accorded substantial leeway in negotiating contracts. * * * Once one of the parties acts in a patently abusive manner, however, the law does provide protection, as, for example, with fraud, duress, and unconscionability.

1. *Fraud*

Negotiated agreements, to be binding, must be entered into by the parties in a knowing and voluntary manner. Lies undermine agreements by removing the "knowing" element from the bargain. That is, one induced by misrepresentations to purchase a relatively worthless item of personal property typically buys the product "voluntarily"—in fact, eagerly—with enthusiasm generated by the false promise of the product's value. The catch is that because of the defrauder's lies, the victim has unfairly lost the opportunity to "know" the precise nature of what he or she has bought. * * *

* * *

Sadly, it appears that lying in negotiations occurs frequently—often to the great advantage of the liar—and dramatically shifts the power balance when it goes undetected. Unfortunately, those who fail to appreciate and take precautions against lies set themselves up to be victimized in their dealings.

Compounding the issue of lying in negotiations is drawing the distinction between what is permissible bluffing, or harmless puffing, and what is truly improper. Traditionally, the distinction, although difficult to draw with precision, is between a factual representation and mere generalized praise or opinion. Factual misrepresentations may constitute fraud, while generalized opinions usually do not. * * *

Lawyers have not always improved the moral climate of bargaining. Indeed, lawyers have adopted ethics rules that permit misrepresentations in certain negotiation settings based on the questionable premise that since the other side has no "right" to know this information, attorneys should not be held to speak honestly about it.

We acknowledge that the lines between proper and improper behavior are difficult to draw at times. We also recognize the general human proclivity to lie, including in negotiations. Nonetheless, we find ourselves persuaded by a careful analysis by Professor Richard Shell that, despite the casual approach that negotiators sometimes take towards the truth, the law actually had adopted a much stronger stance against misrepresentations than is generally recognized. Accordingly, we conclude that there is less room for playing with the truth than many negotiators believe possible.

2. *Duress*

Coercion, whether express or implied, takes many forms. One party, for example, might threaten to take its business elsewhere if its terms are not met. Another might threaten to file suit if its financial claims are not resolved. Still another might insist that it will no longer provide a discount or expedited delivery if a deal cannot be struck. These threats, designed to exert pressure on an opponent to secure his or her cooperation, generally fall into a category that the law would consider to be hard bargaining, but not illegal. At some point, however, coercion becomes objectionable. How does one distinguish between proper and improper behavior? * * *

* * *

Threatened action need not be illegal—even acts otherwise legal may constitute duress if directed towards an improper goal. For example, a threat to bring a lawsuit—normally a legitimate form of coercion—becomes abusive if "made with the corrupt intent to coerce a transaction grossly unfair to the victim and not related to the subject of such proceedings."

Similarly, a threat to release embarrassing, but true, information about another person, although abhorrent, would not constitute duress (in the form of blackmail) unless accompanied by an improper demand for financial or other favors.

Should negotiators with a decided power advantage feel inhibited from pushing for as hard a bargain as they can in light of the law of duress? Generally, no. Judging from the language in the courts' opinions, hard bargainers should have little to fear from the doctrine of duress. * * * Trouble arises only when a party makes threats that lapse into the illegal, immoral and unconscionable. * * *

3.   *Unconscionability*

The doctrine of unconscionability functions to protect bargainers of lesser power from overreaching by dominant parties. * * *

What is an unconscionable contract? * * * At a minimum, an unconscionable contract is one "such as no man in his senses and not under delusion would make on the one hand and no honest and fair man would accept on the other." Unconscionability seeks to prevent two evils: (1) oppression and (2) unfair surprise. * * * Substantive unconscionability includes the actual terms of the agreement; procedural unconscionability refers to the bargaining process between the parties.

Substantive unconscionability occurs where the terms of the contract are so onerous, unreasonable or unfair that someone with common sense hearing the terms could not help exclaiming at the inequality of the agreement. * * *

Procedural unconscionability * * * arises when contracts involve the element of unfair surprise. This typically takes the form of terms hidden in a mass of contract language, terms hidden in small print, or on the back of an agreement where one would not think to look, or the like. Procedural unconscionability also assumes another, less clearly delineated form, that of "oppressive" tactics. When the dominant party uses high-pressure tactics in circumstances that result in unfair control of the situation, the courts will intercede. * * * The abuse falls short of duress, but qualifies for judicial relief under the doctrine of unconscionability.

* * *

How concerned should a negotiator be—especially one with superior bargaining power—that pursuing an advantage in a contract will result in a court ruling that the agreement is unconscionable? Our best answer: some, but not much. For the most part, the courts have taken a cautious approach to finding unconscionability in negotiated agreements. The vast majority of successful unconscionability claims involve poor, often unsophisticated, consumers challenging oppressive adhesion contracts foisted on them by retail merchants or credit sellers. In fact, the courts have generally been unreceptive to unconscionability claims by middle class purchasers or by merchants against other merchants. No doubt this reflects the general view that persons of greater sophistication suffer less contractual abuse and need less protection.

NOTES AND QUESTIONS

1. Adler and Silverstein suggest that the law of undue influence, fraud, duress, and unconscionability impose only minor constraints on a lawyer's negotiation behavior. Do you agree? If so, should these rules be strengthened to further limit how lawyers can bargain? What are the advantages and disadvantages of the status quo?

2. The law of contracts governs behavior toward third parties in negotiations. Most scholars agree that contract law generally imposes no duty of good faith in negotiations. One of the foremost legal scholars on contracts, Allen Farnsworth, argues that the duty of fair dealing does not attach until an agreement is signed:

> * * * Some scholarly writers have generalized from the cases decided on the grounds of misrepresentation and specific promise to argue that a general obligation of fair dealing may arise out of negotiations themselves, at least if the disappointed party has been led to believe that success is in prospect. Thus Summers wrote that if courts follow *Red Owl*, "it will no longer be possible for one party to scuttle contract negotiations with impunity when the other has been induced to rely to his detriment on the prospect that the negotiations will succeed." American courts, however, have been unreceptive to these arguments and have declined to find a general obligation that would preclude a party from breaking off negotiations, even when the success was in prospect. Their reluctance to do so is supported by the formulation of a general duty of good faith and fair dealing in both the Uniform Commercial Code and the Restatement (Second) of Contracts that, at least by negative implication, does not extend to negotiations.

> European courts have been more willing than American ones to accept scholarly proposals for precontractual liability based on a general obligation of fair dealing. But even in Europe it is difficult to find cases that actually impose precontractual liability where an American court would clearly not do so on other grounds. * * *

> It is perhaps not surprising that American courts have rarely been asked to hold that a general obligation of fair dealing arises out of the negotiations themselves when they have reached a point where one of the parties has relied on a successful outcome. Often the reason may be that, as suggested earlier, the disappointed parties to negotiations are unaware of the possibility of a generous measure of precontractual liability. But it may also be that they are not greatly dissatisfied with the common law's aleatory view of negotiations and recognize that the few claims that arise are fairly treated under the existing grounds of restitution, misrepresentation, and specific promise. As long as these grounds are not often invoked and have not been pushed to their

limits, there will be little pressure to add a general obligation of fair dealing.

There is ample justification for judicial reluctance to impose a general obligation of fair dealing on parties to precontractual negotiations. The common law's aleatory view of negotiations well suits a society that does not regard itself as having an interest in the outcome of the negotiations. The negotiation of an ordinary contract differs in this way from the negotiation of a collective bargaining agreement, in which society sees itself as having an interest in preventing labor strife. Although it is in society's interest to provide a regime under which the parties are free to negotiate ordinary contracts, the outcome of any particular negotiation is a matter of indifference.

There is no reason to believe that imposition of a general obligation of fair dealing would improve the regime under which such negotiations take place. The difficulty of determining a point in the negotiations at which the obligation of fair dealing arises would create uncertainty. An obligation of fair dealing might have an undesirable chilling effect, discouraging parties from entering into negotiations if chances of success were slight. The obligation might also have an undesirable accelerating effect, increasing pressure on parties to bring negotiations to a final if hasty conclusion. With no clear advantages to counter these disadvantages there is little reason to abandon the present aleatory view.

Farnsworth, Precontractual Liability and Preliminary Agreements: Fair Dealing and Failed Negotiations, 87 Colum.L.Rev. 217, 239–42 (1987).

Further, the Restatement (Second) of Contracts (1981) § 205, Comment C reflects the absence of a good faith requirement in negotiations:

> c. *Good faith in negotiation.* This section, like Uniform Commercial Code § 1–203, does not deal with good faith in the formation of a contract. Bad faith in negotiation, although not within the scope of this Section, may be subject to sanctions. Particular forms of bad faith in bargaining are the subjects of rules as to capacity to contract, mutual assent and consideration and of rules as to invalidating causes such as fraud and duress. See, for example, §§ 90 and 208. Moreover, remedies for bad faith in the absence of agreement are found in the law of torts or restitution. For examples of a statutory duty to bargain in good faith, see, e.g., National Labor Relations Act § 8(d) and the federal Truth in Lending Act. In cases of negotiation for modification of an existing contractual relationship, the rule stated in this section may overlap with more specific rules requiring negotiation in good faith. See §§ 73, 89; Uniform Commercial Code § 2–209 and Comment.

3. Because contract law does not impose a duty of good faith on negotiators, lawyers still assume, often with good reason, that they are free during negotiations to change direction or walk away at any time. In some cases, however, this freedom may give rise to abuse of the bargaining process, and courts have begun to respond to such abuses. One case that discusses some possible limits for negotiators is Hoffman v. Red Owl Stores, Inc., 26 Wis.2d 683, 133 N.W.2d 267 (1965), a staple of first year contracts classes. In Red Owl, the plaintiff operated a bakery and wanted to set up a grocery store. He contacted Red Owl Stores, which expressed interest in the venture. The Plaintiff stated that $18,000 was all the capital that he had available and the Red Owl negotiators repeatedly assured him that this amount would be sufficient for him to set up a business as a Red Owl Store. On the advice of Red Owl management, plaintiff bought the inventory and fixtures of a small grocery store to give him some experience; before the summer tourist season, he was told to sell his bakery business—that this was the only "hitch" in the entire plan. Time dragged on. At later meetings, the company raised the amount of capital required of plaintiff to $24,000, then to $26,000, and then to $34,000. Finally, the plaintiff had had enough and broke off negotiations. The Wisconsin Supreme Court held Red Owl liable to the franchisee even in the absence of a written agreement, applying the doctrine of promissory estoppel.

Contrast *Red Owl* with the case of Gray v. Eskimo Pie Corp., 244 F.Supp. 785 (D.Del.1965). There plaintiffs had conceived the idea of a circular ice cream product with a hole in the middle, which they referred to as an "ice cream donut." Realizing that mass production would be necessary for any real success, they looked around for a company which had the proper manufacturing equipment and national distribution network. They approached the Eskimo Pie corporation, which, after receiving samples of the product and full details on how it was made, indicated a definite interest in manufacturing and marketing it. For the next two years Eskimo Pie Corporation continued to express enthusiasm for the project, but it put plaintiffs off with an elaborate variety of excuses: its executives were out of the office or on "extended trips;" "preliminary engineering work" had to be done; and "major reorganization activities" were occurring within the company. Often the plaintiffs' urgent calls and telegrams were not returned. Meanwhile, Eskimo Pie had been doing a test run of its own "Eskimo Do-nuts," and eventually it launched this product nationwide. Plaintiffs were left "out in the cold"—without an agreement and ultimately without even any product. Plaintiffs sued.

The court concluded that the defendant was deliberately stalling for time while going forward with its own marketing and development plans. According to the court, "[t]hroughout its negotiations with plaintiffs, defendant failed to act with the degree and candor which honesty, fair dealing and a proper regard for business ethics required. Instead it followed a steadied course of seeming deception."[1] Nevertheless, the court concluded that on the facts the plaintiffs had failed to make a case for relief against the defendant. The plaintiffs had corresponded frequently with other large dairy companies during the time they were negotiating with Eskimo, and this made it reasonably clear that "plaintiffs had decided not to rely solely upon their contacts with defendant as a source of assistance but thereafter they persistently attempted to interest many other concerns in their

---

1. 244 F.Supp. at 794.

'SNONUTS.' "[2] The court also noted that no evidence was presented to show that plaintiffs would have benefited more by doing something other than what they did.

What does good faith mean in the context of these two cases? The Red Owl company appeared to be using the escalation game as a negotiating technique, as its negotiator encouraged Hoffman to increase his investment in successive increments. As Hoffman's sunk costs increased, so did the price of the franchise. To view it in the best light for Red Owl, its negotiator may not have fully appreciated the strategy he was following, or understood its impact, until late in the process. Is the unknowing use of escalation tactics a form of bad faith bargaining? Is the conscious use of such tactics bad faith per se? Perhaps the only mistake Red Owl made was in refusing to conclude a deal of some sort with Hoffman. Is an escalation strategy unethical if an agreement results, regardless of any inequities that might exist?

In contrast to Red Owl, the Eskimo Pie negotiators started out with an obvious intent to deceive plaintiffs and "steal" their idea. Why were they not held accountable for this "bad faith" behavior? The court seems to say that dishonest and deceptive behavior itself is not actionable, that you can benefit by this behavior if the other party either does not fully rely on the deception or cannot prove that it would have been better off absent the deceptive behavior. Does this serve as a realistic limit to bad faith negotiation? Is this consistent with legitimate expectations or custom in business negotiations?

4.   Courts have imposed a good faith bargaining requirement in some statutory contexts, particularly in the labor arena. For example, in the late 1940's the National Labor Relations Act (NLRA) was passed requiring companies and labor unions to bargain in good faith. The General Electric Company's bargaining strategy, which came to be called Boulwarism after the General Electric vice president responsible for it, was ultimately found to violate this requirement. GE's approach to negotiations was simple. The company would collect all the available information about wage rates, economic conditions, market potential and other factors relevant to the negotiations. It would share this information with the union and listen to the union's comments. The management would then prepare a firm, fair and final offer for the labor union. Once submitted, GE refused to negotiate over or change its offer: it was a true take-it-or-leave-it approach. After extensive litigation, General Electric's approach was held to violate the NLRA. See N.L.R.B. v. General Electric Co., 418 F.2d 736 (2d Cir.1969), cert. denied 397 U.S. 965 (1970).

Is this bad faith? Can a take-it-or-leave-it offer ever be an element of good faith bargaining, or must there always be concessions made on both sides? In the General Electric case, the court found that GE had engaged in a variety of additional actions that collectively amounted to bad faith, including developing a sophisticated campaign to sell its opening offer to

----

2. Id. at 795.

union employees, regardless of the employees' wishes or the offer's consequences. In the absence of such coercive measures, would a take-it-or-leave-
it offer constitute bad faith?

b.   A LAWYER'S PROFESSIONAL OBLIGATIONS IN SETTLEMENT NEGOTIATIONS

In addition to the substantive law of contract and tort, various professional codes govern attorneys' conduct in settlement negotiations. The
most prominent standards are those in the ABA's Model Rules of Professional Conduct, promulgated in 1983. Adopted by roughly two-thirds of the
states, the Model Rules replaced the ABA's earlier Model Code of Professional Responsibility, which was created in 1969. That, in turn, replaced
the 1908 Canons of Professional Ethics.

Although the Model Rules are the dominant set of standards for
lawyers, the Code still plays a significant role in many court and disciplinary body decisions. In addition, in 1997 the ABA commissioned a study to
revise the Model Rules. That committee, named "Ethics 2000," has been
circulating new versions of the Rules for consideration, and those revisions
will undoubtedly play a more significant role over time. In addition, the
American Law Institute recently issued its Restatement (Third) of the Law
Governing Lawyers. Finally, a task force of the ABA's Section on litigation
has recently circulated a draft set of Ethical Guidelines for Settlement
Negotiations. Although the Guidelines do not have the binding force of the
Model Rules, in some instances they more clearly articulate standards of
behavior for negotiating lawyers.

In this section we consider some of the basic ethical dilemmas that
lawyers face in negotiations. The first excerpt lays out several hypotheticals
and reviews how they would be handled under the Model Rules. The second
excerpt explores various disciplinary cases in which courts have questioned
attorneys' negotiation behavior. The third excerpt challenges lawyers'
tendencies to describe their lies with euphemisms. The final excerpt considers the ways in which lawyers attempt to justify their negotiation behavior
and whether those justifications are persuasive.

Patrick Emery Longan, Ethics In Settlement Negotiations: Foreward

52 Mercer L.Rev. 807, 810–829 (2001).

II.   LIMITS ON MISLEADING CONDUCT

[There are two initial] issues of truthfulness: misleading statements
and the duty to disclose. Model Rule of Professional Conduct 4.1 covers
these topics:

> In the course of representing a client a lawyer shall not knowingly: (a)
> make a false statement of material fact or law to a third person; or (b)
> fail to disclose a material fact to a third person when disclosure is

necessary to avoid assisting a criminal or fraudulent act by a client, unless disclosure is prohibited by Rule 1.6.

There are two issues lurking within and behind this rule. First, as to misrepresentation, comment two to Rule 4.1 contains a special qualification for statements in the context of settlement negotiations.[5] It exempts from the requirements of Rule. 4.1(a) certain statements that "[u]nder generally accepted conventions in negotiation" are not taken as statements of fact, such as the acceptability of a particular amount in settlement. In other words, there is room in negotiations for puffing and bluffing because those practices are what everyone involved expects. Second, the last phrase of Rule 4.1(b) appears to prohibit disclosure, even to prevent fraud, if Rule 1.6 would prohibit the disclosure. Rule 1.6 forbids disclosure of "information related to the representation of a client," absent client consent and with some very limited exceptions.[7] The exception, therefore, threatens to swallow the rule about disclosure.

Another relevant Model Rule is Rule 1.6(b), which permits a lawyer to withdraw from representation if the client "persists in a course of action involving the lawyer's services that the lawyer reasonably believes is criminal or fraudulent." For example, a client who lies to his or her lawyer and has the lawyer unwittingly repeat the lie to an opposing party may forbid the lawyer to reveal the falsity of the representation already made. The result might be fraud, perpetrated by the client through the lawyer. The attorney ethically may withdraw from the representation under these circumstances.

* * *

A.   The Limits of Representations

[We can consider] these and other issues in the context of three hypotheticals. The first concern[s] a case in which the plaintiff sought lost profits and the lawyer was trying to decide what he or she could say about the lost profits in negotiation in a variety of factual situations:

5. [Comment 2 states:] This Rule refers to statements of fact. Whether a particular statement should be regarded as one of fact can depend on the circumstances. Under generally accepted conventions in negotiation, certain types of statements ordinarily are not taken as statements of material fact. Estimates of price or value placed on the subject of a transaction and a party's intentions as to an acceptable settlement of a claim are in this category, and so is the existence of an undisclosed principal except where nondisclosure of the principal would constitute fraud.

7. Rule 1.6 states * * *:

(a) A lawyer shall not reveal information relating to the representation of a client unless the client consents after consulta-

tion, except for disclosures that are impliedly authorized in order to carry out the representation, and except as stated in paragraph (b).

(b) A lawyer may reveal such information to the extent the lawyer reasonably believes necessary:

(1) to prevent the client from committing a criminal act that the lawyer believes is likely to result in imminent death or substantial bodily harm; or

(2) to establish a claim or defense on behalf of the lawyer in a controversy between the lawyer and the client * * *

You represent a plaintiff in a breach of contract action. You are seeking lost profits. What can you say in negotiations about the lost profits if:

(a) Your expert has come to no conclusion about their cause.

(b) Your expert has told you the breach did not cause the lost profits.

(c) Your expert has given you a range between $2,000,000 and $5,000,000 for the lost profits.

(d) Your expert says the maximum lost profit is $2,000,000.

(e) You do not have an expert; your client says the loss was $5,000,000.

It is common in negotiation for each side to emphasize the strength and persuasiveness of its evidence. On the other hand, each side in discovery has the opportunity to explore the other side's evidence. In this scenario, each side would be entitled to a report and a deposition of the other's testifying expert. Any statement about the expert would be a statement of fact. Because of the importance of expert testimony to this case, any statement of this sort would be material. The lawyer must be careful to tell only the truth to avoid violating Rule 4.1. Good lawyers, however, will test the assertions in discovery, consistent with the now-famous Russian proverb, "Trust, but verify."

Beyond the rules of ethics, however, it is proper to ask what the best strategy is for a lawyer in this negotiation. Here, any statement about the expert's conclusions probably will be the subject of discovery. If the statement is found to be false, the lawyer who made it will lose some credibility. That loss, which will likely survive the conclusion of this particular case and affect negotiations with the other lawyer in future cases, will cause these future negotiations to be more strained, more lengthy, and probably less fruitful. To the extent that the lawyer gains a reputation for untruthfulness as a result of statements about the expert, the lawyer may be impeding all his or her future negotiations. In other words, this hypothetical involves a happy situation in which it is both the right strategy and the smart strategy to tell the truth.

In a continuation of the same hypothetical, [we can consider] questions of representations about settlement authority and statements of fact that are literally true but, in context, potentially misleading:

In this breach of contract action, can you:

(a) tell opposing counsel that you will not settle for less than $3.5 million when you have authority to settle for $2 million?

(b) tell opposing counsel that five major buyers stopped buying from your client after the breach, knowing that they stopped buying for other reasons?

As discussed, comment 2 to Model Rule [4.1] defines statements about settlement authority not to be material. Technically, therefore, the lawyer should feel free to lie about his or her authority. Another strategy, however, and one that may be more effective in the long run, is simply to deflect any questions of authority with statements such as, "You know neither one of us can discuss our authority—let's talk about a fair settlement of this case." The reason a deflection may be more effective in the long run is the same reason exaggerations about the expert's conclusions may cause long term harm. You may be ethically permitted to lie about your authority, but if you do it, and the other lawyer catches you at it, he or she will not trust you again.

The misleading statement about the lost customers raises a persistent and subtle issue for lawyers about the use of language. The statement is literally true. These customers have left, and they did so at a time after the defendant's breach. The only reason the statement is made, however, is in the hope that the defendant will make the leap and conclude that the customers left *because* of the breach or, at least, that the plaintiff will attempt to prove that they did. The statement is, therefore, an intentionally misleading, sly use of language. It is reminiscent of former President Clinton's response to a question before the grand jury about his deposition testimony: "It depends on what the meaning of *is* is." The lawyer who engages in this type of deception is more clever, perhaps, than a straightforward liar, but the lawyer is no less worthy of condemnation. Once again, however, we can rely on the power of reputation to deter lawyers (at least those who care about their reputations) from engaging in these tactics. Word gets around.

B. Disclosure of Factual Errors

The second hypothetical concern[s] a duty to disclose facts when the other lawyer has made a settlement offer containing obvious mistakes:

> You represent the husband in a divorce action. You receive from opposing counsel a proposed property settlement with the following errors: (1) a transcription error that undervalues an asset; (2) an arithmetical error that undervalues an asset; (3) a valuation by purchase price of an asset when market value is much higher. All the errors work to your client's advantage. What, if anything, should you do about them?

To the extent that the first two errors are "scrivener's errors" (the other lawyer missed a typographical error or failed to add the numbers correctly), the lawyer has a duty to correct the mistakes.[15] The third problem may raise more difficult issues because the error may come from opposing counsel's conscious but erroneous judgment about what valuation is best for his or her client.. Can the lawyer in the hypothetical take advantage of his or her adversary's error in judgment?

The question is a species of a fundamental, recurring question in an adversarial system. The lawyer owes a primary duty of loyalty to the client. In most respects, the lawyer is not expected to be his or her brother's keeper. One answer to the particular ethical question presented is to say

15. ABA Comm. on Ethics and Professional Responsibility, Informal Op. 86–1518 (1986).

that it is not the interesting or important question. The client is not perpetrating a fraud or a crime by taking advantage of a bad lawyer on the other side. There is no duty to disclose under Rule 4.1.

Abiding by the rules of ethics, however, is necessary but not always sufficient for good lawyering. Ethically, the lawyer need not correct every misstep of opposing counsel. But sometimes correcting the mistake would be the wise thing to do. For example, if the mistakes involved in the proposal were fundamental mistakes, ones that under the law of contract * * * would provide grounds later to void the transaction, then the lawyer may best serve his or her client by alerting opposing counsel to the mistakes now. If the parties to the transaction will have a continuing relationship, such as shared responsibility for minor children, the best strategy might be to correct the mistakes and buy some trust, which may be sorely needed later. Here, as in many situations, ethics tells you the options available, but the lawyer must still exercise good judgments among the options.

C. Disclosure of Legal Errors

The final hypothetical * * * highlight[s] the fact that Model Rule 4.1 forbids a lawyer from making a material misrepresentation about the law. The hypothetical does so in the context of an interaction with a young lawyer who is operating under a mistake about the state of the law:

> You represent the defendant in a personal injury case. In negotiation with plaintiff's counsel (a young, relatively inexperienced lawyer), it becomes clear to you that this lawyer believes his or her client's potential recovery is limited by a tort reform statute. You know that this statute has been found unconstitutional by the state supreme court. May you, and should you, correct opposing counsel's mistake about the law?

Most practicing lawyers would not think twice about taking advantage of this younger lawyer. Again, the client is not perpetrating fraud or a crime, and the client might be very happy to save some money because his or her adversary's lawyer is clueless. No rule of legal ethics requires the lawyer to be the opposing party's lawyer also. No rule requires that lawyers settle cases only on "fair" terms.

Again, however, the strictly ethical inquiry cannot end the discussion. For example, lawyers might find that taking advantage of the mistake in particular circumstances, such as a horrific injury to a young child, would be morally wrong although ethically permissible. The lawyer is free to counsel the client about nonlegal matters, such as the morality of leaving the injured child unable to obtain the life-long care the child needs. The lawyer is even free to seek to withdraw if assisting in a settlement under these circumstances would be repugnant to the lawyer.[19] Here, as in the

---

19. Model Rule of Professional Conduct 1.16(b) states in relevant part, "[A] lawyer may withdraw from representing a client if ... a client insists upon pursuing an objective that the lawyer considers repugnant or imprudent."

prior examples, the best lawyers consider all the circumstances and determine first whether the rules of ethics require a particular course of action and, if they do not, what under all the circumstances is the wisest choice.

* * *

IV. FAIRNESS IN SETTLEMENT NEGOTIATIONS

* * * Grouped under this heading are concerns about misusing the settlement process, overreaching with other lawyers' clients or an unrepresented party, making improper threats, and using confidential information that has been obtained improperly. The Model Rules deal with most of these issues, although sometimes only indirectly. Model Rule 4.4 forbids a lawyer from using means (not just in settlement, but generally) that "have no substantial purpose other than to embarrass, delay, or burden a third person." Rule 4.2 prohibits lawyers from contacting another lawyer's client without permission. Rule 4.3 contains protections for unrepresented persons and requires lawyers to correct any misunderstanding with these persons about their role. Rule 4.3 also forbids lawyers from stating or implying in this situation that they are disinterested. * * * The Model Rules do not contain a provision about improper threats although ABA Formal Opinions have been issued about threats of criminal prosecution and disciplinary action in civil matters.[37] * * *

* * *

A. Dealing With an Unrepresented Party

* * *

> You represent the defendant in a product liability class action. The plaintiff is seeking class action certification but has not yet received it. You believe that you can settle the claims of many potential members of the class if you can negotiate with them directly. May you make settlement offers directly to them? May you emphasize to them that the cost of litigating their individual claims would be far greater than what they could hope to recover?

The issues are whether any contact is appropriate, and, if it is, what the lawyer can and cannot say.

The lawyer must first ensure that the court has not restricted direct contact. The Supreme Court of the United States has held that district courts can restrict communications with members of a putative class if the order is based upon a clear record and specific findings that the restrictions are necessary. If the court has not restricted communications, the defense lawyer faces another issue. If the class counsel represents the members of the putative class for purposes of Rule 4.2, then the defense lawyer may not

---

37. ABA Comm. on Ethics and Professional Responsibility, Formal Op. 363 (1992) (threats of criminal prosecution); ABA Comm. on Ethics and Professional Responsibility, Formal Op. 383 (1994) (threats of disciplinary action).

contact them directly. There is no consensus whether Rule 4.2 bars this sort of contact [in the class context]. * * *

If the contact is permitted, the lawyer must be wary of Model Rule 4.3's limits on what should be said and of Rule 4.1's prohibition on misleading statements of law or fact. * * *

B. Threats in Negotiations

The [following] hypothetical raises issues about documents that are sent to a lawyer improperly and the use the lawyer can or should make of them:

> Suppose the court certifies a class. During discovery, you receive an unsolicited letter from a former paralegal for the plaintiffs' law firm. The letter encloses a standard set of instructions for the plaintiffs' witnesses. The instructions arguably advise the witnesses to lie under oath about their exposure to the defendant's product. May you use the instructions in settlement negotiations? May you use the threat of a bar disciplinary proceeding or a criminal prosecution for obstruction of justice? In exchange for a favorable settlement, may you agree not to report the instructions the plaintiffs' lawyers had been giving?

* * *

* * * The documents have revealed conduct in violation of the Rules of Professional Conduct. May the lawyer threaten to report the misconduct in order to induce a settlement? The answer appears to be no. As discussed above, in Formal Opinion 94–383, the ABA concluded that the lawyer is "constrained" from using this sort of threat by the mandatory obligation to report the other lawyer's professional misconduct. * * *

The final issue is whether the lawyer can use the threat of a criminal referral in the settlement negotiations. The confidential witness instructions may be evidence of obstruction of justice. The Model Rules of Professional Conduct do not contain a prohibition on using a threat of criminal prosecution to settle a civil claim. However, the ABA has issued a formal opinion in which the lawyer's ability to use these threats is limited to situations in which the criminal and civil matters are related, the criminal charge is warranted on the facts and the law, the lawyer does not try to influence the criminal process, and the threat is not otherwise unlawful. In this situation, one issue would be whether the civil and criminal matters are "related" because the criminal activity arose in connection with the litigation and not the underlying facts of the case. The ABA Formal Opinion requires a relationship between the "facts or transaction" of the underlying civil claim and the criminal activity before a threat of criminal prosecution is permissible. A threat that concerns other activity, such as the way in which the lawyer conducts the litigation, would be improper. * * *

C. Good Faith in Negotiations

The next hypothetical raises a basic question about when and why the lawyer can engage in negotiations:

You choose not to use the plaintiffs' lawyer's instructions in an attempt to settle. In fact, your client has instructed you not to settle this case at all, ever, or even to negotiate. Your client believes any negotiation would be seen as a sign of weakness. You recognize, however, that a complete refusal to negotiate would irritate the magistrate judge assigned to the case. You also realize that you might be able to learn something about how the plaintiffs intend to prove damages if you engage them in negotiations. Your client would also be pleased if negotiations protracted the proceedings. What advice would you give your client about its current settlement posture?

Guideline 4.3.1 states that an attorney "may not employ the settlement process in bad faith." Model Rule 4.4 prohibits a lawyer from using means that only "embarrass, delay, or burden" a third person. What advice should the lawyer give when the client wants to use negotiation to curry favor with the judge, to conduct some informal discovery, and to delay the case?

Nathan M. Crystal, The Lawyer's Duty to Disclose Material Facts in Contract or Settlement Negotiations

87 Kentucky L.J. 1055, 1059–1074 (1998–99).

Any analysis of lawyers' disclosure obligations must begin with the fact that many court decisions have held that under some circumstances lawyers have an ethical duty to disclose information in connection with contract or settlement negotiations. * * *

* * *

Perhaps the most extreme example of nondisclosure occurs when a lawyer fails to reveal the death of a client. *Kentucky Bar Ass'n v. Geisler*[23] was a disciplinary action resulting from litigation arising out of an accident in which the plaintiff was struck by an automobile while he was walking on the street. The plaintiff died as a result of these injuries. Shortly after the plaintiff's death, his attorney contacted opposing counsel and negotiated a settlement. Defense counsel learned of the plaintiff's death when respondent returned the settlement documents signed by the plaintiff's son, who had been appointed as the administrator of his estate. Defense counsel did not attempt to rescind the settlement but instead sent the agreed order of dismissal to the court. However, defense counsel then filed a bar complaint against respondent. The Kentucky Supreme Court found respondent guilty of misconduct. The court reasoned that when the plaintiff died, any further communications by the lawyer without disclosure of the plaintiff's death were the equivalent of a misrepresentation of material fact in violation of Model Rule 4.1(a). * * *

Mississippi Bar v. Mathis[31] illustrates when a lawyer's nondisclosure is both the equivalent of a misrepresentation and a violation of disclosure

---

23. Kentucky Bar Ass'n v. Geisler, 938 S.W.2d 578 (Ky.1997).

31. Mississippi Bar v. Mathis, 620 So.2d 1213 (Miss.1993).

obligations under discovery rules. *Mathis* involved a claim by a beneficiary under accidental death insurance policies. The defendant insurance companies moved to have an autopsy performed to determine whether the insured's death was accidental. The attorney resisted the motion on various grounds. In connection with the motion by the insurance companies, the attorney never revealed that he and his client's son had secretly had an autopsy performed. * * * By failing to comply with discovery rules, Mathis violated DR 7–102(A)(3), which prohibits a lawyer, in his representation of a client, from concealing or knowingly failing to disclose that which he is required by law to reveal. The court also emphasized that Mathis's "failure to disclose is the equivalent of an affirmative misrepresentation." * * *

* * *

When a lawyer changes the terms of a settlement agreement or contract, the lawyer has an ethical obligation to disclose the changes to opposing counsel. In *In re Rothwell*,[44] attorney Rothwell represented a client in negotiations with his former employer. The employer had discharged Rothwell's client after he had moved from Ohio to South Carolina. To facilitate the move, the employer had loaned the employee funds to purchase a house. The company offered to buy back the house and to apply the proceeds to the employee's debt to the company. The company sent Rothwell a deed along with a letter asking Rothwell to have his client sign the deed. The letter stated, "We will expect your call if there are any questions." Rothwell modified the deed by inserting a paragraph discharging his client from all liability to the company. After his client signed the modified deed, Rothwell returned it with a letter to the company stating, "We are returning herewith your package to you duly executed. Once you have filed the deed of record, please forward on a clocked copy of same for our files. Thank you." Rothwell did not inform the company that the deed had been changed. In the disciplinary proceeding, Rothwell argued that he did not have a duty to disclose the change in the deed to the company and that his change was merely a counteroffer. The South Carolina Supreme Court rejected this argument, finding Rothwell in violation of several disciplinary rules * * * Rothwell received a public reprimand.

* * *

If a lawyer makes a representation that is true when made but later learns that the representation is now false, the lawyer has an ethical duty to inform the opposing party of this change. In *In re Williams*,[54] respondent represented a tenant in connection with a dispute with a landlord regarding the maintenance of his house. Williams wrote to the landlord to demand repairs and to inform the landlord that he would hold the rent in escrow until the repairs were made. In a subsequent letter, Williams informed the landlord that the tenant would contract for the repairs and would pay the cost from the rent held in escrow. A few days later, however, the tenant moved out of the house. The lawyer returned a rent check to the

44. *In re* Rothwell, 296 S.E.2d 870 (1982).

54. *In re* Williams, 840 P.2d 1280 (1992).

tenant, but he did not inform the landlord that he had returned the check. The bar conceded that Williams had not engaged in misrepresentation because at the time he wrote to the landlord he intended to hold the rent in escrow. The court accepted this concession and treated the case as one involving nondisclosure rather than affirmative misrepresentation. Nonetheless, the court found Williams guilty of misrepresentation by failing to disclose that he was returning the rent check to the tenant.

* * *

Cases involving the death of a client, surreptitious changes in contracts, or failure to correct representations that are now known to be false are rather extreme situations. Courts, however, have disciplined lawyers for nondisclosure in much less egregious situations. *State ex rel. Nebraska State Bar Ass'n v. Addison*[60] dealt with nondisclosure of insurance coverage. The defendant attorney represented a pedestrian injured in a collision between two automobiles. As a result of his injuries, the client incurred hospital expenses of more than $100,000. The attorney engaged in negotiations with the business manager of the hospital, seeking a release of the hospital's lien in exchange for reduced payment of the client's bills. One driver had a liability policy with $100,000 coverage and a separate umbrella policy of $1 million; the other driver's coverage was limited to $50,000. During these negotiations, the attorney learned that the hospital's business manager was under the mistaken impression that there were only two insurance policies available to pay claims; the manager was unaware of the $1 million umbrella policy. Nonetheless, the attorney negotiated a release of the lien without disclosing the third policy. The Nebraska Supreme Court found that the attorney had violated DR 1–102(A)(4), which prohibits a lawyer from engaging "in conduct involving dishonesty, fraud, deceit, or misrepresentation."

* * *

Nondisclosure of significant mathematical errors has also been the basis for rescission of settlement agreements. For example, *Stare v. Tate*[101] was an action by an ex-wife to reform a property settlement agreement entered into by parties prior to their divorce and to enforce the agreement as reformed. The agreement was the result of extensive negotiations between parties who were both represented by counsel. The parties agreed that community property would be divided equally, but they disagreed about the value of a piece of real estate referred to as the "Holt property." The wife contended that the Holt property was worth $550,000, while the husband argued that the property had a value of no more than $450,000. The property was subject to a mortgage of approximately $300,000. The wife's attorney submitted a settlement offer based on a $550,000 valuation of the Holt property, but the attorney made a mathematical mistake of $100,000 in computing the equity in the property. The husband's lawyer

---

60. State *ex rel.* Nebraska State Bar Ass'n v. Addison, 412 N.W.2d 855 (Neb. 1987).

101. Stare v. Tate, 98 Cal. Rptr. 264 (Ct. App. 1971).

and his accountant spotted the error but did not reveal the mistake to the wife's attorney. They reasoned that the mistake was the equivalent of acceptance of the husband's valuation of the property. Acting on the husband's behalf, they presented a counteroffer that used the mistake by the wife's attorney. After some further negotiation, the parties reached agreement based largely on the terms of the husband's counteroffer. The mistake would probably never have come to light except that after the settlement agreement was signed, the husband sent a note to his wife gloating over the fact that she and her attorney had made a mistake. The California Court of Appeals held that the agreement should be reformed to reflect the wife's intent. * * *

Arthur Isak Applbaum, Ethics for Adversaries: The Morality of Roles in Public and Professional Life

104–108 (1999).

We are now positioned to answer the dangling question about lawyers. Are they liars? Both in the courtroom and out, lawyers—good lawyers—intentionally attempt to convince judges, jurors, litigants, and contracting parties of the truth of propositions that the lawyer believes to be false. The act of intentionally inducing a belief in others that one believes to be false ordinarily counts as deception, whatever else it may count as. When deception is accomplished by making an untrue statement, the deception is a lie. * * * [G]ood lawyers certainly are serial *deceivers*—indeed, deception in one of the core tasks and skills of legal practice. And, because sometimes lawyerly deception is accomplished by making untrue statements, sometimes lawyers—again, good lawyers—deceive by lying. But my stake in showing that many lawyerly deceptions are also lies is poetic, not moral. "Are lawyers deceivers?" doesn't have quite the same ring, but a yes answer does have approximately the same moral force. Since deception also is a presumptive moral wrong, the burden is on the practice of law to justify lawyerly deception as well as lying. The question of moral evaluation cannot be redescribed away.

Consider some examples of clear deception. Many lawyers spend much of their time in contract or settlement negotiations, and several common strategies for reaching agreement when the initial perceived zone of possible agreement is larger than a point involve inducing false beliefs about a number of matters: the alternatives of both parties to settlement, the proper assessment of probabilities when alternatives are uncertain, the proper valuation of those alternatives, the change in alternatives and their valuation over time, the proper assessment of probabilities when the outcome of a proposed agreement is uncertain, and the value of a proposed agreement to both parties. Some manipulation of belief in negotiation counts in the law as fraud, and some counts, both in the law and in positive legal ethics, as "puffing and bluffing." But no institutional redescription can do away with the prior description of "intentionally inducing a false belief," or can block counting intentionally inducing false belief as deception. Though the law and positive legal ethics may count certain representations as mere puffery or bluffery, legal rules and rules of professional practice cannot by themselves undo the prior description of deception. When puffing and bluffing is accomplished by making untrue statements, such as "My client will not accept anything less" when you have good reason to believe that this is not the case, or the disarming "That clause is standard boilerplate" when in fact it was specially drafted to cover a contingency that you have good reason to believe has a substantial chance of occurring, you are lying. That the law has some standard of what counts as a "material" misrepresentation of fact is of no consequence to the prelegal description. Because descriptions persist, the law does not determine what is or is not properly described as a lie.

* * *

The good lawyer claims that, in the practice of lawyering, convincing others to believe the truth of what the lawyer believes to be false no longer counts as deception. Rather, it counts as zealous advocacy. Now, it could be that rules of morality do not count certain untruthful behaviors as deceptions. Morality does not count fiction writing as deception, for instance. But the rules of the practice of *lawyering* cannot redescribe a lie as something else. * * *

The lawyer might concede that, for one side or another, most trials involve deception, but deny that it is the lawyer who is doing the deceiving. It is the client, not the lawyer, who deceives. The lawyer-in-role acts as an artificial person, personating or representing the will of the client, but the natural person who occupies the lawyer's role cannot be described as the author of deception. This, I argued earlier, is untrue. * * *

The lawyer is not lying only. She is also advancing legal rights of her client, fulfilling her professional obligations, taking her part in a system that, in equilibrium, seeks truth and justice—the list goes on. The lies lawyers tell and the deceptions they state may be justified. But that, to repeat the refrain, is an evaluative matter. We cannot evade the hard work of moral evaluation and justification by claiming for the action or actor a different description. Does "liar" misdescribe the lawyer?

Walter W. Steele, Jr., Deceptive Negotiating and High-Toned Morality

39 Vand.L.Rev. 1387, 1390–91 (1986).

* * * In a broad sense, justifications exist for this less than honest standard for negotiating. A lawyer's devotion to a client's interest is so compelling that some lawyers feel justified, if not compelled, to employ some deception when negotiating. This viewpoint assumes that clients have a right to a lawyer who engages in deception. Unfortunately, the Model Code of Professional Responsibility and its modern cousin, the Model Rules of Professional Conduct, do not adequately address whether or not clients have a right to a deceptive lawyer.

Another justification for less than honest and straight-forward negotiating is the belief that a convention exists among lawyers to mislead during negotiations. This viewpoint, when carried to its logical conclusion, means that lawyers expect to negotiate with one another much like the proverbial used car salesperson. What a curious postulate for a learned and "high toned" profession to adopt. One wonders how even the most experienced negotiator in a negotiation can tell the difference between an honest party upon whom he can rely, and a deceitful party, upon whom he should not rely.

A final justification for less than honest and straight-forward negotiating is that deceit in inherent to negotiation. Are misrepresentations essential to negotiations? Certainly non-lawyer negotiators engage is deception from time to time. Should we expect something else from lawyers? Consider the negotiating standards of two holy men, one a willing buyer and the other a willing seller. If their personal commitments to holiness prevented them from making the slightest misrepresentation or from engaging in any abuse of their bargaining positions, how would the ultimate outcome of the negotiations differ from the outcome achieved by two lawyer negotiators? If deceit is truly inherent to negotiation, the outcome achieved by the holy men could not be defined as the product of a negotiation. But if the results achieved by their methods are somehow better or fairer than the result achieved by lawyers, then perhaps the legal definition of negotiation should be changed.

None of these rationalizations of deceptive negotiating is fully satisfactory. As a consequence, each prevaricating negotiator relies upon one or some combination of them. Each negotiator feels more or less justified to deceive or abuse power when negotiating, depending upon how well the chosen rationalizations satisfy the moral imperative of that particular negotiator. The result might be thought of as a disco dance floor full of negotiators, some more adroit than others, some more at ease with the music than others, and each very definitely free to "do his own thing." Obviously, what is missing is a specific and reasonably thorough set of standards for negotiating.

NOTES AND QUESTIONS

1. Although the Model Rules provide some guidance for, and some constraint on, lawyers' behavior, these excerpts illustrate that lawyers still have considerable room to maneuver in ways that you might consider immoral even if they do not run contrary to the profession's ethical standards. Are the Rules sufficiently strict? Should the rules governing negotiation behavior set a minimum standard with which all lawyers must (and should be able to) comply—a floor—or an aspirational standard—a ceiling—at which all lawyers should aim even if they sometimes fail? Do you agree with the following assessment?:

> [T]he reality of the situation supports the notion that the status quo ethical constraints in negotiation are adequate to protect societal and

legal interests. Admittedly, the formal rules of ethical conduct do not directly speak to negotiation behavior, and when they do, they only address the most egregious conduct. However, there are a number of other external factors apart from the vacuum of a particular negotiation setting that act as a check on such unethical negotiation behavior. Among these are the professional forces surrounding a particular attorney's practice, the developing cooperative nature of negotiation itself and the market forces that affect a negotiator's decision. Taken together with formal rules of ethics, these factors insure that ethical standards are met during negotiation, while still honoring the ideals of the adversary system and the zealous advocacy of the client that are deeply imbedded within our existing legal system.

Rosenberger, Laissez-"Fair": An Argument for the Status Quo Ethical Constraints on Lawyers as Negotiators, 13 Ohio St.J. on Dis.Res. 611, 638 (1998).

2. As discussed in the Longan excerpt, Comment 2 to Model Rule 4.1 allows for certain types of misleading statements on the ground that all negotiators expect such behavior from their counterparts. Professor White has long championed that the profession's ethical standards should account for the realities of bargaining:

> A final complication in drafting rules about truthfulness arises out of the paradoxical nature of the negotiator's responsibility. On the one hand, the negotiator must be fair and truthful; on the other hand he must mislead his opponent. Like the poker player, a negotiator hopes that his opponent will overestimate the value of his hand. Like the poker player, in a variety of ways he must facilitate his opponent's inaccurate assessment. The critical difference between those who are successful negotiators and those who are not lies in this capacity both to mislead and not to be misled.

> Some experienced negotiators will deny the accuracy of this assertion, but they will be wrong. I submit that a careful examination of the behavior of even the most forthright, honest, and trustworthy negotiators will show them actively engaged in misleading their opponents about their true positions. That is true of both the plaintiff and the defendant in a lawsuit. It is true of both labor and management in a collective bargaining agreement. It is true as well of both the buyer and the seller in a wide variety of sales transactions. To conceal one's true position, to mislead an opponent about one's true settling point, is the essence of negotiation.

> Of course there are limits on acceptable deceptive behavior in negotiation, but there is the paradox. How can one be "fair" but also mislead? Can we ask the negotiator to mislead, but fairly, like the soldier who must kill, but humanely?

White, Machiavelli and the Bar: Ethical Limitations on Lying in Negotiation, Am.B.Found. Research J. 921, 927–38 (1980). Do you agree? Are the justifications and excuses for lying in negotiations more persuasive than the reasons for candor?

Some research has attempted to determine to what extent the Comment to Model Rule 4.1 actually reflects negotiation practice. Various empirical studies show that lawyers believe that both puffing and misrepresenting one's settlement range are ethical and appropriate. See Dahl, Ethics on the Table: Stretching the Truth in Negotiations, 8 Rev.Litig. 173, 183–93 (1989); Lewicki and Stark, Presentation, What's Ethically Appropriate in Negotiations: An Empirical Examination of Bargaining Tactics 18 (Behavioral Research and Bus. Ethics Conf., Nw.U., July 31–Aug. 4, 1994); Lempert, In Settlement Talks, Does Telling the Truth Have its Limits?, 2 Inside Litig. 1 (1988). Thus, even if an attorney knows her client will settle a personal injury case for $30,000, she can say that the client would like to settle in the $50,000 to $75,000 range.

What about lying about a client's reservation value? For instance, what if an attorney authorized to settle for $30,000 told opposing counsel that her client would settle for no less than $50,000? At first glance, lying about a client's reservation price may seem indistinguishable from misrepresenting a client's settlement range. However, to equate the two requires a broad interpretation of the exceptions to Model Rule 4.1. Lying about one's bottom line differs subtly but significantly from expressing one's desired settlement range. The former is an ultimatum, making an opposing negotiator think that unless she gives in to a demand, no settlement will be possible. It thus exerts leverage on the other side. In contrast, an intended settlement range is as subjective as a wish list, more like an opinion or a value estimate. Accordingly, most negotiators would not directly lie about a reservation value. Instead, they would find ways to artfully evade direct questions about settlement authority. See Dahl, Ethics on the Table: Stretching the Truth in Negotiations, 8 Rev.Litig. 173, 192–93 (1989).

For a survey of cases involving misrepresentation, see Perschbacher, Regulating Lawyers' Negotiations, 27 Ariz.L.Rev. 75 (1985); Shell, When Is It Legal To Lie in Negotiations?, 32 Sloan Mgt.Rev. 93 (Spring 1991).

3.   Lawyers often argue that their role insulates them from moral criticism. As a participant in the adversary system, the argument runs, the lawyer is merely embodying the client's preferences and commands, and is not himself open to moral inquiry about the acceptability of his conduct. Particularly in the negotiation context where common practice may already seem to permit some behavior that would normally seem unethical, do the lawyer's role and the rules of the "game" insulate an attorney from moral scrutiny?

Arthur Applbaum critiques the reasoning of role morality, a prominent justification given by lawyers for conduct that would be considered unethical in other contexts. Applbaum summarizes the argument in favor of role morality:

> [A]ctors occupying professional or public roles are not to make all-things-considered evaluations about the goodness or rightness of their

actions, but rather, they are to act on restricted reasons for action, taking into account only a limited or partial set of values, interests, or fact. * * * Each adversary ought to do so (or more modestly, is permitted to do so) because, in the aggregate, the institution of multiple actors acting from restricted reasons properly takes into account the expansive set of reasons, values, interests, and facts.

Applbaum, Ethics for Adversaries: The Morality of Roles in Public and Professional Life 5–6 (1999). Applbaum is critical of the reasoning of role morality: "Good forms of social organization do not by themselves dictate the forms of moral reasoning particular actors within institutions ought to employ. The gap between what an institution may allow and what an actor within an institution may do is especially great when the action in question deceives, coerces, or violates persons in other ways." Further, Applbaum contends that role morality does not "justify circulating information one believes to be false," undercutting the rationale for allowing certain forms of misrepresentation in negotiation.

4. In addition to the moral questions raised by misrepresentation and nondisclosure, such behavior may cause inefficiencies. According to Howard Raiffa:

> The art of compromise centers on the willingness to give up something in order to get something else in return. Successful artists get more than they give up. A common ploy is to exaggerate the importance of what one is giving up and to minimize the importance of what one gets in return. Such posturing is part of the game. In most cultures these self-serving negotiating stances are expected, as long as they are kept in decent bounds. Most people would not call this "lying," just as they would choose not to label as "lying" the exaggerations that are made in the adversarial confrontations of a courtroom. I call such exaggerations "strategic misrepresentations." The expression is not my own invention; it was used by game theorists and mathematical economists long before I adopted it.

* * *

> * * * Bargainers are often advised that they should purposely add to the negotiation agenda issues that they do not really care about, in the hope that the other side will feel strongly about one of these superfluous issues—strong enough to be willing to make compensating concessions in return for dropping the offending issue. This questionable strategy can, of course, poison the atmosphere of the negotiations, with detriment to both parties.

> Strategic misrepresentation can also cause inefficiencies. Consider a distributive bargaining problem in which there is a zone of agreement in actual, but not necessarily in revealed, reservation prices. An inefficiency can arise only if the parties fail to come to an agreement. By bargaining hard the parties may fail to come to an agreement, even though any point in the zone of agreement would yield a better outcome for both than the no-agreement state. Still, one cannot con-

clude from this observation that a negotiator should unilaterally and truthfully reveal his or her reservation price.

Contrast this situation with an integrative bargaining problem, in which it may be possible for the negotiators to enlarge the pie before cutting it. In order to squeeze out potential joint gains, the negotiators must do some joint problem solving. If both sides strategically misrepresent their value tradeoffs, then inefficient contracts will often result. In complicated negotiations where uncertainties loom large, there may be contracts that are far better for each negotiating party than the no-contract alternative, but it might take considerable skill at joint problem solving to discover those possibilities. Without the right atmosphere and without some reasonably truthful communication of values, such jointly acceptable contracts might never be discerned. It is my impression from observing many negotiation exercises that each negotiator is well advised to behave cooperatively and honestly (for example, by disclosing tradeoffs) in seeking joint gains, but to bargain more toughly when it comes to sharing the jointly created pie.

In general, I would advise negotiators to act openly and honestly on efficiency concerns; tradeoffs should be disclosed (if the adversary reciprocates), but reservation prices should be kept private. * * *

Raiffa, The Art and Science of Negotiation 142–144 (1982).

Even if deception creates market inefficiencies, many scholars contend that economic incentives adequately maintain ethical disclosure in negotiation. Robert Condlin argues that a negotiator with a reputation for cooperating will secure more favorable settlements over time and, consequently, have more clients and income over the long term. See Condlin, Bargaining in the Dark: The Normative Incoherence of Lawyer Dispute Bargaining Role, 51 Md.L.Rev. 1, 82 (1992). The market favors disclosure because the practical risks of not disclosing include injury to the negotiator's reputation. Thus, market forces may preserve ethical conduct because attorneys are concerned about the hidden costs of nondisclosure such as harms to reputation, to future clients, and to professional relationships. See Rosenberger, Laissez-"Fair": An Argument for the Status Quo Ethical Constraints on Lawyers as Negotiators, 13 Ohio St.J. on Dis.Res. 611 (1998). Using economic analysis, Geoffrey Peters advocates heightened disclosure requirements for negotiation. Peters says that in real-world negotiations, deception is almost always inefficient and that it rewards those who are skilled at lying. See Peters, The Use of Lies in Negotiation, 48 Ohio St.L.J. 1 (1987); but see Norton, Bargaining and the Ethic of Process, 64 N.Y.U.L.Rev. 493, 537–38 (contending that certain forms of misrepresentation are efficient and enable negotiators to arrive at accurate information); Wokutch and Carson, The Ethics and Profitability of Bluffing in Business, Westminster Inst.Rev. 77–83 (May 1981) (arguing that some degree of deception through bluffing is necessary to maintain economic profitability).

Are economic incentives sufficient to deter lying and nondisclosure in negotiations? If so, why are the Model Rules, the law of fraud and other ethical codes necessary? Even if market forces encourage candor between lawyers in negotiations, clients may have competing incentives not to disclose. Constrained by client confidentiality, lawyers are pressured by clients to engage in hard-bargaining tactics at the same time that economic incentives encourage them to cooperate—a tension Robert Condlin refers to as the "bargainer's dilemma." How do lawyers deal with the bargainer's dilemma? See Condlin, Bargaining in the Dark: The Normative Incoherence of Lawyer Dispute Bargaining Role, 51 Md.L.Rev. 1, 84–85 (1992) (arguing that stylized, or slightly exaggerated, negotiation behavior is a common solution to the bargainer's dilemma).

5. One of the most common ethical dilemmas in negotiation involves corrective disclosure. Consider the following hypothetical:

> [A] mechanic testifies on the deposition that his customer (the father of a child who was killed in an auto accident after the mechanic worked on the car) did not request that the mechanic check the brakes but asked only for a "general checkup" of the car. Subsequently the mechanic comes to his lawyer and states that he "remembers" that the father of the dead child did tell him to check the brakes.

White, Machiavelli and the Bar: Ethical Limitations on Lying in Negotiation, Am.B.Found. Research J. 921, 936 (1980).

The problem of corrective disclosure is related to nondisclosure, becoming an issue when a representation that was originally true turns out to be false. In such a case, does the attorney have an obligation to provide the now-correct information? In a litigation context, an attorney has an ongoing obligation under Federal Rule of Civil Procedure 26(e) to inform the opposing side when material facts are no longer correct. However, the Model Rules do not explicitly cover negotiation ethics in situations where material facts turn out to be false. A draft proposal for a Model Rule that would have required corrective disclosure in negotiations was rejected. For some, the intentional omission resolves the issue in favor of nondisclosure. Further, White argues that the mechanic's attorney could withhold the information in good faith, reasoning that the faulty "memory" had been induced by a sense of guilt from being connected with the child's death. Scholars are split on the question of whether the mechanic's attorney would be required to disclose. Many cite cases of fraud in which attorneys or their clients were held liable for failing to correct a statement that was initially true. If disclosure is required, the mechanic example above may be a rare case where negotiation ethics are out of step with negotiation practice. White contends that most lawyers would not reveal a witness' recantation, and an empirical study supports his claim.[3]

6. Although misrepresentation and nondisclosure may be the most common ethical issues raised by negotiations, lawyers must consider others as well. In multiparty negotiations, for example, a given lawyer or law firm may represent more than one party, raising conflict of interest and loyalty

---

3. See Dahl, Ethics on the Table: Stretching the Truth in Negotiations, 8 Rev.Litig. 173, 190 (1989).

concerns. Much has been written about the ethical quandaries raised by class action litigation. Concerns include that plaintiffs attorneys often cannot adequately represent all members of a class because of intra-class conflicts, that plaintiffs and defense attorneys may collude in settling for their own advantage and fees but to the detriment of class members, and that settlement classes are sometimes "feigned" or "friendly" actions created by the lawyers on both sides that do not truly meet the "case or controversy" requirement. See e.g., Coffee, Class Action Accountability: Reconciling Exit, Voice, and Loyalty in Representative Litigation, 100 Colum.L.Rev.370 (2000); Coffee, Class Wars: The Dilemma of the Mass Tort Class Action, 95 Colum.L.Rev. 1343 (1996); Hay and Rosenberg, "Sweetheart" and "Blackmail" Settlements in Class Actions: Reality and Remedy, 75 Notre Dame L.Rev. 1377 (2000); Koniak, Feasting While the Widow Weeps: Georgine v. Amchem Products, Inc., 80 Cornell L.Rev. 1045 (1995); Menkel–Meadow, Ethics and the Settlement of Mass Torts: When the Rules Meet the Road, 80 Cornell L.Rev. 1159 (1995).

In addition, multiparty cases sometimes raise ethical concerns about defense representation. When a given defense attorney represents more than one party under what is often known as a "joint defense agreement" or when multiple defendants agree to use separate representation but share costs, conflicts of interest can arise as the lawsuit progresses that may not have been obvious at the beginning of litigation. See Erichson, Informal Aggregation: Procedural and Ethical Implications of Coordination Among Counsel in Related Lawsuits, 50 Duke L.J. 381 (2000); Ashley and Wynne, Dealing with Conflicts in Joint Representation of Defendants in Mass Tort Litigation, 17 Rev.Lit. 469 (1998).

Finally, a particular type of settlement has gained some notoriety. In some cases involving multiple defendants, a plaintiff will settle with a given defendant prior to trial and agree with that settling defendant that any recovery at trial in excess of an amount fixed in the settlement agreement will lower the amount owed by the settling defendant. These agreements, known as Mary Carter agreements after the name of a prominent Florida case, Booth v. Mary Carter Paint Co.,[4] have been questioned for the incentives they provide the settling defendant to reveal confidences to the plaintiff so as to help the plaintiff win its lawsuit against the remaining litigants. In addition, because the settling defendant stays in the lawsuit (despite having "capped" its liability through the settlement device), some question whether such agreements may mislead judge and jury. Although the settling defendant purports to be in an adversarial posture vis-à-vis the plaintiff, their interests actually align. See Entman, Mary Carter Agreements: An Assessment of Attempted Solutions, 38 U.Fla.L.Rev. 521, 529 (1986). Although several states have banned Mary Carter Agreements, some commentators have justified them on economic grounds. See Bernstein and Klerman, An Economic Analysis of Mary Carter Agreements, 83 Geo.L.J. 2215 (1995). In addition, California courts have interpreted state statutes as allowing enforcement of "sliding scale recovery agreements"—

---

4. 202 So.2d 8 (Fla.App.1967).

the California equivalent of Mary Carter Agreements, only if in "good faith." That is, the amount of the settlement must be within the reasonable range of the settling tortfeasor's proportional share of the comparative liability for the plaintiff's injuries. See Tech–Bilt Inc. v. Woodward–Clyde & Assoc., 38 Cal.3d 488, 213 Cal.Rptr. 256, 698 P.2d 159 (1985).

(1) Alternatives

The shortcomings of the existing professional codes have called forth a variety of alternatives from scholars, practitioners and judges. Here we list and consider some of these approaches. As you read, compare the different proposals and consider which seems best suited to governing negotiating lawyers. Are these standards realistic? Operational? Sufficiently aspirational? Do they comport with your understanding of what negotiation requires? Will lawyers obey them? Can they be enforced?

Robert B. Gordon, Private Settlement as Alternative Adjudication: A Rationale for Negotiation Ethics

18 U. Mich.J.L.Ref. 503, 530 (1985).

Fairness to Other Participants

In conducting settlement negotiations,

(A) A lawyer shall at all times act in good faith and with the primary objective of resolving the dispute without court proceedings;

(B) A lawyer shall not

(1) Knowingly make any statement that contains a misrepresentation of material fact or law or that omits a fact necessary to make the statement considered as a whole not materially misleading;

(2) Knowingly fail to

(a) Disclose to opposing counsel such material facts or law as may be necessary to correct manifest misapprehensions thereof; or alternatively,

(b) Give reasonable indication to opposing counsel of the possible inaccuracy of a given material fact or law upon which opposing counsel appears to rely. Such indication may take the form of statements of unwillingness to discuss a particular matter raised by opposing counsel.

Walter Steele, Jr., Deceptive Negotiating and High-Toned Morality

39 Vand.L.Rev. 1387, 1402 (1986).

Obligation of Fairness and Candor in Negotiation

When serving as an advocate in court a lawyer must work to achieve the most favorable outcome for his client consistent with the law and the admissible evidence. However, when serving as a negotiator lawyers should strive for a result that is objectively fair. Principled negotiation between lawyers on behalf of clients should be a cooperative process, not an adversarial process. Consequently, whenever two or more lawyers are negotiating on behalf of clients, each lawyer owes the other an obligation of total candor and total cooperation to the extent required to insure that the result is fair.

James J. Alfini, Settlement Ethics and Lawyering in ADR Proceedings: A Proposal to Revise Rule 4.1

19 N.Ill.U.L.Rev. 255, 270–71 (1999).

Rule 4.1 Truthfulness in Statements to Others

In the course of representing a client a lawyer shall not knowingly:

(a) make a false statement of ~~material~~ fact or law to a third person; or

(b) assist the client in reaching a settlement agreement that is based on reliance upon a false statement of fact made by the lawyer's client; or

(c) fail to disclose a material fact to a third person when disclosure is necessary to avoid assisting a criminal or fraudulent act by a client, unless disclosure is prohibited by Rule 1.6.

COMMENT:

Alternative Dispute Resolution

[2] A lawyer's duty of truthfulness applies beyond formal tribunals (see Rule 3.3) to less formal settings. The obligation to be truthful is particularly essential with the increased use by courts of dispute resolution alternatives such as mediation, arbitration, mini-trial, and summary jury trials to effect settlement. When representing a client in these less formal settings, the lawyer may often encounter situations where both the lawyer and his or her client participate freely in open and frank discussions unconstrained by rules of evidence or procedure. The lawyer should therefore inform the client of the lawyer's duty to be truthful and the lawyer's inability to assist the client in reaching a settlement agreement that is procured in whole or in part as a result of a false statement of material fact or law made by the client.

ABA Litigation Section, Ethical Guidelines for Civil Settlement Negotiations

(Draft 2001).

4.1.1. False Statements of Material Fact.

In the course of negotiating or concluding a settlement, a lawyer may not knowingly make a false statement of material fact (or law) to a third person.

4.1.2. Silence, Omission, and the Duty to Disclose Material Facts.

In the course of negotiating or concluding a settlement, a lawyer must disclose a material fact to a third person when doing so is necessary to avoid assisting a criminal or fraudulent act by a client, unless such disclosure is prohibited by the ethical duty of confidentiality.

4.1.3. Withdrawal in Situations Involving Misrepresentations of Material Fact.

If a lawyer discovers that a client will use the lawyer's services or work product to materially further a course of criminal or fraudulent conduct, the lawyer must withdraw from representing the client and may disaffirm any opinion, document or other affirmation. If a lawyer discovers that a client has used a lawyer's services in the past to perpetuate a fraud, now ceased, the lawyer may, but is not required to, withdraw, but disaffirming his/her prior opinion and work product is not permitted.

4.3.7. Exploiting Opponent's Mistake.

In the settlement context, a lawyer should not attempt knowingly to obtain benefit or advantage for himself or herself or his or her client as a result of an opponent's mistake which has been induced by the lawyer or which is obviously unintentional. Further, a lawyer may have an affirmative duty to disclose information in settlement negotiations if he or she knows that the other side is operating on the basis of a mistaken impression of material fact.

4.3.1. Bad Faith in the Settlement Process.

An attorney may not employ bad faith in the settlement process.

4.3.2. Duress and Extortionate Tactics in Negotiations.

A lawyer may not employ pressure tactics in negotiating a settlement that have no substantial purpose other than to embarrass or burden the opposing party.

Alvin B. Rubin, A Causerie on Lawyers' Ethics in Negotiation

35 LA.L.Rev. 577, 589–91 (1975).

The lawyer must act honestly and in good faith. * * * The lawyer may not accept a result that is unconscionably unfair to the other party.

Discussion Draft of the Model Rules of Professional Conduct

(Jan. 30, 1980).

Rule 4.2—Fairness to Other Participants

(a) In conducting negotiations a lawyer shall be fair in dealing with other participants.

Rule 4.3—Illegal, Fraudulent or Unconscionable Transactions

A lawyer shall not conclude an agreement, or assist a client in concluding an agreement, that the lawyer knows or reasonably should know is illegal, contains legally prohibited terms, would work fraud or would be held to be unconscionable as a matter of law.

Rex R. Perschbacher, Regulating Lawyers' Negotiations

27 Ariz.L.Rev. 75, 133–36 (1985).

5.   *Duty to negotiate in good faith*

Commentators in legal ethics have regularly urged that lawyers owe a duty of fairness to their negotiation adversaries. Even these commentators, however, acknowledge the difficulty in establishing a set of legal rules that express and enforce the general duty of fairness. Fairness either includes or is related to the other restrictions on lawyer-negotiators discussed in this part of the article. But what the commentators have in mind is clearly something that goes beyond simply avoiding fraud, duress, and unconscionability. Judge Rubin suggests negotiating lawyers ought "to act honestly and in good faith."

Without an overhaul of the representational-adversary system, imposing a general good faith obligation on lawyer-negotiators is impossible. In part the problem is technical. Under agency law rules, lawyer-agents are privileged and do not incur liability to their client principals by refusing to perform illegal, unreasonable, or unethical acts. Thus, lawyers can respect their obligations to third parties outlined in this section without thereby violating duties and incurring liability to their clients. Currently, there is no general good faith obligation to third parties, and lawyers cannot act according to such a standard without incurring liability to their clients. If this were the only problem, the solution would be simple: add the general good faith obligation to the ethical rules and lawyers will be privileged to act in accord with it. But there are deeper problems.

There is a structural difficulty inherent in the adversary system. Other than rules of professional etiquette, the duties of negotiating lawyers depend upon the existence of a legally recognized relationship. We do not ordinarily talk in terms of a lawyer's duty of fairness to the client because the legally recognized lawyer-client relationship gives rise to the specific obligations of competence, communication, loyalty, and confidentiality. A duty to third parties is recognized only to the extent that the lawyer must not inflict intentional harm or, in those circumstances where the nominal adversary is dependent on the lawyer, to avoid creating an unreasonable risk of harm to the third party. Under current legal practice standards, expanding these limited third party duty rules is incomprehensible. If lawyers are required to respect their adversaries' rights throughout the course of representation, in the end the lawyer becomes representative of both parties and guarantor of the fairness of the transaction. The adversary system would have to be abandoned in negotiations. However desirable this may be as an ideal, it is unacceptable and unworkable in the profession today.

Although wholesale changes in negotiating lawyers' obligations to third parties are unlikely, incremental changes seem certain. One such change is an expansion of the duty to bargain in good faith. Currently, this obligation is restricted to labor negotiations and insurance, both highly regulated because of perceived special public interests. Most of the elements that comprise good faith bargaining in labor and insurance negotiations are either common to all negotiations, such as the proscription against misrepresentation, or are uniquely dependent on the substantive context, such as mandatory bargaining topics in labor law. Thus labeling them part of good faith bargaining does not carry any implications for a general fairness good faith principle in negotiations.

However, two ideals taken from both insurance and labor collective bargaining suggest possible directions for change. These are (1) limitations on negotiating only for purposes of delay, and (2) obstructing an adversary's access to information material to the negotiation. Even if these ideas do not constitute a duty of good faith bargaining in negotiations, they could eventually become the bases for possible damage claims against lawyers who fail to live up to their requirements. These two elements are similar to already recognized bases for relief under existing law. For example, negotiating solely for delay or to burden a third party resembles the tort of abuse of process. To recover for abuse of process, ordinarily an injured party must show use of legal process for a procedurally improper purpose and malice. Negotiation seldom involves the use of legal process, but by analogy sham negotiating can substitute for the procedurally improper use. Combined with malice such as using sham negotiations to coerce or extort money from a third party, misuse of apparent negotiations could become a part of the abuse of process tort or gain acceptance as a separate duty of good faith negotiation practice.

Obstructing access to information is more difficult to place with assurance. In labor law, access to information has developed in the form of the civil discovery rules. There must be an appropriate demand for the information; it must be relevant to the subjects under negotiation; and the adversary can provide it in several different forms. In good faith insurance settlement negotiations, the duty to provide information is actually part of the lawyer's duty of loyalty to the client—a duty to provide the client with information necessary to make informed choices concerning the subject of the representation. Obviously the duty of providing negotiation information is not one of full disclosure. Such an obligation would create an unresolvable conflict with the lawyer's duties of loyalty and confidentiality to the client. Instead it involves a duty of noninterference that should include familiar proscriptions on destruction or concealment of evidence, and that requires disclosure when the failure to do so would be deceptive or misleading to an adversary. This, then, takes into account the negligence-based duties toward third parties and requires some assessment of the opponent's position and the third party's need to rely on information held exclusively by a lawyer for the adversary. Of course, this duty is unambiguous when the subject of negotiation is litigation (civil or criminal), and the information requested is subject to discovery or must be disclosed under existing constitutional, statutory, or regulatory standards.

NOTES AND QUESTIONS

1. How do you think the legal profession should govern lying, misrepresentation, puffing and bluffing, and nondisclosure in negotiations? Do you prefer the existing Model Rule 4.1, Gordon's approach, or Alfini's proposed rule? Are the ABA's proposed ethical guidelines helpful?

The debate surrounding truthfulness, good faith, and fairness standards in negotiation often centers around the proper role of rules themselves. Two divergent camps advocate alternative views on rulemaking. One side supports a minimalist code of ethics, while the other espouses a "high toned," or aspirational, ethic.

Minimalists contend that a certain amount of deception is inherent in negotiation. Further, enforcement of negotiation rules is more difficult because of the nonpublic setting of most negotiations. In light of the difficulty of achieving consensus on appropriate negotiation standards, most commentators assert that negotiation rules must reflect current negotiation practices. The Model Rules represent an ethical lowest common denominator, and individual negotiators may adopt higher ethical standards at their discretion. Finally, rules that set overly high standards will not be followed, casting all of the rules in doubt. For an example of the minimalist position, see White, Machiavelli and the Bar: Ethical Limitations on Lying in Negotiation, Am.B.Found. Research J. 921, 926 (1980); compare Steele, Deceptive Negotiating and High–Toned Morality, 39 Vand. L.Rev. 1387 (arguing that the intrinsic benefits of aspiring to higher ethical standards outweigh social costs).

In addition to Model Rule 4.1, most legal scholars formerly adopted a minimalist position toward disclosure in negotiations. However, in light of the American Bar Association's Ethics 2000 hearings on revisions to the Model Rules, there has been a recent resurgence in favor of aspirational standards. See e.g. Painter, Rules Lawyers Play By, 76 N.Y.U.L.Rev. 665 (2001) (arguing that aspirational rules could improve ethics norms, especially if combined with public reporting on lawyer compliance); Crystal, The Incompleteness of the Model Rules and the Development of Professional Standards, 52 Mercer L.Rev. 839 (2001) (discussing the recent trend in favor of aspirational standards in response to the limitations of the minimalist Model Rules); ABA Litigation Section, Ethical Guidelines for Civil Settlement Negotiations (Draft 2001) (proposing higher disclosure standards for negotiators).

2. One of the dangers of setting an aspirational standard in the professional ethics rules is that lawyers may then be more constrained in negotiations than non-lawyers. In other words, if the professional ethics codes are more strict than the law of fraud, a client may be disinclined to allow her lawyer to negotiate on her behalf. This argument, however, suggests that Model Rule 4.1 (or any replacement for it) might be unnecessary. Should we just do away with regulating negotiation behavior through professional ethics?

3. In addition to seeking to regulate misrepresentations and nondisclosure, many legal scholars have argued in favor of a fairness standard. Judge Alvin Rubin, for instance, argues in favor of a rule preventing negotiators from accepting "unconscionably unfair" results:

> The lawyer should not be free to negotiate an unconscionable result, however pleasing to his client, merely because it is possible, any more than he is free to do other reprobated acts. He is not to commit perjury to pay a bribe or give advice about how to commit embezzlement. The examples refer to advice concerning illegal conduct, but we do already, at least in some circumstances, accept the principle that some acts are proscribed though not criminal: the lawyer is forbidden to testify as a witness in his client's cause, or to assert a defense merely to harass his opponent; he is enjoined to point out to his client "those factors that may lead to a decision that is morally just." Whether a mode of conduct available to the lawyer is illegal or merely unconscionably unfair, the attorney must refuse to participate. This duty of fairness is owed to the profession and to society; it must supercede any duty owed to the client.

Rubin, A Causerie on Lawyer's Ethics in Negotiation, 35 La.L.Rev. 577, 591–92 (1975).

Arguments in favor of a fairness standard often appeal to the notion that lawyers owe duties to the public. The Model Rules, adopted almost a decade after Rubin's essay, give some support for such a duty. See Model Rules of Professional Conduct Preamble (rules should be "conceived in the public interest") and Rule 2.1 (in rendering advice, a lawyer may refer to "moral, economic, social and political factors").

Does Rubin's proposed rule make a negotiator his brother's (or counterpart's) keeper? Does it deprive the more skilled negotiator the benefits of her negotiating talent and experience? Using Rubin's criteria, what would an unconscionable settlement look like? Where would one draw the line between an unconscionably unfair and a merely unfair settlement?

Contract law allows a party to rescind a contract for an unconscionable agreement. Is in necessary to police unconscionable results before the deal is done? In a negotiation, a lawyer may not always have the ability to step back to assess power imbalances and value differentials. Is that a good enough reason not to impose a rule like Rubin's on the negotiator?

For a discussion of the early legislative history of the Model Rules and the reasons why a rule requiring fairness in negotiations was rejected, see Hazard, The Lawyer's Obligation to Be Trustworthy when Dealing with Opposing Parties, 33 S.C.L.Rev. 181 (1981).

(2) Dealing With Ethical Dilemmas

Robert H. Mnookin, Scott R. Peppet & Andrew S. Tulumello, Beyond Winning: Negotiating to Create Value in Deals and Disputes

286–93 (2000).

What If the Other Side Asks Me a Question I Don't Want to Answer?

Negotiating lawyers are sometimes caught off-guard when asked a question where a truthful answer would disadvantage their client. For example, if you were [negotiating a severance package on behalf of a client named Ed and Ed's employer] asked you "Does Ed have any other job offers?" what could you do to get out of the situation without violating the rules of professional conduct? [What if you feared that disclosing Ed's new job offer would lead to a smaller severance package from his existing employer?]

Attorneys approach such moments in various ways. Many refuse to answer such questions. Some might simply remain silent. Others may say "No comment," "I'm not at liberty to say," or "You'd have to ask my client." A lawyer might indicate that he cannot disclose information because to do so would violate client confidences. Given the exceedingly narrow scope of the Rule 1.6(b) exceptions, Rule 1.6(a)'s broad duty of confidentiality operates as a serious constraint on lawyers. The duty to keep client confidences is one of the central pillars of professional ethics. The attorney-client evidentiary privilege protects the attorney-client relationship from unauthorized revelation of information by an attorney. These walls around the relationship are meant to ensure that clients can talk openly and truthfully with their lawyers without fear that their secrets will become public knowledge.

The weakness of using Rule 1.6 as an excuse in a negotiation is that a client can always authorize a lawyer to disclose anything—and if the other side insists that you answer a question, they'll likely insist that you return to your client for permission to do so. The broader problem is that the other side may interpret your refusal to answer, whether you've invoked the rule explicitly or not, *as* an answer—in this case, that Ed *does* have other opportunities.

As a result, many attorneys try evasion in moments like this. They may try to change the subject. Or, rather than not answer, an attorney might answer a different question than the one asked—the politician's classic interview technique. Or a lawyer might respond by asking a question of his own, either to clarify or to change topics. In Ed's case, a lawyer might try to deflect the question by asking, "Who'd want to hire him?" Or "the job market is pretty tight right now, isn't it?" Of course, alert attorneys might expose such sleight of hand under persistent questioning.

A different sort of problem is posed if the lawyer on the other side asks you the limits of your settlement authority or "What is the least amount Ed is willing to accept as severance pay?" While the Model Rules suggest that an attorney has great leeway to misrepresent such information, it is often far better to refuse to answer and to explain why.

You can name the inherent problem with such difficult questions: they invite you to lie. "You know, I don't find questions like that all that helpful, and here's why. If I asked *you* that, although I think you're a decent person, I'd be setting you up to deceive me. It's just a tough question to answer, and it's tempting to bend the truth. I'd have very little confidence in your answer, and so I'm not sure that the question itself would serve me very well. My suggestion is that we table that question." By naming the strategic problem created by such a question, you can sometimes dissuade the other side from pursuing an answer to it. And you show that you understand the strategic landscape and their motivation for asking. This can take the power out of such inquiries.

The key is to prepare. Before you negotiate, make a list of the nightmare questions the other side might ask. Think of all the inquiries that would make you uncomfortable or tempt you to lie. Then prepare answers that could extricate you from those situations as gracefully as possible. Your answers may not be perfect, but you will be able to react more skillfully than if you simply deceive the other side.

What If I Think the Other Side is Lying or Being Misleading?

In negotiation, often the challenge is the other side's behavior, not yours. Some negotiators boast that they can see through the other side's lies and deception. Others fear that they cannot, and they seek advice on how to distinguish truth from falsehoods. Certainly there are sometimes cues when people lie, and it may be possible to become more skillful at identifying deceit. But research suggests that most people exaggerate their ability to detect lies. The stubborn fact is that people sometimes will lie to you, and often you won't know it. Even more often, you'll be unsure whether to trust the other side. What can you do if you fear that the other side is lying, being misleading, or not telling you material information?

SMOKE OUT DECEPTION

One technique is to smoke out unethical behavior. As we've seen, the Model Rules do not require attorneys to reveal much information voluntarily. As a result, asking direct questions and probing for information is indispensable to successful lawyering. Of course, if the other side doesn't want to answer your question, they may evade or refuse, just as you might if they asked you. And they might lie. But only by asking will you truly test their willingness to respond directly. You can't assume that they will otherwise provide you with material facts. As you probe, you can try to triangulate between the other side's statements to discover inconsistencies that demonstrate deception or an attempt to mislead.

VERIFY INFORMATION

Another way to deal with your doubts about the other side is to verify material information whenever possible. This is why due diligence is so important in deal-making and discovery so important to litigation; each side must independently seek to verify material information about the other. Even if the seller says the house you're purchasing is in good condition, be sure to get an inspection anyway. Even if the other side insists that their company is doing well, have your accountant review their books.

Of course, verifying information is expensive. A strong, trusting relationship is valuable in part because it reduces this cost of doing business: you may not need to spend as much time and money on verification. Nevertheless, independently verifying critical information is often a central part of a lawyer's role.

CRAFT REPRESENTATIONS AND WARRANTIES TO HEDGE RISK

Deception works only if you rely on the other side's falsehood. If you doubt the other side, you can structure your negotiated agreement so that you do not rely upon their statements and so that you hedge the risk if it turns out that they have not told the truth.

Lawyers have a comparative advantage in negotiation because they can use their contracting and drafting skills to seek written representations about material facts. Rather than informally relying on the other side's verbal assurances, lawyers can build representations and warranties into agreements and condition settlement on the veracity of those representations. If the other side was exaggerating or lying, they may balk at making such a written representation. The request then serves to smoke out unethical behavior on the other side.

Warranties can also deter, or remedy, lies and nondisclosure. You should always be on the lookout for the lemons problem, for example. In any purchase and sale, the seller has an incentive to withhold information about the condition of the item in question. Seeking representations and warranties can reduce these risks and decrease the damage to you if they lie.

Contracting is thus the legal negotiator's most helpful tool in discovering and constraining misleading behavior on the other side. Don't just take them at their word—have them write their word down and warrant that it is true.

The danger, of course, is that if you find yourself not trusting the other side, you may be tempted to seek representations and warranties about *everything*. If the other side has demonstrated that they can't be trusted, what would in other cases be over-lawyering may be necessary. But you must calibrate your suspicions. Attorneys too easily get carried away and imagine that a written document provides complete protection. Representations and warranties are not a perfect cure. A breach of warranty must be detected and proved, and enforcement is both costly and imperfect.

GIVE THE OTHER SIDE A WAY TO SAVE FACE

When you've discovered or you suspect that the other side is lying or being misleading, you may want to end the negotiations. We certainly don't want to defend those who lie or mislead, nor to apologize for them. At the same time, before breaking off the negotiations or rubbing the other side's nose in their misdeeds, think carefully about what will best serve your client's overarching interests. If problem-solving is the approach you prefer, it may be more productive to deal with the other side's impropriety while giving them a way to save face.

Why? Because being caught lying is embarrassing. The other side may not want to continue negotiating with you if it is clear that you know they were trying to deceive. Moreover, if you acknowledge that you have found them out, *you* may no longer be able to negotiate with *them*: to preserve your reputation, you can't be known as a person who does business with liars. For example, imagine that you know your employee has falsified a few expense reports. You don't want to fire him, but you want him to change his behavior. However, you can't let him know that you know about the past transgressions, because then you would have to fire him: your company's policy would require it. In this situation, naming the ethical issue would make it harder to work together in the future, even if he was committed to no longer stealing from the company.

Often you can find creative ways to signal or hint to the other side that their unethical behavior won't work or has been found out, while leaving the message ambiguous enough to permit both sides to continue working together.

How Much Do I Have to Tell My Client?

It can be quite easy for a lawyer to manipulate his client to serve his own interests. For example, many lawyers admit to lowballing their clients in order to set achievable expectations. If the client doesn't expect much, then whatever settlement or deal the lawyer reaches will seem like a victory. Some lawyers may even lie to their clients to look good. For example, if the other side has made an oral offer of $50,000 to settle a client's claim, a lawyer might first tell the client that the other side offered $35,000, and then—days later—tell the client that after strenuous negotiations the other side increased the offer to $50,000.

Lawyers may also exaggerate in order to delay settlement and run up fees. An attorney might exaggerate negative comments made by the other side and try to excite his client into continuing litigation. Or he may twist his assessment of the value of the client's claim and argue that an existing settlement offer is insufficient. The lawyer, in short, may manipulate the client's perceptions for the lawyer's own ends.

Finally, lawyers sometimes withhold information for the opposite reason: to make ending a negotiation easier and quicker. This can be done in the name of serving the client's "real" interests. If a lawyer has spent a great deal of time counseling a stubborn and frustrating client, manipulating information may seem easier than continuing these difficult conversations. But his rationalization can also be merely a pretense for advancing the lawyer's interests at the client's expense.

Obviously, a lawyer should not lie to his clients. And saying the other side offered $35,000 when the offer was $50,000 is a lie that most lawyers would consider outrageous. But these situations are often less about lying per se than about shading the truth and not disclosing information. What do the Model Rules say about these issues? Model Rule 1.4 requires lawyers to keep clients "reasonably informed about the status of a matter and promptly comply with reasonable requests for information." Rule 1.4(b) requires lawyers to explain matters "to the extent necessary to permit the client to make informed decisions regarding the representation." And Comment 1 to Rule 1.4 says that when a *written* offer is obtained, the attorney "should promptly inform the client of its substance unless prior discussions with the client have left it clear that the proposal will be unacceptable."

Most commentators go further and urge attorneys to apply Rule 1.4 to a verbal offer as well. Although the Rule doesn't technically apply, the underlying purpose of Rule 1.4 is to keep a client "reasonably" informed about the progress of her legal matter. An attorney's failure to report back to a client should therefore be considered a violation of professional canons if the lawyer's actions leave the client so in the dark that the client cannot be said to be able to make an informed decision. This includes a failure to transmit a verbal settlement offer or an attempt to manipulate the client's impression of a settlement offer through lowballing or other tricks.

At the same time, it is important to note that the Model Rules leave an attorney a great deal of freedom and flexibility to decide for himself what amount of information-sharing should take place with his client. Even if an attorney must transmit both written and verbal settlement offers, there is information that the attorney may *not* be required to share. For example, the codes do not require an attorney to discuss what happened at the negotiation table, what was said, what strategy or tactics the attorney used, or how the other side reacted. If an attorney employs very aggressive hard-bargaining tactics, for example, and the other side reacts negatively and refuses to continue negotiating, is the attorney under a professional obligation to explain what tactics he used and what the consequences were? Or can the attorney merely advise the client that the other side has refused to continue discussions? The codes seem to suggest that if a client *asks* for such information, the lawyer must provide it. In the absence of a direct request, however, the lawyer might not have a duty to disclose such information to the client.

Nevertheless, attorneys should share such information with their clients, or at least negotiate explicitly with their clients about the kind of information that the client *wants*. Being interest-based and client-centered may require a shift in the lawyer's implicit stance toward the client. But at base, effective lawyering requires that a lawyer see her client as a person with valuable information from which the lawyer can learn, and as a person deserving the opportunity to make an informed choice about his legal affairs. The lawyer's job is to provide the client with the information he needs to make such choices.

Aren't I Supposed to Be a "Zealous Advocate"?

An attorney is supposed to champion the client's cause, and as a consequence, many lawyers claim that a duty of "zealous advocacy" requires them to do everything that isn't clearly forbidden. But this often places lawyers in an uncomfortable position. Because defending a client's interests is paramount, attorneys may fear that adopting any negotiating strategy other than extreme hard bargaining violates a basic duty to their client.

Under the Model Rules, this is nonsense. Rule 1.3 requires "reasonable diligence" on behalf of a client. Comment 1 to Model Rule 1.3 states that "a lawyer should act with commitment and dedication to the interests of the client and with zeal in advocacy upon the client's behalf. However, a lawyer is not bound to press for every advantage that might be realized for a client. A lawyer has professional discretion in determining the means by which a matter should be pursued." This comment suggests that attorneys retain significant flexibility in defining the bounds of zealous representation. The client's interests, conceived broadly, may be better served by a more constrained and reasoned approach to negotiation than by initiating a contest of wills or a war of attrition. So long as the client understands the risks and benefits of a problem-solving stance, there is no inherent contradiction between problem-solving and advocacy. Indeed, sometimes blindly going to war—even if the client insists upon it—may disserve the client's broader interests. As Elihu Root once said, "About half the practice of a decent lawyer consists in telling would-be clients that they are damned fools and should stop."

NOTES AND QUESTIONS

1. Many people believe that they can tell when others are lying. In fact, however, studies have found that most people have a very difficult time detecting others' lies. Analyzing nonverbal cues in the deceiver's behavior produces accurate results 45 to 60 percent of the time—roughly equivalent to tossing a coin. See Vrij, Edward, Roberts and Bull, Detecting Deceit Via Analysis of Verbal and Nonverbal Behavior, 24 J. Nonverbal Behavior 239 (2000); DePaulo, Stone and Lassiter, Deceiving and Detecting Deceit, in The Self and Social Life 323–370 (1985). (Some professionals, including law-enforcement officers and psychologists, have been shown to have better than average abilities in detecting lies. See Ekman, O'Sullivan and Frank, A Few Can Catch A Liar, 10 Am.Psychol. Survey 263 (1999).)

In general, most people assume that a liar's behavior will change during deception. See Anderson, DePaulo, Ansfield, Tickle and Green, Beliefs About Cues To Deception: Mindless Stereotypes or Untapped Wisdom?, 23 J. Nonverbal Behavior 67 (1999). We often assume that a deceptive person will become agitated or nervous, and therefore increase her bodily movements. People predict that a liar will avert her eyes, smile less frequently, and shift positions more frequently. People also associate lying with an increase in speech disturbances (such as "ahs" and "ums") and with changes in voice tone or pitch.

Although speech disturbances do generally occur more frequently during deception, liars generally *decrease* their bodily movements while lying. They tend to move deliberately and rigidly, and decrease the number of nonfunctional movements such as hand or leg movements. See Vrij and Mann, Telling and Detecting Lies in a High-stake Situation: The Case of a Convicted Murderer, 15 Applied Cognitive Psych. 187–203 (2001). Liars are often unaware of these changes, see Vrij, Edward and Bull, People's Insight Into Their Own Behavior and Speech Content While Lying, 92 British J. Psych. 373–389 (2001), and, interestingly, even people who have been told in advance that they are likely to decrease their bodily movements when lying—and who are thus trying to compensate for this tendency in order to avoid detection—often fail to incorporate this information and continue to display rigidity and decreased movement when lying. See Vrij, Semin and Bull, Insight Into Behavior Displayed During Deception, 22 Human Commun. Research 544, 545 (1996).

2. Should you lie in negotiations? The discussion in these various excerpts suggests many reasons not to lie, including economic, reputational, moral, and personal costs of lying. If detected, lying may hurt this negotiation, future negotiations, and your reputation generally.

Intriguingly, however, lying may do damage even if *undetected*. Research suggests that even if you are able to lie without detection, your undetected lie can *still* damage the long-term relationship with the other side. Why? Because an undetected liar often will, over time, begin to believe that his *counterpart*—the other person in relationship with him—is being dishonest. "For example, if a husband has an extramarital affair and does not tell his wife, then he may begin to see her as less honest as a result of his own infidelity. This *deceiver's distrust* could occur through one or a combination of three psychological processes: (a) a false consensus effect, in which the liar infers the level of dishonesty in others from his or her own salient behavior; (b) an ego-protective mechanism, in which the liar defends self-image by coming to believe that anyone would have acted the same way; and (c) a belief in a just world, in which the liar derogates the character of the victim of the deceit to maintain the belief that bad outcomes do not afflict good people." Sagarin, Rhoads and Cialdini, Deceiver's Distrust: Denigration as a Consequence of Undiscovered Deception, 24 Personality & Soc.Psychol.Bull. 1167, 1167 (1998).

3. Because of the gaps and conflicting ethical duties in the ethical codes, a negotiator will often face ethical dilemmas that cannot be resolved merely by consulting professional standards. In such a case, what should you do? Each person's moral code differs, and people may reasonably disagree about what constitutes ethical or unethical behavior. To aid in your personal deliberations, however, we reproduce a list of questions that has long circulated as folk wisdom for determining whether a given action is morally permissible. In reading it, think back to the various hypotheticals in the Longan excerpt and the disciplinary cases in the Crystal excerpt. Would the lawyers in those situations have acted as they did if they subjected their behavior to these various tests?

History

How do I guess that future historians are likely to judge conduct like this?

If, years hence, I myself look back at this conduct am I more likely to be proud or ashamed of it?

Will it be cited to my credit or will I have to defend it?

Philosophy

What are guiding principles of which my proposed action is an application?

Are those principles that I would commend to all?

Law

Is the proposed conduct legal?

Would the comparable conduct be legal within most countries?

Would the conduct be consistent with wise laws as they should be established and interpreted?

Religion

Is the proposed conduct consistent with the teachings of the world's religions?

Would the conduct be seen as an example of how a deeply religious person ought to behave?

Literature

How would I have to behave so that if a novelist or dramatist were basing his writing on this incident I might be the hero of that work?

Is the proposed conduct more like that of literary heroes or literary villains?

Family and Friends

Would I be pleased to learn that my father or mother had behaved as I propose to behave?

Would I be proud to learn that my child had behaved this way?

Would I want my child to use this bit of conduct as a guide for his future actions?

Publicity

If, through no doing of mine, a full account of my proposed conduct appeared on the front page of tomorrow's newspaper, is it more likely that I would be proud or embarrassed?

4. Roger Fisher has suggested that because the legal profession's ethical codes do not sufficiently constrain an attorney's behavior and therefore leave an attorney vulnerable to pressure to "cheat" from his or her client, lawyers should begin relations with their clients by laying out their *own* written code of negotiation practice. In a sample letter to a hypothetical client, Fisher suggests explaining the following to a potential client:

I would like to obtain your approval for my accepting this code as providing the general guidelines for any negotiations I may conduct on your behalf. I would also like you to know that I will follow these guidelines in any negotiations that you and I have with each other, for example over the question of fees. * * *

The reason I would like your approval of my following this code in my negotiations as your lawyer is to avoid any future misunderstanding. In addition, I would like to put to rest the canard that because I am a lawyer, I have a "professional" duty to you as my client to engage in sharp or deceptive practices on your behalf—practices that I would not use on my own behalf and ones that might damage my credibility or my reputation for integrity. Let me explain.

The Code of Professional Responsibility approved by the American Bar Association provides that a lawyer should advance a client's interest zealously. The Code * * * does little to clarify this standard, and the Bar Association has failed to adopt proposed changes that would more explicitly permit a lawyer to balance the duty to be a partisan on behalf of a client with the duty to adhere to ethical standards of candor and honesty.

The result is that, in the absence of client approval to do otherwise, it can be (and has been) argued that a lawyer should conceal information, bluff, and otherwise mislead people on behalf of a client even: (a) where the lawyer would be unwilling for ethical reasons to do so on his or her own behalf; and (b) where the lawyer's best judgment is that to do so is contrary to the public interest, contrary to wise negotiation practices, and damaging to the very reputation for integrity that may have caused the client to retain the lawyer.

* * *

I believe that it is not a sound practice to negotiate in a way that rewards deception, stubbornness, dirty tricks, and taking risks. I think it wiser * * * to deal with differences in a way that optimizes the chance of reaching a fair outcome efficiently and amicably; that rewards those who are better prepared, more skillful and efficient, and who have the better case as measured by objective standards of fairness; and that makes each successive negotiation likely to be even better. (This does not mean that a negotiator should disclose everything or make unjustified concessions.)

The attached code is intended to accomplish those goals.

Fisher, A Code of Negotiation Practices for Lawyers, 1 Neg.J. 105–110 (1995). Fisher's code then goes on to outline for lawyers their goals for a given negotiation, including to jointly consider the parties' interests, to seek efficient and creative options, to find a fair or legitimate solution, and to act honorably in ways that promote justice and honesty. Others have recommended that law firms fill the gap left by ethical codes. See e.g. Painter, Rules Lawyers Play By, 76 N.Y.U.L.Rev. 665, 732–740 (2001).

Will Fisher's approach work? How will most clients likely react to a lawyer who disseminates such a personal code? What are the advantages of having given a client such explicit guidance about your negotiation approach? The disadvantages?

c. MALPRACTICE

In addition to the constraints imposed by the substantive law and the professional ethics codes, a lawyer must concern herself with the possibility of a post-settlement malpractice action related to her behavior during the negotiation process. In the following excerpt Professor Epstein considers the viability of such actions.

Lynn A. Epstein, Post–Settlement Malpractice: Undoing the Done Deal

46 Cath.U.L.Rev. 453, 453–60 (1997).

Clients voice their approval to mediators and judges as a settlement agreement is reached. A release is signed, the file is closed, and from the lawyer's perspective, another case ends. The settled case joins an overwhelming majority of civil cases that are resolved in pretrial settlement. Buried within this figure, however, is a more troubling statistic: over twenty percent of civil cases will be resurrected in the form of malpractice actions initiated by dissatisfied clients. In those instances, and for various reasons substantiated by expert opinions, the client will charge that they could have received a better result in the settlement even though the client knowingly and willingly agreed to end the case.

In every state except Pennsylvania, a client is permitted to proceed with the theory that his attorney negligently negotiated an agreement despite the fact that the client consented to settlement. In *Muhammad v. Strassburger, McKenna, Messer, Shilobod & Gutnick*, 587 A.2d 1346 (Pa. 1991), the Pennsylvania Supreme Court determined that an attorney is immune from malpractice based on negligence where the client consented to settle. Court decisions after Muhammad, however, have uniformly rejected immunity for the attorney, permitting post-settlement malpractice actions to proceed in the same manner as the prototypical malpractice case.

* * *

I. Muhammad and its Successors

Conventional wisdom dictates that attorneys settle cases effectively, as an estimated ninety-five percent of civil cases are resolved by settlement. Yet, an emerging trend of post-settlement malpractice claims threatens the integrity of the settlement negotiation process. While malpractice actions are on the rise, most attorneys reasonably believed they were insulated from liability because the client had consented to settlement, and because there was no affirmative wrongdoing by the attorney. Because so many factors influence a client's decision to settle, and because so many individuals, such as judges and mediators, are a part of the process, it would appear fundamentally unfair to hold the attorneys solely responsible for such malpractice claims. This is buttressed by a majority viewpoint which looks unfavorably upon malpractice claims that require the judiciary to infiltrate the negotiation process, a process traditionally viewed as immune from judicial scrutiny.

Balancing these competing interests, the Pennsylvania Supreme Court barred such malpractice actions to foster the negotiation and settlement process. In *Muhammad*, the Pennsylvania Supreme Court held that, absent fraud, an attorney is immune from suit by a former client dissatisfied with a settlement that the former client agreed to enter.

Pamela and Abdullah Muhammad sued the firm of Strassburger, McKenna, Messer, Shilobod and Gutnick for malpractice arising from the settlement of an underlying medical malpractice suit. In the underlying action, the Muhammads sued the physicians and hospital that performed a circumcision on their son who died as a consequence of general anesthesia used during the procedure. The Muhammads retained the Strassburger law firm. The physicians and hospital offered to settle the malpractice claim for $23,000, which was subsequently increased to $26,500 at the suggestion of the trial court. The Muhammads accepted the settlement offer. The Muhammads later grew dissatisfied with the amount received in settlement and instructed the Strassburger law firm to communicate this discontent to defense counsel. An evidentiary hearing ensued where the court upheld the settlement agreement, reasoning that the Muhammads agreed to the settlement amount and, thus, there existed a binding and enforceable contract.

Unable to reopen the medical malpractice proceeding, the Muhammads initiated a claim against the Strassburger law firm alleging legal malpractice, fraudulent misrepresentation, fraudulent concealment, nondisclosure, breach of contract, negligence, emotional distress, and breach of fiduciary duty. The court dismissed the fraud counts because the Muhammads had not pled fraud with specificity. Surprisingly, the court then barred the Muhammads from proceeding with their remaining negligence claim against the Strassburger firm, based on articulated public policy encouraging civil litigation settlement. In granting immunity, the court wrote:

> [W]e foreclose the ability of dissatisfied litigants to agree to a settlement and then file suit against their attorneys in the hope that they will recover additional monies. To permit otherwise results in unfairness to the attorneys who relied on their client's assent and unfairness

to the litigants whose cases have not yet been tried. Additionally, it places an unnecessarily arduous burden on an overly taxed court system.

The court emphasized that this immunity extends to specific cases where a plaintiff agreed to settlement in the absence of fraud by the attorney. This is distinguished from the instance when a lawyer knowingly commits malpractice, conceals the wrongdoing, and convinces the client to settle in order to cover-up the malpractice. According to the court, in this instance, the attorney's conduct is fraudulent and actionable.

In a stinging dissent, Justice Larsen lamented that the majority established a "LAWYER'S HOLIDAY" by barring legal malpractice actions for negligence committed in the negotiation of civil case settlements. Contrasting the new declaration of immunity with the liability exposure of other professionals, Justice Larsen reasoned: "If a doctor is negligent in saving a human life, the doctor pays. If a priest is negligent in saving the spirit of a human, the priest pays. But if a lawyer is negligent in advising his client as to settlement, the client pays." *Muhammad* has suffered widespread criticism and is uniformly rejected in every reported opinion reviewing post-settlement legal malpractice litigation.

For example, in *Ziegelheim v. Apollo*, 607 A.2d 1298 (N.J.1992), the New Jersey Supreme Court rejected Muhammad, permitting a client to sue his attorney even though the client agreed to a settlement amount. Apollo represented Miriam Ziegelheim in a divorce action. The only issues litigated at the trial court level were payment of alimony, identification of marital property, and equitable distribution of that property. After reaching an agreement on these issues, both parties testified in open court "that they understood the agreement, that they thought it was fair, and that they entered into it voluntarily."

After consummation of the agreement, Mrs. Ziegelheim sued Apollo for legal malpractice, contending that he failed to discover information about her husband's assets which would have increased the amount she might have received in settlement. The trial court granted summary judgment for Apollo, holding that Mrs. Ziegelheim entered into the settlement agreement voluntarily with every indication that she clearly understood the terms of the agreement. The appellate division affirmed.

The New Jersey Supreme Court reversed, reasoning that the duty to provide reasonable knowledge, skill, and diligence provides the basis for a legal malpractice action even when the client consents to settlement of the underlying civil action. In addition to Zeigelheim's consent, the family court judge's proclamation that the settlement was "fair and equitable" did not preclude the legal malpractice action. The Supreme Court added:

> The fact that a party received a settlement that was "fair and equitable" does not mean necessarily that the party's attorney was competent or that the party would not have received a more favorable settlement had the party's incompetent attorney been competent.

Thus, in this case, notwithstanding the family court's decision, Mrs. Ziegelheim still may proceed against Apollo in her negligence action.

The New Jersey Supreme Court tempered its decision by qualifying that it did not intend to "open the door" to legal malpractice suits by every former client who had previously agreed to civil suit settlement. The court cautioned that in order to state this genre of legal malpractice, a former dissatisfied client must specify, with particularity, the alleged malpractice. Hence, a general plea by dissatisfied clients who later decide they should have obtained more money in settlement will not be successful. The court also reiterated that an attorney will not be held to an unrealistically infallible standard of securing the maximum outcome in settlement: an attorney's duty remains one of reasonable skill and knowledge.

While most courts are expeditious in determining that an attorney is not absolutely immune from legal malpractice actions when the client consents to settlement, they are also uniform in expressing a desire to foster protection over the negotiation process. In *Prande v. Bell*, 660 A.2d 1055 (Md. Ct. Spec. App. 1995), plaintiff Luisa Prande sued her former attorneys, John T. Bell and Elbert Shore (the Bell firm), alleging they negligently settled claims arising from her motor vehicle personal injury action. The Bell firm represented the plaintiff in two automobile accidents. In the first lawsuit, Prande accepted $7,500 to settle her personal injury suit in which she signed a release. According to the Bell firm, she verbally agreed to settle the second lawsuit for $3,000, but refused to sign the release.

Defendant Wishart then filed a motion to enforce the settlement. The plaintiff's attorney informed Ms. Prande that she should attend the hearing " 'in the event that you seek or wish to contest the matter of whether we had your authorization to accept a settlement.' " Prande failed to appear, and the court granted Wishart's motion, dismissing with prejudice the personal injury lawsuit. Prande then initiated a legal malpractice action against the Bell firm, claiming that it "negligently advised [her] to accept unreasonable and inadequate settlements of her claims." The lower court granted summary judgment for the Bell firm, ruling that the plaintiff merely wished "to relitigate the matters that have already been decided and resolved" by settlement, and concluding that permitting the legal malpractice action to proceed to trial would result in never-ending litigation.

The appellate court reversed, reasoning that when the client voluntarily accepts a settlement, she does not absolve her attorney from liability for negligence committed during settlement negotiation. Rejecting *Muhammad's* hard and fast rule, the court determined that the important public policy of encouraging settlements was outweighed by an attorney's responsibility to advise his client with the same skill, knowledge, and diligence in the negotiation of civil suit settlement as that which an attorney must employ in all other litigation tasks. The court also cautioned, however, that post-settlement malpractice actions involving an attorney's judgment and recommendation whether to settle is not malpractice simply because another attorney would not have recommended settlement. Thus, the court held that to recover, a plaintiff must allege specifically that the attorney's recommendation to settle is one that no reasonable attorney would have made.

Though *Prande* requires a higher standard for alleging malpractice, it focuses solely on the conduct of the attorney. Both *Prande* and *Apollo* ignore the client's role in negotiating civil case settlements, failing to examine the client's reasons for consenting to settlement. While ignoring these important factors, both cases establish guidelines for post-settlement legal malpractice which allow the cause to proceed only if the client alleges specific acts of negligence; typically such allegations are supported by expert testimony. Both courts seek to address the importance of safeguarding the negotiation process in an effort to encourage settlements and discourage clients from seeking redress based on bald assumptions that they should have received more money. * * *

* * *

In review, while other dissatisfied clients alleged they had been unable to comprehend or understand a settlement agreement, it is logical to infer that clients who claim to believe they are entitled to receive more money would have no difficulty "comprehending" the amount of money they did receive. Requiring an attorney to determine whether a client is competent to enter into a settlement agreement when there is no indication otherwise would be tantamount to imposing an unrealistic standard upon the attorney. To anticipate such an unrealistic defense, a properly diligent lawyer would be required to obtain an independent medical evaluation for a client before entering into a settlement agreement or, for that matter, prior to any agreement substantially affecting the course of ongoing litigation. Absent any prior patent evidence of incompetence, a lawyer should not be held to such an unwieldy standard.

NOTES AND QUESTIONS

1. In general, courts have found that a lawyer has both substantive and procedural duties to her client in the settlement process. The procedural duties include the duty to communicate serious settlement offers to the client, the duty to only make settlement offers to the other side with the client's permission, the duty to only accept a settlement offer with the client's consent, and the duty to inform a client of any conflict of interest. In addition, courts have held that an attorney may not use the negotiation process to cover up the lawyer's mistake. In other words, malpractice may be appropriate if a client is forced to accept a lower (or pay a greater) settlement amount because her attorney has encouraged settlement to cover up the attorney's negligence. On the substantive side, as Epstein explains, courts have sometimes found that a lawyer has failed to apply his or her substantive knowledge of the law to the client's case, thereby resulting in a sub-standard settlement agreement. Such malpractice actions are obviously significantly harder to establish. See Baker–Selesky, Negligence in Failing to Settle Lawsuits: Malpractice Actions and Their Defenses, 20 J. Leg. Prof. 191,196–197 (1995–1996).

As Epstein explains, courts have sometimes been reluctant to permit malpractice actions in the settlement context. Is this approach defensible, or is the *Muhammad* rule appropriate? What social policies does each approach promote?

2.   Epstein criticizes the propensity for courts to use the likely result at trial as the standard for measuring whether malpractice has occurred. The jury in a malpractice action is asked to evaluate the settlement agreement about which the plaintiff has claimed malpractice. The jury's assessment of the settlement is said to be an objective standard for measuring a fair outcome. Epstein criticizes this ex post evaluation of the case's value, or "trial within a trial," because it ignores the negotiation process and subjective interests in the earlier negotiation. In the article, Epstein explains,

> Courts that apply the "trial within a trial" method to post-settlement malpractice claims typically ignore the fact that the client voluntarily agreed to settle the case, and instead focus on the result that would have occurred had the case gone to the jury. * * * By definition, however, every aspect of a negotiated settlement, particularly its conclusion, is a subjective evaluation premised on the client's needs and desires, coupled with the various influences that affect that client's ultimate decision to settle. * * *

> * * *

> * * * In post-settlement malpractice litigation analysis, courts tend to focus only on the result obtained (the settlement sum) to gauge the lawyer's liability exposure, ignoring the traditional factors preceding settlement. * * *

Epstein, Post–Settlement Malpractice: Undoing the Done Deal, 46 Cath. U.L.Rev. 453, 463–464 (1997).

If the jurors in a malpractice action are not allowed to consider the negotiation process and parties' interests in the prior settlement, how can they objectively weigh a fair outcome? If the prior settlement was an interest-based negotiation in which non-monetary tradeoffs occurred, how could the jury take that into account? For instance, a divorcing spouse may agree to a reduced monetary settlement for sole custody of the children or for an apology, but in a subsequent malpractice action the jury may not be able to hear about the interest-based tradeoff. Thus, the "trial within a trial" may force a distributive lens on interest-based negotiations.

Epstein suggests that allowing the jury to consider the negotiation process and subjective interests of the parties would allow a jury to see that some settlements that appear one-sided are actually fair. However, there may be problems with this approach. As Epstein notes, courts are reluctant to weigh needs and interests that do not seem to comport with an objective malpractice standard. In addition, judges and legal scholars worry that opening up confidential negotiations to scrutiny will discourage settlement. Further, partisan perceptions and memories will likely cloud what actually happened in the negotiation.

3. To better protect a client's interests and prevent potential malpractice claims, Epstein suggests that attorneys consider the following four factors in settling a client's case:

> * * * The *Prande* court, however, does provide minimum guidelines to which an attorney should adhere in advising a client regarding settlement. *Prande* provides that the lawyer should hold an appreciation of 1) the relevant facts; 2) the present and future potential strengths and weaknesses of his case; 3) the likely costs, both objectively (monetarily) and subjectively (psychological disruption of business and family life) associated with proceeding further in the litigation; and 4) the likely outcome if the case were to proceed further.

Epstein, Post–Settlement Malpractice: Undoing the Done Deal, 46 Cath. U.L.Rev. 453, 471 (1997).

In addition to being aware of the *Prande* factors, an attorney can have a client sign a "release and settlement agreement." Epstein suggests the following model release, which incorporates the *Prande* factors into a comprehensive statement of the case:

Pre–Settlement Statement of Client's Case

Before you, the client, decide to enter into a settlement agreement, you should understand your rights concerning this settlement. The purpose of this statement is to provide you with information concerning your case so that you may make an informed decision to settle your case. This statement is not part of the settlement agreement.

A. Status of Your Case.

1. The relevant facts of your case are _____.

2. The following discovery has been conducted _____.

3. The strengths of your case are _____.

4. The weaknesses of your case are _____.

5. The fees and costs of your case to date _____ until trial _____ through trial _____.

6. The likely verdict of your case at trial is _____.

7. This figure has been based on _____.

8. You have offered/been offered _____ to settle your case.

9. This settlement amount is/is not in the range of settlement figures for cases of your type. This range of settlement figures is based on

_____.

B. Your Rights Concerning Settlement.

You, the client, have the sole decision whether to accept or reject this settlement. While your attorney may offer you advice as to whether to accept or settle your case, you are not obligated or required to follow your attorney's advice.

DO NOT SIGN THIS AGREEMENT if you do not understand any of the information provided to you in this statement.

Your attorney is required to answer any questions you may have concerning the settlement of your case. If you have any questions which your attorney cannot answer to your satisfaction, you have the right to seek the advice from another attorney of your choice or you may contact the bar association at _____. Signing this document does not waive your right to subsequently file a malpractice action against your attorney unless prohibited by state law. However, your attorney may use this document as a defense in a malpractice action if permitted by law.

Date: _____   Signature of Client _____

Date: _____   Signature of Attorney _____

Epstein, Post–Settlement Malpractice: Undoing the Done Deal, 46 Cath. U.L.Rev. 453, 472–474 (1997).

An attorney can use a signed post-settlement release in a subsequent malpractice action. The document sheds light on aspects of settlement that courts routinely ignore in their attempt to consider only "objective" factors in malpractice actions. Is this a reasonable precaution for attorneys to take? Should it be necessary? What implications does it have for the attorney-client relationship? How might it impact the ways attorneys negotiate on behalf of their clients?

4. A number of commentators have noted the difficulty of proving legal malpractice in negotiated settlements. For instance, Rex Perschbacher observes, "Because it is grounded in tort, a malpractice action requires proof of a duty to the plaintiff, a breach of that duty, causation, and damages. Proving this prima facie case is often burdensome for legal malpractice plaintiffs." Perschbacher, Regulating Lawyers' Negotiations, 27 Ariz.L.Rev. 75, 80–81 (1985).

In *Nicolet Instrument Corp. v. Lindquist & Vennum*, 34 F.3d 453, 455 (7th Cir.1994), Chief Judge Posner said that causation is the biggest obstacle to proving legal malpractice in negotiation:

Proof of causation is often difficult in legal malpractice cases involving representation in litigation—the vast majority of such cases—because it is so difficult, yet vital, to estimate what difference a lawyer's negligence made in the actual outcome of a trial or other adversary proceeding. (citation omitted). How many criminal defendants, required as they are to prove that their lawyer's ineffective assistance prejudiced them, succeed in overturning their convictions on this ground? Proof of causation is even more difficult in a negotiating situation, because while there is (at least we judges like to think there is) a correct outcome to most lawsuits, there is no "correct" outcome to a negotiation. Not only does much depend on the relative bargaining skills of the negotiators, on the likely consequences to each party if the negotiations fall through, and on luck, so that the element of the intangible and the unpredictable looms large; but there is no single "right" outcome in a bargaining situation even in principle. Every point within the range bounded by the lowest offer that one party will accept and the highest offer that the other party will make is a possible transaction or settlement point, and none of these points is "correct" or "incorrect."

5. While judgments of legal malpractice in settlement negotiations are rare, they are not unheard of. For example, in *Grayson v. Wofsey, Rosen, Kweskin and Kuriansky*, 231 Conn. 168, 646 A.2d 195 (1994), the Connecticut Supreme Court found a divorce attorney liable for legal malpractice, rejecting Pennsylvania's stringent malpractice standard established in *Muhammad v. Strassburger, McKenna, Messer, Shilobod & Gutnick*, 526 Pa. 541, 587 A.2d 1346 (1991). On the advice of her attorney, Elyn Grayson had agreed to settle a pending divorce suit against her husband. Later she filed a motion to open up the settlement agreement because an affidavit misrepresented the value of her former spouse's assets. The Connecticut Supreme Court affirmed a lower court judgment refusing to open up the settlement agreement.

Ms. Grayson also brought suit against her attorney for legal malpractice for negligently failing to conduct an adequate investigation of her husband's finances and improperly preparing for trial. This time, the Connecticut Supreme Court affirmed a $1.5 million jury verdict. Why would the court allow Ms. Grayson to sue her attorneys but not to open up the settlement agreement? Is the standard for proving legal malpractice easier than the standard for opening up a settlement agreement? The policy of encouraging settlement is undermined both by opening up settlement agreements and by low thresholds for legal malpractice. The *Grayson* court suggests that other policies such as attorney diligence outweigh the policy of encouraging settlement.

In rejecting the *Muhammad* rule, the court said:

> The defendants urge us to adopt a common law rule whereby an attorney may not be held liable for negligently advising a client to enter into a settlement agreement. They argue that, as a matter of public policy, an attorney should not be held accountable for improperly advising a client to settle a case unless that advice is the product of fraudulent or egregious misconduct by the attorney. The defendants contend that the adoption of such a rule is necessary in order to promote settlements, to protect the integrity of stipulated judgments, and to avoid the inevitable flood of litigation that they claim will otherwise result. They claim that such a rule is particularly appropriate if, as here, the court has reviewed and approved the settlement agreement.

> We have long recognized that the pretrial settlement of claims is to be encouraged because, in the vast number of cases, an amicable resolution of the dispute is in the best interests of all concerned. * * *

We reject the invitation of the defendants, however, to adopt a rule that promotes the finality of settlements and judgments at the expense of a client who, in reasonable reliance on the advice of his or her attorney, agrees to a settlement only to discover that the attorney had failed to exercise the degree of skill and learning required of attorneys in the circumstances. * * * Accordingly, like the majority of courts that have addressed this issue, we decline to adopt a rule that insulates attorneys from exposure to malpractice claims arising from their negligence in settled cases if the attorney's conduct has damaged the client.

Furthermore, we do not believe that a different result is required because a judge had approved the settlement of the plaintiff's marital dissolution action. Although in dissolution cases "[t]he presiding judge has the obligation to conduct a searching inquiry to make sure that the settlement agreement is substantively fair and has been knowingly negotiated"; the court's inquiry does not serve as a substitute for the diligent investigation and preparation for which counsel is responsible. * * *

d. STABILITY OF SETTLEMENTS

As we have seen, a client's ability to sue her lawyer for settlement-related malpractice is connected to the courts' approach to post-settlement attempts to reopen a negotiated agreement. Often a client turns to malpractice only as a last resort. First, the client may try to revise the original settlement agreement to improve his or her deal. The courts' reluctance to entertain such claims is directly related to the tendency toward malpractice actions in this arena.

Like any contract, parties are free to modify a settlement agreement by mutual consent. If only one party seeks to change the agreement, however, courts are much more reluctant to acquiesce, because the courts favor and seek to promote the private settlement of disputes and resist undermining the stability of settlements. A party's ability to rescind a settlement agreement depends on whether the settlement is entered into as a private contract or as a consent decree. If parties privately agree to settle, the normal contract rules apply. Grounds for rescission include fraud, misrepresentation, mistake, duress or undue influence, incapacity of the parties, unconscionability, or impossibility. A private settlement ordinarily will not be reopened merely to examine the equities of the agreement, to reinvestigate the facts, or because one of the parties is now dissatisfied.[5]

Conversely, judicially approved settlements are easier to modify or rescind. As Larry Kramer notes, "[I]t is generally easier to obtain modifica-

---

5. Although the grounds for rescinding agreements are limited, in some cases courts have allowed rescission to achieve just results and to serve public policy aims. For example, the Montana Supreme Court allowed an injured worker to rescind a settlement agreement with the state worker's compensation fund on grounds of unilateral mistake of law and mistake of fact because of confusion regarding a subrogation clause with the state fund. *Brown v. Richard A. Murphy, Inc.*, 261 Mont. 275, 862 P.2d 406 (1993).

tion of a consent decree than a contract if circumstances change." For instance, Mnookin and Kornhauser say that in the case of divorce, "A court may at any time during the child's minority reopen and modify the initial decree in light of any subsequent change in circumstances. The parties entirely lack the power to deprive the court of this jurisdiction." However, Mnookin and Kornhauser observe that if no minor children are involved in the divorce, "In some American states a couple may make its agreement binding and final—i.e., not subject to later modification by a court."[6]

Larry Kramer, Consent Decrees and the Rights of Third Parties

87 Mich.L.Rev. 321, 324–31 (1988).

I. THE NATURE OF CONSENT DECREES

What exactly is a consent decree? Opinions have varied over the years, and there is still no consensus. One view is that a consent decree is merely a private contract between the parties. Another view treats a consent decree as a judgment of the court. The dominant modern view is that a consent decree is a hybrid, with elements of both contract and judgment. This view requires the court to decide whether a particular problem implicates the contract or judgment aspect of a consent decree; once the proper category is identified, the rules applicable to that category are applied.

But a consent decree is neither a contract nor a judgment—and it is both. This whole way of thinking about consent decrees is improper, for it leads courts to focus on outer appearance rather than underlying purpose. A consent decree is what it is: an agreement between the parties to end a lawsuit on mutually acceptable terms which the judge agrees to enforce as a judgment. What is critical is why the parties want judicial assistance and why the court agrees (or should agree) to provide it. If contract or judgment rules apply to consent decrees, it is because the nature of the parties' agreement or the reason for judicial assistance is such that the justification for a particular contract or judgment rule also makes sense for consent decrees. But the fact that consent decrees often resemble contracts or judgments does not mean that this will always by the case. There may be instances in which the appropriate rule for a consent decree is different from both contract and judgment rules.

In order to understand consent decrees properly, then, we need a fuller appreciation of the dynamics of the consent decree process: Why do parties want consent decrees? Why should courts agree to enforce them?

One party files a lawsuit against another. Rather than spend time and money and still risk losing at trial, the parties will usually negotiate a

---

6. Mnookin & Kornhauser, Bargaining in the Shadow of the Law: The Case of Di- vorce, 88 Yale L.J. 950, 954–955 (1979).

settlement. Negotiating a settlement is like negotiating any agreement against a background of uncertainty. If the plaintiff's minimum offer is less than the defendant's maximum offer, and if excessive second-guessing does not cause the bargaining process to falter, an agreement will be reached and the case will be voluntarily dismissed.

In this, the typical settlement, there is no further judicial involvement. The agreement by which the plaintiff agrees to dismiss his lawsuit is an ordinary contract, and it can be enforced, modified or set aside as such.

Sometimes, however, the parties ask the court to enter their settlement as a decree. This has some rather important consequences. If either party fails to live up to the agreement, the other party can obtain contempt sanctions without having to file an independent lawsuit on the contract. This allows the party seeking enforcement to avoid some of the expense of a separate lawsuit. Perhaps more importantly, it enables the party seeking enforcement to avoid the court's docket queue and obtain sanctions more quickly than if a new lawsuit had to be filed. In addition, if the settlement is entered as a decree, the court may provide additional assistance (like appointing a monitor to oversee implementation) and will interpret the decree to help the parties resolve disputes before they reach the point of formal litigation.

It is easy, in light of these benefits, to see why a plaintiff might prefer a consent decree to a private contract. By speeding up the process and lowering the cost of enforcement, consent decrees enhance the plaintiff's ability to hold the defendant to his bargain. Indeed, the benefits of a consent decree are often indispensable to plaintiffs in public law or institutional reform litigation. The plaintiffs in these cases are frequently short on resources; they are typically represented by pro bono counsel or by counsel financed through government legal aid; often the class is unorganized and each member has only a small stake in the outcome. In addition, settlements providing for the installation of pollution control devices, the implementation of affirmative action, or the construction of new facilities to house prisoners or mental health patients can be extremely complicated. The parties often anticipate taking years to fulfill the agreement. Moreover, as the agreement grows more complex, it becomes increasingly likely that there will be disputes over its interpretation. Consequently, the availability of a consent decree may make a significant difference in the willingness of the plaintiff to settle.

The defendant's reasons for agreeing to a consent decree are somewhat different. Except in rare instances, the plaintiff's side of the bargain is simply to drop the lawsuit, and the defendant does not need a device to facilitate enforcement. Indeed, if anything, such devices are to the defendant's disadvantage. But the reduced expense of resolving disputes in the implementation phase is advantageous to the defendant as well as the plaintiff. Moreover, it is generally easier to obtain modification of a consent decree than a contract if circumstances change. Most importantly, if the plaintiff wants a consent decree badly enough, the defendant can obtain additional bargaining concessions in return.

But why should the court enter a consent decree? The answer, already suggested by the analysis above, is that making consent decrees available facilitates the settlement of difficult cases that might otherwise go to trial, furthering the strongly held policy favoring settlement over litigation. The reasons for this policy are well known. Settlement is more efficient for the parties, giving them more of what they hoped to gain at less cost. More importantly, settlement allows already overburdened judges to devote time to cases that are not settled voluntarily.

* * *

[A] consent decree is interpreted like a contract. According to the Supreme Court, this is because a consent decree is negotiated like a contract. But the terms of an ordinary judgment are often negotiated by the parties after liability has been determined through litigation, and the Court has never suggested that a litigated decree should be interpreted like a contract. Rather, the reason it makes sense to interpret a consent decree like a contract is that a consent decree represents only what the parties have agreed to do, and the court's participation in enforcing the decree is simply a means of encouraging the parties to make such agreements. The policy protecting justified party expectations that underlies contract law is thus fully applicable. With a litigated decree, by contrast, judicial partic-ipation is compelled by one party's invocation of right under substantive law. The court must therefore interpret the decree in light of what the substantive law requires to remedy a proven violation.

But contract law will not always be appropriate for consent decrees, and the court's participation may sometimes require the development of special procedures. For instance, in *Local 93, International Association of Firefighters v. City of Cleveland*, 478 U.S. 501 (1986), the Supreme Court held that a court cannot approve a consent decree unless it (1) determines that the consent decree "springs from and serves to resolve a dispute within the court's subject-matter jurisdiction"; (2) ensures that the consent decree comes "within the general scope of the case made by the pleadings"; and (3) satisfies itself that the consent decree "furthers the objectives of the law upon which the complaint was based." The exact reason for these requirements has puzzled some commentators, but they follow naturally from an understanding of consent decrees as a method of facilitating settlement by making judicial resources available, under certain circum-stances, to help the parties enforce their agreement. The court is not "a recorder of contracts" from whom parties can freely purchase injunctions. The court only agrees to "record" and enforce a particular kind of contract: one that saves judicial resources by settling a lawsuit. The requirements for approval set forth in *Local 93* help insure that only such contracts are entered as consent decrees.

Moreover, the court is concerned with other interests in addition to facilitating settlement, and the pursuit or protection of these interests may impose limits on the consent decree device. Consider, for example, the question of modifying a consent decree over the objection of one of the parties. One might extend the argument for interpreting consent decrees according to principles of contract law to modification. But the Supreme Court held contract law inapplicable to consent decree modification in *United States v. Swift & Co.*, 286 U.S. 106 (1932). The Court explained that a consent decree is a "judicial act," an unsatisfying explanation made even more so by the fact that the Court articulated a test for modifying a consent decree that is stricter than the test for modifying judgments entered after litigation. How, then, does one explain the rules governing consent decree modification?

An argument can be made that entering the parties' agreement as a judgment associates the court with a consent decree in a way that is not true of ordinary contracts. This, in turn, gives the court an institutional stake in the consent decree beyond protecting the parties' expectations, and justifies retaining additional power to modify the decree if, in the words of Justice Cardozo, the court is "satisfied that what it has been doing has been turned through changing circumstances into an instrument of wrong."

The hard question is deciding how broad this power should be. The *Swift* Court apparently thought that a narrow power would suffice. Courts today are often willing to modify consent decrees on a less stringent showing. I do not address this issue here. My point is simply to illustrate that beyond the question of whether a particular rule facilitates settlement lies the additional question of whether further adjustments are necessary because of the court's involvement in the enforcement process.

NOTES AND QUESTIONS

1. Formerly, consent decrees, sometimes referred to as "confession of judgments," were used primarily in antitrust cases. In recent years, the consent decree has been used in a wide range of cases. Consent decrees have been used to achieve broad institutional reforms such as school desegregation, environmental regulation and housing reform. See Note, The Modification of Consent Decrees in Institutional Reform Litigation, 99 Harv.L.Rev. 1020, 1020–21 (1986). In an effort to clear clogged dockets, courts have also increasingly filed consent decrees in lawsuits between private parties. Further, courts are often responsible for approving divorce settlements, a legal proceeding resembling a consent decree. See generally Mnookin and Kornhauser, Bargaining in the Shadow of the Law: The Case of Divorce 88 Yale L.J. 950, 954–55 (1979). Thus, judicially approved settlements are a common feature of the legal system.

2. Whether consent decrees in civil rights and institutional reform cases can bind similarly situated non-parties is an issue of much controversy. This is an important consideration for counsel in deciding whether to negotiate a consent decree, rather than going to trial. In Martin v. Wilks, 490 U.S. 755, 109 S.Ct. 2180, 104 L.Ed.2d 835 (1989), white firefighters were allowed to make a collateral attack on a consent decree entered in a suit brought by seven black firefighters that established goals for hiring blacks. The Court stated: "A judgment or decree among parties to a lawsuit resolves issues as among them, but it does not conclude the rights of strangers to those proceedings." Although there was no evidence that the settlement was collusive, any consent decree raises concerns that parties may sacrifice the interests of others in reaching a compromise settlement. See Laycock, Consent Decrees Without Consent: The Rights of Nonconsenting Third Parties, 1987 U.Chi.L. Forum 103. The Civil Rights Act of 1991, 42 U.S.C.A. § 2000e–2(n)(1), provides that "an employment practice that implements and is within the scope of a litigated or consent judgment or order that resolves a claim of employment discrimination under the Constitution or Federal civil rights laws may not be challenged" by a person who had actual notice of the proposed judgment sufficient to apprise him that it might adversely affect him or who was adequately represented by another person who had previously challenged the judgment.

3. Why should the consent decree be interpreted like a contract generally but like a judicial act when parties request modification? Courts encourage freely negotiated private settlements, yet they are more willing to actively administer agreements on which they put their seal of approval. Contract law encourages market activity through the freedom to contract. Similarly, courts encourage parties to craft their own negotiated settlements. In most cases, parties assume the risks of changing circumstances in private contracts. Thus, parties are normally responsible for evaluating exchanges and risks. A bad bargain or a foreseeable risk, therefore, will normally not allow for contract modification. However, when a court gets involved in the contracting process by accepting a consent decree, it often assumes the responsibility of ensuring that a bargain is at least nominally fair. For instance, a negotiated divorce settlement often must be judged to be fair or at least not unconscionable before a court will approve it. See Mnookin and Kornhauser, Bargaining in the Shadow of the Law: The Case of Divorce 88 Yale L.J. 950, 954 n. 15 (1979). If circumstances change to the detriment of one party, the court will be more likely to provide relief.

4. Andrew Kull argues that the availability of rescission as a remedy in settlement agreements has an important consequence in settlement negotiations. Rescission acts as a powerful deterrent against breach of the settlement agreement at the same time that it promotes opportunistic behavior:

> Let us assume (i) a breach by the defendant giving rise to a right of rescission on the part of the plaintiff, (ii) the absence of any broader relationship that would constrain the parties in their post-breach behavior, and (iii) mutual recognition that the cost of rescission to the defendant would exceed the harm to the plaintiff from the defendant's breach. Such circumstances, which are not particularly rare, make an opportunistic threat of rescission an implicit part of any settlement negotiations. Indeed, the practical consequences of a rescission alternative will predominantly be realized, not through the infrequent judicial decrees granting rescission and restitution, but in terms of enhanced settlement leverage for those plaintiffs for whom rescission is a credible option.

Kull, Restitution as a Remedy for Breach of Contract, 67 S.Cal.L.Rev. 1465, 1512–14 (1994).

e. JUDICIAL SANCTIONS

In addition to the threat of malpractice and the possibility of a settlement agreement unraveling after completion, parties and their attorneys must take into account the threat of judicial sanctions for improper litigation conduct. Judicial sanctions are available in a federal court under 28 U.S.C.A. § 1927, which permits sanctions for "multipl[ying] the proceedings in any case unreasonably and vexatiously." The discovery rules were amended in 1980 to provide for sanctions for failure to cooperate in discovery.[7] In 1983, Federal Rule of Civil Procedure Rule 11 was amended to provide broad new sanctions for a variety of litigation conduct. The risk of these sanctions constitutes a check on excessively adversarial behavior. This rule, amended again in 1993, sets forth the following requirements for representations made to a court:

> *Representations to Court.* By presenting to the court (whether by signing, filing, submitting, or later advocating) a pleading, written motion, or other paper, an attorney or unrepresented party is certifying that to the best of the person's knowledge, information, and belief, formed after an inquiry reasonable under the circumstances,
>
> (1) it is not being presented for any improper purpose, such as to harass or to cause unnecessary delay or needless increase in the cost of litigation;
>
> (2) the claims, defenses, and other legal contentions therein are warranted by existing law or by a nonfrivolous[8] argument for the extension, modification, or reversal of existing law or the establishment of new law;
>
> (3) the allegations and other factual contentions have evidentiary support or, if specifically so identified, are likely to have evidentiary support after a reasonable opportunity for further investigation or discovery; and
>
> (4) the denials of factual contentions are warranted on the evidence or, if specifically so identified, are reasonably based on a lack of information or belief.

Several 1993 changes to Rule 11 softened the Rule's impact. First, the 1993 version of Rule 11 creates a "safe harbor" by requiring that a Rule 11 motion be served separately from other papers and that the served party be given twenty-one days to withdraw the challenged statement or submission. In other words, a lawyer or client can avoid sanctions by withdrawing any questionable representation to the court. Second, the 1993 amendments were intended to incent litigants to file Rule 11 motions quickly after an

---

7. Fed.R.Civ.Proc. 37(b)(2).

8. The 1983 version of Rule 11 required that such arguments be in "good faith," a standard that seemed overly subjective and was thus replaced in 1993 with the word "nonfrivolous."

alleged violation, rather than waiting until after final judgment to raise Rule 11 issues. If a litigant delays in raising Rule 11 issues, they may be found untimely.[9] Third, the 1993 amendments were clearly intended to make Rule 11 a tool to deter improper litigation conduct, not to compensate the alleged victim of that conduct.[10] Fourth, the amended rule permits factual assertions that are "likely to have evidentiary support after a reasonable opportunity for further investigation or discovery" or denials that are "reasonably based on a lack of information or belief." These "reasonable ignorance" provisions permit attorneys to pursue a case (or defend it) despite incomplete factual information about the issue at hand.

In the following case the court applies the 1993 version of Rule 11 to a litigant and his lawyer, ultimately holding that neither should be sanctioned under the Rule. What effects will this holding have on the negotiation behavior—and the lawyer-client relationships—of litigants?

Hadges & Kunstler v. Yonkers Racing Corp.

United States Court of Appeals, Second Circuit, 1995.
48 F.3d 1320.

■ Before FEINBERG, KEARSE AND ALTIMARI, CIRCUIT JUDGES.

■ FEINBERG, CIRCUIT JUDGE:

[The Plaintiff George Hadges had filed various actions against defendant Yonkers Racing Corp. (YRC) for its alleged unfair refusal to permit him to pursue his career as a harness racehorse driver, trainer and owner. In 1989, the New York State Racing and Wagering Board had suspended Hadges's racing license for six months after determining that he had illegally passed wagering information to a member of the betting public at a race. Although the Racing Board then reissued his license, YRC denied him the right to work at the Yonkers racetrack. The district court granted summary judgment for YRC in 1990 (Hadges I). In 1992, Hadges began another suit against YRC in New York state court, but lost on all claims. He then appealed that decision. In 1993 he brought a § 1983 action in federal district court against the Meadowlands racetrack, alleging that the Meadowlands had barred him because of YRC's ban. He settled that suit. With a state court appeal pending regarding the New York state court suit, Hadges then brought a Rule 60(b) action in federal court in New York seeking to vacate Hadges I. He alleged that YRC had perpetrated fraud on the court by claiming that Hadges could continue to work at other tracks despite the YRC ban—which Hadges claimed was false. The district court ruled against Hadges and granted summary judgment for YRC. The district court also imposed sanctions under Rule 11 against Hadges and his lawyer Kunstler.]

---

9. See Ridder v. City of Springfield, 109 F.3d 288, 295 (6th Cir.1997).

10. See Advisory Committee Notes to the 1993 Amendments.

B. Facts underlying Rule 11 sanctions

In support of his claim for relief in the Rule 60(b) action, Hadges submitted a sworn statement that 1993 was his "fifth year ... out of work, with the boycott by Yonkers still in effect." In addition, he stated that "there was a secret agreement among all of the racetracks, that barring a licensee from one, will result in his being barred from all." Plaintiff's memorandum of law, signed by Kunstler, also asserted that Hadges "has not worked for more than four years." Hadges claimed that he had applied to race at other tracks in New York State, but that these tracks refused to act upon the applications, thereby barring him from racing. He also asserted that upon the advice of a former attorney, Joseph A. Faraldo, he had written to the general managers of these tracks to apply for driving privileges in mid–1990 but received no reply. Hadges presented the court with an affidavit of Faraldo stating that Faraldo had so advised Hadges.

In response, YRC produced documents revealing that Hadges had in fact raced at Monticello Raceway five times in 1991 and seven times in 1993. The most recent race took place less than one month before Hadges submitted his affidavit stating that he had been banned from racing by all tracks in New York State for more than four years. YRC also submitted letters of current and former Racing Secretaries from race tracks in Saratoga, Batavia Downs, Fairmount Park, Vernon Downs and Buffalo who asserted that Hadges had not applied (or they had no recollection of his having applied) for racing privileges at their respective tracks in the relevant time period.

In a memorandum of law and notice of motion to dismiss the Rule 60(b) action, YRC requested that the court impose sanctions on Hadges and, if warranted, on his counsel for this misrepresentation and for failing to disclose the state court action to the district court. This method of requesting Rule 11 sanctions was, as set forth below, contrary to the procedural requirements of Rule 11 that took effect on December 1, 1993, five days before Hadges filed his complaint in the Rule 60(b) action and 15 days before YRC requested sanctions.

After YRC requested sanctions, Hadges submitted an affidavit dated December 28, 1993, admitting that he had raced in Monticello in 1991 and 1993, but explaining that he considered the races insignificant because he had earned less than $100 in the two years combined. That affidavit also described a so-called "scratching incident" that Hadges claimed had taken place at Yonkers Raceway on October 31, 1989. He stated that although his state racing license had been restored in 1989, New York State Racing Board judges "scratched" him from that race, in which he was to have ridden the horse "Me Gotta Bret." After this scratching incident, YRC informed him of its independent ban. Hadges argued to the district court that this sequence of events supported his theory that YRC was acting as a state agent in banning him and thus could be held liable in a § 1983 action. Hadges submitted to the court a "scratch sheet," purporting to document his version of the event.

YRC then submitted what the district court later described as "overwhelming proof" that the scratch sheet did not refer to an October 1989 race, but rather to a November 1987 race.

In its decision on the merits of the Rule 60(b) action, the district court found that Hadges had raced at Monticello in 1991 and 1993 but that he had made only a "minimal" amount of money. 845 F. Supp. at 1041. It also found that the legal basis for Hadges's Rule 60(b) action was not "so frivolous as to warrant Rule 11 sanctions." Id. However, the court was "quite concerned" that Hadges and Kunstler had attempted "to indicate that [Hadges] had not raced in four years when, in fact, he had privileges at Monticello in both 1991 and 1993." Id. The court stated that Hadges had "made matters worse by attempting to strengthen his claim of state involvement alleging that he was scratched from driving Me Gotta Bret on October 31, 1989 by the judges of the racing board." Id. The court further found that submission of the undated scratch sheet was a "flagrant misrepresentation . . . suggesting the need for sanctions, certainly against the plaintiff and possibly against his counsel." Id. The judge invited Hadges and Kunstler to submit papers opposing the imposition of sanctions. The court did not refer to the nondisclosure of the state court action as a possible basis for sanctions.

Thereafter, Hadges submitted an affidavit admitting that he had made a misstatement about the scratching incident but expressing his objection to sanctions. He stated that this error was the result of a simple memory loss, and that the scratch sheet involved was bona fide proof of his having been scratched in 1987 rather than in 1989. He went on to describe yet another 1989 incident in which he had been scratched from racing the horse "Dazzling GT" at YRC. Hadges also submitted an affidavit of his then-assistant Erik Schulman, which also described the 1989 Dazzling GT scratching incident. Further, Hadges repeated that he had written to the General Managers (not the Racing Secretaries relied upon by YRC) of the various tracks to request driving privileges but had received no reply. He attached copies of the letters along with copies of postal receipts.

Kunstler also submitted a sworn response, which stated that he "had no idea" that the scratch sheet was from 1987 rather than 1989, and set forth the facts of the Dazzling GT incident. Kunstler maintained that the error regarding the date of the scratch sheet was unintentional but would not have affected the outcome of the case in any event. Regardless of its date, he argued, the scratch sheet was evidence that YRC was acting as an agent of the state Racing Board and could therefore be held liable in a § 1983 action. Thus, he maintained that submission of the document was not sanctionable. Kunstler's affidavit did not describe the efforts he had undertaken to verify his client's factual claims. YRC then submitted further affidavits stating that it had no records concerning the alleged Dazzling GT incident.

Thereafter, in the second ruling on appeal to us, the judge imposed a Rule 11 sanction of $2,000 on Hadges as an appropriate sanction for his misrepresentations. The judge also censured Kunstler under Rule 11 for failing to make adequate inquiry as to the truth of Hadges's affidavits and for failing to inform the court of the pending state court litigation. In the course of his opinion, the judge stated:

> Mr. Kunstler is apparently one of those attorneys who believes that his sole obligation is to his client and that he has no obligations to the court or to the processes of justice. Unfortunately, he is not alone in this approach to the practice of law, which may be one reason why the legal profession is held in such low esteem by the public at this time.

Kunstler responded in a letter to the court, in which he argued that the court erred in sanctioning his client $2,000 and in censuring him. In particular, he objected to the court's characterization of him as an attorney "who believes that his sole obligation is to his client," and he objected to the court's charge that his approach to law practice was in part responsible for the low public esteem for the legal profession. Kunstler went on to state his opinion that the court's comment was "generated by an animus toward activist practitioners who, like myself, have, over the years, vigorously represented clients wholly disfavored by the establishment."

* * *

This appeal from the judgment for YRC in the Rule 60(b) action and from the two April 1994 rulings on sanctions followed.

II.   Discussion

* * *

B.   Rule 11 sanctions

As we have already noted, not only did the district court rule against Hadges regarding his claims of fraud on the court in Hadges I, but it went on to impose Rule 11 sanctions on both Hadges and Kunstler for their own misrepresentations and omissions. This determination was based on two principal grounds: (1) misstatement of the date of the alleged "scratching" incident and (2) misstatement regarding Hadges's lack of work in the years since the YRC ban. In addition, the court based Kunstler's censure on his failure to inform the court of the state court action. The court also found that Hadges's sanction was justified in part by the disqualification motion, referred to in note 2 above, which the court characterized as "bizarre." Hadges and Kunstler argue that the district court abused its discretion in imposing the Rule 11 sanctions.

As noted above, an amended version of Fed.R.Civ.P. 11 came into effect on December 1, 1993, five days before Hadges filed his complaint in the Rule 60(b) action in the district court.

* * *

1.   Hadges's sanction

Hadges argues that the district court abused its discretion in imposing sanctions on him. YRC argues that the sanctions were justified. We believe that Hadges is correct.

In imposing sanctions, the district court apparently did not take into account YRC's failure to comply with the revised procedural requirements of Rule 11. In this case, YRC did not submit the sanction request separately from all other requests, and there is no evidence in the record indicating that YRC served Hadges with the request for sanctions 21 days before presenting it to the court. Thus, YRC denied Hadges the "safe-harbor" period that the current version of the Rule specifically mandates. See advisory committee note to 1993 amendment * * *

If Hadges had received the benefit of the safe-harbor period, the record indicates that he would have "withdrawn or appropriately corrected" his misstatements, thus avoiding sanctions altogether. Hadges did in fact correct one of his misstatements by admitting in an affidavit, sworn to on December 28, 1993, just 12 days after YRC asked for sanctions, that he had raced at Monticello in 1991 and 1993. Thus, this misstatement is not sanctionable.

Hadges also explained and corrected his misstatement about the 1989 date of the first scratching incident and described another scratching incident in 1989 involving another horse (Dazzling GT). This correction was supported by his own affidavit sworn to on March 17, 1994, and the affidavit of Erik Schulman, sworn to on March 16, 1994. Both were filed with the district court on March 21, 1994, just one week after the court issued its order stating that it was considering imposition of sanctions. Apparently, YRC had not previously requested sanctions on the basis of the scratching incident. Although YRC subsequently questioned whether the Dazzling GT incident described by Hadges and Schulman had taken place, the district court did not rely on this as a basis for imposing sanctions. We note that Kunstler also filed an affidavit making similar retractions.

In addition to sanctioning Hadges for his factual misrepresentations, the district court ruled that sanctions were justified in part by the disqualification motion filed on Hadges's behalf. See note 2 above. In relying on the latter ground, the court imposed monetary sanctions on a represented party for making a legal contention that the court believed was not warranted by existing law or by a nonfrivolous argument for a change in existing law. Revised Rule 11 specifically prohibits imposition of monetary sanctions on the party on this basis. Fed.R.Civ.P. 11(b)(2) & 11(c)(2)(A).

Rule 11 also provides that a court may impose sanctions on its own initiative. Fed.R.Civ.P. 11(c)(1)(B). If a court wishes to exercise its discretion to impose sanctions sua sponte, it must "enter an order describing the specific conduct that appears to violate subdivision (b) and directing an attorney, law firm, or party to show cause why it has not violated subdivision (b) with respect thereto." Id. In this case, the court indicated that it was imposing sanctions in response to YRC's request and did not state that it was imposing sanctions on Hadges sua sponte. We doubt that sua sponte sanctions would have been justified here. The advisory committee note on the 1993 amendment specifically states that such sanctions "will ordinarily be [imposed] only in situations that are akin to a contempt of court." Hadges's conduct did not rise to that level.

Thus, under all the circumstances, particularly the failure to afford Hadges the 21–day safe-harbor period provided by revised Rule 11, we believe that the sanction of Hadges should be reversed.

2. Kunstler's censure

Like Hadges, Kunstler did not receive the benefit of the safe-harbor period. The district court imposed sanctions on Kunstler for failing to adequately investigate the truth of Hadges's representations prior to submitting them to the court and for failing to disclose that Hadges had brought an action against YRC in New York state court. Kunstler argues that the court's censure of him was an abuse of discretion because the court was motivated by a personal or political animus against him and because his conduct was not sufficiently egregious to justify imposition of sanctions.

In our decisions concerning the former version of Rule 11 we have had occasion to address the reasonableness of an attorney's reliance on information provided by a client. In Kamen v. American Tel. & Tel. Co., 791 F.2d 1006 (2d Cir.1986), the plaintiff brought suit against her employer and supervisors under the Rehabilitation Act of 1973 and state law. Employers are not liable under the Rehabilitation Act unless they receive "federal financial assistance." 29 U.S.C. § 794. The employer sent letters to the plaintiff's attorney asserting that it did not receive federal financial assistance, but her attorney persisted in prosecuting the Rehabilitation Act suit. The district court agreed with the employer and dismissed the claims. Although plaintiff's attorney had submitted an affirmation stating that his client had advised him that the employer received federal grants, the district court imposed sanctions. We found that the district court abused its discretion because the attorney's reliance on his client's statements was reasonable. Kamen, 791 F.2d at 1007–12.

A few years later, we relied on Kamen in holding that "an attorney is entitled to rely on his or her client's statements as to factual claims when those statements are objectively reasonable." Calloway v. Marvel Entertainment Group, 854 F.2d 1452, 1470 (2d Cir.1988), rev'd in part on other grounds sub nom. Pavelic & LeFlore v. Marvel Entertainment Group, 493 U.S. 120, 107 L. Ed. 2d 438, 110 S. Ct. 456 (1989). This interpretation is in keeping with the advisory committee notes on former Rule 11, which indicates that the reasonableness of an inquiry depends upon the surrounding circumstances, including

> such factors as how much time for investigation was available to the signer; whether he had to rely on a client for information as to the facts underlying the pleading ...; or whether he depended on forwarding counsel or another member of the bar.

Advisory committee note on 1983 amendment to Fed.R.Civ.P. 11.

In Calloway, at least one of the plaintiff's claims "was never supported by any evidence at any stage of the proceeding," and we affirmed the district court's imposition of sanctions. Calloway, 854 F.2d at 1470 & 1473.

However, we went on to set forth a procedure for district courts to follow in analyzing whether an attorney has conducted a reasonable inquiry into the facts underlying a party's position.

> In considering sanctions regarding a factual claim, the initial focus of the district court should be on whether an objectively reasonable evidentiary basis for the claim was demonstrated in pretrial proceedings or at trial. Where such a basis was shown, no inquiry into the adequacy of the attorney's pre-filing investigation is necessary.

Id. at 1470.

The new version of Rule 11 makes it even clearer that an attorney is entitled to rely on the objectively reasonable representations of the client. No longer are attorneys required to certify that their representations are "well grounded in fact." Fed.R.Civ.P. 11 (1983) amended 1993. The current version of the Rule requires only that an attorney conduct "an inquiry reasonable under the circumstances" into whether "factual contentions have evidentiary support." Fed.R.Civ.P. 11(b) & (b)(3). Thus, the new version of Rule 11 is in keeping with the emphasis in Calloway on looking to the record before imposing sanctions.

In its first sanction decision in April 1994, the district court here stated:

> With respect to plaintiff's counsel, William M. Kunstler, the situation is not quite as clear. There is nothing to indicate that, on the serious factual misrepresentations made in plaintiff's papers, Mr. Kunstler had independent knowledge of their falsity. However, it is equally clear that he made no attempt to verify the truth of the plaintiff's representations prior to submitting them to the court.

Apparently, the district court did not focus, as Rule 11 now requires, on whether the pretrial proceedings provided "evidentiary support" for the factual misrepresentations with which the court was concerned.

It is clear that the record before the district court contained evidentiary support for Kunstler's incorrect statements. As to the scratching incident, the record included a sworn statement by Hadges describing an October 1989 incident in which he claimed to have been scratched from driving the horse "Me Gotta Bret." A scratch sheet, which did not reveal the year in which it was made out, was also part of the record. Kunstler later submitted an affidavit admitting the error and stating that he had no idea that the 1989 date was wrong. He further maintained that regardless of its date, the scratch sheet was relevant to show collaboration between the Racing Board and YRC in 1987, which would subject the latter to § 1983 liability. Moreover, it appears to be undisputed that most of the evidence YRC produced to persuade the court that the event had taken place in 1987 was within its possession, not Hadges's. See Kamen, 791 F.2d at 1012 (noting reasonableness of relying on client representations where "the relevant information [is] largely in the control of the defendants").

We also believe that the record contained evidentiary support for the claim that Hadges had not worked for four years. At the time the district court granted YRC summary judgment in Hadges's 60(b) action, it had before it Hadges's affidavit asserting that he had written to racetrack General Managers asking for driving privileges and had not received any replies. The record also contained attorney Faraldo's affidavit asserting that Hadges had followed his advice in writing these letters. Moreover, Kunstler represented Hadges in the Meadowlands suit in which Meadowlands admitted banning Hadges based upon the YRC ban. We believe that in light of his familiarity with the Meadowlands litigation and the sworn statements of his client and another attorney, Kunstler had sufficient evidence to support a belief that Hadges had not participated in harness horseracing in New York since the YRC ban. * * *

The district court also believed that censure of Kunstler was justified because "he had to be aware of the recent state court litigation, still on appeal, but made no mention of it in his initial papers." Kunstler concedes that he was aware of this litigation but maintains that he did not believe that it was necessary to bring the proceedings to the court's attention because the New York Supreme Court had not ruled on the merits of the state law blackballing claim. As noted above, we agree with the view that the state court opinion was not a decision on the merits of that issue. Even if it were, there would be no tactical advantage in not mentioning the state court ruling to the district court since YRC was a party to both actions (indeed, it was represented by the same law firm and the same attorney in both actions) and could be expected to inform the district court of the state court action if it were helpful.

Moreover, the portion of the court's opinion in the Rule 60(b) action that listed the possible bases for imposition of sanctions omitted any reference to Kunstler's nondisclosure of the state court action. Rule 11 specifically requires that those facing sanctions receive adequate notice and the opportunity to respond. See Fed.R.Civ.P. 11(c)(1)(A) & (B). Although YRC had requested sanctions on this ground, as discussed above, that request was procedurally improper. Thus, although Kunstler would have been wiser to alert the court to the state court proceedings, the nondisclosure was not a proper ground for sanctioning him.

YRC maintains that sanctions were justified because the motions to reargue and to disqualify the district court judge were frivolous. As noted above, the court referred to the disqualification motion as a reason for sanctioning Hadges. However, the court did not rely upon it as a ground for the censure of Kunstler, and we decline to do so here.

Finally, the remarks of the district court, which we have quoted in substantial part above, contribute to our conclusion that the sanction of Kunstler was unjustified. These remarks have the appearance of a personal attack against Kunstler, and perhaps more broadly, against activist attorneys who represent unpopular clients or causes. We find the court's criticism of Kunstler's law partner, Ronald L. Kuby, for his activities in another case, especially unwarranted. For all these reasons, we reverse the imposition of the sanction of censure on Kunstler.

III. Conclusion

We have considered all of the parties' remaining arguments and find that they are without merit.

We affirm the ruling of the district court denying Rule 60(b) relief. We reverse the Rule 11 sanction of Hadges and the censure of Kunstler.

NOTES AND QUESTIONS

1. How should the possibility of sanctions affect negotiations between parties? Should a party who believes his opponent's case is based on a frivolous claim or defense raise the possibility of sanctions as a means of getting a more favorable settlement? Would a party's willingness to talk settlement indicate that the opponent's case really isn't frivolous? Would an actual offer of settlement so indicate?

2. In applying the 1993 version of Rule 11, the *Hadges* court ultimately rejects sanctions against both the plaintiff and his lawyer on procedural grounds. In other words, both were saved by the safe harbor provision created in 1993 and by the diminished requirements regarding investigation of factual assertions. Is this justified? Given the extensive (and perhaps excessive) litigation waged by Mr. Hadges and the numerous seemingly unsupported assertions he made to the court, should the court have been able to use Rule 11 in this instance? Should the court have sanctioned him using 28 U.S.C.A. § 1927, which permits sanctions for "multipl[ying] the proceedings in any case unreasonably and vexatiously"?

What effects will the *Hadges* opinion have on lawyer-client relationships? What assumptions does the court make about how lawyers and clients should prepare for litigation or negotiation?

3. Rule 11 has been interpreted as imposing an objective standard for frivolousness. Does that mean that any party who loses a suit is a likely candidate for imposition of sanctions? Does this discourage parties from seeking redress when the present law seems to be against them or where the potential witnesses are biased in favor of their opponent?

4. Is there a way to factor in a value for the possibility of Rule 11 sanctions in determining the settlement value of a case? What considerations would go into determining the size of that discount? How should a lawyer factor the possibility of sanctions into a decision tree?

5. The federal rules were also amended in 1983 to encourage use of sanctions for violation of the discovery rules. One of the reasons was a feeling that lawyers would not seek, and judges would not award, sanctions. A federal district judge commented: "A lawyer who wants the option to abuse discovery when it is to his client's advantage will hesitate to seek sanctions when his client is the victim of such practices—especially if the sanctions are imposed on the attorney instead of, or in addition to, the client. As a result, a kind of gentlemen's agreement is reached, with the tacit approval of the bench, which is extremely convenient for the attorneys who avoid the just imposition of sanctions and extremely unfair to the litigants who pay more and wait longer for the vindication of their rights than they should." Renfrew, Discovery Sanctions: A Judicial Perspective, 67 Cal.L.Rev. 264, 272 (1979). Today, however, requests for such sanctions are commonplace. Have the beefed-up sanctions rules gone too far the other way, encouraging further disputes involving great personal acrimony over collateral matters like discovery?

f.   FEE AND COST–SHIFTING AND OFFERS OF JUDGMENT

Parties must also consider the affects of an award of legal fees or other costs when deciding whether to press forward with litigation or seek settlement. The following excerpt explains the traditional "American Rule" regarding such awards, the ways in which offer of judgment rules work, and the incentives they create for bargaining parties.

Edward F. Sherman, From Loser Pays to Modified Offer-of-Judgment Rules: Reconciling Incentives to Settle With Access to Justice

76 Tex.L.Rev. 1863, 1863–77 (1998).

The "American rule" that parties will bear the cost of their own attorneys' fees in litigation, whether or not they win or lose, has a long pedigree going back to the earliest days of our republic. It stands in sharp contrast to the "English rule," long followed in Great Britain and most European nations, that the loser must pay the successful party's attorneys' fees. Historical explanations for the American departure from the English rule, such as the spirit of individualism in frontier societies, the conception of lawsuits as sporting contests, and hostility toward lawyers, are not very persuasive today. "Even if distrust of lawyers does survive," Professor John Dawson observed, "it provides no reason for denying indemnity to their clients." Indeed, the American rule cuts against a basic assumption of American remedies law—that a party with a valid claim should be made whole—because requiring a successful claimant to pay his own attorneys' fees considerably diminishes his remedy.

I.   "Access to the Courts" Justification for the American Rule

Perhaps the strongest historical justification for the American rule is centered in the American faith in liberal access to the courts for righting wrongs. If a wronged party is deterred from filing and prosecuting a suit by the risk that he will have to pay the opposing party's attorneys' fees if the suit is unsuccessful, there is a concern that many wrongs could go unremedied in our society. That rationale is essentially pro-litigation, indeed pro-plaintiff, in the sense that it reflects a view that access to the courts by claimants should not be discouraged by the threat of substantial, potential penalties for losing. This view also reflects a certain wealth consciousness, particularly in this century when defendants in lawsuits have increasingly been corporations, business entities, institutions, and governmental bodies that are generally more able to bear the risk of penalties for losing than are plaintiffs. Thus, underlying the American rule is a concern that a well-heeled defendant is less likely to be deterred from defending a weak suit by the threat of having to pay its opponent's attorneys' fees than a plaintiff from prosecuting a possibly meritorious suit. Since plaintiffs are generally more risk averse than defendants, a "loser pays" rule impacts disproportionately on plaintiffs' access to the courts.

The pro-plaintiff nature of the American rule (or perhaps more properly pro-claimant, since a loser who is not required to pay the winner's attorneys' fees may be a counterclaimant or cross-claimant rather than a plaintiff) is particularly apparent in the way the rule has been applied in the twentieth century.

First, various common-law doctrines have accorded exceptions to the American rule, permitting recovery of attorneys' fees by a claimant (but not a defending party) against a losing party under certain circumstances—for example, under the theories of "common fund" and "private attorney general." The breach of the American rule in circumstances that only benefit plaintiffs gives added emphasis to the "access to the courts" rationale for the rule. One common-law doctrine that is an exception to the American rule does apply equally to claimants and their opponents—the "bad faith" doctrine that allows recovery of attorneys' fees when an opponent has acted "in bad faith, vexatiously, wantonly, or for oppressive reasons." The rationale is punitive, and fees may be awarded for bad faith either in filing and prosecuting a case or in defending it. This doctrine provides one of the few vehicles for shifting attorneys' fees to a victorious defendant, but "bad faith" is a more demanding standard than the "prevailing party" standard that usually governs fee shifting of plaintiffs' attorneys' fees.

Second, a large number of statutes have been passed since the 1930s to allow recovery of attorneys' fees by a prevailing party despite the American rule. Most of these statutes apply only to prevailing plaintiffs. The justification for such fee shifting has been based on providing an incentive for parties to vindicate their rights under the particular statute (for example, the Civil Rights Act) and to make them whole by not diminishing their damage award through a requirement that they pay their own attorneys. Thus the "access to the courts" concern underlies the departure from the American rule in most attorney's fee shifting statutes, serving as an exception that actually reinforces the pro-plaintiff rationale of the American rule.

II.   Attack on the American Rule Gives Way to Modified Offer of Judgment
       Proposals

Although the American rule remains a bedrock of American jurisprudence, it has increasingly come under attack in recent years. In the early 1980s, Florida passed a "loser pays" rule that shifted legal fees to the losing party in medical malpractice suits as part of "malpractice reforms" sought by doctors and insurance companies. "The rule was not at all what the doctors expected," however, and they "quickly came to the support of its repeal when many fee awards proved uncollectable—except for those against losing doctors." The "tort reform" and "competitiveness" movements of the 1980s and 1990s, particularly supported by business interests, mounted a new attack on the American rule, calling for state legislatures and Congress to replace it with the English "loser pays" rule. Little headway was made, however, until the Republican "Contract with America" burst upon the political scene with the GOP sweep of the congressional elections in 1994.

One of the major planks of the Contract with America was the "loser pays" rule. Early in its first hundred days, the 104th Congress introduced the Common Sense Legal Reforms Act of 1995 which required the application of the "loser pays" rule in actions arising under state law but brought in federal courts under diversity jurisdiction. The proposed rule was modified by provisions that attorneys' fees recovered by the winning party could not exceed those of the losing party, and that the court could limit awards under special circumstances. Along the way, however, resistance to the "loser pays" rule arose, and its advocates shifted to an offer of judgment procedure as an acceptable substitute. A bill was introduced to replace the "loser pays" provision in the Common Sense Legal Reforms Act with a provision that allowed any party to make an offer of judgment to an opposing party. If this offer of judgment were refused, and the ultimate judgment were not more favorable than the original offer, the offeree would have to pay the offeror's costs, including its attorneys' fees up to an amount equal to the offeree's attorneys' fees.

The House of Representatives passed this bill on March 7, 1995, prompting the American Bar Association to convene a task force to study and report back quickly on the desirability of this expanded offer of judgment practice. The task force report presented an alternative proposal * * * that would expand the offer of judgment to allow plaintiffs to invoke it and to allow shifting of attorneys' fees. However, it also included safeguards to ensure that access to the courts and the parties' right to trial by jury would not be chilled. That report was narrowly adopted by the ABA House of Delegates in the spring of 1995, after it debated whether the alternative proposal would adequately guarantee access to the courts. Meanwhile the bill that had been passed by the House stalled in the Senate, and the congressional session ended without action being taken. A similar bill was introduced in 1997 in the 105th Congress, the ABA again opposed it, and it did not become law.

This legislative history highlights the nexus between "loser pays" and expanded offer of judgment rules. Both accomplish the shifting of attorneys' fees—under the "loser pays" rule automatically to the winner, while under the offer of judgment rule to an offeree who refused his opponent's offer to settle and did not do better at trial. Both deter parties' willingness to prosecute a suit by threatening to shift the successful party's attorneys' fees. The offer of judgment rule, however, requires an additional step—a party must first make an offer of judgment to settle for a certain sum as a prerequisite to being allowed to invoke the fee shifting provisions. Offer of judgment thus has an added settlement potential because, in order to invoke it, a party must be prepared to settle if his offer is accepted. Because fee shifting will only occur if the offeree does not do better in the final judgment than in the offer, the offeror has an incentive to make an offer that will be better than what he expects the judgment might be. The offer of judgment rule is thus less directly punitive than the "loser pays" rule, and the manner in which it creates incentives is more complex. It is also more susceptible to fine-tuning, although the drafting job to create the desired incentive structure and to factor for competing policies is enormously complicated.

III. Incentives Under Fee Shifting Structures

The incentives created by fee shifting have been the subject of considerable analysis but limited empirical research. The most traditional form of fee shifting is the shifting of court costs to the losing party upon the completion of a trial or appeal. "Loser pays" and offer of judgment rules are an extenuation of that concept. But while the justification for fee shifting of court costs is based on fairness and making the winning party whole, fee shifting of attorneys' fees is viewed today as a significant means of inducing settlement. Incentives for settlement have thus become the principal focus for analysis of these rules.

A. "Loser Pays" Rule

There has been much debate in the law and economics literature over the effect of fee shifting rules on settlement. Richard A. Posner and Steven Shavell have concluded that fee shifting of the English "loser pays" type would decrease the likelihood of settlement. They viewed parties as pursuing litigation because they are overly optimistic about their chances at trial, which causes them to discount the amount of attorneys' fees they will have to pay, and thus makes settlement less attractive. This position has been challenged by John J. Donohue III, who argued that Posner and Shavell failed to consider the Coase theorem and instead presented a model showing that the settlement rate would be identical under the American and British rules. John C. Hause also argued that fee shifting rules raise the stakes, creating an incentive to spend more at trial and, by increasing the projected costs, a heightened expectation of benefits from settlement. Keith N. Hylton differentiated between a "filing effect" and a "settlement effect." He concluded that "defendants who can credibly commit to large litigation expenses are less likely to be sued under the British than under the American rule," while "the incentive to litigate rather than to settle a dispute is greater under the British than under the American rule." Perhaps the most that can be said with confidence is that the variables and details affecting incentives are sufficiently complex that, as Donohue remarked, "until a better empirical foundation has been established, the existing theoretical arsenal is still too weak to resolve many of the ultimate questions of interest."

* * *

There is, however, reason to believe that the "loser pays" rule can have a disproportionate impact depending on the wealth of a litigant. "Loser pays" has the effect of a blunderbuss rather than a rifle because it shifts all of the winning party's attorneys' fees to the loser no matter their relationship to the amount of damages in issue. The prospect of having to pay the winner's attorneys' fees, plus one's own lawyer, presents a formidable risk to any litigant. It falls equally on plaintiffs and defendants. An individual or small business with limited means, whether a plaintiff or defendant, is likely to be more severely affected by the risk than a well-heeled opponent, especially one who is a repeat player (such as an insurance company) capable of spreading risk over a large number of cases. The rule could encourage a well-heeled party to raise the stakes by hiring more expensive counsel in anticipation of shifting its cost to its opponent (although this assumes that increased attorneys' fees will necessarily improve chances of winning, and it is not at all clear that a rational prosperous litigant would always make that assumption). Much more likely is that a poorly financed litigant would accept an unfavorable settlement because of the relative degree of risk imposed by potential fee shifting. "The rule would deter some litigation," Judge Schwarzer concludes, "but it would do so more on the basis of a litigant's risk averseness than the merits of the litigant's case." Based on this disparate impact, the Economist in 1995 called for the abolition of the English rule on the grounds that it makes no economic sense and denies judicial access to most citizens.

* * *

B. Offer of Judgment

The offer of judgment device was included in Rule 68 when the Federal Rules of Civil Procedure were adopted in 1938. It was new to federal procedure, being borrowed from the practice of a few states. Today twenty-nine states and the District of Columbia have rules similar in language and effect to Rule 68.

Rule 68 provides that any party defending a claim may make a settlement offer to the plaintiff. If the plaintiff rejects the offer and does not receive a more favorable judgment at trial, he must pay the defendant's court costs and fees incurred after the date of the offer. The final judgment must result from an actual trial and not by way of settlement or voluntary dismissal.

An offer of judgment must meet a few simple criteria. It must be served on the adverse party more than ten days before the trial begins and must be for a definite sum, including "costs then accrued." The requirement for a definite sum aims at fostering settlement; an "ambiguous" offer does not give the plaintiff sufficient information to "make reasonable decisions regarding the conduct of litigation." Ambiguous offers, however, are open to clarification, including oral clarification, and clarifications are generally not treated as attempted revocations.

The Rule 68 offer of judgment procedure has been subjected to a great deal of analysis relating to its legal administrative feasibility and economic justification. It is a paradigm for lawyers and academics to try their hand at modeling, structuring, and drafting in hopes of achieving myriad goals. Let us consider some of the features of its incentive structure.

1. Limitations Reducing Its Usefulness.—Two factors have particularly limited parties' resort to Rule 68: only defendants may use it, and only court costs, and not attorneys' fees, are shifted. The Judicial Conference of the United States proposed in 1983 and 1984 to amend the rule because it "has rarely been invoked and has been considered largely ineffective as a means of achieving its goals." The amendments would have made the Rule available to both parties, allowed an offer to be made up to thirty days before trial, and required that the offer remain open for thirty days. A party who refused an offer and did not obtain a more favorable judgment would have to pay the costs and expenses (including reasonable attorneys' fees) incurred by the offeror after making the offer. The rigor of the fee shifting would be lessened by allowing a reduction to the extent that the fees shifted were found by the court to be excessive or unjustified, and by prohibiting fee shifting if the offer was found to have been made in bad faith. These proposals were never adopted by the Rules Advisory Committee.

Although proposals for changes in Rule 68 have primarily focused on expanding it to apply to offers by plaintiffs and recovery of attorneys' fees, a number of proposals have also tinkered with the basic terms of what triggers cost shifting. One of the more interesting proposals came from the local rule experimentation fostered by the Civil Justice Reform Act of 1990 (CJRA). For example, the CJRA-generated plan adopted in 1993 by the United States District Court for the Eastern District of Texas provides that "a party may make a written offer of judgment" and "if the offer of judgment is not accepted and the final judgment in the case is of more benefit to the party who made the offer by 10%, then the party who rejected the offer must pay the litigation costs incurred after the offer was rejected." "Litigation costs" is defined to include "those costs which are directly related to preparing the case for trial and actual trial expenses, including but not limited to reasonable attorneys' fees, deposition costs and fees for expert witnesses." If the plaintiff recovers either more than the offer or nothing at trial, or if the defendant's offer is not realistic or in good faith, the cost shifting sanctions do not apply. Chief Judge Robert M. Parker reported that in the rule's first two years, hundreds of parties made offers of judgment, generally resulting in settlement at a subsequently negotiated figure. No sanctions had to be granted under the rule for failure of the offeree to have obtained a judgment less than 10% better than the offer. There is a question, however, as to whether such a local federal rule is inconsistent with Rule 68, and similar modification of Rule 68 has not been followed in other local rules.

2. Extension of Rule 68 to Attorney Fee Shifting Statutes.—Although Rule 68's limitation of shifting court costs has provided little incentive for parties to make an offer because the potential recovery is so small, that defect also diminishes the concern that the Rule will have the effect of denying access to the courts. A 1985 Supreme Court interpretation of Rule 68, however, directly impacts a plaintiff's willingness to go to a full trial in a case in which a prevailing plaintiff may be entitled to attorneys' fees. In *Marek v. Chesny*,[79] the Court held that when a statute awards attorneys' fees to a prevailing party "as part of" costs (as does the Civil Rights Attorney's Fees Award Act of 1976 which was applicable in *Marek*), a prevailing plaintiff who does not obtain a judgment more favorable than the defendant's offer loses the right to recover his attorneys' fees. The Court read the word "costs" which the offeree is required to pay under Rule 68, as "intended to refer to all costs properly awardable under the relevant substantive statute or other authority." Thus whenever a statute awards attorneys' fees to a prevailing party "as part of costs," or with similar language, a plaintiff offeree who obtains a favorable judgment on liability that is less favorable than the offer loses his right to attorneys' fees as prevailing party. The dissent expressed doubt that the rule was intended to condition fee shifting on whether particular statutes passed over the years referred to attorneys' fees as "part of costs," often without an appreciation of the impact of such language on the application of Rule 68.

Marek has been viewed by the plaintiffs' bar, and particularly the pro-bono and civil-rights bar, as a backdoor way to deny prevailing plaintiffs their attorneys' fees, and thus, as a hindrance to access to the courts. It did create the potential for strategic use of a Rule 68 offer by defendants. A defendant can put the plaintiff's recovery of his attorneys' fees in jeopardy by making a lump sum offer and specifying that this sum is intended to include costs. The dilemma of the plaintiff's lawyer in such a situation can be intense: Any statutory attorneys' fees it might recover can be a negotiable item on the table, and his client, who has no liability for those statutory fee amounts if not awarded, has discretion to accept or reject the settlement offer.

The Court intensified this dilemma in *Evans v. Jeff D.*[89] That case involved a section 1983 class action suit which the defendant would only settle if the plaintiff's lawyer waived his statutory fees. The plaintiff's reluctant agreement to the settlement was conditioned on the court's specific approval of the waiver along with the settlement, both of which the district court provided. On appeal, the Ninth Circuit reversed, holding such agreements unfair per se, barring unusual circumstances, because of inherent conflicts that the negotiation tactic generates between the plaintiff and his lawyer. The Supreme Court reversed, holding that a settlement offer may link the merits with a waiver of statutory attorneys' fees, confirming "the possibility of a tradeoff between merits relief and attorney's fees."

Evans enables defendants in pro-bono and civil-rights cases to offer a settlement in which the plaintiffs waive attorneys' fees for which they have no personal liability. This poses a classic conflict between the interests of

---

79. 473 U.S. 1 (1985).   **89.** 475 U.S. 717 (1986).

settlement and access to courts. It is true that by jettisoning their attorneys' right to recover attorneys' fees, plaintiffs may more often be able to achieve an attractive settlement. Yet the practice may make many lawyers, including even public interest groups, unwilling to take cases in reliance on statutory sources for adequate fees. Especially in civil-rights cases, in which clients often are unable to pay for legal services, lawyers may rely on statutory attorneys' fees. Several bar associations responded to the decision in *Evans* by adopting ethics opinions insisting that a defense lawyer violates the code of ethics by making a settlement contingent on the plaintiff's lawyer waiving or limiting his rights to a statutory fee. Congressional attempts to overrule *Marek v. Chesny*, however, have failed.

3. Applicability to a Defendant's Verdict.—Rule 68 provides that cost shifting will take place "if the judgment finally obtained by the offeree is not more favorable than the offer." This language seems to apply only when the offeree obtains a verdict less favorable than the offer; it makes no reference to the situation when the verdict is in favor of the defendant. In *Delta Air Lines, Inc. v. August*,[96] the Supreme Court held that "the plain language of Rule 68 confines its effect to . . . [cases] in which the plaintiff has obtained a judgment" which is for less than the offer of judgment.[97] There is irony in this interpretation of Rule 68: a plaintiff who suffers a defendant's judgment at trial might end up better off under the attorney's fee shifting provision than if there had been a plaintiff's verdict that was less favorable than the offer that the plaintiff turned down. The virtue of this literal interpretation of the rule, however, is to prevent defendants from making token, rather than serious, offers for small amounts (say $1) in order to invoke cost shifting in every case in which there is a defendant's verdict. For this reason, proposals to change Rule 68 generally have chosen to leave the Delta interpretation intact.

4. The Offer Process.—Under Rule 68, offers last only a short period of time, but can be renewed. The offeree has ten days to accept an offer. Acceptance is carried out by serving notice on the offeror, must be unconditional, and cannot purport to accept only part of the offer tendered. While Rule 68 does not expressly provide that the offer is irrevocable during the ten-day period, this seems to be the best interpretation and has been adopted by at least one federal court. However, in "exceptional" circumstances, such as fraud on the part of the plaintiff, the court may approve revocation of an offer. An offer that is unaccepted at the end of ten days is "deemed withdrawn." An unaccepted offer is not admissible for anything other than establishing costs, should the offeree obtain a judgment that is less favorable than the offer.

Rule 68 does not preclude the possibility of multiple offers. Once an offer is deemed withdrawn, the offeror is free to make another as long as it is made at least ten days before the beginning of trial. According to the Advisory Committee Note to the 1946 Amendment of the rule, if the offeror makes several successive offers, the offer which is "equal to or greater than

---

96. 450 U.S. 346 (1981).   **97.** *Id.* at 351.

the judgment ultimately obtained" sets the date for determining the defendant's cost savings.

5.   When a Judgment is "Less Favorable" Than the Offer.—To determine whether an offer is more favorable than the judgment, Rule 68 requires a comparison of the offer (including pre-offer costs) with the "judgment finally obtained." It has been said that the Supreme Court favors a comparison that would include pre-offer costs on both sides of the comparison, adding these costs to the jury award and to the offer of judgment. But that approach has also been criticized as contrary to the language of the rule that only speaks of comparing the "judgment finally obtained," arguably meaning that pre-offer costs should not be added to the judgment for purposes of comparison. In a 1986 civil rights case, the Seventh Circuit held that pre-offer costs and attorneys' fees should be added to the jury award for comparison with the offer of judgment.

When comparing the offer to the judgment, courts are divided as to how to quantify any nonmonetary relief which was obtained. Some courts have declined to attempt to put any value on nonmonetary relief. Other courts, however, try to take nonmonetary relief into account and have found it sufficient to offset a substantial difference between a monetary offer and a judgment that includes nonmonetary relief.

NOTES AND QUESTIONS

1.   Various commentators have examined the effect of fee-shifting procedures on settlement behavior. See e.g., Donohue, The Effects of Fee Shifting on the Settlement Rate, 54 Law & Contemp.Probs. 195 (1991). One observer concludes that Rule 68's primary effect "is not to encourage settlement but to benefit defendants and harm plaintiffs by shifting downward the relevant settlement range." Miller, An Economic Analysis of Rule 68, 15 J.Leg.Stud. 93 (1986). The argument is as follows: A defendant will make a lower settlement offer under Rule 68 than he would otherwise, knowing the effect that the added impact of cost-shifting will have on the plaintiff's decision. The plaintiff, for his part, will accept something less than he otherwise would, knowing the increased cost of not surpassing the offer at trial. Thus, the entire settlement range is shifted downward. The effect is even more pronounced if the plaintiff is risk-averse (as many are) and the defendant is risk-neutral. See Chung, Settlement of Litigation Under Rule 68: An Economic Analysis, 25 J.Leg.Stud. 261 (1996).

2.   In a recent article Bruce Merenstein has argued that the only legitimate benefit of Rule 68 is the discouragement of vexatious or frivolous litigation, a benefit that can be captured using the more discretionary standards found in Federal Rule of Civil Procedure 11. Merenstein contends that Rule 11, which permits a court to sanction attorneys, law firms, or parties that submit papers to the court for an improper purpose—such as to harass or cause unnecessary delay—could be extended to "provide that all offers of settlement and refusals of such offers must not be presented for any improper purpose, as well as be 'warranted by existing law or by a nonfrivolous argument for the extension, modification, or reversal of existing law or the establishment of new law' and be supported by evidence obtained after a reasonable pre-offer (or pre-refusal) inquiry." Merenstein, More Proposals to Amend Rule 68: Time to Sink the Ship Once and For All, 184 F.R.D. 145 (1999). This would eliminate the gambling quality of Rule 68 while still punishing the most egregious problems of litigation abuse.

Is cost-shifting—and fee-shifting—a wise approach to managing the problem of excessively adversarial or bad faith litigation behavior? Do you favor a strict rule-bound approach, such as Rule 68, or a more discretionary approach, such as that permitted to judges under Rule 11?

g.   CONFIDENTIALITY

Lawyers and litigants must also consider the possibility that information exchanged during settlement discussions could adversely affect future litigation. The following excerpt considers the rules that govern the confidentiality of settlement-related information. Given the "minefield" the excerpt describes, will lawyers and clients be significantly constrained as they negotiate for fear that their statements may later be used against them?

Jane Michaels, Rule 408: A Litigation Mine Field

19 Litig. 34, 34–38, 71 (Fall 1992).

Suppose that you have three settlement negotiations to conduct. In each, a client will send you on a mission requiring detailed, but slightly different, knowledge of Rule [of evidence] 408. Before beginning the negotiations, your first step is to review the Rule carefully, along with the policies supporting it. Rule 408 reads as follows:

> Evidence of (1) furnishing or offering or promising to furnish, or (2) accepting or offering or promising to accept, a valuable consideration in compromising or attempting to compromise a claim which was disputed as to either validity or amount, is not admissible to prove liability for or invalidity of the claim or its amount. Evidence of conduct or statements made in compromise negotiations is likewise not admissible. This rule does not require the exclusion of any evidence otherwise discoverable merely because it is presented in the course of compromise negotiations. This rule also does not require exclusion when the evidence is offered for another purpose, such as proving bias or prejudice of a witness, negativing a contention of undue delay, or proving an effort to obstruct a criminal investigation or prosecution.

After reading, and re-reading, Rule 408, you manage to distill its language into a useful checklist. The first two sentences of the Rule exclude two kinds of evidence. They provide that the Rule may be used to exclude: (a) offers of compromise; and (b) conduct and statements made in compromise negotiations, if four requirements are met:

(1) there is an actual dispute;

(2) the dispute is over validity or amount of the claim;

(3) efforts are made to compromise the dispute; and

(4) the evidence is offered to prove the validity or amount of the claim.

The third and fourth sentences of Rule 408 have been labeled by some as exceptions to the general exclusionary rule. More properly considered, however, these sentences merely clarify the limits of the Rule's application. The third sentence confirms that Rule 408 is not a discovery privilege. The fourth states that settlement evidence is not automatically excluded if offered to prove something other than the validity or amount of the claim, and so it actually reiterates one of the four requirements of the general rule.

Knowing the policies behind a rule can help guide its application. Two reasons are commonly advanced for the exclusion of compromise evidence: (a) a desire to encourage the extrajudicial resolution of disputes; and (b) lack of relevance.

* * *

Your first mission begins Monday morning. You have a meeting with a potential client, Austek, Inc., which has invented a revolutionary computer chip. Megabite Corp., a manufacturer of personal computers, had entered into an oral agreement with Austek in which Megabite purchased the right to use the computer chip in exchange for Megabite's promise to pay Austek 10 percent of the gross receipts from the sales of computers containing the Austek chip. Megabite has refused to remit the 10 percent royalty. Austek asserts it is owed $5 million in royalties, but does not have underlying documentation to support the amount. The president of Austek has come to you for help.

Was There a Dispute?

In reviewing what has already happened, you learn that, two weeks ago, Megabite called your client and said that it was sending a check for $150,000, which would satisfy the entire amount owed.

The $150,000 is an offer of compromise that will be excluded by Rule 408, right?

Wrong. The offer will not be excluded under Rule 408 because there was not an actual dispute when the offer was made. The language of Rule 408 does not mention a dispute requirement, but the courts have read one in. The reasoning is simple: In order to compromise a dispute, there must be a dispute to compromise. * * *

Not surprisingly, the actual dispute requirement has been litigated frequently. Having to look for, or define, the precise moment when a difference becomes a "dispute" has produced scattered results. Facts matter a lot, and formulas are not helpful. The Federal Circuit has held, for example, that an acknowledged "probability" of an eventual court battle is not sufficient to invoke Rule 408 protection if the claim has not yet been contested. *Deere & Co. v. International Harvester Co.*, 710 F.2d 1551, 1556 (Fed.Cir.1983).

* * *

Since there has been no explicit assertion of conflicting rights in your case, you decide that there is probably no dispute, even under the more liberal *Alpex [Computer v. Nintendo Co., Ltd.*, 770 F. Supp. 161 (S.D.N.Y. 1991),] standard. Thus, you conclude Megabite's $150,000 offer will be admissible if there later is litigation.

On Tuesday morning, you set up a conference call to discuss a settlement between your client and Megabite. Before the meeting, Megabite's attorney—doing a little study of his own—looks at the second sentence of Rule 408, which states that "Evidence of conduct or statements made in compromise negotiations is likewise not admissible." He thinks everything he is about to say will never be heard in court. That turns out to be a mistake.

During the negotiations, Megabite offers $200,000 for a release of all claims. You refuse this offer on Austek's behalf and threaten to enjoin Megabite from using the Austek chip. Megabite knows that your client does not have the money to engage in protracted litigation. In pure mockery, Megabite's lawyer admits that it owes the $5 million, but simply refuses to pay. He tells you that unless Austek accepts the $200,000 offer, Megabite will tie the case up so long that it will get all the benefits it wants out of Austek's computer chip. Your client is concerned because the chip will be obsolete in three years.

Megabite's admission of liability is protected by the second sentence of Rule 408 because it was made in compromise negotiations, right?

Wrong. Megabite has stepped on a Rule 408 mine. You happily inform your client that Megabite's statements are admissible because Megabite has admitted that there is no dispute over the "validity or amount" of the claim. Megabite's admission of liability for the full $5 million bars exclusion under Rule 408, and the admission itself can be introduced at trial. *See Cassino v. Reichhold Chemicals, Inc.*, 817 F.2d 1338 (9th Cir.1987).

You jot down some notes to support this exception, just in case you have to argue it at trial. You find support in a careful reading of the Rule itself. The second sentence of Rule 408 says that "statements made in compromise negotiations" are "likewise not admissible." The word "likewise" refers back to the restrictions on offers of compromise contained in the first sentence of Rule 408. Thus, statements made in compromise negotiations are excluded on the same basis as the offers themselves. The first sentence states that an offer to compromise a claim that was "disputed as to either validity or amount" is not admissible. The word "likewise" then makes a dispute "as to either validity or amount" a condition precedent to exclusion of statements made in negotiations as well.

* * *

Megabite has unconditionally admitted liability and the amount due, but refuses to settle. You realize that Megabite is strong-arming your client with a threat of litigation attrition. Megabite hopes to chisel down the amount required to settle. In effect, Megabite is trying to force a buy-out of Austek's rights in the chip.

Having Megabite's admission of full liability safely in your pocket as admissible evidence, you should now have some leverage. But, still undaunted, Megabite refuses to settle. There will be a trial. Suppose for a moment you can go ahead in time to that proceeding.

Megabite lists Mr. Third as a potential trial witness. Mr. Third had once been in the same position as your client, Austek. Mr. Third had sold Megabite the right to install his microprocessors in the same computers as the Austek chips, in exchange for 5 percent of the gross revenues of all computers sold with his microprocessors. Like your client, Mr. Third had not received any royalty payments. Six months ago, Mr. Third told you that Megabite sold 10,000 computers containing both his microprocessors and your client's chips. In fact, Mr. Third offered to testify on behalf of your client.

You learn, however, that at trial Mr. Third intends to testify that Megabite sold only 200 computers containing Austek's chips. This undermines your entire damages theory. Your heart races; your mind grapples for a solution.

During pretrial investigations, you have also discovered that Mr. Third settled his claim with Megabite two months ago. You immediately approach the judge and seek permission to use evidence of the settlement to impeach the credibility of Mr. Third.

Megabite's counsel confidently recites the general rule that evidence of making or accepting a settlement offer is excluded by Rule 408. Opposing counsel correctly states that settlements with third parties are also excluded under Rule 408.

Bias or Prejudice

But you hold the trump card. The fourth sentence of Rule 408 states that settlement evidence is not excluded when offered to prove something other than the validity or amount of the claim. The evidence is admissible to prove bias or prejudice of a witness. Having settled his own dispute with a party, a third-party witness might be swayed toward, or occasionally against, the litigant. The paradigm example is a Mary Carter agreement. Such a settlement agreement may give the witness a financial stake in the outcome of the trial. See Brocklesby v. United States, 767 F.2d 1288, 1293 (9th Cir.1985). In extreme cases, you may be able to show that a very generous settlement is fundamentally payment for testimony, rather than a resolution of liability.

You have correctly understood the exception, but you have not won the argument yet. A conflict exists between the right to cross-examine a witness for bias and the policy of encouraging settlement. Rule 408 makes an explicit exception for proof of "bias or prejudice" and seems to set that as a policy superior to encouraging settlements. Nonetheless, trial courts strike a balance between these competing policies. Regardless of the purpose for which the evidence is offered, there is a danger that the jury may view the evidence as an implied admission, creating a possibility that future settlement may be deterred. *See Weir v. Federal Ins. Co.*, 811 F.2d 1387, 1395 (10th Cir.1987). Sometimes the evidence may not come in, even to show bias.

Opposing counsel also reminds the court that Rule 408 is a rule of exclusion, not admissibility. Although Rule 408 may not bar settlement evidence if offered to show bias, the evidence must still satisfy all the other rules of evidence. That includes Rule 403, which permits a court to refuse evidence that is unduly confusing or prejudicial. The trial judge must weigh the need for the settlement evidence against the potential of discouraging compromise negotiations and the chance of unfair prejudice. Rule 403 may require exclusion in many instances.

Limited Admissibility

You retort that Mr. Third had previously agreed to testify for Megabite. After listening to arguments from both attorneys, the judge determines that the chance of jury confusion is outweighed by your interest in revealing Mr. Third's bias. He allows you to present evidence of the settlement with Mr. Third.

Even though you seem to have won, the judge warns you that the settlement with Mr. Third will not be admissible to impeach a Megabite representative. The bias exception takes on a different character if the witness to be impeached is a party, because such a witness has an obvious interest in the outcome of the trial. For such a witness, the additional proof of bias offered by settlement evidence is probably minimal; it will more likely be seen as an admission of liability. As a result, settlement evidence offered to impeach Megabite will be excluded under a combination of Rules 408 and 403.

* * *

* * * A prior inconsistent statement made during a settlement discussion may not be used for impeachment. Although the Rule does not expressly prohibit the use of settlement evidence for other methods of impeachment, admitting prior inconsistent statements for such a purpose would eviscerate Rule 408.

After this excursion through the lawbooks, you return to the Austek/Megabite litigation. Through discovery, you have obtained an intraoffice report in which Megabite's sales manager admits that Megabite owes your client "$4 million or $5 million." Will this smoking gun document be admissible? Megabite claims that it must be excluded under Rule 408, because the report was specifically prepared for use in compromise negotiations after the lawsuit was filed. If the report was actually prepared for settlement purposes, the policies of Rule 408 will require its exclusion. *See Ramada Development Co. v. Rauch*, 644 F.2d 1097 (5th Cir.1981).

The intent of the party making the report is an important question. Were it otherwise, the Rule would be open to abuse. An unscrupulous party seeking to keep a damaging report out of evidence could do so by merely saying that the report was produced for settlement purposes. Courts, however, do not accept this argument absent objective, good-faith evidence of settlement intent. For example, in *Blue Circle Atlantic, Inc. v. Falcon Material, Inc.*, 760 F.Supp. 516 (D.Md.1991), the court ruled that Rule 408 does not apply to intraoffice memoranda unless communicated to the other side in an attempt to settle.

After hearing more about the context of the sales manager's preparation of the report, the court excludes it from evidence. However, effective impeachment of Mr. Third, combined with Megabite's pre-suit admissions of liability, convince the jury that your client deserves full recovery. In the final analysis, Megabite was blown away in the Rule 408 mine field.

Come back now to the present and embark upon your second settlement mission of the week. Wednesday afternoon brings a reunion with an old friend who seeks your assistance. The friend, Ms. Reliable, was unexpectedly discharged from her job. She asks you if she has a suit. After reviewing the facts, you determine that she has a strong chance of proving wrongful discharge or sex discrimination. You file the claim.

As you will soon learn, counsel for the defendant employer is more familiar with the intricacies of Rule 408 than Megabite's lawyer. Defendant's counsel telephones to suggest a settlement conference Thursday over breakfast. Since conduct and statements made during compromise negotiations are inadmissible under Rule 408, you agree.

During the compromise negotiation, the employer admits that most of the employees it has let go recently were women. Is this statement admissible?

No. In its greatest departure from the common law, the second sentence of Rule 408 provides that statements of fact made in compromise negotiations are inadmissible. * * *

The common law rule had two main problems. First, the admissibility of factual statements hindered the negotiation process because parties could not speak freely. Second, often fights occurred over which comments fell within a prefatory "without prejudice" statement.

Rule 408 solves these problems by excluding all conduct and statements made in compromise negotiations. Thus, parties can speak freely about the facts of the disputed matter without fear of the subsequent admissibility of those conversations.

Your client's former employer has come to this settlement meeting with an objective. The company wants to generate evidence that will limit backpay damages if the matter goes to trial. Specifically, it wants to demonstrate that Ms. Reliable has rejected a reasonable offer of reinstatement.

Opposing counsel knows that the definition of the word "compromise" provides an implicit exception to Rule 408's evidentiary ban. A compromise is an agreement reached by mutual concession. Each side agrees to relinquish something to which it believes itself entitled. If an offer does not require Ms. Reliable to release her legal claim against the employer, then it seeks no compromise within the meaning of Rule 408, and there is no exclusion. In other words, offers not requiring a release are not excluded by Rule 408. * * * Presenting Ms. Reliable with an offer that does not require a release would be easy. But the company wants to have it both ways: It wants to create evidence of the reinstatement offer to cut off backpay damages, but not have to pay additional salary should Ms. Reliable accept the offer.

* * *

By now, as a Rule 408 veteran, you see exactly what is happening. The employer plans to circumvent the Rule 408 exclusion by resorting to ambiguity. If the terms of the offer are ambiguous, Ms. Reliable will be uncertain as to whether acceptance requires her to waive her legal claim. The former employer wants to make the terms of the offer vague, but just clear enough to convince a judge that Ms. Reliable was not being asked to release her claim, so that the offer will not be excluded under Rule 408.

Fortunately, you have just read a case holding that offers presented during compromise negotiations are inadmissible, unless the offering party can prove that the offer did not require a release of claims. *See Pierce v. F.R. Tripler & Co.*, 955 F.2d 820 (2d Cir.1992). The burden of clarifying ambiguity should fall on your adversary. You inform opposing counsel of the *Pierce* case.

Your opponent is not easily deterred, however. Later in the negotiations, she says "We are making a reinstatement offer without prejudice." This time, opposing counsel has skillfully used the language of Rule 408, creating admissible evidence that could limit the damages awarded to your client. Because the offer was made "without prejudice," its acceptance would not have required Ms. Reliable to waive her claim against the employer. Falling outside the purview of Rule 408, the offer is admissible. Of course, to set up this evidence, opposing counsel had to take the risk that Ms. Reliable might accept. Disregarding your sound advice, however, Ms. Reliable rejects the offer.

At trial, Ms. Reliable wins on the liability issue, but the offer of reinstatement "without prejudice" is admitted. Opposing counsel's careful use of Rule 408's compromise requirement has limited the damages awarded to your client.

Name Theft

Your third and final mission comes from an old and dear client: A–One Airlines. A–One has come to you because a small air cargo company is operating under the name "A–One Cargo." Your client is a first-class operation that scorns any association with a slipshod outfit like A–One Cargo. The airline owns the right to use the name "A–One," and it wants you to get the cargo company to change its name—quickly.

Your client wants to avoid an ugly battle in the courts and would prefer to settle. You call counsel for the cargo company and set up a meeting. You suggest that all parties sign a written agreement in advance, stating their intent to meet in a compromise negotiation under Rule 408.

During negotiations, the cargo company says it will change its name if your client pays $20,000, plus the expenses of a new logo design and reprinting the company stationery. Your client likes the idea but is reluctant to pay any money. After all, there might be another A–One operation out there. Your client fears that the terms of the settlement might be revealed if a future plaintiff makes a discovery request.

You consult the third sentence of Rule 408, which states: "This rule does not require the exclusion of any evidence otherwise discoverable merely because it is presented in the course of compromise negotiations." From reading the Rule and interpretive case law, you conclude that, while the intent of Rule 408 is to foster settlement negotiations, there is only one means used to effectuate that policy: exclusion from evidence at trial. Rule 408 does not create a broad discovery privilege. *NAACP Defense and Education Fund, Inc. v. United States of Justice,* 612 F. Supp. 1143, 1146 (D.D.C.1985).

Doing more research, you determine that your client does have some protection. Third parties will not be able to compel discovery of settlement material if their sole aim is to expose your client's prior negotiations with others. A–One Airlines is not required to disclose settlement material unless, as required by Rule 26(b)(1), there is a showing that the material sought through discovery will be relevant to the issues in another case or will lead to the discovery of evidence admissible there. *See Morse/Diesel, Inc. v. Trinity Indus., Inc.,* No. Civ. 5781 (SWK), 1992 WL 76896 (S.D.N.Y. April 10, 1992).

* * *

Discovery of Settlements

Assessing the risks, you advise your client that future litigants might be able to compel discovery of the A–One Cargo settlement, but that it cannot be used against A–One Airlines in a later suit to prove the validity or amount of the claim. You must, however, warn your client of certain risks. For example, factual admissions made during compromise negotiations are more likely to be discoverable in another suit, because they are more likely to lead to admissible evidence. In addition, the settlement could be subject to discovery if the evidence will be used to demonstrate bias. With these concerns reviewed and carefully examined, your client signs the settlement papers, satisfied that the risks have been well identified.

At the end of your various settlement discussions, you take a moment to reflect. Although intended to encourage settlement negotiations and to assure that negotiators can speak freely during settlement discussions without creating admissible evidence, Rule 408 contains numerous exceptions. They make it a mine field—but one that can be negotiated successfully.

NOTES AND QUESTIONS

1. The Michaels article begins by referring to the policy of encouraging settlement. In judicial opinions concerning settlement practice, the policy of encouraging settlement is an overriding concern. In close cases regarding post-settlement issues such as malpractice, confidentiality, and collateral attack, the policy of encouraging settlement often tips the scales in favor of one side. Thus, parties in post-settlement disputes are well advised to discuss the ways in which their legal position favors, or at least does not discourage, settlement.

2. Whether to discourage similar suits, prevent future liability, or preserve a positive public image, parties often seek to protect the terms of private settlements. In such a case, the public's right to know may outweigh the policy of encouraging settlement. Carrie Menkel–Meadow has discussed the policy questions raised by confidential settlement. While parties may prefer private settlement terms, many groups claim a right to know stemming from the First Amendment and the common law. Public interest groups and the media attempt to disclose public harms. Public officials encourage open discussion of issues pertaining to the public interest. Plaintiff's lawyers want to share information with others and to prevent some plaintiffs from trading large settlements for promises of secrecy. In response to the controversy, many state legislatures have adopted "sunshine laws" precluding confidential settlements in cases involving public issues. See Menkel–Meadow, Public Access to Private Settlements: Conflicting Legal Policies, 11:6 Alt. to the High Cost of Litig. 85 (Jun. 1993). For further discussion, including an analysis of the legal procedures available to parties seeking to protect settlement terms, see Dore, Secrecy by Consent: The Use and Limits of Confidentiality in the Pursuit of Settlement, 74 Notre Dame L.Rev. 283 (1999).

3. As Michaels' article makes clear, Federal Rule of Evidence 408 leaves many statements made in settlement negotiations subject to discovery. However, parties can mutually agree through private contract to maintain the confidentiality of settlement negotiations. The degree of deference a court will afford such a contract depends on the circumstances. Contracts that violate public policy are routinely disregarded. Courts may also view private contracting as infringing on the court's power to consider evidence or as conflicting with Rule 408. As Wayne Brazil notes, "Confidentiality contracts that threaten none of these more compelling public policies, however, may be enforceable * * *" See generally Brazil, Protecting the

Confidentiality of Settlement Negotiations, 39 Hastings L.J. 955, 1026–28 (1988).

4.   The Advisory Committee that drafted Rule 408 made no recommendation about whether parties should be able to use lies in settlement negotiations to impeach their opponents at trial. Some legal scholars have suggested that allowing parties to impeach their counterparts with inconsistent statements made during negotiations would not undercut the policy rationale behind Rule 408, and it would promote ethical negotiation behavior. See Rambo, Impeaching Lying Parties with their Statements during Negotiation: Demysticizing the Public Policy Rationale Behind Evidence Rule 408 and the Mediation–Privilege Statutes, 75 Wash.L.Rev. 1037 (2000); Hjelmeset, Impeachment of Party by Prior Inconsistent Statement in Compromise Negotiations: Admissibility Under Federal Rule of Evidence 408, 43 Clev.St.L.Rev. 75 (1995).

The exclusion provided in Rule 408 must be read in conjunction with the standards for discovery in the Federal Rules. Rule 26(b) allows discovery "regarding any matter, not privileged, which is relevant to the subject matter involved in the pending action." Furthermore, that rule states that "[I]t is not ground for objection that the information sought will be inadmissible at the trial if the information sought appears reasonably calculated to lead to the discovery of admissible evidence." This broad scope of discovery could be seen to come into conflict with the Rule 408 exclusion for offers in compromise. Consider the following case:

Young v. State Farm Mutual Automobile Insurance Company

U.S. District Court, S.D. West Virginia 1996.
169 F.R.D. 72.

■ FEINBERG, UNITED STATES MAGISTRATE JUDGE.

This is a civil action in which Plaintiffs, a partnership of attorneys, seek to recover legal fees in connection with the representation of Defendant Michael Pritchard, who was seriously injured in an automobile accident at the conclusion of a high speed chase involving Fayetteville, West Virginia police officers and a Fayette County Deputy Sheriff.

Defendants State Farm Mutual Insurance Company and State Farm Fire and Casualty Company (collectively referred to as "State Farm") insured the automobile in which Pritchard was riding when he was injured. Plaintiff Ralph Young served as local counsel in the trial of Pritchard's case against the driver of the automobile. *Michael Pritchard, Jr. v. Town of Fayetteville,* No. 5:89–1457 (S.D.W.Va. Aug. 30, 1993). Defendant Sutherland was Pritchard's lead attorney at the trial. The jury awarded Pritchard more than $15 million in damages payable by the driver, Smith.

Subsequently, Smith, Pritchard, and the owner of the automobile sued State Farm for unlawful trade practices and bad faith in connection with the Pritchard case, *Smith v. State Farm Mut. Auto. Ins. Co.*, No. 94–C–54–S (Cir.Ct. McDowell Co., W.Va.), removed to United States District Court, No. 1:95–0100 (S.D.W.Va. Mar. 13, 1996). Plaintiffs notified the *Smith v. State Farm* litigants of their claim to attorneys' fees. State Farm then settled with Smith, Pritchard and the owner, and the unlawful trade practices/bad faith case was dismissed. The *Smith v. State Farm* parties agreed that their settlement agreement would be confidential.

It is clear to the Court that all parties to the *Pritchard v. City of Fayetteville* case recognized that the insurance policy limits on the automobile driven by Smith were totally inadequate to compensate the damages suffered by Mr. Pritchard. The trial of *Pritchard v. City of Fayetteville* was conducted for the purpose of establishing the amount of damages, not the issue of liability, which was conceded. It is also clear that State Farm was the only available source of money to satisfy the verdict in favor of Pritchard, if recovery could be had against State Farm on the bad faith/unlawful trade practices claim. The underlying action and the insurance action were two separate cases, involving some different attorneys, but they were related.

In this civil action, Plaintiffs claim that they are owed a share of the settlement paid by State Farm to Pritchard on behalf of Smith. Plaintiffs sue Defendants Sutherland and Pritchard for breach of contract of an oral contingency fee agreement (Count I), and for *quantum meruit* (Count II); they sue all Defendants for enforcement of attorney's lien (Count III). Defendants Sutherland and Pritchard admit that Plaintiff Ralph Young is entitled to receive a reasonable attorney's fee according to the legal doctrine of *quantum meruit* but deny any liability based on a contingency. State Farm has moved to dismiss pursuant to Fed.R.Civ.Proc. 12(b)(6), asserting lack of privity of contract with Plaintiffs, and lack of services rendered by Plaintiffs to State Farm.

Now pending before the Court are Plaintiffs' Motions to Compel and the Motion for Protective Order filed by Defendants Sutherland and Pritchard. Plaintiffs seek disclosure by Defendants Sutherland and Pritchard of [certain matters, including the] amount and terms of the settlement between Mr. Pritchard and State Farm, the amount of all attorneys' fees received by Mr. Sutherland,* * * or by any other person, from the above settlement proceeds; whether funds were escrowed; [and] any portion of the file maintained by Sutherland in connection with the bad faith action. * * *

Plaintiffs request the following information from State Farm: "the amount and terms of the settlement in question, the escrow-related information, if any, and information concerning the identity of the person or persons at State Farm who made a decision not to honor plaintiffs' attorneys' fee lien."

State Farm resists disclosure based upon relevancy and the confidentiality provision of the settlement agreement. No privilege is asserted. * * *

The issues posed by the Complaint in this case are:

1. Did Plaintiffs have an agreement with Defendants Sutherland and Pritchard concerning the amount of Plaintiffs' attorneys' fees for services rendered?

2. If so, what were the terms of that agreement?

3. If attorneys' fees are payable to Plaintiffs, how much is payable, and who is liable for the payment?

The issues raised by the pending Motions are:

1. Should the settlement agreement between Sutherland/Pritchard and State Farm be disclosed to Plaintiffs, despite the agreement's provision to maintain its confidentiality?

2. Should the Court compel Defendants Pritchard, Sutherland and State Farm to answer the additional discovery requested by Plaintiffs concerning the settlement?

These discovery issues are of first impression in the Fourth Circuit and the District Courts within that Circuit.

* * *

When the requested discovery concerns a confidential settlement agreement, the majority of courts considering the issue have required the requesting party to meet a heightened standard, in deference to Federal Rule of Evidence 408, and the public policy to encourage settlements and to uphold confidentiality provisions. In Bottaro v. Hatton Associates, *96 F.R.D. 158, 159 (E.D.N.Y.1982)*, the court noted that *Rule 26(b)* itself provides that "[i]t is not ground for objection that the information sought will be inadmissible at the trial if the information sought appears reasonably calculated to lead to the discovery of admissible evidence." The Bottaro court held as follows:

> Given the strong public policy of favoring settlements and the congressional intent to further that policy by insulating the bargaining table from unnecessary intrusions *[Fed.R.Evid. 408]*, we think the better rule is to require some particularized showing of a likelihood that admissible evidence will be generated by the dissemination of the terms of a settlement agreement. The Bottaro court found that the showing had not been made, and refused disclosure.

In Morse/Diesel, Inc. v. Fidelity and Deposit Co. of Maryland, *122 F.R.D. 447, 451 (S.D.N.Y.1988)*, the court used the heightened standard analysis, found that the required showing had been made, and ordered disclosure of the settlement materials. A similar result was reached in Fidelity Federal Savings and Loan Ass'n v. Felicetti, *148 F.R.D. 532, 534 (E.D.Pa.1993)*. The Felicetti court characterized the heightened standard as "switch[ing] the burden of proof from the party in opposition to the discovery to the party seeking the information." In Lesal Interiors, Inc. v. Resolution Trust Corp., *153 F.R.D. 552, 562 (D.N.J.1994)*, the court applied the heightened standard, and refused disclosure.

In Vardon Golf Co. v. BBMG Golf Ltd., *156 F.R.D. 641, 650–51 (N.D.Ill.1994)*, the court concluded that the Bottaro standard overstated the nature of the proponent's burden. Rather than require a "particularized showing," the court noted that *Rule 26(b)* considers what is "reasonably calculated to lead to the discovery of admissible evidence."

> "[W]e hold that where information sought in discovery would not be admissible due to an exclusionary rule in the Federal Rules of Evidence, the proponent of discovery may obtain discovery (1) by showing that the evidence is admissible for another purpose other than that barred by the Federal Rules of Evidence or (2) by articulating a plausible chain of inferences showing how discovery of the item sought would lead to other admissible evidence. The proponent may do this by simply articulating what kind of information it reasonably expects to find in the documents sought and how this will lead to other admissible evidence. The proponent need not show that the information expected is in fact in the items sought, but need only articulate why it is reasonable to believe that information of that nature would be revealed were discovery permitted."

Despite the lessened standard, the court refused disclosure in Vardon Golf.

At least one court has rejected the Bottaro heightened standard, has applied the normal relevancy standard of *Rule 26(b)*, and has placed the burden on the party opposing discovery to establish some good cause or sound reason for withholding the material. Bennett v. La Pere, *112 F.R.D. 136, 140 (D.R.I.1986)*. In Bennett, the court found that the requested documents were relevant and not privileged and that no sound reason had been shown to withhold them from disclosure. Moreover, the Bennett court opined that disclosure would enable the parties to appraise the case realistically, to consider settlement, and to avoid protracted litigation. "So long as the policy of the Rules is the promotion of the 'just, speedy, and inexpensive' resolution of cases, then fair settlements must always be encouraged. Fairness cannot be achieved when one said is needlessly blindfolded." Id. *at 141.*

The case which is closest in its facts to the instant action is McCullough v. Nichols, *No. 9404CV0093, 1995 WL 679265, *2 (Mass.Dist.Ct. Aug. 3, 1995)*, in which the plaintiff-attorneys sued their former clients for breach of contract and, alternatively, in *quantum meruit,* for failure to honor a written fee agreement and to pay attorneys' fees. Defendants counterclaimed, alleging failure of adequate representation. The court held as follows:

> [I]t is my view that when private parties to a civil action enter into an agreement providing for the non-disclosure of settlement terms, the privilege from disclosing those terms that is thereby created must yield to a request for discovery by a third party attorney in an independent action for recovery of counsel fees against one of the settling parties for services performed in connection with the subject matter of the case that was settled in circumstances in which the terms and conditions of the prior settlement are central to the third party cause of action.

The threshold question is whether the requested discovery, including the disclosure of the confidential settlement agreement, is relevant to this litigation. Any discussion of relevancy in the context of discovery must begin with *Fed.R.Civ.Proc. 26(b)*, which provides that "[p]arties may obtain discovery regarding any matter, not privileged, which is relevant to the subject matter involved in the pending action...." *Federal Rule of Evidence 401* defines "relevant evidence" as "evidence having any tendency to make the existence of any fact that is of consequence to the determination of the action more probable or less probable than it would be without the evidence." "All relevant evidence is admissible." *Fed.R.Evid. 402.* Courts have construed *Rule 26(b)* to permit very broad discovery, encompassing "any matter that bears on, or that reasonably could lead to other matter that could bear on, any issue that is or may be in the case." Oppenheimer Fund, Inc. v. Sanders, *437 U.S. 340, 351, 98 S.Ct. 2380, 2389, 57 L.Ed.2d 253 (1978).*

Review of the pleadings in the instant case reveals that Plaintiffs allege that there was an oral contingency fee contract between Plaintiff Young and Defendant Pritchard's attorneys, with the fee to be determined upon the successful outcome of both the underlying action and the insurance action. Defendants Pritchard and Sutherland admit that there was an implicit agreement to compensate Plaintiff Young for his services, and that the amount of the fee was not agreed. They deny the existence of a contingency fee agreement, and contend that Plaintiff Young can recover a fee based only on *quantum meruit.*

* * *

It is evident, and the Court so finds, that the requested discovery material is relevant to the issues in this case. Contrary to Defendants' position, a District Court's determination of an attorney's fee is not a simple mathematical calculation of "percentage multiplied by verdict," or "number of hours multiplied by hourly rate." A District Court's responsibility in a dispute over attorneys' fees requires review of each attorney's performance and role in the cases which are relevant to the dispute, in light of the Johnson factors. In determining whether the fee is fixed or contingent (factor 6), Plaintiffs should be able to examine Defendant Sutherland's file and to question him concerning his understanding as to whether Plaintiff Young's fee was fixed or contingent. The results obtained (factor 8) cannot be determined without knowing what State Farm paid to settle with Pritchard, Sutherland, and Smith. A large verdict has little value unless the judgment is actually paid in whole or in part.

Having determined that the requested discovery material is relevant, the next question is whether it is privileged. As noted above, Defendants Sutherland and Pritchard have waived the attorney-client and work product privileges as to discovery [requested of them]. State Farm does not assert any privilege. Therefore, the Court concludes that the requested discovery material is relevant and not privileged.

The next inquiry is whether the requested discovery material is admissible. * * * If the confidential settlement agreement or related discovery material were offered into evidence at the trial of this case, it would not be offered to prove State Farm's liability for bad faith or unfair trade practices, nor to prove the invalidity of the claim that State Farm engaged in bad faith or unfair trade practices, nor to prove the amount of the claim against State Farm. Presumably the settlement agreement and the related discovery materials would be offered into evidence for other purposes, that is, to prove the nature of the agreement with Plaintiff Young, and the results obtained in the subject cases. While it is the decision of the presiding District Judge to determine whether evidence is admissible, this Magistrate Judge considers it probable that the confidential settlement agreement and the related discovery materials would be admissible for the purposes stated. At a minimum, the Court finds that the confidential settlement agreement and the related discovery materials constitute information which is reasonably calculated to lead to the discovery of admissible evidence. *Fed.R.Civ.Proc. 26(b)*.

Having determined that the discovery requests are relevant and not privileged, and that the discovery material is probably admissible (or likely to lead to admissible evidence), the Court notes that applicable cases support disclosure. Bottaro, *96 F.R.D. at 160;* Morse/Diesel, Inc., *122 F.R.D. at 451;* Vardon Golf Co., *156 F.R.D. at 650–51;* McCullough, supra, *1995 WL 679265, at *2.* The weight of authority and *Rule 26(b)* itself impose upon the requesting party a greater burden to establish the relevancy, and to gain discovery, of otherwise inadmissible non-privileged confidential settlement documents. But if the requesting party shows that the "information appears reasonably calculated to lead to the discovery of admissible evidence," then it is probably discoverable. It is appropriate to protect confidential settlement agreements, but not if such protection prevents necessary discovery.

The settlement agreement contains specific terms bearing on the disposition of files and the relationships among attorneys and represented parties which directly affect this litigation. Moreover, the hand-written note attached to document #63 suggests that Plaintiff Young and Pritchard's first attorney discussed Young's receiving a contingent fee based on the outcome of both the underlying action and the insurance action if verdicts were rendered. If the confidentiality provision were enforced against Plaintiffs, then Plaintiffs would probably be blocked in their efforts to obtain documentary and testamentary evidence concerning any agreement concerning their fees.

For the reasons stated and after careful consideration of the terms of the settlement agreement, the facts of the underlying and insurance actions, and all the cited cases, the Court holds that the confidential settlement agreement signed by Defendants Sutherland, Pritchard and State Farm, and the other discovery materials that it protects by its confidentiality provision, are discoverable because Plaintiffs have demonstrated their relevance and probable admissibility (or likelihood of leading to admissible evidence). The Court concludes that the requested discovery, including the settlement agreement, is likely to lead to the discovery of admissible evidence relevant to the issues posed by this case, i.e., the existence, terms, and proper enforcement of any agreement between Plaintiffs, on the one hand, and Defendants Sutherland and Pritchard, on the other hand.

For these reasons, it is hereby **ORDERED** that Plaintiffs' Motions to Compel with respect to Defendants Pritchard and Sutherland * * * are granted in part * * *

It is further **ORDERED** that Plaintiffs' Motions to Compel with respect to State Farm * * * are granted as follows, but any disclosure shall be subject to a protective order:

1.   Amount and terms of the settlement: granted;

2.   Escrow-related information: granted; and

3.   Identity of person who decided not to honor the attorney's lien: granted.

It is further **ORDERED** that no disclosure shall be made unless and until all parties execute an agreed protective order.

NOTES AND QUESTIONS

1.   Are Rule 408 and Rule 26(b) in conflict? Were they properly reconciled in this case? How should courts respond to discovery requests pertaining to previous settlement agreements?

2.   The plaintiffs in *Young* claim that the settlement agreement was relevant to their claim for attorneys' fees which were contingent upon success in both the underlying claim and the bad faith action. What is the link between the agreement and their claim for fees? Was it critical that the agreement contained "specific terms bearing on the disposition of files and relationships among attorneys and represented parties?" Would that be admissible to prove that plaintiff Young had a contingent fee contract, or would it just lead to admissible evidence?

3.   How does the court deal with the conflict in the case law concerning the standard to apply under the interface between Rule 408 and Rule 26(b), i.e., *Bottaro* requires "some particularized showing of a likelihood that admissible evidence will be generated by the dissemination of the terms of a settlement agreement," while *Bennett* rejected such a heightened standard and simply applied the "relevancy" standard of Rule 26(b)? The court states that Rule 26(b) imposes "upon the requesting party a greater burden to establish the relevancy, and to gain discovery, of otherwise inadmissible non-privileged confidential settlement documents." Did it find that plaintiffs discharged that burden, or did its finding that the information was reasonably calculated to lead to the discovery of admissible evidence result in its applying a lesser standard?

4. In *Bottaro*, non-settling defendants sought to discover the nature of the plaintiff's settlement agreement with a settling defendant. How could discovery of the terms of the settlement reasonably lead to admissible evidence? Defendants argued that it might lead to admissible evidence on the question of damages. However, the court found that there was no particularized showing of a likelihood of leading to admissible evidence and refused to compel disclosure of the settlement agreement. Could the fact that the settling defendant paid the plaintiff a large sum lead to admissible evidence concerning damages? Might it not indicate that plaintiff had a stronger case than the defendants thought (or if the settlement was small, that he had a weaker case). The court in *Bennett* required disclosure to a non-settling defendant Hospital of a settlement agreement between the plaintiff and defendant Physicians, stating "the damages which the plaintiffs can collect from the Hospital if they successfully prosecute what remains of the case will depend to some extent on the terms, amount, and value of the Physicians' settlement."

5. In *Bottarro*, would the details of the settlement agreement be relevant to determining whether, and in what amount, remaining defendants would be entitled to contribution against a settling defendant? The *Bottaro* decision, however, stated that "while it is true that a settling defendant's liability for contribution depends on whether he paid his share of any damage award, this determination cannot be made until a final judgment has been rendered." It further stated that "even then, the settlement would not be evidence relevant to any issue in this case other than a ministerial apportionment of damages, a mathematical computation which the Court rather than the jury will perform." Must a defendant wait until a final judgment to discover the settlement amount for purposes for determining contribution? Would the interests of settlement be better served by allowing discovery of that information earlier so that all claims might be resolved at one time? What if the state procedure provides for comparing the negligence of settling defendants with that of the remaining defendants in the primary suit (see Tex. Civ.Prac. & Rem.Code § 33.003 et seq.)?

6. Rule 408 clearly prohibits introduction of the fact or amount of a settlement for the purpose of proving liability or the amount of damages due. But it may be introduced for "another purpose, such as proving bias or prejudice or interest of a witness or a party." Could the defendants in *Bottaro* have succeeded on a theory that they wanted to use the settlement information to impeach the settling defendant if he testified? When there is a "Mary Carter agreement" between plaintiff and a settling defendant (an agreement by which the settling defendant retains a financial interest in the plaintiff's recovery against non-settling defendants), evidence of the agreement may be introduced for the purpose of impeaching the settling defendant. See General Motors Corp. v. Simmons, 558 S.W.2d 855, 858 (Tex.1977). Should the same be true when there is no "Mary Carter agreement," but the defendant desires to show that the settling defendant was "paid off" in return for testimony favorable to the plaintiff?

7. The discovery rules also offer the possibility of protection of confidentiality through a court protective order, as in incorporating a mediation agreement of confidentiality or in sealing a mediation record. Rule 26(c) provides that a court may "for good cause shown ... make any order which justice requires to protect a party or person from annoyance, embarrassment, oppression, or undue burden or expense." Rule 26(c)(7) specifically provides for a protective order that "a trade secret or other confidential research, development, or commercial information not be disclosed or be disclosed only in a designated way."

2. JUDICIAL PROMOTION OF SETTLEMENT

A lawyer's efforts to use litigation procedures to help assure a more successful negotiation can be made more effective if a judge assumes responsibility for managing the litigation with a goal of resolving the dispute voluntarily, fairly, and efficiently. Judicial administrators at both the federal and state levels currently emphasize the judge's role in promoting settlement.[11]

Federal Rule of Civil Procedure 16, adopted in 1938, provides the primary tool for judicial supervision of litigation through the pretrial conference. It was amended in 1983 to provide for two types of pretrial conferences—"scheduling and planning" and "final." Among the subjects to be discussed at pretrial conference are "establishing early and continuing control so that the case will not be protracted because of lack of management," "discouraging wasteful pretrial activities," "improving the quality of the trial through more thorough preparation," and "facilitating settlement."

Rule 16(c)(9) now expressly provides that "settlement and the use of special procedures to assist in resolving the dispute when authorized by statute or local rule" may be considered and acted upon during pretrial conferences. Explicit reference to settlement was added to Rule 16 in 1983; as the Advisory Committee then acknowledged, it had "become commonplace to discuss settlement at pretrial conferences." In 1993 the treatment of settlement promotion was expanded, and the Advisory Committee explained this expansion as follows:

> Even if a case cannot immediately be settled, the judge and attorneys can explore possible use of alternative procedures such as mini-trials, summary jury trials, mediation, neutral evaluation, and non-binding arbitration that can lead to consensual resolution of the dispute without a full trial on the merits.

But these devices can be employed only when authorized by statute or local rule. This reflects in part the decentralization accomplished by the Civil Justice Reform Act, 28 U.S.C.A. § 471 et seq., which allowed each district to authorize, or not, the use of alternative dispute resolution. A sizable

---

11. See Miller, The August 1983 Amendments to the Federal Rules of Civil Procedure: Promoting Effective Case Man- agement and Lawyer Responsibility 11–34 (Fed.Judicial Center 1984).

number of districts decided to adopt such ADR methods, but some specifically rejected them.

a. THE PROPER ROLE OF THE JUDGE

Judicial encouragement of settlement has long been practiced in federal and many state courts; until the advent of the ADR movement, this was primarily accomplished through a settlement conference with the judge who used a combination of jaw-boning and veiled threats to move the parties towards settlement.[12] The courts have uniformly held that such settlement procedures must not have the effect of coercing the parties into settling.

In a typical case, *Kothe v. Smith*,[13] the Second Circuit reversed sanctions against the defendant after he refused to settle before trial (on the judge's recommendation of a $20,000 to $30,000 settlement figure), but settled for $20,000 after one day of trial. The Second Circuit concluded that an "attorney should not be condemned for changing his evaluation of the case after listening to [the opponent's] testimony during the first day of trial."[14] The process used in *Kothe* was a judicial settlement conference, authorized by Federal Rule of Civil Procedure 16, which the appellate court viewed as "designed to encourage pretrial settlement discussions," but not to "impose settlement negotiations on unwilling litigants." "Pressure tactics to coerce settlement," it said, "simply are not permissible."[15]

An ABA-sponsored study of lawyers in four federal districts concluded that "85 percent of the responding attorneys from the entire four-district sample agree that involvement by federal judges in settlement discussions is likely to improve significantly the prospects of achieving settlement."[16] The data, summarized in the following selection, provide interesting insight into the relationships of lawyers and judges in the negotiation area.

Wayne D. Brazil, Settling Civil Disputes
44–46 (1985).

Why do lawyers say that judicial involvement can significantly improve prospects for achieving settlement? Our data do not provide a definitive answer, but they offer clues and suggest hypotheses. Even though a large percentage of cases ultimately settle, the process through which the parties eventually reach agreement often is difficult to launch, then can be awkward, expensive, time-consuming, and stressful. The route to resolution can be tortuously indirect and travel over it can be obstructed by emotion, posturing, and interpersonal friction. Counsel and clients can be distracted by irrelevancies and resources can be consumed by feints or maneuvers

---

12. See E. Donald Elliott, Managerial Judging and the Evolution of Procedure, 53 U.Chi.L.Rev. 306 (1986); Paul Reidinger, Then It's Settled, A.B.A.J., July 1989, at 92.

13. 771 F.2d 667 (2d Cir.1985).

14. Id. at 670.

15. Id. at 669.

16. Wayne D. Brazil, Settling Civil Suits 39 (1985).

designed primarily to save face with opponents or to retain credibility with the people paying the bills. Parties and lawyers can be slow to feel confidence in the wisdom or fairness of proposals developed through such an awkward, adversarial process, a process in which people assume that their opponents are not disclosing significant information and are offering only self-serving assessments of the implications of evidence and the relative strengths of competing positions.

Since at least some of these problems burden private settlement negotiations in many cases, lawyers well might feel that federal judges can make significant contributions to the settlement process by reducing frictions and removing obstacles that otherwise would impede it. As we will demonstrate, the pattern of lawyer responses to our questions suggests an important unifying hypothesis; judicial involvement is likely to improve prospects for achieving settlement because judges are professional decision makers.

Litigators, by contrast, are professional advocates. The skills that are central to the litigator's professional self-image and role revolve around marshalling evidence and arguments for one side, selecting and packaging information to make it as persuasive as possible. Lawyers are trained to uncover evidence, then to arrange its display to others; the others have ultimate responsibility to decide what the evidence means. Thus the litigator's job is to present persuasively, not to judge dispassionately.

Judges, on the other hand, are paid to make decisions, and to do so rationally and impartially. Good judges know that their central responsibility is to resolve disputes fairly, to terminate conflicts by making neutral decisions. Judges also know that the data on which they must make decisions will be presented to them by advocating litigators seeking persuasive advantages. To achieve their objective of making rational decisions in this environment, good judges become skillful at cutting through verbal and emotional camouflage to identify pivotal issues, at ferreting out key evidence, assessing credibility and analyzing strengths and weaknesses of arguments. The pursuit of fair solutions teaches judges to probe, to ask about matters not presented. The responsibility to make decisions puts a premium on efficiency. The responsibility to decide rationally sharpens the judge's analytical edge.

A judge who enters the settlement dynamic with these instincts and skills is in a position to make unique and valuable contributions. The presence of a judicial officer can create an expectation of decision making and can help overcome lawyers' and litigants' natural resistance to realistically assessing their positions. The judge can initiate settlement discussions earlier than counsel otherwise would and can relieve lawyers of the onus of being the first to suggest discussion of settlement. Some lawyers are reluctant to initiate settlement talks because they are afraid that raising the issue of settlement will be perceived by their opponents as a sign of weakness. That fear might help explain why so many of our respondents think settlement conferences should be mandatory in most actions in federal court and that judges should take steps to encourage settlement even when no one has asked them to do so.

Our data indicate, however, that lawyers believe that initiating dialogue about settlement is by no means the principal contribution judges can make to the process. What judges have to contribute to settlement that lawyers value most is skill in judging. Lawyers value penetrating, analytical exposition and thoughtful, objective, knowledgeable assessment. They want the judges' opinions. They want the judges' suggestions. They want the perspective of the experienced neutral. Data we discuss in a subsequent section shows that a judge's opinion that a settlement offer is reasonable is likely to have a great effect on a recalcitrant client, especially if that client is not often involved in litigation.

There also are many ways judges can contribute to the quality of the settlement dialogue itself: they can defuse emotions, set a constructive and analytical tone, help parties focus on the pertinent matters, and ask questions that expose underdeveloped areas. Judges can help keep litigants talking when they otherwise might retreat into noncommunication. In these and other ways, a judicial officer can improve the civility, efficiency, and efficacy of the negotiation process.

Thus, we infer that when lawyers say judicial involvement is likely to improve significantly prospects for achieving settlement, they mean that the right kind of judicial activism can initiate the process earlier, expedite it, and lead to earlier agreement by improving litigant and lawyer confidence in the fairness or wisdom of specific settlement proposals.

NOTES AND QUESTIONS

1. The survey data showed that a majority of litigators (90% in one judicial district) preferred that judges in settlement conferences "actively offer suggestions and observations" for the settlement of the case. Opinions were sharply divided, however, as to whether the "settlement judge" should be the same judge who would ultimately try the case. What reasons might litigators have for wanting a different judge at trial than at the settlement conference?

2. Two sitting judges, speaking to an audience of other judges, used the following language to describe the judge's role in settlement negotiations:

> One of the fundamental principles of judicial administration is that, in most cases, the absolute result of a trial is not as high a quality of justice as is the freely negotiated, give-a-little, take-a-little settlement. * * * Therefore, it is essential as part of your procedures to provide some techniques that will maximize the possibility of freely negotiated settlements in cases for which you are responsible. * * *

> There's no point in talking about settlement at a time when the parties are not well enough informed to rationally discuss the elements in the case, and so that they can tell you enough about it so you can make an intelligent contribution to an evaluation of the case. * * *

If you get to that point, then you are faced with the question as to what your role should be. I always say, "Do you want me to participate in your discussions, or do you want to go off and have them by yourselves?" This is because * * * the use of judge time in settlement negotiations is valuable only if desired. * * *

We are catalysts in settlement. Our role is not that of a traditional judge. Our role at that stage is that of a mediator.

Panel Discussion, Comments by Judge Hubert L. Will, The Role of the Judge in the Settlement Process (Fed. Judicial Center 1983).

I thought it might be well for us to examine our own experiences as practicing lawyers, and think a little bit about why cases settle, because I think that helps us best to analyze the judge's role in the settlement process. * * *

[T]here appear to be two primary factors that lead to settlement. One is anxiety, and the other is the necessity for doing something. Now, none of us like anxiety. * * * It's not a desirable human emotion. * * * [A]nd lawyers, sharing with their clients the desire to eliminate anxiety, want to get rid of it. We eliminate anxiety, of course, by replacing uncertainty with certainty.

But that alone of itself won't settle anything because we are capable of tolerating anxiety for long periods. So, the second thing that seems to me to be an important component of the settlement process is the need to do something by a certain time. All settlement procedures are more efficient if there is a more or less inexorable trial date.

Panel Discussion, Comments by Judge Alvin B. Rubin, The Role of the Judge in the Settlement Process (Fed. Judicial Center 1983).

3. A Colorado state district court issued an administrative order that parties in civil cases who settle after the case has been scheduled for trial shall be assessed a fine of no less than $550 for failure to resolve the case in a timely manner. Do you see any problems, either in terms of policy or due process, with this rule? See Raymond Lloyd Co. v. District Court for the Twentieth Judicial District, 732 P.2d 612 (Colo.1987).

Agent Orange Settlement Conference

In 1967 the United States military forces faced serious obstacles in their efforts to support the Government of South Vietnam. The war, which had begun (for the U.S.) in the early 1960's and had been escalating rapidly since 1965, included an estimated 500,000 American military personnel and showed few signs of completion. A major problem was the infiltration of North Vietnamese guerillas throughout South Vietnam under cover of heavy forestation and undergrowth. An obvious solution, recognizable immediately to the military mind, was to create and apply a chemical that would eliminate the foliage, thereby exposing the enemy to rifle fire.

Several American chemical firms prepared the defoliant, named Agent Orange, and the U.S. military used it to spray enormous forested areas in rural South Vietnam. The results were not only disappointing in terms of military strategy, but disastrous (at least allegedly) for the health of those required to live and work in an Agent Orange environment.

In 1978, three years after the last Americans left Vietnam, many veterans and their families filed individual and class action lawsuits in federal court against the chemical companies responsible for manufacturing and distributing Agent Orange. The plaintiffs complained of multiple diseases caused by exposure to the defoliant. By the conclusion of the district court case in 1985, it involved a plaintiff class of over 2.4 million veterans and family members, seven defendant corporations, the U.S. Government as a potential indemnitor, a docket sheet containing 375 pages and roughly 6,000 entries, and one entire room full of filed documents.

The lawyers settled this complex case on Monday, May 7, 1984, the date set for trial to begin, after intense nonstop settlement discussions led by Judge Jack B. Weinstein throughout the weekend. In the following selection, Professor Schuck describes the final three months:

Peter H. Schuck, The Role of Judges in Settling Complex Cases: The Agent Orange Example

53 U.Chi.L.Rev. 337, 344–348 (1986).

In February 1984, Weinstein requested and obtained permission to retain, at the defendants' expense, an unnamed consultant to develop a settlement strategy and plan. That consultant was later revealed to be Ken Feinberg, a lawyer whom Weinstein knew and trusted. Feinberg was not only knowledgeable about toxic tort litigation, but also had a reputation as an effective mover, shaker, and conciliator. By mid-March, he had prepared a settlement plan. It stated no dollar amount but contained three sections: an analysis of the elements for determining the aggregate settlement amount, especially the various sources of uncertainty and the likely number and nature of claims; a discussion of alternative criteria for allocating any liability among the chemical companies; and a discussion of alternative criteria for distributing any settlement fund to claimants. This document, which the judge made available to the lawyers, occasioned considerable disagreement but succeeded in setting the terms for the negotiations that followed.

On April 10, less than three weeks before trial, Weinstein appointed three special masters for settlement. Feinberg and David I. Shapiro, a prominent class action expert and skillful negotiator, would work with the lawyers. Leonard Garment, a Washington political insider, would explore what resources the government might contribute to a settlement. Feinberg and Shapiro immediately identified three major obstacles to settlement: the parties were more than *a quarter of a billion dollars* apart; each side was deeply divided internally over whether and on what terms to settle (and in defendants' case, how to allocate liability); and the government was manifestly unwilling to contribute toward a settlement fund or even to participate in settlement negotiations.

The judge and special masters decided to convene an around-the-clock negotiating marathon at the courthouse during the weekend before the trial. The lawyers were ordered to appear on Saturday morning, May 5, with their "toothbrushes and full negotiating authority." On that morning, while preliminary jury selection work was proceeding in another room, Weinstein met with the lawyers and gave them a "pep talk" about settlement. Then the special masters undertook a grueling two-day course of shuttle diplomacy, holding separate meetings with each side interspersed with private conferences with Judge Weinstein. On several occasions, the judge met privately with each side.

Several features of the discussion were particularly salient in generating the settlement agreement. First, the court did not permit the two sides to meet face-to-face until the very end, after the terms of the deal had been defined. This strategy preserved the court's control over the negotiations and prevented them from fragmenting. In particular, it stymied the plaintiffs' lawyers in their last-ditch effort to improve on the deal by settling with five of the defendants and isolating Monsanto and Diamond Shamrock, the two companies they thought most vulnerable to liability and punitive damages.

Second, the masters attempted to break log-jams in the negotiations by helping the lawyers to predict the consequences of the various approaches under consideration, and by proposing alternative solutions. For example, when the chemical companies' lawyers expressed the fear that a settlement would be rendered worthless if a large number of veterans decided to opt out of the class and sue on their own, Shapiro devised a "walk-away" provision that would minimize those concerns. The tax implications of a settlement were also questions that the masters helped to clarify.

Third, when especially difficult issues arose that threatened to derail the settlement, the parties agreed to be bound by the judge's decision. The most important example of the judge acting as arbitrator involved perhaps the most difficult question facing the defendants—how to allocate liability among themselves. Another example involved the question of one of the defendants' "ability to pay" its share.

Fourth, the judge and his special masters, while being careful not to be duplicitous, did emphasize different things to each side. In their discussions with plaintiffs' lawyers, they stressed the weakness of the evidence on causation, the novelty of many questions of law in the case, the consequent risk of reversal on appeal of a favorable verdict, the prospect that they might lose everything if they rejected settlement, and the enormous costs of continued litigation. To the defendants' lawyers, they stressed the presumed pro-plaintiff sympathies of Brooklyn juries, the reputational damage that protracted litigation and unfavorable publicity would cause their clients, and the high costs of the trial and of the inevitable appeals.

Fifth, a common theme in all discussions was the pervasive *uncertainty* that surrounded the law, the facts, the duration and ultimate outcome of the litigation, and the damages likely to be awarded. By almost all accounts, it was this uncertainty that proved to be the decisive inducement to settlement. On one count, however, Judge Weinstein left little doubt in the lawyers' minds: the court, having crafted and taken responsibility for the settlement, was in a position to make it stick.

Sixth, the imminence and ineluctability of trial "concentrated the minds" of the lawyers as nothing else could have done. This deadline imparted to their deliberations an urgency and a seriousness that swept aside objections that might have undermined negotiations in less compelling circumstances. The lawyers' growing physical and mental exhaustion during that weekend of feverish intensity abetted the conciliatory effect. As one plaintiff's lawyer later complained in his challenge to the validity of the settlement, "the Judge wore us all down with that tactic."

Seventh, the judge and special masters displayed a degree of skill, sophistication, imagination, and artistry in fashioning the settlement that almost all the participants viewed as highly unusual. But even this would not have availed had Judge Weinstein not inspired an extraordinary measure of respect, even awe, in the lawyers, and had the special masters not been viewed as enjoying the authority to speak and make commitments for him.

Eighth, the settlement was negotiated without any agreement (or even any serious discussion) of how the settlement fund would be distributed among the claimants, and without reliable information as to the number of claims that would be filed. The first, of course, was of great interest to the plaintiffs and a matter of indifference to the defendants. The second, however, was significant to both sides. It is not at all certain that settlement could have been reached had the parties been required to resolve these issues in advance. The problem was not simply that preparation of a distribution plan required an immense amount of analysis. A protracted process of political compromise and education was also needed to gain support for the plan, a process whose results even now remain doubtful and perhaps legally vulnerable.

Ninth, the lawyers on the PMC [Plaintiffs' Management Committee] at the time of the settlement possessed very different personalities, ideologies, and incentives than those of the group of lawyers that had launched the case and carried it through its first five years. These differences likely affected the lawyers' disposition to settle. The veterans' passionate desire for vindication at trial, quite apart from their wish for compensation, had strongly driven their chosen lawyer, Victor Yannacone, during the earlier stages of the litigation. Yet the PMC's deliberations concerning the settlement were strongly influenced by lawyers who had only the most attenuated relationship to the veterans. And under the terms of an internal fee-sharing agreement, these lawyers would be secured financially by even a "low" settlement.

Finally, the court was prepared to allocate substantial resources to the quest for a settlement. Judge Weinstein devoted a great deal of his own time to thinking through and implementing a settlement strategy. His three special masters for settlement commanded high compensation and worked long hours. Their billings to the court totaled hundreds of thousands of dollars, even excluding the massive amount of work they later invested in connection with the distribution plan.

According to virtually all of the lawyers who participated in the negotiation of the Agent Orange settlement, Judge Weinstein's distinctive intervention was essential to the settlement. It is possible, of course, that the lawyers are wrong, and that a pretrial settlement would have been reached even without Weinstein's intervention—or, at the very least, that a settlement would have been reached after some witnesses had testified and "blood" had been drawn. But the court's settlement activity was regarded as crucial by those in the best position to know.

NOTES AND QUESTIONS

1. The Agent Orange settlement cannot be used as a guide for lawyers in the typical lawsuit since the case was anything but typical. Several lessons, however, emerge: 1) the settlement process in a complex litigation often needs a manager—if a lawyer does not serve in that role (in addition to his role as advocate), the judge or a master may; 2) creativeness and flexibility are frequently indispensible to settlement; 3) a judge has many available and appropriate resources which can improve the climate for settlement; 4) the judge can easily assume the role of a "mediator with muscle," giving rise to charges of possible overreaching and coercion; and 5) a trial deadline is perhaps the single most effective tool promoting settlement.

2. One ambitious form of structured negotiation and settlement is the Asbestos Claims Facility, created in 1984 by representatives of insurance companies and manufacturers of asbestos products in an attempt to resolve the tens of thousands of asbestos cases pending (and still to be filed) in state and federal courts around the country. The Facility, governed by a Board of Directors with equal representation from manufacturers and insurers, provided adjusters who made offers of compensation to asbestos victims who submitted claims to it. If the claimant rejected the offer, he could pursue relief in court. The Facility also provided ADR procedures for claims by producers against insurers. See description in Richard L. Marcus & Edward F. Sherman, Complex Litigation 835–36 (1985). The Facility had a modest success in resolving claims, but some asbestos manufacturers and insurers and many plaintiffs chose to stay out. Why would claimants spurn such a non-binding settlement process?

b. FORM OF PARTICIPATION REQUIRED

Lawyers recognize that judicial involvement can improve the chances for settlement, and they welcome "the right kind of judicial activism," as Judge Brazil's article notes. A central issue is, of course, what form of participation by parties and their lawyers is helpful to achieving the goal of a fair settlement efficiently arrived at. To what degree can a court require such participation in judicial settlement conferences without distorting the existing balance of interaction of the parties? These same questions are equally important for other mandated forms of ADR, such as mediation and evaluative and "trial run" processes.

Edward F. Sherman, Court–Mandated Alternative Dispute Resolution: What Form of Participation Should Be Required?

46 SMU L.Rev. 2079, 2089–92, 2094–96 (1993).

Over the past several years some judges in ordering parties to participate in ADR proceedings have included a provision that they must participate in good faith. A number of states have also adopted, by statute or rule, a good faith participation requirement for mediation or ADR.[17] A good faith participation requirement is obviously premised on the belief that since ADR is non-binding, it will be a futile exercise unless the parties engage in it with willingness to present their best arguments and to listen to those of the other side with an open mind.

1.   Inadequacy of Case Precedents for Policy Guidance

There is remarkably little case law that examines policy issues as to the propriety of a requirement of good faith participation in ADR. A good faith standard first appeared in a 1983 amendment to Rule 16, the pretrial conference rule on which the authority for federal courts' annexation of ADR processes has been based. Rule 16(f) provides for sanctions, upon motion or a judge's own initiative, for a party's or its attorney's failing to obey a scheduling or pretrial order, being "substantially unprepared to participate in the conference," or failing "to participate in good faith." There have been few reported cases on the application of the Rule 16 good faith participation requirement. It is usually failure to appear[18] or lack of preparation[19] rather than the quality of participation, that has resulted in sanctions. That is not surprising since a settlement conference with a judge is usually informal, leaving both the judge and attorneys considerable

---

17. *See, e.g.,* Me.Rev.Stat.Ann. tit. 19 § 214 (West Supp.1992) (requiring a good faith effort to mediate in mandatory domestic mediation); Minn.Stat.Ann. § 583.27 (West 1988 & Supp.1992) (requiring good faith mediation in farm mortgage mediations with authority in mediator to determine that a party is "not participating in good faith").

18. *See* Barsoumian v. Szozda, 108 F.R.D. 426 (S.D.N.Y.1985) (sanction of $300 attorney fees and $200 court costs imposed on plaintiff's attorney for failure to appear at pre-trial conference); In re McDowell, 33 B.R.

323 (Bankr.N.D.Ohio 1983) (default judgment entered against defendant for failure of his lawyer to appear at pre-trial conference).

19. *See* Flaherty v. Dayton Elec. Mfg. Co., 109 F.R.D. 617, 618–19 (D.Mass.1986) (sanction of payment of opposing counsel's fees and costs of preparation for pre-trial conference entered against plaintiff's attorney who was "substantially unprepared" in not knowing her client's injuries, medical expenses, lost earnings, or whether worker's compensation payments had been received).

leeway in how they will participate.[20] Only recently has there been an emphasis on attendance and participation by the parties themselves, raising a host of new issues about participation. Thus Rule 16 precedents offer little guidance as to the scope of the good faith participation requirement in ADR.

* * *

2. Inadequacy of the Collective Bargaining Analogy

A possible source for policy guidance in applying the "good faith participation" requirement is collective bargaining. Under the labor laws, unions and management that are required to engage in collective bargaining must bargain in good faith.[21] Is that an apt analogy for ADR? Both ADR and collective bargaining would undoubtedly benefit from the parties' good faith participation. But there are differences in ADR which suggest that such participation is not as critical to the process as in collective bargaining and that the content of "good faith participation" is more difficult to determine.

First, the necessity for demanding good faith participation is less in ADR than in collective bargaining. The failure of an ADR proceeding simply means that the parties are relegated to their basic constitutional right to a trial. Failure of collective bargaining, on the other hand, can have severe social consequences—labor unrest, non-cooperation, and strikes. The fact that there is no reasonable fall-back process after unsuccessful collective bargaining underlines the importance of forcing the parties to meet a certain level of participation.

Second, the labor laws impose positive duties on management and labor to participate in collective bargaining that do not exist in the procedural context of ADR. Negotiation in good faith is viewed as critical to labor's rights to share in the determination of contract provisions. The good faith participation duty in collective bargaining refers to "a *bilateral* procedure whereby the employer and the bargaining representative *jointly* attempt to set wages and working conditions for the employees."[22] In effect, the conduct of the collective bargaining process itself is a playing out of the substantive rights guaranteed in the labor laws.

There is no similar substantive entitlement of parties in an ADR proceeding. A party has no right to force another party to accept its participation in shaping a settlement agreement. The authority for ADR in court rules and orders is only procedural, with express limitations on enlarging or modifying substantive rights. If the ADR is not successful, it

20. *See* R. Lawrence Dessem, Pretrial Litigation: Law, Policy and Practice 477–83 (1991).

21. 29 U.S.C. §§ 158(a)(5), (b)(3); (d) (1988).

22. Charles Morris, The Developing Labor Law 574 (2d ed. 1983) (referring to General Elec. Co., 150 NLRB 192 (1964)), *enforced,* 418 F.2d 736 (2d Cir.1969), *cert. denied,* 397 U.S. 965 (1970) (emphasis in original).

will be followed by a trial where the parties' substantive rights can be vindicated.

* * *

3. Incompatibility with Values and Objectives of Litigation

If the ADR and collective-bargaining precedents provide little policy analysis, they do at least demonstrate that too expansive a "good faith participation" requirement may not be compatible with the four principles underlying the values and objectives of court-mandated ADR [which were set out earlier in the article]. Although in a nonbinding ADR proceeding, a broad participation requirement may not be *coercive* in the *Kothe* sense in which a judge attempts to impose his settlement figure on the parties, the higher the level of participation required, the greater the coercion by forcing a party to present its case in a manner not of its choosing. This shades into an invasion of *litigant autonomy* by interfering with the party's choice as to how to present its case. A legitimate claim of litigant autonomy can be made as to those matters of case presentation as to which the parties have superior expertise and can best perform in the interests of accuracy and efficiency. Under the principle of providing the *equivalent of a day in court*, the good faith participation requirement could result in a freer exchange of information and views, but, by requiring the parties to participate as they might not have chosen to do in a trial, it does not necessarily enhance their feeling of having had a fair proceeding. For the equivalent of a day in court, no greater degree of participation should be required than is needed for fairness under the ADR process (which places a high value on litigant autonomy and lack of coercion). This shades into the fourth principle—*calculated to achieve its process purposes*—which insists that the parties not be required to perform unnecessary or futile acts that are not reasonably likely to result in settlement. Imposing collective-bargaining kinds of good faith requirements on the parties seems as likely to result in satellite litigation over sanctions as to improve the possibility of settlement.

EXCHANGE OF POSITION PAPERS AND OBJECTIVE INFORMATION

If a "good faith participation" requirement is undesirable in ADR, there are forms of participation that would enhance the likelihood of success that rely on objective conduct and therefore are more easily enforced by courts. For any form of ADR to succeed, there must be some indication of the parties' positions on the relevant issues and some exchange of basic factual information. Requiring the parties to provide each other and the third-party neutral with position papers and other relevant information lays a basis for meaningful consideration of the case without mandating specific forms of presentation or interaction with the other party. It encourages further oral participation and interaction without having to specify its form, since once having submitted a position paper, parties and counsel are less likely to refuse to discuss their positions at the ADR proceeding.

A reasonable order would be that the parties provide a position paper in advance of the ADR proceeding which would include a plain and concise statement of: (1) the legal and factual issues in dispute, (2) the party's position on those issues, (3) the relief sought (including a particularized itemization of all elements of damage claimed), and (4) any offers and counter-offers previously made.[23] This is a shortened list of the kinds of items that are routinely required by federal courts in proposed pretrial orders under the authority of the Rule 16 pretrial conference rule.

The order might also require the parties to provide to the other side in advance, or to bring to the ADR proceeding, certain documents, such as current medical reports or specific business records. It would thus also serve as a discovery or subpoena order. Such an order may not be necessary if discovery has already been conducted in the normal course of the litigation (although updating of documents, such as medical records, is still often necessary). Courts should be aware of the interplay between on-going discovery in the case and any production provisions contained in an ADR order. The two should be coordinated so as not to conflict. When ADR is ordered early in the litigation before discovery, some form of abbreviated discovery may be necessary if the ADR proceeding is to be meaningful.[24] On the other hand, there is a growing tendency for courts to stay ordinary discovery if a scheduled ADR proceeding could make full discovery unnecessary.[25] Courts should take care to insure that ADR not be used strategically as a vehicle to delay or frustrate normal discovery. If a stay of discovery is granted, the court should require the ADR proceeding to take place within a reasonably short time period.

MINIMAL MEANINGFUL PARTICIPATION

Although exchange of position papers and objective information often provides an alternative to mandating a specific level of participation in ADR, there can still be a need for a minimal level of oral participation by the parties if the process is to have a genuine hope of success. It is not easy to fashion a term to describe what that minimal level should be because the necessary degree of participation varies with the type of ADR process involved. For want of a better term, I have adopted the language used by some courts that require the parties to participate "in a meaningful

---

23. Fed.R.Civ.P. 16(a), (b), & (c). These items are culled from a larger list required by Local Rule 235–7 of the U.S. District Court for the Northern District of California.

24. Abbreviated discovery may be accomplished by court order or agreement of the parties. Consider the following description of discovery in "fast track settlement" in automobile product liability cases:

In a fast track settlement, the plaintiff and defendant agree shortly after the defendant has answered the lawsuit to forego formal discovery and court action for a specified period to pursue settlement. It usually in-

volves the plaintiff voluntarily producing the vehicles to the defendant for inspection and voluntarily producing documents and other information requested by the defendant, which it needs for its settlement evaluation.

W. Douglas Matthews & Timothy F. Lee, *Identifying and Developing a Crashworthiness Case*, 26 Texas Trial Lawyers Forum No. 4, 17, at 21 (1992).

25. *See* Wagshal v. Foster, 1993 WL 86499 (D.D.C.1993) (discovery stayed pending parties' resort to mandatory ADR procedure with "case evaluator").

manner."[26] Although hardly a model of certainty and precision, a "minimal meaningful participation" standard avoids the subjectivity of "good faith participation" by suggesting that the degree of participation required to be "meaningful" is related to the goal of the ADR procedure. Since the methodology and objectives of ADR processes vary a good deal, the "minimal meaningful participation" standard allows flexibility of participation depending on the particular process involved in each case.

NOTES AND QUESTIONS

1. What "minimal meaningful participation" should be required of a party in a settlement conference? What more is required than simply attending?

2. Should "good faith participation" ever be required for a settlement conference?

3. Consider the following settlement conference rule from the U.S. District Court for the Central District of California:

Rule 23. Mandatory Settlement Procedures

23.1. Policy. It is the policy of the Court to encourage disposition of civil litigation by settlement when such is in the best interest of the parties. The Court favors any reasonable means to accomplish this goal. Nothing in this rule shall be construed to the contrary. The parties are urged first to discuss and to attempt to reach settlement among themselves without resort to these procedures.

23.2. Proceeding Mandatory. Unless exempted by this rule or otherwise ordered by the Court, the parties in each civil case shall participate in one of the settlement procedures authorized by this rule.

* * *

23.2.2. Excuses. A judge either on application of a party or sua sponte may excuse counsel in any case from compliance with this rule.

23.3. Time for Proceedings. No later than forty-five (45) days before the final Local Rule 9 pretrial conference, the parties shall participate in one of the approved settlement procedures set forth in this rule and selected by the parties. Except in the case of Settlement Procedure No. 1, a Notice of Settlement Procedure Selection, signed by counsel for both sides, shall be filed not later than fourteen (14) days before the date scheduled for the settlement procedure. The notice shall state the settlement procedure selected, the name of the settlement officer and the date, time and place of the settlement procedure.

23.4. Court–Ordered Proceedings. If the parties do not file a timely Notice of Settlement Procedure Selection (and the Court has not consented

---

26. *See, e.g.,* W.D.Tex.R. CV–87(f)(2) (providing for "appropriate sanctions" against a party who "fails to participate in the [court-annexed] arbitration process in a meaningful manner").

to engage in Settlement Procedure No. 1), the Court may order the parties to participate in any of the settlement procedures approved by this rule.

23.5.   Approved Settlement Procedures.

23.5.1.   Settlement Procedure No. 1. With the consent of all parties and the concurrence of the Court, the parties shall appear before the judge assigned to the case for such settlement proceedings as the judge may conduct.

23.5.2.   Settlement Procedure No. 2. With the consent of the Court, the parties shall appear before a judge of the Court, other than the judge assigned to the case, or a magistrate judge for settlement proceedings.

23.5.3.   Settlement Procedure No. 3. The parties shall appear before an attorney for settlement proceedings. If the parties agree on this procedure but are unable to agree upon an attorney to conduct it, an attorney shall be appointed by the Court.

23.5.4.   Settlement Procedure No. 4. The parties shall appear before a retired judicial officer or other private or non-profit dispute resolution body for mediation-type settlement proceedings.

23.6.   Requirements for Settlement Procedures. Regardless of the settlement procedure selected, the parties shall:

23.6.1.   Submit in writing to the settlement officer, in camera (but not file), a letter (not to exceed five (5) pages) setting forth the party's statement of the case and the party's settlement position, including the last offer or demand made by that party and a separate statement of the offer or demand the party is prepared to make at the settlement conference. This confidential settlement letter shall be delivered to the settlement officer, at least five (5) days before the date of the conference. Such confidential settlement letters shall be returned to the submitting party at the conclusion of the settlement proceedings.

23.6.2.   Each party shall appear at the settlement proceeding in person or by a representative with full authority to settle the case, except that parties residing outside the District may have such an authorized representative available by telephone during the entire proceeding.

23.6.3.   Each party shall be represented at the settlement proceeding by the attorney who is expected to try the case, unless excused by the settlement officer.

23.6.4.   Each party shall have made a thorough analysis of the case prior to the settlement proceeding and shall be fully prepared to discuss all economic and non-economic factors relevant to a full and final settlement of the case.

23.7.   Optional Requirements for Settlement Procedures. Without limitation, the settlement officer may require any of the following procedures in any settlement proceeding:

(a) An opening statement by each counsel.

(b) With the agreement of the parties, a "summary" or "mini-trial", tried either to the settlement officer or to a jury.

(c) Presentation of the testimony, summary of testimony or report of expert witnesses.

(d) A closing argument by each counsel.

(e) Any combination of the foregoing.

23.8. Report of Settlement. If a settlement is reached it shall (i) be reported immediately to the judge's courtroom deputy clerk, and (ii) timely memorialized.

23.9. Confidentiality of Proceedings. All settlement proceedings shall be confidential and no statement made therein shall be admissible in any proceeding in the case, unless the parties otherwise agree. No part of a settlement proceeding shall be reported, or otherwise recorded, without the consent of the parties, except for any memorialization of a settlement.

c. OBLIGATION TO ATTEND

Edward F. Sherman, Court–Mandated Alternative Dispute Resolution: What Form of Participation Should Be Required?

46 SMU L.Rev. 2079, 2103–08 (1993).

Court orders that the parties participate in ADR proceedings often provide that they must attend with "full authority to settle the case" and, in the case of a corporate party or governmental body, that a representative attend who has authority to settle. Such orders raise questions, first, as to what persons are included when parties are ordered to attend, and, second, as to what kind of settlement authority the parties and/or attorneys must have.

1. Mandatory Client Attendance

The conviction that it is essential for the parties to attend settlement proceedings has been relatively late in coming. The original pretrial conference rule (Rule 16), promulgated in 1937, authorized federal courts only to "direct the attorneys for the parties to appear before it for a conference." In 1983 it was amended to include, in addition to the attorneys, "any unrepresented parties."[27] Increasingly, however, courts have come to the conclusion that attendance of the parties themselves, whether represented by counsel or not, increases the possibility of success of both settlement

---

27. Fed.R.Civ.P. 16(a), as amended, 1983. The Manual for Complex Litigation 365 (2d ed. 1985) provides in its Sample Order Setting Initial Conference: "Each party represented by counsel shall appear through its attorney who will have primary responsibility for its interests in this litigation. Parties not represented by counsel are expected to appear in person or through a responsible officer."

conferences and newly emerging ADR proceedings. A 1993 amendment to the rule allows courts to require that "a party or its representative be present or reasonably available by telephone in order to consider possible settlement of the dispute." (Rule 16(c)(16)).

Professor Riskin has made an examination of the advantages and disadvantages of client attendance that offers useful guidance for courts. Advantages include giving the client a chance to tell his story in his own words, learning about the strengths and weaknesses of both sides, permitting him to act on new information, allowing cooperation and momentum to build in the offer process, clearing up miscommunications about facts and interests between lawyers and clients, and providing the information to spot opportunities for problem-solving solutions. Disadvantages include the risk that the client may give away valuable information that could leave him vulnerable to exploitation or weaken his case, that exposure to the other side's behavior will anger or harden some clients, or that direct communication will cause a flare-up and loss of objectivity.[28]

On balance, required attendance of individual parties at ADR proceedings is consistent with the four principles of court-mandated ADR.[29] Client participation reduces coercion by providing full information to the person who must ultimately decide whether to settle and enhances litigant autonomy by allowing the client to participate in the presentation of his own case. It strengthens the feeling of the parties that they have had their day in court. Its compatibility with the ability of the ADR process to achieve its objectives varies with the process. It is certainly consistent with the objectives of "facilitative" ADR* by including the client as an active participant in searching for solutions. It may not be as important in "evaluative" or "trial run" ADR,† as the attorney usually plays the key role in summarizing and presenting the case, but the client can often add a

---

28. Riskin, The Represented Client in a Settlement Conference: The Lessons of G. Heileman Brewing Co. v. Joseph Oat Corp., 69 Wash.U.L.Rev. 1059, 1099–1102 (1991).

29. *Id.* at 1107 n. 167. Riskin concludes that client attendance is more likely to be useful in an ADR process that has such features as "participatory lawyer-client relationships, problem-solving negotiation, and judicial interventions emphasizing facilitation rather than pressure." *Id.* at 1106. He recommends that the "judicial host" in a settlement conference should "1. routinely require attendance of represented clients, and representatives of organizational clients with full settlement authority, in the absence of a suitable, and suitably presented objection, and 2. take appropriate measures to ensure that the client's presence is worthwhile to the client." *Id.* at 1106–07.

* [In "facilitative" ADR, the neutral views her role only as facilitating communica-
tion, and avoids giving an evaluation of the strengths of the parties' cases, opinions as to outcome in a court, or recommendations for terms of settlement. Judicial settlement conferences and mediation are often "facilitative" depending on the approach of the judge or mediator.—Eds.]

† [In "evaluative" ADR, the neutral may provide an evaluation of the strengths of the cases, opinions as to outcome, and recommendations for settlement. Examples are early neutral evaluation (ENE) and settlement conferences and mediations in which an "evaluative" approach is taken. In "trial run" ADR, the parties are provided with an opportunity to present their cases in shortened form to a neutral or neutrals who render a non-binding decision. Examples are court-annexed arbitration, mini-trial, and summary jury trial.—Eds.]

critical aspect to both the case presentation and the negotiation that is expected to follow.

An exception to this analysis is when a named party has no real interest in the case. This frequently arises in personal-injury or property-damage cases filed against a fully insured defendant. Under standard insurance policy provisions, the insurance company has sole authority over the defense of cases, including whether to settle or go to trial. The insurance company representative, therefore, is the crucial person on the defense side for settlement negotiations. The insured defendant may have some interest in the case since its conduct is in question, but determination of that issue may have no monetary consequences to it. Most insured defendants are content to leave settlement matters to the insurance company, with no interest in devoting time and emotional capital to participating in settlement negotiations. An appropriate court order, therefore, would not require an insured defendant to attend when it has no realistic exposure over policy limits and when its consent to settle is not required. It is quite different, however, if there is any realistic possibility of recovery against the defendant above policy limits. The paradigm example arises when a plaintiff offers to settle within policy limits in a state that provides for recovery against an insurance company for bad faith failure to settle. [Then] the defendant has a significant interest to preserve in the settlement negotiations, and, in fact, its desire to escape exposure by having the insurance company settle within policy limits may provide an interesting dynamic in the settlement proceedings.

Difficult questions also arise when the client is not an individual but a corporation. A broad range of issues in this context was explored by a Seventh Circuit en banc decision, *G. Heileman Brewing Co., Inc. v. Joseph Oat Corp.*

* * *

2. Scope of Settlement Authority

Courts also routinely include in ADR orders a requirement that the parties and counsel come to the proceeding with settlement authority.[30] This is based on the frequent experience that a settlement is less likely to be achieved if persons not in attendance must approve the settlement agreed upon. Coming without full settlement authority has also been seen as an illegitimate tactic used by parties, particularly insurance companies, to allow the negotiator to claim inability to bargain outside of a prescribed range and to allow absent officials to disavow agreements made by their negotiating representative as outside their authority.[31]

30. *See, e.g., In re Air Crash Disaster at Stapleton International Airport,* 720 F.Supp. 1433, 1441 (D.Colo.1988) (settlement conference order that "Representatives of all parties, with full settlement authority, shall attend the settlement conference and participate fully in all negotiations. The court expressly notes that the presence of counsel of record does not fulfill the requirement of the presence of an individual with settlement authority.").

31. *See* Chester L. Karrass, Give and Take 96–97 (1974).

Lockhart v. Patel provides an extreme example of an insurance company's noncompliance with such an order. After a non-binding summary jury trial that awarded the plaintiff $200,000 for a lost eye in a medical malpractice case, the plaintiff agreed to settle for $175,000, but the attorney for the doctor's insurer told the judge he was only authorized to offer $125,000 and not to negotiate any further. The judge then called a settlement conference, directing the defense attorney to bring the home-office representative of the insurance company who had issued these instructions and a representative with equal authority. He said: "Tell them not to send some flunky who has no authority to negotiate. I want someone who can enter into a settlement in this range without having to call anyone else."[32]

The defense attorney brought an adjuster from the local office who advised the court that her instructions from the home office were to reiterate the previous offer "and not to bother to call them back if it were not accepted." The judge then made findings that the insurer "had deliberately refused to obey the order of the court," striking the pleadings of the defendant, declaring him in default, and ordering a show cause hearing why the insurer should not be punished for criminal contempt. Later that day, the insurer settled for $175,000. At the contempt hearing, the judge accepted the assurances of the insurer that "it had all been a misunderstanding" and permitted it to purge itself with a letter of apology from its Chief Executive Officer.

Lockhart is an appropriate fact situation for sanctions. Defendant's refusal to send a representative with any settlement authority at all, other than to reiterate the previous offer, insured that the conference would be a futile proceeding. Requiring settlement authority does not coerce a party into settling for any specific amount, and litigant autonomy cannot justify ignoring a requirement directed at avoiding wasteful negotiation tactics.

The hard cases arise when the representative's settlement authority is more ambiguous than in *Lockhart*. Assume that an insurance company sends a representative with authority to settle only up to $10,000, on the basis that it has thoroughly reviewed the case and is convinced that there is no liability at all and, that, in any event, the reasonable damages are much smaller than that amount. Surely the company should not be required to give its representative authority to settle at a higher amount when it has concluded that there is no justification for doing so. But the key inquiry is what the representative's instructions are. If he is sent without authority to consider any settlement above $10,000, this is essentially a "no authority" case as in *Lockhart*. A court should be entitled to require that the representative at least be open to hearing the arguments of the other side with the possibility of settling at any amount found to be persuasive, even though the representative understands that the company has evaluated the case as not worth more than $10,000. If his authority and instructions are

---

32.   115 F.R.D. 44, 45 (E.D.Ky.1987).

so limited that he is deaf to any persuasion, then he is not the proper representative with adequate authority that the court has ordered.

A further question, however, is whether the representative must himself possess full authority to settle. Would it be sufficient to have a representative at the regional office with broader settlement authority be available by phone? What is troubling with this approach is that the person with the ultimate authority cannot be subjected to the discussion that takes place in the settlement conference, thus undermining the effectiveness of the process. On the other hand, requiring the representative to be the person with ultimate settlement authority can impose enormous burdens on that official's time or force her to delegate the authority further down the line than she finds it prudent to do.

G. Heileman Brewing Co., Inc. v. Joseph Oat Corp. wrestled with these issues. * * *

G. Heileman Brewing Co. v. Joseph Oat Corp.

United States Court of Appeal, Seventh Circuit.
871 F.2d 648.

■ Before BAUER, CHIEF JUDGE, CUMMINGS, WOOD, JR., CUDAHY, POSNER, COFFEY, FLAUM, EASTERBROOK, RIPPLE, MANION and KANNE, CIRCUIT JUDGES.

■ KANNE, CIRCUIT JUDGE.

May a federal district court order litigants—even those represented by counsel—to appear before it in person at a pretrial conference for the purpose of discussing the posture and settlement of the litigants' case? After reviewing the Federal Rules of Civil Procedure and federal district courts' inherent authority to manage and control the litigation before them, we answer this question in the affirmative and conclude that a district court may sanction a litigant for failing to comply with such an order.

I.   Background

A federal magistrate ordered Joseph Oat Corporation to send a "corporate representative with authority to settle" to a pretrial conference to discuss disputed factual and legal issues and the possibility of settlement. Although counsel for Oat Corporation appeared, accompanied by another attorney who was authorized to speak on behalf of the principals of the corporation, no principal or corporate representative personally attended the conference. The court determined that the failure of Oat Corporation to send a principal of the corporation to the pretrial conference violated its order. Consequently, the district court imposed a sanction of $5,860.01 upon Oat Corporation pursuant to Federal Rule of Civil Procedure 16(f). This amount represented the costs and attorneys' fees of the opposing parties attending the conference.

II. The Appeal

Oat Corporation appeals, claiming that the district court did not have the authority to order litigants represented by counsel to appear at the pretrial settlement conference. Specifically, Oat Corporation contends that, by negative implication, the language of Rule 16(a)(5) prohibits a district court from directing represented litigants to attend pretrial conferences. That is, because Rule 16 expressly refers to "attorneys for the parties and any unrepresented parties" in introductory paragraph (a), a district court may not go beyond that language to devise procedures which direct the pretrial appearance of parties represented by counsel. Consequently, Oat Corporation concludes that the court lacked the authority to order the pretrial attendance of its corporate representatives and, even if the court possessed such authority, the court abused its discretion to exercise that power in this case. Finally, Oat Corporation argues that the court abused its discretion to enter sanctions.

A. Authority to Order Attendance

First, we must address Oat Corporation's contention that a federal district court lacks the authority to order litigants who are represented by counsel to appear at a pretrial conference. Our analysis requires us to review the Federal Rules of Civil Procedure and district courts' inherent authority to manage the progress of litigation.

Rule 16 addresses the use of pretrial conferences to formulate and narrow issues for trial as well as to discuss means for dispensing with the need for costly and unnecessary litigation. As we stated in Link v. Wabash R.R., 291 F.2d 542, 547 (7th Cir.1961), aff'd, 370 U.S. 626, 82 S.Ct. 1386, 8 L.Ed.2d 734 (1962):

> Pre-trial procedure has become an integrated part of the judicial process on the trial level. Courts must be free to use it and to control and enforce its operation. Otherwise, the orderly administration of justice will be removed from control of the trial court and placed in the hands of counsel. We do not believe such a course is within the contemplation of the law.

The pretrial settlement of litigation has been advocated and used as a means to alleviate overcrowded dockets, and courts have practiced numerous and varied types of pretrial settlement techniques for many years. Since 1983, Rule 16 has expressly provided that settlement of a case is one of several subjects which should be pursued and discussed vigorously during pretrial conferences.

The language of Rule 16 does not give any direction to the district court upon the issue of a court's authority to order litigants who are represented by counsel to appear for pretrial proceedings. Instead, Rule 16 merely refers to the participation of trial advocates—attorneys of record and pro se litigants. However, the Federal Rules of Civil Procedure do not completely describe and limit the power of the federal courts. HMG

Property Investors, Inc. v. Parque Indus. Rio Canas, Inc., 847 F.2d 908, 915 (1st Cir.1988).

The concept that district courts exercise procedural authority outside the explicit language of the rules of civil procedure is not frequently documented, but valid nevertheless. The Supreme Court has acknowledged that the provisions of the Federal Rules of Civil Procedure are not intended to be the exclusive authority for actions to be taken by district courts. Link v. Wabash R.R., 370 U.S. 626, 82 S.Ct. 1386, 8 L.Ed.2d 734 (1962).

In *Link,* the Supreme Court noted that a district court's ability to take action in a procedural context may be grounded in " 'inherent power,' governed not by rule or statute but by the control necessarily vested in courts to manage their own affairs so as to achieve the orderly and expeditious disposition of cases." 370 U.S. at 630–31, 82 S.Ct. at 1389 (footnotes omitted). This authority likewise forms the basis for continued development of procedural techniques designed to make the operation of the court more efficient, to preserve the integrity of the judicial process, and to control courts' dockets. Because the rules form and shape certain aspects of a court's inherent powers, yet allow the continued exercise of that power where discretion should be available, the mere absence of language in the federal rules specifically authorizing or describing a particular judicial procedure should not, and does not, give rise to a negative implication of prohibition.

Obviously, the district court, in devising means to control cases before it, may not exercise its inherent authority in a manner inconsistent with rule or statute. As we stated in Strandell v. Jackson County, 838 F.2d 884, 886 (7th Cir.1988), such power should "be exercised in a manner that is in harmony with the Federal Rules of Civil Procedure." This means that "where the rules directly mandate a specific procedure to the exclusion of others, inherent authority is proscribed."

In this case, we are required to determine whether a court's power to order the pretrial appearance of litigants who are represented by counsel is inconsistent with, or in derogation of, Rule 16. We must remember that Rule 1 states, with unmistakable clarity, that the Federal Rules of Civil Procedure "shall be construed to secure the just, speedy, and inexpensive determination of every action." This language explicitly indicates that the federal rules are to be liberally construed. There is no place in the federal civil procedural system for the proposition that rules having the force of statute, though in derogation of the common law, are to be strictly construed.

"[The] spirit, intent, and purpose [of Rule 16] is ... broadly remedial, allowing courts to actively manage the preparation of cases for trial." In re Baker, 744 F.2d 1438, 1440 (10th Cir.1984) (en banc), cert. denied, 471 U.S. 1014, 105 S.Ct. 2016, 85 L.Ed.2d 299 (1985). Rule 16 is not designed as a device to restrict or limit the authority of the district judge in the conduct of pretrial conferences. As the Tenth Circuit Court of Appeals sitting en banc stated in Baker, "the spirit and purpose of the amendments to Rule 16 always have been within the inherent power of the courts to manage their affairs as an independent constitutional branch of government." Id. at 1441.

We agree with this interpretation of Rule 16. The wording of the rule and the accompanying commentary make plain that the entire thrust of the amendment to Rule 16 was to urge judges to make wider use of their powers and to manage actively their dockets from an early stage. We therefore conclude that our interpretation of Rule 16 to allow district courts to order represented parties to appear at pretrial settlement conferences merely represents another application of a district judge's inherent authority to preserve the efficiency, and more importantly the integrity, of the judicial process.

To summarize, we simply hold that the action taken by the district court in this case constituted the proper use of inherent authority to aid in accomplishing the purpose and intent of Rule 16. We reaffirm the notion that the inherent power of a district judge—derived from the very nature and existence of his judicial office—is the broad field over which the Federal Rules of Civil Procedure are applied. Inherent authority remains the means by which district judges deal with circumstances not proscribed or specifically addressed by rule or statute, but which must be addressed to promote the just, speedy, and inexpensive determination of every action.

B. *Exercise of Authority to Order Attendance*

Having determined that the district court possessed the power and authority to order the represented litigants to appear at the pretrial settlement conference, we now must examine whether the court abused its discretion to issue such an order.

At the outset, it is important to note that a district court cannot coerce settlement. Kothe v. Smith, 771 F.2d 667, 669 (2d Cir.1985).[33] In this case, considerable concern has been generated because the court ordered "corporate representatives with authority to settle" to attend the conference. In our view, "authority to settle," when used in the context of this case, means that the "corporate representative" attending the pretrial conference was required to hold a position within the corporate entity allowing him to speak definitively and to commit the corporation to a particular position in the litigation. We do not view "authority to settle" as a requirement that corporate representatives must come to court willing to settle on someone else's terms, but only that they come to court in order to consider the possibility of settlement.

As Chief Judge Crabb set forth in her decision which we now review:

---

33. Likewise, a court cannot compel parties to stipulate to facts. J.F. Edwards Constr. Co. v. Anderson Safeway Guard Rail Corp., 542 F.2d 1318 (7th Cir.1976) (per curiam). Nor can a court compel litigants to participate in a nonbinding summary jury trial. Strandell, 838 F.2d at 887. In the same vein, a court cannot force a party to engage in discovery. Identiseal Corp. v. Positive Identification Sys., Inc., 560 F.2d 298 (7th Cir.1977).

There is no indication ... that the magistrate's order contemplated requiring Joseph Oat ... to agree to any particular form of settlement or even to agree to settlement at all. The only requirement imposed by the magistrate was that the representative [of Oat Corporation] be present with full authority to settle, should terms for settlement be proposed that were acceptable to [Oat Corporation].

If this case represented a situation where Oat Corporation had sent a corporate representative and was sanctioned because that person refused to make an offer to pay money—that is, refused to submit to settlement coercion—we would be faced with a decidedly different issue—a situation we would not countenance.

The Advisory Committee Notes to Rule 16 state that "[a]lthough it is not the purpose of Rule 16(b)(7) to impose settlement negotiations on unwilling litigants, it is believed that providing a neutral forum for discussing [settlement] might foster it." These Notes clearly draw a distinction between being required to attend a settlement conference and being required to participate in settlement negotiations. Thus, under the scheme of pretrial settlement conferences, the corporate representative remains free, on behalf of the corporate entity, to propose terms of settlement independently—but he may be required to state those terms in a pretrial conference before a judge or magistrate.

As an alternative position, Oat Corporation argues that the court abused its discretion to order corporate representatives of the litigants to attend the pretrial settlement conference. Oat Corporation determined that because its business was a "going concern":

It would be unreasonable for the magistrate to require the president of that corporation to leave his business [in Camden, New Jersey] to travel to Madison, Wisconsin, to participate in a settlement conference. The expense and burden on the part of Joseph Oat to comply with this order was clearly unreasonable. Consequently, Oat Corporation believes that the district court abused its authority.

We recognize, as did the district court, that circumstances could arise in which requiring a corporate representative (or any litigant) to appear at a pretrial settlement conference would be so onerous, so clearly unproductive, or so expensive in relation to the size, value, and complexity of the case that it might be an abuse of discretion. Moreover, "[b]ecause inherent powers are shielded from direct democratic controls, they must be exercised with restraint and discretion." However, the facts and circumstances of this case clearly support the court's actions to require the corporate representatives of the litigants to attend the pretrial conference personally.

This litigation involved a claim for $4 million—a claim which turned upon the resolution of complex factual and legal issues. The litigants expected the trial to last from one to three months and all parties stood to incur substantial legal fees and trial expenses. This trial also would have preempted a large segment of judicial time—not an insignificant factor. Thus, because the stakes were high, we do not believe that the burden of requiring a corporate representative to attend a pretrial settlement conference was out of proportion to the benefits to be gained, not only by the litigants but also by the court.

Additionally, the corporation did send an attorney, Mr. Fitzpatrick, from Philadelphia, Pennsylvania to Madison, Wisconsin to "speak for" the principals of the corporation. It is difficult to see how the expenses involved in sending Mr. Fitzpatrick from Philadelphia to Madison would have greatly exceeded the expenses involved in sending a corporate representative from Camden to Madison. Consequently, we do not think the expenses and distance to be traveled are unreasonable in this case.

Furthermore, no objection to the magistrate's order was made prior to the date the pretrial conference resumed. Oat Corporation contacted the magistrate's office concerning the order's requirements and was advised of the requirements now at issue. However, Oat Corporation never objected to its terms, either when it was issued or when Oat Corporation sought clarification. Consequently, Oat Corporation was left with only one course of action: it had to comply fully with the letter and intent of the order and argue about its reasonableness later.

We thus conclude that the court did not abuse its authority and discretion to order a representative of the Oat Corporation to appear for the pretrial settlement conference on December 19.

C. Sanctions

Finally, we must determine whether the court abused its discretion by sanctioning Oat Corporation for failing to comply with the order to appear at the pretrial settlement conference. Oat Corporation argues that the instructions directing the appearance of corporate representatives were unclear and ambiguous. Consequently, it concludes that the sanctions were improper.

Absent an abuse of discretion, we may not disturb a district court's imposition of sanctions for failure of a party to comply with a pretrial order. The issue on review is not whether we would have imposed these costs upon Oat Corporation, but whether the district court abused its discretion in doing so.

Oat Corporation contends that the presence of Mr. Fitzpatrick, as an attorney authorized to speak on behalf of the principals of Oat Corporation, satisfied the requirement that its "corporate representative" attend the December 19 settlement conference. Oat Corporation argues that nothing in either the November 19, 1984 order or the December 14, 1984 order would lead a reasonable person to conclude that a representative or principal from the Joseph Oat Corporation was required to attend the conference personally—in effect arguing that sanctions cannot be imposed because the order failed to require a particular person to attend the conference.

We believe that Oat Corporation was well aware of what the court expected. While the November order may have been somewhat ambiguous, any ambiguity was eliminated by the magistrate's remarks from the bench on December 14, the written order of December 18, and the direction obtained by counsel from the magistrate's clerk.

III. Conclusion

We hold that Rule 16 does not limit, but rather is enhanced by, the inherent authority of federal courts to order litigants represented by counsel to attend pretrial conferences for the purpose of discussing settlement. Oat Corporation violated the district court's order requiring it to have a corporate representative attend the pretrial settlement conference on December 19, 1984. Under these circumstances, the district court did not abuse its discretion by imposing sanctions for Oat Corporation's failure to comply with the pretrial order.

■ POSNER, CIRCUIT JUDGE, dissenting.

Rule 16(a) of the Federal Rules of Civil Procedure authorizes a district court to "direct the attorneys for the parties and any *unrepresented* parties to appear before it for a [pretrial] conference." The word I have italicized could be thought to carry the negative implication that no represented party may be directed to appear—that was the panel's conclusion—but I hesitate to so conclude in a case that can be decided on a narrower ground.

The main purpose of the pretrial conference is to get ready for trial. For that purpose, only the attorneys need be present, unless a party is acting as his own attorney. The only possible reason for wanting a represented party to be present is to enable the judge or magistrate to explore settlement with the principals rather than with just their agents. Some district judges and magistrates distrust the willingness or ability of attorneys to convey to their clients adequate information bearing on the desirability and terms of settling a case in lieu of pressing forward to trial. The distrust is warranted in some cases, I am sure; but warranted or not, it is what lies behind the concern that the panel opinion had stripped the district courts of a valuable settlement tool—and this at a time of heavy, and growing, federal judicial caseloads. The concern may well be exaggerated, however. The panel opinion may have had little practical significance; it is the rare attorney who will invite a district judge's displeasure by defying a request to produce the client for a pretrial conference.

The question of the district court's power to summon a represented party to a settlement conference is a difficult one. On the one hand, nothing in Rule 16 or in any other rule or statute confers such a power, and there are obvious dangers in too broad an interpretation of the federal courts' inherent power to regulate their procedure. One danger is that it encourages judicial high-handedness ("power corrupts"); several years ago one of the district judges in this circuit ordered Acting Secretary of Labor Brock to appear before him for settlement discussions on the very day Brock was scheduled to appear before the Senate for his confirmation hearing. The broader concern illustrated by the Brock episode is that in their zeal to settle cases judges may ignore the value of other people's time. One reason people hire lawyers is to economize on their own investment of time in resolving disputes. It is pertinent to note in this connection that Oat is a defendant in this case; it didn't want its executives' time occupied with this litigation.

On the other hand, die Not bricht Eisen ["necessity breaks iron"]. Attorneys often are imperfect agents of their clients, and the workload of our district courts is so heavy that we should hesitate to deprive them of a potentially useful tool for effecting settlement, even if there is some difficulty in finding a legal basis for the tool. Although few attorneys will defy a district court's request to produce the client, those few cases may be the very ones where the client's presence would be most conducive to settlement. If I am right that Rule 16(a) empowers a district court to summon unrepresented parties to a pretrial conference only because their presence may be necessary to get ready for trial, we need not infer that the draftsmen meant to forbid the summoning of represented parties for purposes of exploring settlement. The draftsmen may have been unaware that district courts were asserting a power to command the presence of a represented party to explore settlement. We should hesitate to infer inadvertent prohibitions.

The narrowly "legal" considerations bearing on the question whether district courts have the power asserted by the magistrate in this case are sufficiently equivocal to authorize—indeed compel—us to consider the practical consequences for settlement before deciding what the answer should be. Unfortunately we have insufficient information about those consequences to be able to give a confident answer, but fortunately we need not answer the question in this case—so clear is it that the magistrate abused his discretion, which is to say, acted unreasonably, in demanding that Oat Corporation send an executive having "full settlement authority" to the pretrial conference. This demand, which is different from a demand that a party who has not closed the door to settlement send an executive to discuss possible terms, would be defensible only if litigants had a duty to bargain in good faith over settlement before resorting to trial, and neither Rule 16 nor any other rule, statute, or doctrine imposes such a duty on federal litigants. There is no federal judicial power to coerce settlement. Oat had made clear that it was not prepared to settle the case on any terms that required it to pay money. That was its prerogative, which once exercised made the magistrate's continued insistence on Oat's sending an executive to Madison arbitrary, unreasonable, willful, and indeed petulant. This is apart from the fact that since no one officer of Oat may have had authority to settle the case, compliance with the demand might have required Oat to ship its entire board of directors to Madison. Ultimately Oat did make a money settlement, but there is no indication that it would have settled sooner if only it had complied with the magistrate's demand for the dispatch of an executive possessing "full settlement authority."

* * *

■ COFFEY, CIRCUIT JUDGE, with whom EASTERBROOK, RIPPLE and MANION, CIRCUIT JUDGES, join, dissenting.

* * * Unlike the majority, I am convinced that Rule 16 does not authorize a trial judge to require a represented party litigant to attend a pretrial conference together with his or her attorney because the rule mandates in clear and unambiguous terms that only an unrepresented party litigant and attorneys may be ordered to appear.

[The opinion goes on to reject "inherent authority" to compel the presence of represented parties.]

■ Easterbrook, Circuit Judge, with whom Posner, Coffey, and Manion, Circuit Judges, join, dissenting.

Our case has three logically separate issues. First, whether a district court may demand the attendance of someone other than the party's counsel of record. Second, whether the court may insist that this additional person be an employee rather than an agent selected for the occasion. Third, whether the court may insist that the representative have "full settlement authority"—meaning the authority to agree to pay cash in settlement (maybe authority without cap, although that was not clear). Even if one resolves the first issue as the majority does, it does not follow that district courts have the second or third powers, or that their exercise here was prudent.

The proposition that a magistrate may require a firm to send an employee rather than a representative is puzzling. Corporate "employees" are simply agents of the firm. Corporations choose their agents and decide what powers to give them. Which agents have which powers is a matter of internal corporate affairs. Joseph Oat Corp. sent to the conference not only its counsel of record but also John Fitzpatrick, who had authority to speak for Oat. Now Mr. Fitzpatrick is an attorney, which raised the magistrate's hackles, but why should this count against him? Because Fitzpatrick is a part-time rather than a full-time agent of the corporation? Why can't the corporation make its own decision about how much of the agent's time to hire? Is Oat being held in contempt because it is too small to have a cadre of legal employees—because its general counsel practices with a law firm rather than being "in house"?

At all events, the use of outside attorneys as negotiators is common. Many a firm sends its labor lawyer to the bargaining table when a collective bargaining agreement is about to expire, there to dicker with the union (or with labor's lawyer). Each side has a statutory right to choose its representatives. 29 U.S.C. § 158(b)(1)(B). Many a firm sends its corporate counsel to the bargaining table when a merger is under discussion. Oat did the same thing to explore settlement of litigation. A lawyer is no less suited to this task than to negotiating the terms of collective bargaining or merger agreements. Firms prefer to send skilled negotiators to negotiating sessions (lawyers are especially useful when the value of a claim depends on the resolution of legal questions) while reserving the time of executives for business. Oat understandably wanted its management team to conduct its construction business.

As for the third subject, whether the representative must have "settlement authority": the magistrate's only reason for ordering a corporate representative to come was to facilitate settlement then and there. As I understand Magistrate Groh's opinion, and Judge Crabb's, the directive was to send a person with "full settlement authority". Fitzpatrick was deemed inadequate only because he was under instructions not to pay money. E.g.: "While Mr. Fitzpatrick claimed authority to speak for Oat, he stated that he had no authority to make a [monetary] offer. *Thus,* no representative of Oat or National having authority to settle the case was present at the conference as the order directed" (magistrate's opinion, emphasis added). On learning that Fitzpatrick did not command Oat's treasury, the magistrate ejected him from the conference and never listened to what he had to say on Oat's behalf, never learned whether Fitzpatrick might be receptive to others' proposals. (We know that Oat ultimately did settle the case for money, after it took part in and "prevailed" at a summary jury trial—participation and payment each demonstrating Oat's willingness to consider settlement.) The magistrate's approach implies that if the Chairman and CEO of Oat had arrived with instructions from the Board to settle the case without paying cash, and to negotiate and bring back for the Board's consideration any financial proposals, Oat still would have been in contempt.

Both magistrate and judge demanded the presence not of a "corporate representative" in the sense of a full-time employee but of a representative with "full authority to settle". Most corporations reserve power to agree (as opposed to power to discuss) to senior managers or to their boards of directors—the difference depending on the amounts involved. Heileman wanted $4 million, a sum within the province of the board rather than a single executive even for firms much larger than Oat. Fitzpatrick came with power to discuss and recommend; he could settle the case on terms other than cash; he lacked only power to sign a check. The magistrate's order therefore must have required either (a) changing the allocation of responsibility within the corporation, or (b) sending a quorum of Oat's Board.

Magistrate Groh exercised a power unknown even in labor law, where there is a duty to bargain in good faith. 29 U.S.C. § 158(d). Labor and management commonly negotiate through persons with the authority to discuss but not agree. The negotiators report back to management and the union, each of which reserves power to reject or approve the position of its agent. We know from Fed.R.Civ.P. 16—and especially from the Advisory Committee's comment to Rule 16(c) that the Rule's "reference to 'authority' is not intended to insist upon the ability to settle the litigation"—that the parties cannot be compelled to negotiate "in good faith". A defendant convinced it did no wrong may insist on total vindication. Rule 68, which requires a party who turns down a settlement proposal to bear costs only if that party does worse at trial, implies the same thing. Yet if parties are not obliged to negotiate in good faith, on what ground can they be obliged to come with authority to settle on the spot—an authority agents need not carry even when the law requires negotiation? The order we affirm today compels persons who have committed no wrong, who pass every requirement of Rules 11 and 68, who want only the opportunity to receive a decision on the merits, to come to court with open checkbooks on pain of being held in contempt.

Settling litigation is valuable, and courts should promote it. Is settlement of litigation more valuable than settlement of labor disputes, so that courts may do what the NLRB may not? The statutory framework—bona fide negotiations required in labor law but not in litigation—suggests the opposite. Does the desirability of settlement imply that rules of state law allocating authority within a corporation must yield? We have held in other cases that settlements must be negotiated within the framework of existing rules; the desire to get a case over and done with does not justify modifying generally applicable norms.

*   *   *

■ RIPPLE, CIRCUIT JUDGE, with whom COFFEY, CIRCUIT JUDGE, joins, dissenting.

I join the dissenting opinions of Judge Coffey and Judge Manion. I write separately only to emphasize that the most enduring—and dangerous—impact of the majority's opinion will not be its effect on the conduct of the pretrial conference, but on the relationship between the Judiciary and the Congress in establishing practice and procedure for the federal courts. Recognizing that the line between substance and procedure is at best an indistinct and vague one, the two branches of government have established a long tradition of shared responsibility for this aspect of governance. That tradition is embodied principally—although not exclusively—in the Rules Enabling Act. 28 U.S.C. § 2072. That Act was designed to foster a uniform system of procedure throughout the federal system, supplemented but not altered, by local rules to take care of local problems. Experimentation at the local level in areas where policy choices have not been made at the national level is permitted. Moreover, there is no question that the judicial officer retains a substantial degree of inherent authority to deal with individual situations—as long as that authority is exercised in conformity with the policies embodied in the national rules. However, the Rules Enabling Act hardly contemplates the broad, amorphous, definition of the "inherent power of a district judge" articulated by the majority.

NOTES AND QUESTIONS

1. The majority opinion in Heileman conceded that circumstances could arise in which requiring a corporate representative to appear "would be so onerous, so clearly unproductive, or so expensive in relation to the size, value, and complexity of the case that it might be an abuse of discretion." However, it found no such situation here, where the claim was sizable ($4 million) and turned on complex factual and legal issues, where the trial was expected to be lengthy (one to three months), and where the corporation had sent an attorney from Philadelphia to speak for the principals, whose expenses would not have exceeded sending a corporate representative from

Camden. Would any of these facts, if changed, have made the attendance order impermissible?

2. Judge Posner, dissenting, expressed the concern "that in their zeal to settle cases judges may ignore the value of other people's time." Surely there are circumstances when an attorney can adequately represent a party and when requiring a non-attorney representative is unnecessarily wasteful. How does the majority opinion deal with this point? Do the efficiency and proportionality considerations identified by the majority provide appropriate guidance for case-by-case determinations?

3. Judge Easterbrook, also dissenting, argued that many firms send their lawyer to negotiate in collective bargaining or merger talks, and that a lawyer is no less suited to negotiating in a settlement conference. It is important to have in attendance the person who will make the ultimate decision to settle so that she can hear, see, and participate in the proceedings, in short, so that she can be affected by the discussion and interaction with the other side and the judge? Would an appropriate test be that if a lawyer is the sole representative she should be essentially the alter ego of the corporate decisionmaker, with the same knowledge, interests, and settlement authority?

4. Can a court require an insurer to attend a settlement conference? In In re Novak, 932 F.2d 1397 (11th Cir.1991), the district court in a malpractice action directed the defendant's lawyer to find out who at the defendant's insurer had "full settlement authority" after the lawyer stated in a pretrial conference that he would have to check with the insurer before increasing defendant's settlement offer. On being told that the person with such authority was Novak, the judge ordered him to appear for a settlement conference and fined him when he did not. The appellate court agreed with *Heileman* that there is inherent power to require a party to send a person with full settlement authority to a pretrial conference, but held that there is no similar authority to require a nonparty insurer to attend. It added, however, that the court could threaten sanctions against the insured party as a way to coerce cooperation from the party's insurer. Id. at 1406–08.

5. The 1993 amendments to Rule 16(b) provide that "[i]f appropriate, the court may require that a party or its representative be present or reasonably available by telephone in order to consider possible settlement of the dispute." The note also mentioned that this might include "a representative from an insurance company." Citing *Heileman,* the note states that the telephone provision "is not intended to limit the reasonable exercise of the court's inherent powers."

FURTHER REFERENCES

In addition to the principal selections throughout this book, there are other sources that may be useful to the reader for reference. These books and articles are listed by chapter.

Chapter I

Books:

Abel, Richard L. (ed.), The Politics of Informal Justice: The American Experience (2 vols. 1982).

Brunet, Edward, & Charles B. Craver, Alternative Dispute Resolution: The Advocate's Perspective (1997).

Carbonneau, Thomas E., Alternative Dispute Resolution: Melting the Lances and Dismounting the Steeds (1989).

Dauer, Edward A., Manual of Dispute Resolution (1994).

Ellickson, Robert C., Order Without Law: How Neighbors Settle Disputes (1991).

Galanter, Marc, & Joel Rogers, The Transformation of American Business Disputing?. Some Preliminary Observations (Disputes Processing Research Program 1991).

Goldberg, Stephen B., Frank E.A. Sander, & Nancy H. Rogers, Dispute Resolution: Negotiation, Mediation and Other Processes (3d ed. 1999).

Kheel, Theodore W., The Keys to Conflict Resolution: Proven Methods of Settling Disputes Voluntarily (1999).

Lieberman, Jethro K., The Litigious Society (1981).

Olson, Walter, The Litigation Explosion (1991).

Riskin, Leonard L. & James E. Westbrook, Dispute Resolution and Lawyers (2d ed. 1998).

Roth, Bette J., Randall W. Wulff & Charles A. Cooper, The Alternative Dispute Resolution Practice Guide (1993).

Singer, Linda R., Settling Disputes: Conflict Resolution in Business, Families, and the Legal System (2d ed. 1994).

Stone, Katherine, Private Justice: The Law of Alternative Dispute Resolution (2000).

Trachte–Huber, E. Wendy & Stephen K. Huber, Alternative Dispute Resolution: Strategies for Law and Business (1996).

Ware, Stephen J., Alternative Dispute Resolution (2001).

Wilkinson, John H. (ed.), Donovan Leisure Newton & Irvine ADR Practice Book (1990).

Articles:

Bordone, Robert C., Electronic Online Dispute Resolution: A Systems Approach—Potential, Problems, and a Proposal, 3 Harv. Negotiation L. Rev. 175 (Spring 1998).

Baruch Bush, Robert A., Dispute Resolution Alternatives and the Goals of Civil Justice: Jurisdictional Principles for Process Choice, 1984 Wis. L.Rev. 893.

Brunet, Edward, Questioning the Quality of Alternate Dispute Resolution, 62 Tul.L.Rev. 1 (1987).

Cochran, Robert F., Jr., ADR, the ABA, and Client Control: A Proposal that the Model Rules Require Lawyers to Present ADR Options to Clients, 41 S. Tex. L. Rev. 183 (Winter 1999).

Dauer, Edward A., Justice Irrelevant: Speculations on the Causes of ADR, 74 So. Cal. L. Rev. 83 (2000).

Delgado, Richard, Chris Dunn, Pamela Brown, Helena Lee & David Hubbert, Fairness and Formality: Minimizing the Risk of Prejudice in Alternative Dispute Resolution, 1985 Wis.L.Rev. 1359.

Edwards, Harry T., Alternative Dispute Resolution: Panacea or Anathema?, 99 Harv.L.Rev. 668 (1986).

Frey, Martin A., Representing Clients Effectively in an ADR Environment, 33 Tulsa L.J. 443 (Fall 1997).

Galanter, Marc, Why the "Haves" Come Out Ahead: Speculations or, the Limits of Legal Change, 9 Law & Soc'y Rev. 95 (1974).

——, Reading the Landscape of Disputes: What We Know And Don't Know (And Think We Know) About Our Allegedly Contentious and Litigious Society, 31 UCLA L.Rev. 4 (1983).

——, Justice in Many Rooms: Courts, Private Ordering, and Indigenous Law, 19 J. Pluralism & Unofficial L. 1 (1981).

—— & Mia Cahill, Most Cases Settle: Judicial Promotion and Regulation of Settlements?, 46 Stan.L.Rev. 1339 (1994).

Garth, Bryant G., Privatization and the New Market for Disputes: A Framework for Analysis and a Preliminary Assessment, 12 Stud. Law Pol. & Soc'y 367 (1992).

Kupfer Schneider, Andrea, Building a Pedagogy of Problem–Solving: Learning to Choose Among ADR Processes, 5 Harv. Negotiation L. Rev. 113 (Spring 2000).

Lind, E. Allen, Robert Maccoun, Patricia Ebener, William Felstiner, Deborah Hensler, Judith Resnik, & Tom Tyler, In the Eye of the Beholder:

Tort Litigants' Evaluations of Their Experiences in the Civil Justice System, 24 Law & Soc'y Rev. 953 (1990).

Menkel–Meadow, Carrie, Pursuing Settlement in an Adversary Culture: A Tale of Innovation Co–Opted or "the Law of ADR", 19 Fla.St.U.L.Rev. 1 (1991).

___, What Will We Do When Adjudication Ends? A Brief Intellectual History of ADR, 44 UCLA L. Rev. 1613 (August 1997).

Picker, Bennett G., New Roles: Problem Solving ADR: New Challenges, New Roles, and New Opportunities, 72 Temple L. Rev. 833 (Winter 1999).

Polythress, Norman G., Procedural Preferences, Perceptions of Fairness and Compliance with Outcomes: A Study of Alternatives to the Standard Adversary Trial Procedure, 18 Law & Hum.Behav. 361(1994).

Resnik, Judith, Many Doors? Closing Doors? Alternative Dispute Resolution and Adjudication, 10 Ohio St.J. on Disp.Res. 211 (1995).

Sander, Frank E.A., Varieties of Dispute Processing, 70 F.R.D. 111 (1976).

___, Fitting the Forum to the Fuss: A User–Friendly Guide to Selecting an ADR Procedure, 10 Negotiation J. 49 (1994).

Shavell, Steven, Alternative Dispute Resolution: An Economic Analysis, 24 J. Leg. Stud. 1 (1995).

Special Edition: Alternative Dispute Resolution and Procedural Justice, 46 S.M.U.L.Rev. (1993)

Stempel, Jeffrey W., Reflections on Judicial ADR and the Multi–Door Courthouse at Twenty: Fait Accompli, Failed Overture, or Fledgling Adulthood?, 11 Ohio St. J. on Disp. Res. 297 (1996).

Sternlight, Jean R., Is Binding Arbitration a Form of ADR?: An Argument That the Term "ADR" Has Begun to Outlive its Usefulness, 2000 J. Disp. Resol. 97 (2000).

Stipanowich, Thomas J., The Multi–Door Contract and Other Possibilities, 13 Ohio St. J. on Disp. Res. 303 (1998).

Symposium Issue, Quality of Dispute Resolution, 66 Denv.U.L.Rev. No. 3(1989).

Symposium, The Lawyer's Duties and Responsibilities in Dispute Resolution, 38 South Texas Law Review No. 2 (1997).

Symposium, Dispute Resolution in the Law School Curriculum: Opportunities and Challenges, 50 Fla. L. Rev. No. 5 (1998).

Symposium, ADR and the Professional Responsibility of Lawyers, 28 Fordham Urban L.J. No. 4 (2001).

Wangerin, Paul T., The Political and Economic Roots of the "Adversary System" of Justice and Alternative Dispute Resolution, 9 Ohio St.J. on Disp.Res. 203 (1994).

Ware, Stephen J. & Sarah Rudolph Cole, Introduction: ADR in Cyberspace, 15 Ohio St. J. on Disp. Res. 589 (2000).

Chapter II

Books:

Arrow, Kenneth J. et al. (eds.), Barriers to Conflict Resolution (1995).

Axelrod, Robert M., The Evolution of Cooperation (1984).

Bazerman, Max H., & Roy J. Lewicki, Negotiating in Organizations (1983).

____, & Margaret A. Neale, Negotiating Rationally (1991).

Brams, Steven J., & Alan D. Taylor, The Win–Win Solution: Guaranteeing Fair Shares to Everybody (1999).

____, & Alan D. Taylor, Fair Division: From Cake–Cutting to Dispute Resolution (1996).

Brazil, Wayne D., Effective Approaches to Settlement: A Handbook for Lawyers and Judges (1988).

Breslin, J. William, & Jeffrey Z. Rubin (eds.), Negotiation Theory and Practice (1991).

Cialdini, Robert B., Influence: Science and Practice (3d ed. 1993).

Cloke, Kenneth, & Joan Goldsmith, Resolving Personal and Organizational Conflict: Stories of Transformation and Forgiveness (2000).

Dixit, Avinash K., & Barry J. Nalebuff, Thinking Strategically: The Competitive Edge in Business, Politics, and Everyday Life (1991).

Fisher, Roger, & William J. Ury, with Bruce Patton, Getting to Yes (2d ed. 1991).

Freund, James C., Smart Negotiating: How to Make Good Deals in the Real World (1992).

Goleman, Daniel, Emotional Intelligence (1995).

Hammond, John S., Ralph L. Keeney, & Howard Raiffa, Smart Choices: A Practical Guide to Making Better Decisions (1999).

Heifitz, Ron, Leadership Without Easy Answers (1994)

Isaacs, William, Dialogue and the Art of Thinking Together (1999)

Kahneman, Daniel, Paul Slovic, & Amos Tversky, Judgment under Uncertainty: Heuristics and biases (1982).

Kritzer, Herbert M., Let's Make a Deal: Understanding the Negotiation Process in Ordinary Litigation (1991).

Kolb, Deborah M., & Judith Williams, The Shadow Negotiation: How Women Can Master the Hidden Agendas That Determine Bargaining Success (2000).

Lax, David, & James K. Sebenius, The Manager as Negotiator (1986).

Lewicki, Roy J., David M. Saunders, & John W. Minton, Negotiation (3d ed. 1999).

Mnookin, Robert, Scott Peppet, & Andrew Tulumello, Beyond Winning: Creating Value in Negotiating Deals and Disputes (2000)

___, & Lawrence E. Susskind (eds.), Negotiating on Behalf of Others (1999).

Nelken, Melissa L., Understanding Negotiation (2001).

Raiffa, Howard, The Art and Science of Negotiation (1982).

Rogers, Carl, On Becoming a Person (1961).

Schelling, Thomas C., Strategies of Conflict (1960).

Schon, Donald, The Reflective Practitioner (1987)

Stone, Douglas, Bruce Patton, & Sheila Heen, Difficult Conversations: How to Discuss What Matters Most (1999).

Ury, William L., Getting Past No: Negotiating With Difficult People (1991).

Walton, Richard E., Joel E. Cutcher–Gershenfeld, & Robert B. McKersie, Strategic Negotiations: A Theory of Change in Labor–Management Relations (1994).

Articles:

Gross, Samuel R., & Kent D. Syverud, Getting to No: A Study of Settlement Negotiations and the Selection of Cases for Trial, 90 Mich.L.Rev. 319 (1991).

Guernsey, Thomas F., Truthfulness in Negotiation, 17 Univ.Rich.L.Rev. 99 (1982).

Korobkin, Russell, & Chris Guthrie, Psychological Barriers to Litigation Settlement: An Experimental Approach, 93 Mich.L.Rev. 107 (1994).

Menkel–Meadow, Carrie, Toward Another View of Legal Negotiation: The Structure of Problem Solving, 31 UCLA L.Rev. 754 (1984).

Mnookin, Robert H., & Ronald J. Gilson, Disputing Through Agents: Cooperation and Conflict Between Lawyers in Litigation, 94 Colum.L.Rev. 509 (1994).

Murray, John S., Understanding Competing Theories of Negotiation, 2 Negotiation J. 179 (1986).

Perschbacher, Rex R., Regulating Lawyers' Negotiations, 27 Ariz.L.Rev. 75 (1985).

Peters, Geoffrey M., The Use of Lies in Negotiation, 48 Ohio St.L.J. 1 (1987).

Watson, Carol, Gender versus Power as a Predictor of Negotiation Behavior and Outcome, 10 Negotiation J. 117 (1994).

Wetlaufer, Gerald B., The Ethics of Lying in Negotiation, 76 Iowa L.Rev. 1219 (1990).

White, James J., Machiavelli and the Bar: Ethical Limitations on Lying in Negotiation, 1980 Am.Bar.Found. Research J. 926.

*

APPENDIX A

FEDERAL RULES OF CIVIL PROCEDURE

Rule 11.

SIGNING OF PLEADINGS, MOTIONS, AND OTHER PAPERS; SANCTIONS

(a) Signature. Every pleading, written motion, and other paper shall be signed by at least one attorney of record in the attorney's individual name, or, if the party is not represented by an attorney, shall be signed by the party. Each paper shall state the signer's address and telephone number, if any. Except when otherwise specifically provided by rule or statute, pleadings need not be verified or accompanied by affidavit. An unsigned paper shall be stricken unless omission of the signature is corrected promptly after being called to the attention of the attorney or party.

(b) Representations to Court. By presenting to the court (whether by signing, filing, submitting, or later advocating) a pleading, written motion, or other paper, an attorney or unrepresented party is certifying that to the best of the person's knowledge, information, and belief, formed after an inquiry reasonable under the circumstances,—

    (1) it is not being presented for any improper purpose, such as to harass or to cause unnecessary delay or needless increase in the cost of litigation;

    (2) the claims, defenses, and other legal contentions therein are warranted by existing law or by a nonfrivolous argument for the extension, modification, or reversal of existing law or the establishment of new law;

    (3) the allegations and other factual contentions have evidentiary support or, if specifically so identified, are likely to have evidentiary support after a reasonable opportunity for further investigation or discovery; and

    (4) the denials of factual contentions are warranted on the evidence or, if specifically so identified, are reasonably based on a lack of information or belief.

(c) Sanctions. If, after notice and a reasonable opportunity to respond, the court determines that subdivision (b) has been violated, the court may, subject to the conditions stated below, impose an appropriate sanction upon the attorneys, law firms, or parties that have violated subdivision (b) or are responsible for the violation.

(1) How Initiated.

(A) By Motion. A motion for sanctions under this rule shall be made separately from other motions or requests and shall describe the specific conduct alleged to violate subdivision (b). It shall be served as provided in Rule 5, but shall not be filed with or presented to the court unless, within 21 days after service of the motion (or such other period as the court may prescribe), the challenged paper, claim, defense, contention, allegation, or denial is not withdrawn or appropriately corrected. If warranted, the court may award to the party prevailing on the motion the reasonable expenses and attorney's fees incurred in presenting or opposing the motion. Absent exceptional circumstances, a law firm shall be held jointly responsible for violations committed by its partners, associates, and employees.

(B) On Court's Initiative. On its own initiative, the court may enter an order describing the specific conduct that appears to violate subdivision (b) and directing an attorney, law firm, or party to show cause why it has not violated subdivision (b) with respect thereto.

(2) Nature of Sanction; Limitations. A sanction imposed for violation of this rule shall be limited to what is sufficient to deter repetition of such conduct or comparable conduct by others similarly situated. Subject to the limitations in subparagraphs (A) and (B), the sanction may consist of, or include, directives of a nonmonetary nature, an order to pay a penalty into court, or, if imposed on motion and warranted for effective deterrence, an order directing payment to the movant of some or all of the reasonable attorneys' fees and other expenses incurred as a direct result of the violation.

(A) Monetary sanctions may not be awarded against a represented party for a violation of subdivision (b)(2).

(B) Monetary sanctions may not be awarded on the court's initiative unless the court issues its order to show cause before a voluntary dismissal or settlement of the claims made by or against the party which is, or whose attorneys are, to be sanctioned.

(3) Order. When imposing sanctions, the court shall describe the conduct determined to constitute a violation of this rule and explain the basis for the sanction imposed.

(d) Inapplicability to Discovery. Subdivisions (a) through (c) of this rule do not apply to disclosures and discovery requests, responses, objections, and motions that are subject to the provisions of Rules 26 through 37.

As amended 1983, 1987, 1993.

Rule 16.

PRETRIAL CONFERENCES; SCHEDULING; MANAGEMENT

(a) Pretrial Conferences; Objectives. In any action, the court may in its discretion direct the attorneys for the parties and any unrepresented parties to appear before it for a conference or conferences before trial for such purposes as

(1) expediting the disposition of the action;

(2) establishing early and continuing control so that the case will not be protracted because of lack of management;

(3) discouraging wasteful pretrial activities;

(4) improving the quality of the trial through more thorough preparation, and;

(5) facilitating the settlement of the case.

(b) Scheduling and Planning. Except in categories of actions exempted by district court rule as inappropriate, the district judge, or a magistrate judge when authorized by district court rule, shall, after receiving the report from the parties under Rule 26(f) or after consulting with the attorneys for the parties and any unrepresented parties by a scheduling conference, telephone, mail, or other suitable means, enter a scheduling order that limits the time

(1) to join other parties and to amend the pleadings;

(2) to file motions; and

(3) to complete discovery.

The scheduling order may also include

(4) modifications of the times for disclosures under Rules 26(a) and 26(e)(1) and of the extent of discovery to be permitted;

(5) the date or dates for conferences before trial, a final pretrial conference, and trial; and

(6) any other matters appropriate in the circumstances of the case.

The order shall issue as soon as practicable but in any event within 90 days after the appearance of a defendant and within 120 days after the complaint has been served on a defendant. A schedule shall not be modified except upon a showing of good cause and by leave of the district judge or, when authorized by local rule, by a magistrate judge.

(c) Subjects for Consideration at Pretrial Conferences. At any conference under this rule consideration may be given, and the court may take appropriate action, with respect to

(1) the formulation and simplification of the issues, including the elimination of frivolous claims or defenses;

(2) the necessity or desirability of amendments to the pleadings;

(3) the possibility of obtaining admissions of fact and of documents which will avoid unnecessary proof, stipulations regarding the

authenticity of documents, and advance rulings from the court on the admissibility of evidence;

(4) the avoidance of unnecessary proof and of cumulative evidence, and limitations or restrictions on the use of testimony under Rule 702 of the Federal Rules of Evidence;

(5) the appropriateness and timing of summary adjudication under Rule 56;

(6) the control and scheduling of discovery, including orders affecting disclosures and discovery pursuant to Rule 26 and Rules 29 through 37;

(7) the identification of witnesses and documents, the need and schedule for filing and exchanging pretrial briefs, and the date or dates for further conferences and for trial;

(8) the advisability of referring matters to a magistrate judge or master;

(9) settlement and the use of special procedures to assist in resolving the dispute when authorized by statute or local rule;

(10) the form and substance of the pretrial order;

(11) the disposition of pending motions;

(12) the need for adopting special procedures for managing potentially difficult or protracted actions that may involve complex issues, multiple parties, difficult legal questions, or unusual proof problems;

(13) an order for a separate trial pursuant to Rule 42(b) with respect to a claim, counterclaim, cross-claim, or third-party claim, or with respect to any particular issue in the case;

(14) an order directing a party or parties to present evidence early in the trial with respect to a manageable issue that could, on the evidence, be the basis for a judgment as a matter of law under Rule 50(a) or a judgment on partial findings under Rule 52(c);

(15) an order establishing a reasonable limit on the time allowed for presenting evidence; and

(16) such other matters as may facilitate the just, speedy, and inexpensive disposition of the action.

At least one of the attorneys for each party participating in any conference before trial shall have authority to enter into stipulations and to make admissions regarding all matters that the participants may reasonably anticipate may be discussed. If appropriate, the court may require that a party or its representative be present or reasonably available by telephone in order to consider possible settlement of the dispute.

(d) Final Pretrial Conference. Any final pretrial conference shall be held as close to the time of trial as reasonable under the circumstances. The participants at any such conference shall formulate a plan for trial, including a program for facilitating the admission of evidence. The conference shall be attended by at least one of the attorneys who will conduct the trial for each of the parties and by any unrepresented parties.

(e) Pretrial Orders. After any conference held pursuant to this rule, an order shall be entered reciting the action taken. This order shall control the subsequent course of the action unless modified by a subsequent order. The order following a final pretrial conference shall be modified only to prevent manifest injustice.

(f) Sanctions. If a party or party's attorney fails to obey a scheduling or pretrial order, or if no appearance is made on behalf of a party at a scheduling or pretrial conference, or if a party or party's attorney is substantially unprepared to participate in the conference, or if a party or party's attorney fails to participate in good faith, the judge, upon motion or the judge's own initiative, may make such orders with regard thereto as are just, and among others any of the orders provided in Rule 37(b)(2)(B), (C), (D).* In lieu of or in addition to any other sanction, the judge shall require the party or the attorney representing the party or both to pay the reasonable expenses incurred because of any noncompliance with this rule, including attorney's fees, unless the judge finds that the noncompliance was substantially justified or that other circumstances make an award of expenses unjust.

As amended 1983, 1987, 1993.

Rule 45.

Subpoena

(a) Form; Issuance.

(1) Every subpoena shall

(A) state the name of the court from which it is issued; and

(B) state the title of the action, the name of the court in which it is pending, and its civil action number; and

(C) command each person to whom it is directed to attend and give testimony or to produce and permit inspection and copying of designated books, documents or tangible things in the possession, custody or control of that person, or to permit inspection of premises, at a time and place therein specified; and

(D) set forth the text of subdivisions (c) and (d) of this rule.

---

* ["(B) An order refusing to allow the disobedient party to support or oppose designated claims or defenses, or prohibiting that party from introducing designated matters in evidence; (C) An order striking out pleadings or parts thereof, or staying further proceedings until the order is obeyed, or dismissing the action or proceeding or any part thereof, or rendering a judgment by default against the disobedient party; (D) In lieu of any of the foregoing orders or in addition thereto, an order treating as a contempt of court the failure to obey any orders except an order to submit to a physical or mental examination." Rule 37(b)(2).]

A command to produce evidence or to permit inspection may be joined with a command to appear at trial or hearing or at deposition, or may be issued separately.

(2) A subpoena commanding attendance at a trial or hearing shall issue from the court for the district in which the hearing or trial is to be held. A subpoena for attendance at a deposition shall issue from the court for the district designated by the notice of deposition as the district in which the deposition is to be taken. If separate from a subpoena commanding the attendance of a person, a subpoena for production or inspection shall issue from the court for the district in which the production or inspection is to be made.

(3) The clerk shall issue a subpoena, signed but otherwise in blank, to a party requesting it, who shall complete it before service. An attorney as officer of the court may also issue and sign a subpoena on behalf of

   (A) a court in which the attorney is authorized to practice; or

   (B) a court for a district in which a deposition or production is compelled by the subpoena, if the deposition or production pertains to an action pending in a court in which the attorney is authorized to practice.

(b) Service.

(1) A subpoena may be served by any person who is not a party and is not less than 18 years of age. Service of a subpoena upon a person named therein shall be made by delivering a copy thereof to such person and, if the person's attendance is commanded, by tendering to that person the fees for one day's attendance and the mileage allowed by law. When the subpoena is issued on behalf of the United States or an officer or agency thereof, fees and mileage need not be tendered. Prior notice of any commanded production of documents and things or inspection of premises before trial shall be served on each party in the manner prescribed by Rule 5(b).

(2) Subject to the provisions of clause (ii) of subparagraph (c)(3)(A) of this rule, a subpoena may be served at any place within the district of the court by which it is issued, or at any place without the district that is within 100 miles of the place of the deposition, hearing, trial, production, or inspection specified in the subpoena or at any place within the state where a state statute or rule of court permits service of a subpoena issued by a state court of general jurisdiction sitting in the place of the deposition, hearing, trial, production, or inspection specified in the subpoena. When a statute of the United States provides therefor, the court upon proper application and cause shown may authorize the service of a subpoena at any other place. A subpoena directed to a witness in a foreign country who is a national or resident of the United States shall issue under the circumstances and in the manner and be served as provided in Title 28, U.S.C. § 1783.

(3) Proof of service when necessary shall be made by filing with the clerk of the court by which the subpoena is issued a statement of the date and manner of service and of the names of the persons served, certified by the person who made the service.

(c) Protection of Persons Subject to Subpoenas. * * *

(3) (A) On timely motion, the court by which a subpoena was issued shall quash or modify the subpoena if it

(i) fails to allow reasonable time for compliance;

(ii) requires a person who is not a party or an officer of a party to travel to a place more than 100 miles from the place where that person resides, is employed or regularly transacts business in person, except that, subject to the provisions of clause (c)(3)(B)(iii) of this rule, such a person may in order to attend trial be commanded to travel from any such place within the state in which the trial is held, or

(iii) requires disclosure of privileged or other protected matter and no exception or waiver applies, or

(iv) subjects a person to undue burden.

(B) If a subpoena

(i) requires disclosure of a trade secret or other confidential research, development, or commercial information, or

(ii) requires disclosure of an unretained expert's opinion or information not describing specific events or occurrences in dispute and resulting from the expert's study made not at the request of any party, or

(iii) requires a person who is not a party or an officer of a party to incur substantial expense to travel more than 100 miles to attend trial, the court may, to protect a person subject to or affected by the subpoena, quash or modify the subpoena or, if the party in whose behalf the subpoena is issued shows a substantial need for the testimony or material that cannot be otherwise met without undue hardship and assures that the person to whom the subpoena is addressed will be reasonably compensated, the court may order appearance or production only upon specified conditions. * * *

(e) Contempt. Failure by any person without adequate excuse to obey a subpoena served upon that person may be deemed a contempt of the court from which the subpoena issued. An adequate cause for failure to obey exists when a subpoena purports to require a non-party to attend or produce at a place not within the limits provided by clause (ii) of subparagraph (c)(3)(A).

Rule 68.

OFFER OF JUDGMENT

At any time more than 10 days before the trial begins, a party defending against a claim may serve upon the adverse party an offer to allow judgment to be taken against the defending party for the money or property or to the effect specified in the offer, with costs then accrued. If within 10 days after the service of the offer the adverse party serves written notice that the offer is accepted, either party may then file the offer and notice of acceptance together with proof of service thereof and thereupon the clerk shall enter judgment. An offer not accepted shall be deemed withdrawn and evidence thereof is not admissible except in a proceeding to determine costs. If the judgment finally obtained by the offeree is not more favorable than the offer, the offeree must pay the costs incurred after the making of the offer. The fact that an offer is made but not accepted does not preclude a subsequent offer. When the liability of one party to another has been determined by verdict or order or judgment, but the amount or extent of the liability remains to be determined by further proceedings, the party adjudged liable may make an offer of judgment, which shall have the same effect as an offer made before trial if it is served within a reasonable time not less than 10 days prior to the commencement of hearings to determine the amount or extent of liability.

As amended 1948, 1966, 1987.

FEDERAL RULES OF CRIMINAL PROCEDURE

Rule 11.

PLEAS

(e) Plea Agreement Procedure.

(1) In general. The attorney for the government and the attorney for the defendant—the defendant when acting pro se—may agree that, upon the defendant's entering a plea of guilty or nolo contendere to a charged offense, or to a lesser or related offense, the attorney for the government will:

(A) move to dismiss other charges; or

(B) recommend, or agree not to oppose the defendant's request for a particular sentence or sentencing range, or that a particular provision of the Sentencing Guidelines, or policy statement, or sentencing factor is or is not applicable to the case. Any such recommendation or request is not binding on the court; or

(C) agree that a specific sentence or sentencing range is the appropriate disposition of the case, or that a particular provision of the Sentencing Guidelines, or policy statement, or sentencing factor is or is not applicable to the case. Such a plea agreement is binding on the court once it is accepted by the court.

The court shall not participate in any discussions between the parties concerning any such plea agreement.

(2) Notice of such agreement. If a plea agreement has been reached by the parties, the court shall, on the record, require the disclosure of the agreement in open court or, on a showing of good cause, in camera, at the time the plea is offered. If the agreement is of the type specified in subdivision (e)(1)(A) or (C), the court may accept or reject the agreement, or may defer its decision as to the acceptance or rejection until there has been an opportunity to consider the presentence report. If the agreement is of the type specified in subdivision (e)(1)(B), the court shall advise the defendant that if the court does not accept the recommendation or request the defendant nevertheless has no right to withdraw the plea.

(3) Acceptance of a plea agreement. If the court accepts the plea agreement, the court shall inform the defendant that it will embody in the judgment and sentence the disposition provided for in the plea agreement.

(4) Rejection of a plea agreement. If the court rejects the plea agreement, the court shall, on the record, inform the parties of this fact, advise the defendant personally in open court or, on a showing of good cause, in camera, that the court is not bound by the plea agreement, afford the defendant the opportunity to then withdraw the plea, and advise the defendant that if the defendant persists in a guilty plea or plea of nolo contendere the disposition of the case may be less favorable to the defendant than that contemplated by the plea agreement.

(5) Time of plea agreement procedure. Except for good cause shown, notification to the court of the existence of a plea agreement shall be given at the arraignment or at such other time, prior to trial, as may be fixed by the court.

(6) Inadmissibility of pleas, plea discussions, and related statements. Except as otherwise provided in this paragraph, evidence of the following is not, in any civil or criminal proceeding, admissible against the defendant who made the plea or was a participant in the plea discussions:

(A) a plea of guilty which was later withdrawn;

(B) a plea of nolo contendere;

(C) any statement made in the course of any proceedings under this rule regarding either of the foregoing pleas; or

(D) any statement made in the course of plea discussions with an attorney for the government which do not result in a plea of guilty or which result in a plea of guilty later withdrawn.

However, such a statement is admissible (i) in any proceeding wherein another statement made in the course of the same plea or plea discussions has been introduced and the statement ought in fairness be considered contemporaneously with it, or (ii) in a criminal proceeding for perjury or false statement if the statement was made by the defendant under oath, on the record, and in the presence of counsel.

As amended Dec. 1, 1999.

Federal Rules of Evidence

Rule 408.

COMPROMISE AND OFFERS TO COMPROMISE

Evidence of (1) furnishing or offering or promising to furnish, or (2) accepting or offering or promising to accept, a valuable consideration in compromising or attempting to compromise a claim which was disputed as to either validity or amount, is not admissible to prove liability for or invalidity of the claim or its amount. Evidence of conduct or statements made in compromise negotiations is likewise not admissible. This rule does not require the exclusion of any evidence otherwise discoverable merely because it is presented in the course of compromise negotiations. This rule also does not require exclusion when the evidence is offered for another purpose, such as proving bias or prejudice of a witness, negativing a contention of undue delay, or proving an effort to obstruct a criminal investigation or prosecution.

Rule 409.

PAYMENT OF MEDICAL AND SIMILAR EXPENSES

Evidence of furnishing or offering or promising to pay medical, hospital, or similar expenses occasioned by an injury is not admissible to prove liability for the injury.

Rule 410.

INADMISSIBILITY OF PLEAS, PLEA DISCUSSIONS, AND RELATED STATEMENTS

Except as otherwise provided in this rule, evidence of the following is not, in any civil or criminal proceeding, admissible against the defendant who made the plea or was a participant in the plea discussions:

(1) a plea of guilty which was later withdrawn;

(2) a plea of nolo contendere;

(3) any statement made in the course of any proceedings under Rule 11 of the Federal Rules of Criminal Procedure or comparable state procedure regarding either of the foregoing pleas; or

(4) any statement made in the course of plea discussions with an attorney for the prosecuting authority which do not result in a plea of guilty or which result in a plea of guilty later withdrawn.

However, such a statement is admissible (i) in any proceeding wherein another statement made in the course of the same plea or plea discussions has been introduced and the statement ought in fairness be considered contemporaneously with it, or (ii) in a criminal proceeding for perjury or false statement if the statement was made by the defendant under oath, on the record and in the presence of counsel.

As amended 1975, 1980.

APPENDIX D

AMERICAN BAR ASSOCIATION MODEL RULES OF PROFESSIONAL CONDUCT

RULE 1.1 Competence

A lawyer shall provide competent representation to a client. Competent representation requires the legal knowledge, skill, thoroughness and preparation reasonably necessary for the representation.

RULE 1.2 Scope of Representation

(a) A lawyer shall abide by a client's decisions concerning the objectives of representation, subject to paragraphs (c), (d) and (e), and shall consult with the client as to the means by which they are to be pursued. A lawyer shall abide by a client's decision whether to accept an offer of settlement of a matter. In a criminal case, the lawyer shall abide by the client's decision, after consultation with the lawyer, as to a plea to be entered, whether to waive jury trial and whether the client will testify.

(b) A lawyer's representation of a client, including representation by appointment, does not constitute an endorsement of the client's political, economic, social or moral views or activities.

(c) A lawyer may limit the objectives of the representation if the client consents after consultation.

(d) A lawyer shall not counsel a client to engage, or assist a client, in conduct that the lawyer knows is criminal or fraudulent, but a lawyer may discuss the legal consequences of any proposed course of conduct with a client and may counsel or assist a client to make a good faith effort to determine the validity, scope, meaning or application of the law.

(e) When a lawyer knows that a client expects assistance not permitted by the rules of professional conduct or other law, the lawyer shall consult with the client regarding the relevant limitations on the lawyer's conduct.

RULE 1.6 Confidentiality of Information

(a) A lawyer shall not reveal information relating to representation of a client unless the client consents after consultation, except for disclosures that are impliedly authorized in order to carry out the representation, and except as stated in paragraph (b).

(b) A lawyer may reveal such information to the extent the lawyer reasonably believes necessary:

(1) to prevent the client from committing a criminal act that the lawyer believes is likely to result in imminent death or substantial bodily harm; or

(2) to establish a claim or defense on behalf of the lawyer in a controversy between the lawyer and the client, to establish a defense to a criminal charge or civil claim against the lawyer based upon conduct in which the client was involved, or to respond to allegations in any proceeding concerning the lawyer's representation of the client.

RULE 1.8   Conflict of Interest: Prohibited Transactions

(a) A lawyer shall not enter into a business transaction with a client or knowingly acquire an ownership, possessory, security or other pecuniary interest adverse to a client unless:

(1) the transaction and terms on which the lawyer acquires the interest are fair and reasonable to the client and are fully disclosed and transmitted in writing to the client in a manner which can be reasonably understood by the client;

(2) the client is given a reasonable opportunity to seek the advice of independent counsel in the transaction; and

(3) the client consents in writing thereto.

(b) A lawyer shall not use information relating to representation of a client to the disadvantage of the client unless the client consents after consultation, except as permitted or required by Rule 1.6 or Rule 3.3.

(c) A lawyer shall not prepare an instrument giving the lawyer or a person related to the lawyer as parent, child, sibling, or spouse any substantial gift from a client, including a testamentary gift, except where the client is related to the donee.

(d) Prior to the conclusion of representation of a client, a lawyer shall not make or negotiate an agreement giving the lawyer literary or media rights to a portrayal or account based in substantial part on information relating to the representation.

(e) A lawyer shall not provide financial assistance to a client in connection with pending or contemplated litigation, except that:

(1) a lawyer may advance court costs and expenses of litigation, the repayment of which may be contingent on the outcome of the matter; and

(2) a lawyer representing an indigent client may pay court costs and expenses of litigation on behalf of the client.

(f) A lawyer shall not accept compensation for representing a client from one other than the client unless:

(1) the client consents after consultation;

(2) there is no interference with the lawyer's independence of professional judgment or with the client-lawyer relationship; and

(3) information relating to representation of a client is protected as required by Rule 1.6.

(g) A lawyer who represents two or more clients shall not participate in making an aggregate settlement of the claims of or against the clients, or in a criminal case an aggregated agreement as to guilty or nolo contendere pleas, unless each client consents after consultation, including disclosure of the existence and nature of all the claims or pleas involved and of the participation of each person in the settlement.

(h) A lawyer shall not make an agreement prospectively limiting the lawyer's liability to a client for malpractice unless permitted by law and the client is independently represented in making the agreement, or settle a claim for such liability with an unrepresented client or former client without first advising that person in writing that independent representation is appropriate in connection therewith.

(i) A lawyer related to another lawyer as parent, child, sibling or spouse shall not represent a client in a representation directly adverse to a person whom the lawyer knows is represented by the other lawyer except upon consent by the client after consultation regarding the relationship.

(j) A lawyer shall not acquire a proprietary interest in the cause of action or subject matter of litigation the lawyer is conducting for a client, except that the lawyer may:

(1) acquire a lien granted by law to secure the lawyer's fee or expenses; and

(2) contract with a client for a reasonable contingent fee in a civil case.

RULE 2.2 Intermediary

(a) A lawyer may act as intermediary between clients if:

(1) the lawyer consults with each client concerning the implications of the common representation, including the advantages and risks involved, and the effect on the attorney-client privileges, and obtains each client's consent to the common representation;

(2) the lawyer reasonably believes that the matter can be resolved on terms compatible with the clients' best interests, that each client will be able to make adequately informed decisions in the matter and that there is little risk of material prejudice to the interest of any of the clients if the contemplated resolution is unsuccessful; and

(3) the lawyer reasonably believes that the common representation can be undertaken impartially and without improper effect on other responsibilities the lawyer has to any of the clients.

(b) While acting as intermediary, the lawyer shall consult with each client concerning the decision to be made and the considerations relevant in making them, so that each client can make adequately informed decisions.

(c) A lawyer shall withdraw as intermediary if any of the clients so request, or if any of the conditions stated in paragraph (a) is no longer satisfied. Upon withdrawal, the lawyer shall not continue to represent any of the clients in the matter that was the subject of the intermediation.

RULE 3.1 Meritorious Claims and Contentions

A lawyer shall not bring or defend a proceeding, or assert or controvert an issue therein, unless there is a basis for doing so that is not frivolous, which includes a good faith argument for an extension, modification or reversal of existing law. A lawyer for the defendant in a criminal proceeding, or the respondent in a proceeding that could result in incarceration, may nevertheless so defend the proceeding as to require that every element of the case be established.

RULE 3.3 Candor Toward the Tribunal

(a) A lawyer shall not knowingly:

(1) make a false statement of material fact or law to a tribunal;

(2) fail to disclose a material fact to a tribunal when disclosure is necessary to avoid assisting a criminal or fraudulent act by the client;

(3) fail to disclose to the tribunal legal authority in the controlling jurisdiction known to the lawyer to be directly adverse to the position of the client and not disclosed by opposing counsel; or

(4) offer evidence that the lawyer knows to be false. If a lawyer has offered material evidence and comes to know of its falsity, the lawyer shall take reasonable remedial measures.

(b) The duties stated in paragraph (a) continue to the conclusion of the proceeding, and apply even if compliance requires disclosure of information otherwise protected by Rule 1.6.

(c) A lawyer may refuse to offer evidence that the lawyer reasonably believes is false.

(d) In an ex parte proceeding, a lawyer shall inform the tribunal of all material facts known to the lawyer which will enable the tribunal to make an informed decision, whether or not the facts are adverse.

RULE 3.8 Special Responsibilities of a Prosecutor

The prosecutor in a criminal case shall:

(a) refrain from prosecuting a charge that the prosecutor knows is not supported by probable cause;

* * *

(d) make timely disclosure to the defense of all evidence or information known to the prosecutor that tends to negate the guilt of the accused or mitigates the offense, and, in connection with sentencing, disclose to the defense and to the tribunal all unprivileged mitigating information known to the prosecutor, except when the prosecutor is relieved of this responsibility by a protective order of the tribunal;

(e) exercise reasonable care to prevent investigators, law enforcement personnel, employees or other persons assisting or associated with the prosecutor in a criminal case from making an extrajudicial statement that the prosecutor would be prohibited from making under Rule 3.6.

* * *

RULE 4.1   Truthfulness in Statements to Others

In the course of representing a client a lawyer shall not knowingly:

(a) make a false statement of material fact or law to a third person; or

(b) fail to disclose a material fact to a third person when disclosure is necessary to avoid assisting a criminal or fraudulent act by a client, unless disclosure is prohibited by Rule 1.6.

RULE 4.4   Respect for Rights of Third Persons

In representing a client, a lawyer shall not use means that have no substantial purpose other than to embarrass, delay, or burden a third person, or use methods of obtaining evidence that violate the legal rights of such a person.

RULE 5.6   Restrictions on Right to Practice

A lawyer shall not participate in offering or making:

(a) a partnership or employment agreement that restricts the right of a lawyer to practice after termination of the relationship, except an agreement concerning benefits upon retirement; or

(b) an agreement in which a restriction on the lawyer's right to practice is part of the settlement of a controversy between private parties.

RULE 8.4   Misconduct

It is professional misconduct for a lawyer to:

(a) violate or attempt to violate the Rules of Professional Conduct, knowingly assist or induce another to do so, or do so through the acts of another;

(b) commit a criminal act that reflects adversely on the lawyer's honesty, trustworthiness or fitness as a lawyer in other respects;

(c) engage in conduct involving dishonesty, fraud, deceit or misrepresentation;

(d) engage in conduct that is prejudicial to the administration of justice;

(e) state or imply an ability to influence improperly a government agency or official; or

(f) knowingly assist a judge or judicial officer in conduct that is a violation of applicable rules of judicial conduct or other law.

†